P9-DSX-261

Where
the
Money
Was

---

by WILLIE SUTTON
with Edward Linn

BALLANTINE BOOKS • NEW YORK

*Some of the names of the people mentioned in this book have
been changed.*

Copyright © 1976 by Royal Production Corporation

All rights reserved. Published in the United States by Ballantine Books, a division of Random House, Inc., New York, and
simultaneously in Canada by Ballantine Books of Canada,
Ltd., Toronto, Canada. Originally published by The Viking
Press, 1976.

Acknowledgment is made to THE NEW YORK TIMES for
the limerick written by Meyer Berger (1952). © 1952 by The
New York Times Company. Reprinted by permission.

Library of Congress Catalog Card Number: 76-3725

ISBN 0-345-25371-X-195

Manufactured in the United States of America

First Ballantine Books Edition: June 1977

Contents

Where
the
Money
Was

Where the Money Was

What am I doing, I ask myself, standing on a corner at six o'clock in the morning freezing my ass off? Hell, I am almost forty-nine years old. I have been a fugitive for three full years now. I am number one on the FBI Wanted List. If I am caught I will go back to prison for life. They don't even have to catch me for another bank robbery, all they have to do is get their hands on me.

Even to me it makes no sense. I have a safe harbor in Staten Island. I have fifty thousand dollars or so stashed around that I could get my hands on with a couple of phone calls. And still, I am out here on a cold winter morning putting it all on the line in order to rob a bank for money that I neither want nor need. The most brilliant student of the criminal mind that I have ever known once told me that banks would always present an irresistible challenge to me, and any doubts I may have had about that are now gone. I am not only determined to get this bank, I am determined to get it my way, even though my modus operandi is so distinctive that I might just as well be leaving my calling card behind.

Maybe not, though. The Willie Sutton trademark has always been to get inside the bank by wearing the kind of uniform that would lead the guard to open the door for me without question. On this one—if everything goes exactly right—I am going to get in without a uniform and it is a prospect that excites me more than anything has excited me in years.

The bank is the Manufacturers Trust Company in Sunnyside, Queens, and everything about it is ideal.

All around me along Queens Boulevard during the next two hours is the traffic of a city on its way to work. Thousands of residents are pouring out of the high-rise apartment houses. Thousands of cars are passing on their way toward the Queensboro Bridge and Manhattan. On the corner of Forty-fourth Street there is a bus stop. Directly across the street is an elevated subway station. Also a taxicab stand in which dozens of cabs are lined up. I like to work in crowds, that's another of my trademarks. The more that is going on outside the bank, the less chance there is that anybody is going to bother to look in. And if despite all my planning something should go wrong, only a psychopathic cop would shoot into a crowd.

All that activity also makes it easier to case the place. For three weeks now I have been charting the arrival of the employees, changing my vantage point daily so as to attract no attention. Wearing different clothes and different disguises. The land alongside the rising elevated structure is used by neighborhood people and commuters alike as one huge parking lot, and some mornings I would simply pull in and sit there in my car. Sometimes I would mingle with the crowd at the bus stop. Other times I would go up on the elevated structure and look down into the bank.

There is one other thing that makes the Manufacturers Trust perfect for me. On every other bank I have ever taken, the first employee, the man who opened the bank, arrived at eight o'clock, the time lock to the vault released at eight-thirty, and the bank opened to the public at nine. Between eight-thirty and nine, that was the half hour I always looked upon as my time.

At the Manufacturers Trust, the guard arrived at eight-thirty, the time lock was released at nine o'clock, and the doors weren't opened to the public until ten. That was going to give me half an hour to take the employees under control, and another full hour to clean the place out.

There are seventeen people who will have to be taken care of, sixteen employees (eleven men and five women) and a mailman. By now I know them all so intimately that I haven't bothered to bring my note-

2

book with me. People are, above all things, victims of habit, especially when it comes to time. They set their alarm for the same time, catch the same train or bus, and arrive at their job within the same minute. There is also a pecking order in a bank which is unfailing. The employees will always arrive in reverse order to their importance. Weston, the guard, who evidently lives nearby, rounds the corner at 8:30 on the dot. Mr. Hoffman, the manager, arrives at 9:01. He is a heavy set man who always reminds me of a wrestler who has allowed himself to go fat.

The only man who has changed his pattern is the outsider, the mailman. For the first few days he hadn't come to the door until somewhere around 9:40, which could have presented a minor problem. Apparently he has changed his route, though, and for at least a week now he has been arriving between 8:45 and 8:55.

It is the routine of the guard, though, which has particularly fascinated me. One last time I want to watch him, because tomorrow is the day. At exactly 8:30 he comes walking down from Forty-fifth Street in his uniform, gun and all, turns into the boulevard and walks west for half a block, picks up a newspaper at the stand outside the variety store two doors from the bank, drops his coin, takes the key out of his pocket and walks on, so completely engrossed in the paper that he is oblivious to everything around him. With his head still in the paper he puts the key into the lock, pushes the door open, and enters.

Twenty times out of twenty he has done exactly the same thing. Tomorrow, I am betting that he is going to make it twenty-one out of twenty-one.

After Mr. Hoffman arrives, I drive across the Queensboro Bridge to Manhattan where Tommy Kling, my crime partner, has a room. The main weakness of my M.O., as I know only too well, is that it calls for the use of two other people. Two times I have gone to prison because I have been betrayed by partners whom I had every reason to trust. But Tommy is the best partner I have ever had. Small but tough. He will follow orders without question. If you told him to stay on that corner, he'd stay there if he had to beat

3

off an army to do it. Down at the docks where he had been a strong-arm man for the union his nickname was Mad Dog. As small as he is—he is only five foot six—he would take on heavyweights and they would have had to kill him to beat him. When I first met him in prison his hands were like claws, that's how hard he hit. The nerves on both hands had been damaged. A rough kid. Tomorrow he will be wearing elevator shoes to add four inches to his height.

Tommy's weaknesses are the usual weaknesses of thieves: booze and broads. He spent money the way he fought. All out. He did everything all out. Tommy couldn't just pick up a prostitute, he had to shack up with her. He couldn't just shack up with her, he had to fall in love. And so although I trusted Kling as much as I trusted anybody in the world, I would not tell him where I was living. And even though he understood the reason for it, he resented it bitterly.

We hop into the car and drive back across the bridge to Flushing where the third man of the team, John De Venuta (usually referred to as either Dee or Venuta) has taken a furnished room. Since the room is less than a mile from the Manufacturers Trust we have to ride right past it. By this time Queens Boulevard has converted back into the main street of a lazy suburban community. Very little traffic on the wide street. A few housewives here and there carrying shopping bags and wheeling baby carriages. Even the bank looks kind of middle-class and settled.

Although De Venuta was in for a full share of any job he was on, I never looked upon him as a crime partner. He was a functionary, that's all. I never contacted him directly; that was left to Tommy. And although Tommy had recommended him—Tommy had served time with both Dee and his brother, Nick, in Trenton—they didn't get along at all. Which wasn't too surprising in that Venuta was unlike any other thief I have ever known. He was a miser. With his share of the robberies we had already committed in Pennsylvania and New Jersey, he had purchased two modern delicatessen stores in Newark and then hired the cheapest help he could find so that he could continue to work in a sweatshop pressing marine overcoats at thirteen cents per coat.

"You couldn't believe two brothers would be so different," Tommy was always saying. "Nick is such a square, stand-up guy. This sonofabitch is so cheap he won't even eat his own food. You know what he takes to work with him every day? Two soggy tuna-fish sandwiches in a paper bag."

"That's his business," I would say. "It wouldn't hurt you to put a dollar aside yourself instead of throwing it away on those whores of yours." To me, Venuta's cheapness was an asset. The cheaper the better. Nobody is going to get into trouble or create suspicion by working hard and spending nothing.

The real trouble between them had arisen, predictably, when Tommy had tried to borrow some money. Tommy was sore that Venuta wouldn't lend it to him, and Venuta was incensed that Tommy should even ask. Fortunately, Venuta was afraid of Tommy—even though he was four inches taller and at least thirty pounds heavier—and whenever the hostility between them threatened to erupt, Venuta could be counted upon to back off.

"We'll probably find him counting his money," Tommy said as we parked the car a couple of blocks from the house. "The sonofabitch has the first dollar he ever made buried in a potato field somewhere."

Actually, Venuta was waiting for us at the front door. A dark, balding, hawk-nosed man. Tomorrow he would be wearing a toupee. After we had gone over the job one last time, I wanted to test the getaway car. Acting on my instructions, Venuta had stolen a new Pontiac, out of state, and stashed it away in a private garage a few blocks away. I had then bought a junk car for about a hundred bucks, registered it under an assumed name, and dumped it. Now that I had a pair of legitimate plates, all I had to do was make out my own registration, inserting the motor number of the junked car (who was going to check on that?) and the make, type, and year of the stolen car. If we should happen to get stopped for a traffic violation, I would be able to show a registration to match the car. And also a driver's license with the same name that was on the registration. Getting the registration form had been no problem at all. In those days, you could walk into any motor-vehicle bureau and pick them up by the dozen. The rubber stamps that would make it official were no problem either if you knew where to go. (Unfortunately, the rubber stamps were found in my room when I was arrested, and the motor-vehicle bureau changed their whole system. You can't pick up blank forms any more; you get the registration with the license plates at the window and it comes with a water mark that is impossible to duplicate.)

The getaway car, Venuta assured me, was ready to go. He had put the license plates from his own Plymouth on it and driven it around to a filling station to have it greased and oiled and filled with gas. Never mind. I still wanted to test it out myself. The garage was at the end of a row of tin structures just off Queens Boulevard. At my suggestion, we dusted the inside of the car to remove any latent fingerprints, and then we all put on gloves and drove around for a while, testing its speed and maneuverability. Perfect. We would meet at the garage tomorrow at seven o'clock sharp.

Before going to bed, I dyed my hair to a very light brown, almost bordering on blond. The following morning, I slipped out of bed early and began to work on my face. I stained my skin to a dark, olive complexion. I thickened my eyebrows with mascara. I inserted a couple of hollowed-out corks up my nostrils to broaden my nose. From the closet, I took a light gray suit which was padded and cut to alter my silhouette. (Not that it would matter, I knew. The police would undoubtedly know that it was me, and if they wanted an identification they knew how to get it. But if it might not help, it certainly wouldn't hurt. And anyway . . . disguising myself has always been a part of a robbery to me, and I am a victim of habit, too.)

Once I was satisfied with my appearance, I put the license plates and a dog chain into my briefcase and slipped out of the house.

The frost was still sparkling on the front lawns of Westerleigh, Staten Island, as I heated up the motor of my car. The streets were deserted. The ferry slip, which would become choked with traffic in another hour, was empty. This early in the morning, Willie Sutton was the only resident of Staten Island going to work.

De Venuta was already at the garage, thickening his own eyebrows, when Kling and I arrived. While I was attaching the New York plates, De Venuta pulled on four or five heavy sweatshirts to make himself look heavier. I wanted to get there early to make sure we got a parking space on Forty-fourth Street.

At eight-twenty, we synchronized our watches and left the car. Tommy and I attached ourselves to the fringe of the crowd waiting for the bus, and Venuta took his position under the elevated across the street.

At precisely eight-thirty, Weston, the guard, turned the corner at Forty-fifth Street. At the same moment, I detached myself from the crowd and started to walk toward him. As always, he picked up the newspaper, dropped his coin, took out his key, and, with his head in the paper, walked on toward the bank. As he turned toward the door I turned too, so close behind him that I could have been his shadow. So close that if he had so much as glanced up while he was inserting the key he would have caught my reflection in the glass door. While he was pushing the door open I was turning with him, describing a semicircle behind his back that actually placed me in front of him in the bank.

And still he didn't know that I was there. He closed the door, locked it, turned around, and his mouth fell open. All I had to do was reach down and take his pistol out of the holster. Cold as it was, the sweat began to pour out of him. "Come inside," I said, in the kind of voice that knows it is going to be obeyed. "I want to talk to you."

Once I had explained the situation to him, I impressed upon him that any attempt on his part to thwart the holdup would result in somebody being injured and possibly even killed. "All right," I told him, after he had agreed to cooperate. "Within a few minutes my partners will come to the door and you will let them in just as if they were bank employees."

Once they were safely in, I took Weston back to the cage so that he could turn on the lights, as he always did, and point out the alarm-system buttons to me. Off to the side of the main area of the bank, there was a flight of stairs leading down, something I had always been curious about. "Let's take a look," I told him. It was a conference room. A beautiful conference room with one of those big shiny tables surrounded by all of those big comfortable chairs. Oh, very nice. We were going to have ourselves a conference after it was over. ("Ladies and gentlemen, we are gathered here to-day . . .")

While the guard had been giving me the tour, Kling and Venuta had been lining up seventeen chairs, in two rows, in front of the executive area, with the backs to the rail so that they were facing toward the vault. There was not the slightest danger of their being seen from the street; the whole area was shielded from the prying eyes of the passersby by a five-foot wooden partition topped by a foot and a half of frosted glass.

During my first examination of the bank I had noted with interest the radiator in the vestibule just inside the door. Out of my coat pocket I took the dog chain. One end was very quickly attached to the radiator grille, the other end I attached to Weston's ankle. Every time he opened the door he'd be one step from the street, and I didn't want him to get any ideas.

With the first employee due to arrive at any minute, I stationed myself almost directly behind him in a kind of blind spot along the right-hand side of the door. Tommy was behind the partition, where he could pick them up after they were inside, and Venuta was stationed alongside the chairs. As the first four or five employees entered, singly and right on schedule, Weston opened the door for them and locked it again behind them. They were in the bank and past me before they realized they had walked into an ambush. Tommy took them by the elbow and explained what was going on while he was walking them toward the chairs. The bank was being robbed, he told them. All the employees would remain together in the rows of chairs while we were waiting for Mr. Hoffman to arrive and open the vault for us. Nothing was going to

8

happen to anybody, he told them, as long as we received their full cooperation. After that, Tommy simply took each of the new arrivals by the arm and informed them that their fellow employees would tell them all about it as soon as they sat down.

The system was absolutely foolproof. Once they were in the bank, they were always between two of us. Either between me and Tommy or between Tommy and Venuta. Where there were two of them coming in together, Tommy would simply take each of them by an arm. If there were three, he would conduct two of them to the chairs and leave the third one standing there under my surveillance.

Knowing what is happening has a calming effect on people; it's the unknown that causes fear. I wanted them obedient but not frightened, because frightened people can do foolish things. For much the same reason, I welcomed any kind of diversion that would break the tension. When the mailman arrived I stepped out of my hiding place, invited him to join the party, and, leaving Kling to take care of the guard, walked him over to the chairs myself. "Too bad you had to change your route," I told him. "But don't worry, we'll get you out of here as quick as possible. I wouldn't want to get into trouble for interfering with the U.S. mail."

Once you've taken control of the bank, it doesn't really matter who comes to the door. A trio of painters once arrived unexpectedly while I was taking a bank in Pennsylvania, and I simply told them to spread out their drop-cloths and go to work. "The pay you guys get, the bank can't afford to have you hanging around doing nothing. They're insured against bank robbers but nobody would insure them against you robbers." All during the robbery I was able to keep up a line of chatter about how I could have retired by now if we bank robbers had as strong a union as they did. Everybody had a good time, and by the time we walked out the door with the money they had one of the walls completely painted.

After the double row of chairs at the Manufacturers Trust had pretty well filled up, I went strolling over there again. "Don't worry, folks," I said. "It's only money. And it isn't your money." Wherever possible I threw in a little banking lingo to let them know we knew what we were doing. Acting for all the world as if we belonged there. We were going to have to keep them there, I told them, until Hoffman and the assistant manager, Sands, came in to open the vault for us. "We know that for security reasons each of them has half of the combination. Boy, I wonder how Mr. Hoffman is going to react. He's going to be in for quite a surprise."

Sands arrived right on schedule. This was the day, naturally, that Hoffman had to be late. "Gee," I grinned as the tension began to mount, "maybe he's having a session with his wife or something. I sure hope he comes pretty soon. For his wife's sake as well as ours."

I had already removed the chain from Weston's leg and told him that after he let Hoffman in he was to step back and walk into the bank alongside me. When Hoffman finally did show up, four minutes late, he walked absently to the partition, saw all of his people sitting there, and pulled up short. A look of complete bewilderment came over him. "What's this?" was all he was able to say.

"This is a bank holdup," I said, from directly in back of him. "Come on, I want to talk to you."

The handling of the manager is the critical part of the operation. The guard is deflated as soon as you take his gun. The other employees have very mixed feelings about the bank anyway. But the manager represents authority. He's in charge, his status is involved, and he is the man who has to take the positive action of opening the vault.

"Mr. Hoffman," I said, before we sat him down, "you're the bank manager. We know all about this place. We know what your duties are and we know what all your employees' duties are. You have the first three numbers of the combination, and Mr. Sands, your assistant manager, has the last three. You are going to open the vault for us. If you give me any trouble, I want you to know that some of these here employees of yours will be shot. I don't want you to have any false illusions about that. Now perhaps you

10

don't care about your own safety, but the health of these here employees of yours are your responsibility. If anything happens to them, the blame will be yours, not mine."

The psychological bribe there is twofold. I was not only giving him the opportunity to save face in front of his employees, I was giving him the opportunity to tell himself that if it was only his own safety that was involved he would have unquestionably and unhesitatingly attempted to thwart the robbery.

"All right," I said, flinging my arm forward like the wagon master in "Wagons West," "Mr. Hoffman and Mr. Sands, get us in."

Once the vault is open, it isn't just a matter of walking in and scooping up the cash. The money is kept in a series of compartments which are really interior safes with their own combination locks. My immediate targets were the "teller banks," the boxes where the three paying tellers set aside their allotment of money to open for business. After Sands had "primed" each of the locks with his master key, Kling brought in each of the tellers, in turn, and remained behind to scoop the bills into his black silk bag. Once that had been done, I had Hoffman open up all the other compartments. There was one compartment, up in the right-hand corner, which he conspicuously tried to avoid. That, I knew, would be the reserve compartment, which can contain as much, or more, as all the other compartments combined. "You'll have to open that too, Mr. Hoffman," I told him. "You know, I'm a pro at this. I'm not going to miss the big money."

Oh, yes I was. For some reason which I never did find out, the reserve compartment was empty. Barren. Bare. Boy, what a disappointment.

Still, the bag was almost completely filled. I had estimated the job was going to be worth around $150,000. A hundred grand wasn't going to be so bad, either. Back out in the front of the bank, I whispered to Kling that I was going to bring everybody down to the conference room. "As soon as I'm out of sight," I told him, "you and Dee leave and get the car ready."

Having marched all seventeen of them down the stairs in front of me, I sat them around the conference

11

table and gave them a speech. "Now, you people have been very good up to now," I began. "You have co-operated fully. All this money is insured by the bank, you don't have to worry about that. Or about getting the bank open. Your funds will be replenished probably within an hour from one of your other offices. Now, lookit, I'm going to go upstairs now and check on something with my partners. But I want you to know that I'll be back in a couple of minutes. If you got any ideas, you'd better get them out of your head."

Without a backward glance I walked up the stairs, through the bank, and out the front door. The time was nine forty-five. As I got into the car on Forty-fourth Street the motor was already running. "Everything is under control," I said. "Just take it easy, Dee. I don't want you to hit anybody."

The Queensboro Bridge was the final risk point. My time schedule called for us to reach the bridge in five or six minutes. As we were approaching the ramp, right on schedule, a couple of police cruisers were just taking off in the other direction with their sirens going. If the police had an emergency plan for setting up a road block at the Manhattan exit, there was still the possibility that they could react quickly enough to seal it off. It wasn't until we came off the side ramp on the Manhattan side that I knew we were home free.

We swung the car around to First Avenue and drove up a dozen blocks to where Seventy-second Street turns into York Avenue, alongside the East River, before we dumped the car. I took the plates off and put them in the bag with the money. Before I got home that night I would have hammered them into small squares and dropped them over the side of the ferry. For the time being, we separated. Tommy and I started to walk in the general direction of his apartment, which was on Forty-fourth Street all the way over on the west side of Manhattan. The plan was to put a good distance between ourselves and the car before we caught a cab, but the bag was so heavy that we had to take turns carrying it, and we probably hadn't gone more than half-a-dozen blocks before we said, "To hell with this," hailed a cab, and had the driver drop us a couple of blocks away from Tommy's apartment.

In every profession there are unwritten rules. Although neither of us was close to De Venuta, the bag remained on the bed, unopened, until he had arrived. When at last I turned the bag over and saw the money come cascading out, I was sure that we had $100,000 there, easy. When I started to stack the bills, though, each denomination in a separate pile, the piles that kept growing higher and higher were the wrong ones. The ones, fives, and tens. The final count came to just a few dollars under $64,000. Only $21,000-plus apiece. An artistic success, but a commercial disappointment.

But that wasn't what gave me such a let-down feeling. Twenty thousand or forty thousand, what was the difference? I always felt that way when it was over. Emotionally drained and physically exhausted. Which is understandable enough, I suppose. During the planning of a robbery, you are in a constant state of excitement. From the time you disarm the guard to the time you enter the vault, all of your juices are flowing. And then comes the exhilaration of getting into the vault, the satisfaction of the escape, and a temporary sense of happiness that it has come off exactly as you had planned.

And then suddenly it's over. Clarence Darrow wrote something that has always lived with me. The expectation of doing something, he said, gives you much more happiness than you can ever get from actually doing it. Or, I would add, from having done it.

The Manufacturers Trust job didn't end there for me, though. It was the crime for which I was tried and convicted when I was captured two years later. People always ask me whether I'd do the same thing if I had my life to live over, and it's a meaningless question. What they are really saying is: "If you knew then what you know now, would you do it again?" And it was impossible for me to know then what I know now.

Taking the question at face value, though, I certainly wouldn't. Although not for the reasons that would bring any comfort to moralists. If I had worked alone, it would have been nothing more than sticking a gun into the teller's cage and taking whatever was on hand. Not very much satisfaction there, and not very much money either. Working with others, you are at the mercy of your crime partners, and honor among thieves is a myth. You involve yourself with a very low grade of person when you become a thief. The vast majority is basically unstable and therefore unpredictable. I was convicted of the Manufacturers Trust job because for the third time in my life one of my crime partners betrayed me. Against all logic; against his whole track record. Against, even, his own self-interest.

Which brings me to the other question that I have frequently been asked. How could I have been such a terrible judge of character?

Given my own background and my own standards of loyalty, I don't think that I was.

PART ONE

Breaking In

Irishtown Made Me

I was born on June 30, 1901, on the corner of Nassau and Gold in a section along the Brooklyn docks known as Irishtown. When I was three, we moved over one block to High Street, between Gold Street and Bridge Street, and about five years later we moved down the block from 183 High to 227 High. Irishtown was wedged in between the East River on the north, the Navy Yard on the east, and the Washington Street entrance approach to the Brooklyn Bridge off to the west. To pin my own neighborhood down more closely, the Manhattan Bridge was built while I was nine or ten and we kids used to drive everybody crazy by clambering up the structural ironwork which was going up only a block away from my house.

It was a workingman's neighborhood of one- and two-family dwellings and small neighborhood stores in which credit was extended from payday to payday. We weren't bad off, considering. My father, William Francis Sutton, Sr.—I'm William Francis, Jr.—was a hard-working blacksmith who earned fifteen dollars a week, which was not a bad salary in those days. A blacksmith at that time was like an automobile mechanic today. No matter how bad the times got, there was always a place somewhere for a good one. My mother's father, who was totally blind, lived with us, and so did her brothers, John and Jim, plus John's wife, my Aunt Alice. My grandfather had gone blind from working over the coffee roasters for the A & P stores, and he had a pension. The others all worked and contributed to the upkeep of the house. We were the first family in the neighborhood to have a Victrola, a brand-new Victor in which the music was produced from round cylinders and projected through a cone-shaped horn.

It was a tough neighborhood, but it was a toughness without any strut or swagger. There was constant warfare for control of the docks, because to control the docks meant that you controlled the gambling, the loan-sharking, the pilfering, and the kickbacks. Plus the loading racket, which was the sweetest racket of all. Two rackets really. A flat rate, otherwise known as extortion, was levied against the importer, and then another charge was levied against the truckers for every crate they loaded. Lead pipes and brass knuckles were standard equipment. Murder was commonplace. No one was ever convicted. A code of silence was observed in Irishtown more faithfully than *omertá* is observed by the Mafia.

A code of silence that was to have a powerful influence on my life.

Since it was all muscle, the gang members were generally in their late teens or early twenties and therefore very easy for a kid to identify with. The dock boss—the leader—would usually be a little older, all the way up into his mid-twenties, maybe. They gained control by killing their predecessors, and they in turn were killed by their successors. Two years was a long time for a dock boss to stay alive; the turnover was very rapid. They were beaten to a pulp on a dark street; they were shot or stabbed and dumped into the water.

Bill Lovert, my first idol, held power longer than most. A slim man, not very tall, with a sure sense of command and a vibrant personality. Or, at any rate, he was before he had his head bashed in along the docks one night. His successor, Dinny Meehan, was the only dock boss I can remember who died in bed. By which I mean that somebody slipped in through his bedroom window while he was asleep and put a bullet in his brain.

It wasn't only the gangs that were at war with the police. Everybody was. If a man was arrested, his whole family would run alongside the paddy wagon screaming:

"Stop beating my husband!"

17

"Stop beating my son!"

"They're murdering my daddy!"

The word would go out and in a matter of minutes all his friends would gather outside the police headquarters at Poplar Street and set up a clamor:

"Murderers! Cowards! Leave the lad alone!"

The lad was going to be beaten up anyway. Everybody knew that. The theory was that if you could show the police that there were people on the outside who were interested in his welfare the beating would be less severe.

Either way, all the police ever got out of him was the exercise. Nobody ever talked in Irishtown.

The Italian section began on the other side of the Tillary Street Slaughterhouse, and as far as the kids were concerned we got along very nicely. Probably, now that I think of it, because PS 5 was situated right on the border, and neither group had to fight its way through. The Irish mobs and the Italian mobs were something else. The Irish, having got there first, ran the docks, and the Italians were always fighting for their piece of the action. They didn't get very far. Scarface Al Capone was a member of the Italian mob, and it was common knowledge in later years that he had gone to Chicago because the Irish mob played too rough. Although there was one occasion I distinctly remember where the Irish mob invaded an Italian social club down at Union Street and Fourth Avenue in South Brooklyn, and several of the Irish were brought back dead.

If the docks were a battleground, the East River was both our playground and our lifeline. We swam through the raw untreated garbage which was dumped regularly into the river. We dove off the cargo barges as they were being pulled toward shore, against the tide, by their little tugboats. Before I was out of my early teens I was swimming to Manhattan and back with such ease that on three separate occasions I was able to rescue friends of mine who couldn't make it. If I hadn't been such a powerful swimmer in my youth I would never have been able to save myself, years

18

later, when an attempt to escape from a Pennsylvania prison through the main sewer went all wrong.

Everything came in by barge, including the livestock that was headed for the Tillary Street Slaughterhouse. A cattle drive through the narrow cobblestone streets of Irishtown? I saw it often. The barges, carrying cattle or sheep, would dock a couple of blocks from St. Ann's, the first school I attended. The cattle would be driven down Hudson Avenue, past the tenement houses and the neighborhood stores, to the slaughterhouse, which was actually on Hudson Avenue, a little east of Tillary, a block away from PS 5, the second school I attended. The sheep didn't have to be driven. They would follow the Judas sheep, which, at this slaughterhouse anyway, was literally a black sheep. Two big iron doors would swing open and the sheep, baaing piteously, would be crowded into the building.

The slaughtering was done in open view on what could be compared to the loading platform of a factory. And it was slaughter on an assembly line. One of the workers would hit the cattle on the head with a sledgehammer to knock him off his feet and stun him and another would immediately slit his throat. With the sheep, they would simply run a long knife through the throat. The workers would be standing there in hip boots on a floor that was awash with blood, and every now and then one of them would stop to scoop up a cupful of the warm blood and drink it down. They were big, powerful men, and they believed that it gave them extra strength. That's what they told me, anyway. A couple of times while I was standing there watching, they even offered me a cup. I didn't like the taste of it much, but since I was never a kid to turn down a challenge I'd drink it.

I had nothing against the workers. They were German immigrants, most of them, with heavy accents. A job was a job. But that Judas sheep, I came to hate it. I swear that he knew what he was doing. There was an expression of exaggerated innocence on its face that no other sheep had. I hated it so much that I got all of my friends together and planned to drown it when the next load of sheep arrived. After the gangplank of the barge had been lowered we came running forward, swinging sticks and throwing rocks, and drove the black sheep right into the river. It had never occurred to any of us that the other sheep were going to follow it right into the river. What a mess!

I have never forgotten the Judas sheep, though. Or ever stopped hating it. How could I? I kept seeing that same expression of exaggerated innocence in the faces of the hired killers, the woman stranglers, and the sex fiends I ran across in prison.

We were not a family that ever had any trouble with the police. Nobody before me. And nobody except me. My mother was a deeply religious woman who filled the house with religious paintings and artifacts and was always stuffing rosary beads and religious medals into my pockets. We were regular churchgoers, and my brother, Jimmy, who was 15 months older than me, and my sister Helen remained very active in religious affairs all of their lives.

Over all of us hung the memory of the family tragedy, the death of my little sister Agnes. Agnes had been one year younger than me, a beautiful little girl with a headful of curls, the darling of the family. Such an outstanding little beauty that people were always commenting on it. When she was seven years old, she fell off the stoop in front of the house, split the back of her head open, and contracted meningitis.

Two or three days, that's all it took. She died there in the house. In those days in that neighborhood, our people didn't trust the hospitals. Any more than they trusted anything else that smacked of officialdom. People went into the hospital and died, that's all they knew. "The Bellevue Disease," they would say with a shudder. And then cross themselves. "The Black Bottle," they'd whisper knowingly. For it was common gossip in my neighborhood that if they happened to need a bed or something at Bellevue, they would pick out a poor Irish patient and give him the Black Bottle. Poison.

Not that it would have mattered in Agnes's case. The doctors knew almost nothing about meningitis in those days, except that it was so highly contagious that the law required that the body be placed in a sealed coffin, lined with lead, and buried within twenty-four hours.

The casket was placed in the parlor, within a bower of flowers. There was a small glass window in it just large enough so that you could see her face. Even in death, everybody could see how beautiful she was.

When the time came to take her away, my mother hurled herself upon the men from the funeral home. The priest tried to hold her back. My father tried to reason with her. Her closest friends begged and pleaded. It was such a hysterical scene that even now, sixty-five years later, I can see it so vividly that I can smell the sweet and heavy odor of the flowers and feel the emptiness in my stomach.

Nothing anybody could say or do could dissuade her. The men from the funeral home finally had to remove the screws, open the clamps, and then back quickly away while my mother lifted the lid and leaned down to kiss her darling daughter one last time.

For the next few weeks I wheeled my sister Helen up and down the streets, being extremely watchful of her. Although the concept of death was beyond my grasp, I did know that it meant I was never going to see my sister Agnes again, an idea which I found so wholly unacceptable that I doubt whether I could have allowed it to fully penetrate.

I also knew that my mother was prostrate with grief. She remained in a deep state of depression for a long, long time, and though she eventually did come out of it and begin to sing again the lovely Irish ballads that I loved so well, it was never again with quite the same sweet, lilting brogue.

My mother's maiden name was Mary Ellen Bowles. She had been born in Ireland. She was a small woman with sparkling brown eyes and jet-black hair. There was a saying in those days that a woman's work was never done. And it was true. There was no electricity at that time, not in Irishtown anyway. Nor hot water. You'd heat the water on the coal stove in the kitchen and dump it into a big open tub. The washing was done with Fels-Naptha, a yellow scouring soap that left its disinfectant smell in the very walls, with each piece of clothing being rubbed clean on a corrugated metal washboard and then wrung dry by cranking it through a pair of rollers.

My father was a slim, wiry man with a walrus mustache. A strong, silent man who worked fourteen to sixteen hours a day, six days a week, and came home so goddamned tired that he could just about have dinner and read a few of the headlines before he'd doze off to sleep.

He was never able to refuse any of us anything. For as long as I could remember, he was trying to save a few bucks for a rainy day, which wasn't easy because about the only way he could save anything was by cutting down on his tobacco or occasional glass of beer. And my mother was always conning him out of it. The ritual never changed. His bankroll was kept in his pants pocket with a rubber band around it, and since a wife was not supposed to know how much money her husband had—what a laugh!—he would go into the next room to create the impression that he was counting out the money and then come back and solemnly hand it to her. It was, of course, every penny he had. As my mother, having gone through his pants pockets the night before, very well knew.

I used to feel so sorry for him because he had to work so hard. And then angry. When I went out into the world myself, at the age of fifteen, my first job was in a bank. I'd see these poor people coming in early in the morning, putting their nickels and dimes in their accounts, and then at about eleven o'clock the bank president would be driven up in his limousine, his chauffeur would open the door for him, and in he would come—morning clothes, derby hat, cane hooked over his arm—nodding at everybody without looking at anybody—and it infuriated me.

I loved my father, and I couldn't touch him. My father loved me, and he couldn't touch me. He had so little talent for communication that I knew almost nothing about him. It was only years later—after he had died—that my sister, Helen, told me that my father's father had been an itinerant actor who had gone from woman to woman and that my father had been left to shift for himself from the time he was ten years old.

I could look back then and see that he was always a man alone. When Agnes died I doubt whether it occurred to anyone that he might have been suffering as much as my mother. When I began to get into trouble, he never called me down or lectured me. And I always felt he was suffering more than if he had been able to express his concern, his disappointment, and, goddammit, his anger. As strong as he was—he could lift the heaviest furniture we had and carry it across the room by himself—the man never once raised his voice or lifted a hand toward me.

What it was, I think, was that his place in the household had been usurped. In our patriarchal, three-generational household, the unquestioned head of the house, the arbiter of all disputes, was my grandfather James Bowles. Three of the other four adults in the house were, after all, his children, and blind though he was, he was an autocratic figure. My mother absolutely adored him. His sons had a healthy respect for him. He'd give them the back of his hand—just reach out and whack them—and as big and tough as they were, they accepted it without question as the natural course of things.

As a very young boy I was given the job of taking him wherever he wanted to go. He had friends from the old country living on the east side of New York, and I would sometimes take him over the Brooklyn Bridge on the horse-drawn trolley cars. Usually, though, he would be wanting to go down to Carney's saloon, a few blocks away, to have a beer or two with his cronies. I would sit at the table behind them, sipping a soft drink, and sooner or later the talk would always get back to the troubles in Ireland. My grandfather dominated every discussion, and his voice would turn thunderous as he damned the English. When we were alone, he would fill me with stories of Ireland's fight for independence, telling me about the martyrs who were being shot down in the streets like dogs. And I would burn with resentment.

Inside the house, you would never have known that he was blind. Whenever his sons would come home drunk, he'd be waiting behind the door for them with his shillelagh. My mother would come running down to try to save them but he'd whale the tar out of them. With me, he was altogether different. I wasn't a son. I was a grandson and he doted on me. He never hit me, never chastised me. When I did something wrong he would lecture me about developing proper values. When I began to get into trouble he'd admonish me not to be hanging around with bad company. He and my mother were very much alike in that way. Nothing I did was ever my fault. It was always somebody else's.

Even when I stole money from him. Flying pigeons was a favorite pastime in my neighborhood. The rooftops of Irishtown were alive with pigeon coops and the sound of cooing birds. It was fiercely competitive. The owner of one flock would send his birds out to capture strays from his neighbor's flock, and prestige was measured far more by the number of birds that you were able to capture than by the number of birds you bought. Pigeon races were big sporting events, attracting large crowds. The birds would be released miles away and sizable wagers were laid on which bird would get back to its coop first.

I doubt whether I was ten years old when I made myself a coop out of some scrap lumber and screening and got the twenty-five cents I needed to buy a pigeon by stealing it from the loose change my grandfather kept on his bureau. A big, beautiful bird whom I promptly named Skyflier. The first time I took him out of the cage to wash him down, I handed him to one of my friends to hold while I was refastening the door —and that was the end of Skyflier. There was a violent fluttering of the wings, and the next thing I knew he was circling the roof twice to get his bearings and streaking for his former home. I had been sold a "homer," a bird which had been trained to return to its original coop.

I was so heartbroken that I went crying to my grandfather and made a full confession. I had stolen the money from him, and I had been cheated and now the pigeon was gone. "Don't cry, Willie," he said. There, there, Willie. He wiped away my tears, patted me on the head and gave me another quarter so that I could buy another pigeon.

The other powerful figure of my youth was my uncle John. Like his father, he was a powerfully built man. Over six feet tall, redheaded, and a fighter. He was a boss tinsheet worker and also a strong union man at a time when union activity could get a man shot or, at best, badly beaten by the Pinkertons. Nobody ever wanted to tangle with my uncle John, though. He was a very well respected figure all up and down the Atlantic coast. (It isn't so surprising, incidentally, that a foreman would also be a union organizer. A very casual reading of the history of the union movement in America shows that it was usually the more skilled craftsmen who became the leaders, if only because the skilled workers were the ones the owners could least afford to fire.)

Unlike my mother and grandfather, my uncle John was no particular admirer of the clergy. St. Ann's was, of course, a parochial school and corporal punishment was a routine part of the curriculum. The brothers and the nuns all carried bamboo sticks, and you didn't have to misbehave to feel the sting of them. If a pupil didn't know his lesson, he could get his head knocked off.

When I was in the fifth grade I got into a fight during recess and came back into the classroom with a beaut of a black eye. I admitted quite readily that I had been fighting, but when the brother demanded to know who the other boy was the code of silence took over. "You'll tell me," he said, flexing the bamboo.

"No, I won't," I said.

He gave me such a terrible beating that I finally broke away and ran all the way home. As it happened, my uncle John was there. He took one look at me, made me take off my shirt, and when he saw the welts all over my body he took me by the hand and didn't stop walking until we were back in the classroom. He asked the brother one question: "Did you hit him?"

The brother said, "Yes," and the next thing he knew he was on the floor, holding his jaw.

The next thing I knew, I was going to school at PS 5.

The greatest thing my uncle John did for me,

though, was to marry my aunt Alice. I was quite young when he brought her into the house, and I fell in love with her at first sight. She was a very beautiful woman with extraordinarily delicate features. Billie Burke, who later became a Follies star and married Flo Ziegfeld, was her half sister and the resemblance was very strong. As much as I loved my uncle John, I couldn't help but wonder how such a fragile and obviously cultured woman could have married a roughneck like him.

And that was exactly what she was. Delicate and cultured. She had attended a finishing school as a young girl, and she dressed in the latest fashions and practiced the social graces. She used a very delicate perfume that appealed to me so strongly that I would practically evaporate along with it.

By the standards of the day, it was a remarkably liberated marriage. She had worked as a social secretary and governess for some of the wealthiest families in New York, practically running their lives for them, and whenever the spirit moved her she would go back to one of them, sometimes even living with them for a while. She was so sought after that she could work when she felt like working, and come and go as she pleased. My uncle John was so sure of himself that he was perfectly willing to let her have a life of her own.

When she was living at the house, I tried to be around her as much as possible. On her part, she took me by the hand and opened up an entirely new world to me. She had, after all, been a governess. The best governess, probably, in New York. I was a very bright boy and I always got excellent marks in school. Not because I was a scholar but because I had such a retentive memory that I was able to get straight As without ever bringing a book home. My brother, Jimmy, on the other hand, had left school very early and gone to work in a coal yard. He was stolid, uncomplicated, and hard-working, very much like my father. Aunt Alice saw me as the member of the family with the greatest potentiality, and her natural inclinations took over.

By the time I was ten or twelve, she was buying me suits that cost twelve or fourteen dollars, which was as much as short-pants suits could cost. She took me to Broadway shows and the best New York restaurants. We would walk down Fifth Avenue, and people would turn their heads to look at her. We would walk into the Waldorf, which was located on Thirty-fourth Street at that time, right where the Empire State Building stands today, and the head waiter would come bustling over and automatically conduct us to a window table. She just had that air about her.

She tutored me in the social graces. Proper etiquette. The manners of a gentleman. And, along with it, the more valuable lesson that manners and etiquette were important not so much in the acts themselves as in the statement you were making about yourself. The first time I dropped a piece of silverware, she let me go reaching for it. And then she said: "If you ever drop anything again, let the waiter pick it up."

I once asked her to define the word *class* for me. "I hear people say that some people have it and some people don't. What do they mean?"

She said: "The best way I can illustrate that, Willie, is to say that if you buy a two-dollar linen handkerchief and put it in your pocket, nobody knows it's there but you. Nobody else has to."

It was the same with everything. Don't be showy. Keep your own counsel. Know your own worth. I listened carefully and I took it all to heart. More than anybody else, it was Aunt Alice who set my style of living and my attitudes. Unlike most thieves, I never flashed a big roll of bills. I never went after people, I let them come after me. Although I loved clothes, I was never a flashy dresser. If anything, I was always careful to be a little understated. But understated or not, I dressed so well, even while I was still living at home, that my mother began to call me The Dude. "Here comes The Dude," she would say. And my father would never fail to say in response, "Well, every family has to have a sport. It might as well be Willie as anyone else."

The Navy Yard had its impact upon me too. Sands Street, the sailors' honky-tonk, ran just parallel to High Street and directly into the Navy Yard three blocks away. A three-block carnival. Three blocks of whore-houses and street hookers, free-flowing liquor and noisy revelry. It was a street of happily blended sounds. The music pouring from the dance hall, the sea chanteys arching over the swinging doors of the saloons, the ricky-ticky piano telling of great happenings at the nickelodeon, and the high-pitched laughter from the throats of waist-holding couples as they paused for a moment to look into the shop windows. The sailors and their girls would slip into the nickelodeon or crowd into the penny arcades to have their pictures taken, shoot clay pigeons, or have their fortunes told.

It was a street of bars and taverns. In the morning, the paddy wagon would come around and pick up the debris. Those who had sobered up enough would be taken to the Navy YMCA, which was right there on Sands Street too. The others would be deposited in the police station overnight.

It was also a hangout for the toughs of the neighborhood, the same guys, for the most part, who were running the docks. A ship would pull in after months at sea, the sailors would come pouring out looking for girls, and, inevitably, somebody would go for the wrong one. And then it would become a street of wild brawls. There were full-scale riots there. The fighting wouldn't come to an end until the sailors had been chased right back into the Yard.

I was about ten when I began to hang around Sands Street with my school chums Charlie McCarthy and Eddie Lynch. They were just as fascinated by the street as I was, and we eagerly absorbed the exciting tales being told by the lush rollers, the burglars, the gamblers, and the gangsters. They became my first heroes. They wore good clothes, their shoes were always shined, and they looked as if they belonged in them, not awkward and uncomfortable like the working men of Irishtown in their Sunday go-to-church suits.

Charlie McCarthy and I found ourselves planning our first burglary as if it were the most natural thing in the world. It was a small department store in the neighborhood, and we planned every detail as if we were seasoned criminals. On the scheduled night we scurried through a dark alley, over a fence, and up the fire escape to the roof. We pried open a skylight and tied a rope to the frame, and then Charlie began to lower himself into the darkness. The next thing that happened hadn't been planned on. A loud crash and a tremendous clatter. Charlie had lost his grip and fallen right into the crockery department. Windows started going up all around us. People began shouting out questions. I had flattened myself against the roof, and after a while I could hear Charlie's voice calling faintly from below. I slid down the rope, waded through the broken crockery, and found him standing there, unharmed. "Come on," he said. "Let's get the cash register."

For the next two weeks Charlie and I were the kings of the neighborhood, buying ice cream and candy for all our friends and treating them to the movies. But it was a funny thing. When the money was gone, there was not a thought about pulling another job. We had done it to see if we could do it, that's all.

The next time I stole anything, I did it entirely on my own. I was twelve years old when I was transferred to PS 5, courtesy of my uncle John. Every morning my teacher, Miss Grilli, would place a quarter on her desk. Her lunch money. Every day as the class filed out for lunch I would see it sitting there. More and more I began to wonder what would happen if I took it.

The day came when I puttered around at my desk long enough to make sure I would be at the very end of the line, and as quick as a wink the quarter was in my pocket.

Miss Grilli was a very pretty, very emotional young woman with a huge bosom. Which, upon our return, she began to pound with both fists. Someone had stolen her quarter, she shouted, and she knew who it was. She surveyed the entire class, letting an accusing eye fall on each of us. "I'm going to give the person a chance to return the money," she announced, at last. "And if he doesn't, I'll expose him to the class."

I knew nobody had seen me, and I had not the slightest temptation to give it back. Not that I wanted the damn quarter. I just wanted the thrill of having pulled it off exactly as I had planned.

Miss Grilli said nothing more about it. But the next day there was another quarter on the desk. Christ, you couldn't learn anything. It was like a magnet. Everybody's mind was on that desk. For a full week the game went on. And on into the next week. And then, when I was convinced that the interest had died down, I dropped back to the end of the line and stole it again. Holy Christ, what a commotion when the kids came out of the cloak room and saw that it was gone again.

Miss Grilli herself said not a word. Just put another quarter on the desk. Another week went by, and I couldn't stand it. Nothing in the world could have stopped me from going after it, and this time she caught me red-handed.

I wouldn't admit I had stolen the other two quarters. I denied it indignantly. If I hadn't been caught red-handed, I wouldn't have admitted to the third one, either. They sent for my mother, and it was touch-and-go for a while whether I was going to be expelled.

That wasn't the end of it, though. The family held a meeting in the parlor, which pointed up the enormity of my offense right there. We were kitchen people. The parlor was for company. The punishment that was decided upon was worse, as far as I was concerned, than any beating could have been. The silent treatment. For a full week, nobody in the family would speak a word to me. I was being excommunicated. I wasn't even allowed to go to church.

It was only because I had such good marks, I suppose, that I hadn't been expelled. Being that good a student, and a naturally friendly kid anyway, I was one of the few kids who had free passage between the good boys and the bad boys. My best friend, in fact, had always been Johnny Mahoney, who was an altar boy. The best student and the best-behaved kid in the neighborhood. When I was fourteen we moved to Park Slope, about two miles away. It wasn't upward mobility, either. We were moving to a drab eight-family tenement on Thirteenth Street, a block away from Prospect Park. Within a month or two the

Mahoneys moved to the same block, and Johnny and I became closer than ever. We would lie on the sloping hills of Prospect Park enjoying the incredibly beautiful floral arrangements. Or go swimming in the waters off Red Hook, just as we had always done. Exchanging our boyhood confidences, our secret dreams. Johnny's ambition was to be a priest. Mine was to become a criminal lawyer.

That's right, a criminal lawyer. And it wasn't as illogical as it may seem. Through all the years that I was growing up, the big, running story in the papers was the murder of Herman Rosenthal, who had been subpoenaed to testify before a grand jury investigating corruption in city government, and the subsequent trial of Lieutenant Charles Becker, a crooked police officer who was accused of hiring the murderers and fingering the victim. Becker was convicted on the testimony of the actual assassins, Gyp the Blood, Dago Frank, Lefty Louie, and Whitey Lewis. The story seemed to go on forever. The appeals, the clemency petitions to the governor, who happened to be the same man who had prosecuted him years earlier as district attorney, and, finally, the execution.

In Irishtown, the sympathy was all with Becker. Not that we had any love for crooked cops but only because we despised the gunmen who had turned rat—and who ended up in the chair along with Becker anyway.

Actually, my interest in the law had been sharpened even earlier. When I was very young, my father was hit by a truck while he was crossing a street in lower Manhattan. His collarbone was broken, among other things, and so he hired an attorney and brought suit. While we were waiting for the case to come to trial, we lived on dreams of the new life that was going to be opened up to us by all that money we were going to get. Just before the case was scheduled to go to trial, the lawyer settled for a few hundred dollars. My mother, always the philosopher, believed the lawyer when he told her how lucky we had been to get anything. I always had the sneaking suspicion that he had sold us out. (In later years, when I learned how the game was played, I became sure of it.)

31

I was going to be a lawyer for the poor people, I'd tell Johnny. A fighter for justice. Another Clarence Darrow. Boy, I was going to get everybody off.

I came closer to being a lawyer than Johnny ever came to being a priest. He drowned a few feet off the shore in Red Hook. I was supposed to have gone with him that day, but I had begged off. Our neighbors, the Jantzens, had just bought a new Ford, the first automobile on the street. On the day it arrived, Al Jantzen, who was about my age, allowed me to sit in the back seat with him, and, boy, what a thrill that was. This was in 1915, remember; I had never actually ridden in a car before in my life. When he came in later to tell me I was being invited to drive to Coney Island with them the next day . . . well, you can imagine. Hell, I could go swimming with Johnny Mahoney anytime. As Johnny himself agreed. Don't worry, he told me. He'd go by himself. While Al and I were in the car waiting for the rest of his family to come out, Johnny came by, carrying his bathing suit, and stood there talking to us until we were ready to leave.

When we came back in the evening, I learned that he hadn't come home. His mother had been to the house to ask whether Johnny had changed his mind and gone with us. In the morning, the word came that his body had been found wedged in a milk can beneath the water.

My mother and I went to the morgue with Mrs. Mahoney to identify the body. A terrible experience. When the attendant pulled out the slab and lifted the sheet, his face was so bloated that he was practically unrecognizable. "That's not my Johnny!" his mother screamed. "It's not! That's not Johnny!" While my mother was trying to comfort her, they took me into the office and showed me the clothes that had been found on the dock, plus the crucifix and ring that had been removed from the body. Johnny's graduation ring from St. Ann's. It was Johnny, all right.

I had taught Johnny how to swim, and if I had been with him—as I had promised—I would have been able to save him. I was so consumed with guilt that I began to make excuses not to go to church. Not because I blamed God or anything like that, but because I just couldn't bear to look at the altar boy.

My ambition died a less dramatic death. When I was fifteen I graduated from grammar school—PS 10 —which was as far as most kids went at that time. My diploma was the first one that had ever come into the Sutton family, and it was the ambition of my parents that I would go on to become a high-school graduate and maybe even enter college. Over the summer, though, I decided to get a job and earn some money. I had a new friend by then, Tommy McGovern, and we had discovered girls. Tommy and I both went to work for the Title Guarantee Company. I was the office boy for the vice-president, a job which permitted me to roam through every department of the vast organization, including the banking department. I became so friendly with the cashiers and the tellers that they allowed me to watch the opening of the massive doors of the vault every morning and to help wheel the money into the cages for the beginning of each day's business. Although it never occurred to me that I might slip a few packets into my pocket and go on my way, whistling merrily, neither is it completely irrelevant that my first job should have involved such intimate association with vaults and banking procedure. That knowledge was there in my mind, ready to be used when I needed it.

Before the summer was over, something else happened. Unknown to me, one of my friends had sent in a coupon to a correspondence school in Chicago, enrolling me in their law course. When I came home from work and saw those books I became so excited that I can still remember the address. LaSalle Street. In those days you didn't need a degree from a law school. All you had to do was pass the bar exam. There probably weren't more than half-a-dozen law schools in the whole country. The customary way to become a lawyer was to apprentice yourself to a practicing lawyer, read law on your own, and learn about trial work by carrying the old man's bag into court. The old-timers will tell you that while the apprentice system didn't turn out particularly good book lawyers, it produced trial lawyers far superior to those you have today.

My excitement didn't last for long. "You'll have to send the books back," my mother said. "They cost too much." I kept the books for a couple of weeks anyway, poring through them every night and hoping against hope that she might change her mind. But finally my mother packed them back in the box herself, and there was nothing for me to do but send them back.

When the summer came to an end, I didn't go back to school. Instead, I got another job. At the Metropolitan Insurance Company. Six months later, the United States declared war on Germany, and with good-paying jobs becoming available everywhere, I left home for good.

I have often wondered whether my life wouldn't have been entirely different if I had been allowed to keep those law books. So much that happens to you is the result of sheer accident. You're walking in a park, you take the left path instead of the right path, and you meet a girl who you later marry. And your whole life has been changed. Who knows what had been happening that had my mother feeling so insecure—which wasn't like her—at that particular moment. Maybe she just didn't like the idea of somebody taking it upon himself to order books for me. If it had been my own idea, if I had sat around the kitchen table and said, "Look, I want to become a lawyer and there's this correspondence school in Chicago . . ." My guess is that she would have reacted every bit as enthusiastically as I did. At the very least she would have said, "Let's find out a little more about it first."

I'd have been a good lawyer, I'm sure of that. I know I'd have made a good book lawyer because, in a manner of speaking, I was. I got dozens of my fellow inmates out of prison, in later years, by drawing up their appeals. And I always had the flair for dramatics, the sense of humor and the instinctive judgment about people that the really good trial lawyers have.

The line between a bank robber and a lawyer is a

very thin one, anyway. In robbing a bank I always planned the job carefully, leaving nothing to chance. It's the same thing in trying a case. "Preparation is everything," lawyers say. Once you're inside the bank, you have to see everything, guard yourself against everybody. While he is putting in his case, the lawyer has to be equally alert, equally on guard against anything the other side might throw at him. In both professions, it helps to be a little paranoid.

And whatever they might say in the law schools, it also helps to have a grudge against society. The criminal lawyer, like the criminal, is the enemy of Law and Order. The criminal attacks society head on; the lawyer is trying to set you free after you have been caught so that you can go out and steal some more. Whether he succeeds or not, he profits from your crime. The only way you can pay him is out of the money you have got away with at one time or another, everybody knows that. It isn't called his share of the loot, of course. It's called "the fee." But that's only because he has a license that entitles him to do what he's doing, and you haven't.

At other times, however, it seems to me that whatever path I had happened to take, the destination would have been the same. I never had anything against stealing. The only thing that bothered me after I had robbed that department store with Charlie McCarthy, at the age of ten, was that I had to lie to my mother about why I had come home so late. As far as the robbery itself was concerned, I felt just great. The same thing happened, in a way, while I was working at the Metropolitan Insurance Company. I was an interior messenger in the mailing department and in no time at all I was doubling my salary by stealing rolls of postage stamps and cashing them in at their face value. The only pangs of conscience I suffered came when I learned that two of my coworkers had been arrested. After a few sleepless nights, I came to the conclusion that if the code of silence meant that it wasn't permissible to rat on anybody it also meant that it wasn't permissible to allow innocent people to take the rap for you. Just as I was about to turn myself in, I discovered that they had confessed. They had been stealing stamps too. Hell, half the people in the place had been stealing them. In one way, I felt relieved. In another, all the pleasure I had felt about having figured out such a foolproof scheme had been taken away.

But it's funny. I was already set against society, there's no doubt in my mind about that. And yet, when the United States declared war against Germany, a few weeks later, I was as ferocious a little patriot as you could have found anywhere. There's a dichotomy there that I can't explain except to say that I've seen it often among prisoners. I spent all of World War II in a Pennsylvania prison, and it seemed that hardly a day went by without my hearing somebody say, "You know what General MacArthur said, don't you? 'When I want the best ten soldiers in any camp for a really dangerous assignment I always know exactly where I can find them. I go to the stockade.' " Society seems to be one thing; the country something altogether different. I tried desperately to enlist in the army, but they wouldn't take me because I was too young. Neither would the navy or the marines. I tried to join the Canadian Army, which had an enlistment office over on Forty-second Street, and was told that they weren't taking American citizens any more. I was still so determined to get into uniform that I altered my birth certificate so that I could register in the draft. All the time that I was making good money in defense factories I was only marking time until I was called.

I was in Wheeling, West Virginia, working in a munitions factory when I received a telegram from my mother informing me that the draft board had finally ordered me to report for induction. As I got off the train the following afternoon and walked through the depot, there was an excitement in the air. An electric buzz. The word *armistice* seemed to be all around me, a word that I had never heard before. What it meant, I was told, was that the war was over.

Talk about mixed emotions. I couldn't help but be happy that the war was over and we had won, and yet my overriding emotion was one of terrible disappointment that I had been deprived of the chance to play any part in it.

36

Three months later, I was in jail. What had begun as a lark, and a romantic lark at that, had ended in charges of burglary, grand larceny, and abduction. My real career had begun.

On the Matter of Unlawful Entry

I met Carrie Wagner at a Brooklyn dance hall shortly after my return. She was fifteen years old, and a very protected fifteen. I knew about her in the way you knew about everybody in such a tight, inbred neighborhood. Her father owned and operated a spar yard down in Red Hook; that is, a yard for repairing the spars on sailing ships. Her mother had died when she was quite young, and her father had brought her up very strictly.

I was seventeen. A very experienced seventeen. Before I left Brooklyn, Tommy McGovern and I had been hitting Broadway regularly, crashing the dances at the better hotels or trying out the dance halls. Tommy was a handsome devil, with curly hair and dimples. I was blondish and not bad-looking, and if we didn't beat them off with a stick it was only because we didn't want to.

During my entire stay in Wheeling, West Virginia, I was living with a gorgeous southern blonde. Bell worked at the control table at the head of the assembly line, sorting out the defective shell casings as they came by, a job which allowed a certain amount of shaking and jiggling to go on underneath her coveralls when she was interested. First day at work, she looked at me and I looked at her and we recognized each other.

Her apartment was located in a very nice section of town, and if it was rather small it was beautifully furnished. My original assessment of her had been quite correct, though. At the age of fourteen she had run away from home, knowing that there had to be something more in life than a grubby little Georgia farm and knowing what she was going to use to get it. As soon as she stepped off the bus in Atlanta she was picked up by a sharpie who took her home with him. A few days later, he had her out hustling for him. She was such an eager pupil that within a matter of months he took her off the streets and had her giving exhibitions before selected audiences of the leading figures in the city. Before the year was over, she told me with pride, she had become almost as well known as the mayor. I could believe it. She was a virtuoso of the bedroom arts. An acrobat. The only thing she didn't like about it was that the pimp was taking all the money. When he landed in the hospital with a fractured skull, she grabbed the first train out of town. Somewhere along the line she met up with a small-time hood and part-time pimp named Johnny Kabouris. Also, she discovered, a drug addict. In a matter of months he was shot to death in an East End nightclub and lucky Bell fell heiress to the few thousand dollars he had stashed under the floorboards.

Now that she had a stake, she wasn't going to sell herself cheaply any more. She had bought some smart clothes, rented the apartment, and was keeping her eyes open for somebody who would set her up in a penthouse apartment in New York.

Six months I spent with her, living in high style off Kabouris's stash. She knew every action place in Wheeling and she had a roving eye that turned every visit to a bar into an adventure. Inevitably, that look she had given me the first day would fall upon someone else. He would straighten his tie and come strolling over, she would affect an air of injured innocence, and I would have to be ready to fight.

Six racking months.

Her greatest performance, however, was saved for the farewell scene after the telegram had arrived from my mother. Having thrown a going-away party for me which lasted through the night, she insisted upon going to the station with me so that she could pledge her undying love in the proper moving-picture setting and have us exchange our promises that we would get back together when I returned from the war—presumably so that we could go shopping for that penthouse in Manhattan. A truly magnificent performance, considering that we both had massive hangovers. With any luck at all, I thought, just before I dozed off in the train, she'd have another guy before she left the station.

Carrie, at age fifteen, was every bit as well developed as Bell. Which is saying something. While we were dancing I felt her lips brush my cheek. "Sounds great, doesn't it?" she whispered.

"What?" I asked gallantly. "The beat of my heart?"

"No, silly, the music."

I looked at her and she was blushing. After Bell, the blush, the innocence of that word *silly,* the freshness, the trembling of her body as she pressed closer to me, appealed to me beyond anything I had ever experienced before.

When the music stopped I took her around the waist and walked her over to the corner stand where the soft drinks were sold. She had a way of smiling, a slow smile that came up under lowered eyes. She had a cute little way of running the tip of her tongue across her upper lip that tried to tell you she wasn't quite as innocent as you might have thought.

I fell in love with her right there.

Before the night was over she was telling me all about her troubles with her father. If he had his way he would have locked her up in the house. He allowed her to go to the dances and movies with her two close girl friends, May Wallace and Lil Lavin, but in order to go out with boys she had to lie to him. Not that it did very much good. He'd be waiting for her at the door and if he saw her with the same boy twice he'd frighten him away.

"He can only frighten someone who's willing to be frightened," I said pointedly. "If you'd stand up to him yourself," I said, even more pointedly, "there wouldn't be a thing he could do about it."

We began to meet secretly, using her friends, May and Lil, as blinds. Sometimes we'd go out with them and their boyfriends. Sometimes we'd go out alone. Sooner or later, the confrontation was going to have to come, and, sure enough, one night as we were returning from the Prospect Theatre, a neighborhood vaudeville house, there he was. A block before we got to the house. If he ever saw me around his daughter again, he thundered, he was going to have me arrested.

I didn't back off an inch. "I love your daughter," I told him. "I'm going to keep going with her as long as she wants to go with me." So why didn't he be sensible about it, I said, and let me pick her up at the house and bring her home to the door?

You just couldn't talk to the man, though. He went into an absolute rage. "If I ever see you around here again," he yelled, "I'll give you so much trouble you won't know what hit you!" And he wasn't necessarily talking about the police, either.

And he was so wrong. If his worst fears hadn't come about it was only because the Catholic upbringing was still so strong in me that I was the one, far more than she, who wanted to wait until she was my wife. And it was driving us both crazy. Our plan was to elope as soon as I could get together a couple of hundred dollars. It was all we ever talked about. I had a job working part time for a florist, decorating churches for weddings mostly, and at the rate I was able to put anything away it was going to take forever. Well, one night when we were out with May Wallace and her boyfriend, Bill Lavin, Carrie suddenly came out with the information that her father always kept at least a couple of hundred dollars in his office safe.

All I asked was one question: Could she get the key? All four of us became very excited. We'd go down the next night, we decided, take a couple of hundred dollars, and, when the opportune moment came, run off and get married. After we had given her father a little time to cool off, we figured, we could come back and confront him with a fait accompli.

By the next night May Wallace had lost her nerve. Bill, however, was still game for anything. It was a dark, overcast night. Carrie inserted the key and opened the door that let us into the yard. I could distinguish the dim outlines of the ships tied to the dock and hear the sucking sound of the water pushing against the hulls. Small lights on the decks of the ships rose and fell with the rhythm of the incoming tide, and the odd shapes of the marine machinery around the yard cast weird shadows on the ground.

And then, all of a sudden, I was practically jumping out of my shoes. Two enormous dogs had come leaping out of the darkness, barking ferociously. Carrie had told me about them, and I had completely forgotten. They were the dogs her father kept in the yard to guard the office. She called to them by name, knelt down, put her arms around them, and in a second they were wagging their tails and trying to lick her face.

The office was in a small wooden building. Across the room was an old-fashioned safe that opened with a key. The money was in a large tin box in the back corner. We were expecting, remember, to find two or three hundred dollars. I opened the cover and it was full to the top. Overflowing with money. They were all small bills, I found out later—fives, tens, and twenties —but there were so many of them there that it came to sixteen thousand dollars. Immediately, I slammed the cover shut. In that moment, my plans had changed. We were going to take it, box and all, and start a new life somewhere else. Carrie was all aglow. Bill was so excited that he insisted upon coming along to be our best man.

It had all happened so quickly that when we got to Grand Central Station we didn't have the slightest idea where we were going. I looked up at the departure board, saw that the next train was going to Albany, and Albany it was.

Frankly, Carrie was in a gayer mood on the way up than I was. For although I was very easily able to blame her father for forcing us to steal the money, I wasn't quite able to convince myself that he was going to take the loss of both his daughter and his money without moving heaven and earth to find us.

It wasn't until we were safely settled in our rooms at the Ten Eyck Hotel—Carrie and I in one room and Bill in another—that the original gaiety, the sense of adventure, returned. We were going to stay in Albany only long enough to buy a car and a few provisions, then head for California. Bill was still with us all the way.

The next morning we had breakfast sent up to the room. I felt like a king, and I had the money to live like one. Carrie, having become a woman, was transformed. We spent the day on a wild shopping spree. Complete new wardrobes for all three of us. A squirrel coat for Carrie costing nine hundred dollars. A wedding ring costing twenty-five hundred. Everything Aunt Alice had told me about class was forgotten. We spread money around lavishly. A haircut cost fifteen cents, and I tipped the barber five dollars. The taxi driver, twenty-five dollars.

The next day we took a taxi to the adjoining town, Olean, and drove back in a brand-new Reo coupe costing twelve hundred dollars. I had been behind the wheel of a car perhaps two or three times in my whole life, but in those days you didn't have to have a license and I saw no reason why I couldn't learn as I went along. Brakes were screeching all around me; other drivers were screaming. By the time we got back to the hotel, Carrie and Bill were nervous wrecks.

In 1919, a cross-country trip by automobile was a long and precarious journey. The best way to get to California, we had been advised by the automobile dealer, was to set out from Washington, D.C. In the morning, we started out, holding our breaths as we drove through New York. When we arrived in Philadelphia we registered at the Bellevue-Stratford, spent the day visiting the places of historic interest, and then went to the theater and made the rounds of the night spots. We wandered around Washington for a couple of days too, visiting the museums and art galleries. Although I wasn't quite the menace on the roadway that I had been, I wasn't really that eager to drive all the way across the country any more. A better idea came to me. Why not go to Canada? It was safer, it was closer, and it would probably even be easier for a couple of underage Americans to get married.

So now we retraced the route and headed north. As we were passing through New Jersey a terrible clatter developed in the motor. Nobody had told me that a car had to be oiled, and with all that driving we had burnt out a bearing.

By this time, most of the sixteen thousand dollars was gone and I was growing more and more uneasy about putting off the wedding. As we set out again, after the repairs had been made, I told Carrie that we were going to get married at whatever city we happened to stop off to spend the night. We drove right through New York City for a second time, passed through Westchester, and at five in the evening I pulled up to the entrance of the Windsor Hotel in the middle of Poughkeepsie. Any number of people were passing by; it was a busy hour on a busy street. I picked out one particularly pleasant-looking fellow and asked if he could tell me where the marriage-license bureau was. "Sure," he said. He turned around and pointed to a building only two blocks away. "But," he said, smiling, "it's closed for the day." It would open again at nine in the morning.

Carrie had come out of the car right behind me. She had the wedding ring wrapped in a handkerchief, and while I was thanking him she took the handkerchief out of her purse and the ring dropped to the sidewalk. The stranger picked it up and handed it back to her. And smiled at us, in the way people smile at young lovers, as we entered the hotel.

All three of us were so exhausted that we dined in the hotel and planned to retire early so that we could be first in line when the marriage bureau opened. Bill had scarcely gone back to his room when there was a knock at the door. Our friend, the pleasant-looking stranger, was standing there. He was the chief of police, he announced as pleasantly as ever, and part of his job was to question everybody who came to town.

Soon enough he let us know why he was really there: A bulletin had been sent out for a young man, answering my description, who had stolen some money from a man in Brooklyn and abducted his daughter. He knew it was us. We admitted it.

There was nothing to do except go back to police headquarters with him and wait for the detectives who would be sent up from Brooklyn to take us back. The small room in police headquarters contained a rolltop desk and a few hard chairs. Every policeman on duty must have come in while we were there, and while ostensibly it was to offer us a few words of sympathy, you could see by the way they looked Carrie over what they were really saying among themselves. Carrie drew closer and closer to me and finally turned her head against my shoulder, put her arm around my neck, and held on.

When the detectives arrived from Brooklyn and her father wasn't with them, I was terribly disappointed in him. I couldn't believe that he thought so little of his daughter that he wouldn't even come up to bring her home himself. When we reached Grand Central, Carrie was taken one way and Bill and I another. We were taken to the Raymond Street jail, which had the look of an ancient fortress. Turreted walls and all. The stones were heavily rutted and coated with the grime of a century. My cell contained a latticed steel bunk suspended from the wall on two heavy chains. The two thin blankets gave off an odor as pungent as the smell of the disinfectant that seemed to be everywhere. I sat up through the long night praying devoutly that one night was all I was going to have to spend there. It wasn't. In the morning we learned that Carrie's father had bailed her out—which made me feel better about him—and also that he was determined to press charges. Which he didn't. It was three weeks before we were brought to court, and by the third or fourth night I was not only sleeping on the bunk, I was sleeping like a babe.

My first experience in jail. The food that was brought to us in the cell was at the barest subsistence level; a tasteless mush, some meatless stew and a watery soup. The first time we were brought out into the yard for exercise, however, we were tipped off that if you had the money you could buy anything. There was a regular price list. Order anything you want, pay up, and it would be brought in from the outside, still steaming. Fresh sheets and towels could be bought from the linen man. Toilet articles too if you wanted them.

When we were finally brought into court and assigned a lawyer we were told that all three of us had been indicted for burglary and grand larceny, and that Bill and I had also been indicted for abduction. To make the picture even gloomier, we were up in front of Judge Dike, who was known far and wide as the toughest judge in Brooklyn. Carrie and her father both kept their eyes straight ahead. Whether Mr. Wagner had agreed to a deal I never did learn, but Judge Dike allowed all three of us to plead guilty to unlawful entry—which may or may not have been judicial humor—sentenced each of us to one year in the reformatory, and then immediately suspended sentence. The terms of my probation were that I was to get a job and stay away from Carrie. The terms of her probation were that she was to stay away from me. If we tried to contact each other in any way, the judge told us sternly, we would both be arrested and made to serve out the full year.

Carrie's father took her firmly by the arm and marched her out. Our lawyer seemed to want to get us out of there before Judge Dike could change his mind. As we came out to the top of the steps, Carrie glanced back fleetingly in my direction. And then her father was hurrying her away. I saw her only twice again in my life.

I was able to get a job at the P. T. Morse Shipyard as an apprentice burner. Which meant that I was working with an acetylene torch, cutting steel plate, burning out rivets, and the like. I threw myself into the work so totally that within a few months I was promoted to a full burner, which allowed me all the overtime I wanted. The ease with which it was possible to cut through the steel hull of an ocean liner fascinated me. I'd be standing on a platform, suspended from the deck of an ocean liner, with a canvas tent around me to shield me from the sharp winds coming off the river. Every now and then I'd have to lift the canvas to let the wind blow away the gaseous fumes, but while I was working I was in a world of my own. As the molten metal bubbled and smoked beneath the blue flame of the torch, the ship's hull would become a bank vault in my mind. I made the connection quite consciously, not merely to pass the time in harmless fantasy but in conscious training for something I

45

wanted to do. I already knew a great deal about vaults and the inner workings of a bank. I never doubted that I was going to be putting all this specialized knowledge to the best possible use.

To perfect my technique I'd sometimes work around the clock, twenty-four hours straight. It was going to catch up with me, of course, and it did. I collapsed at work, literally keeled over, and the foreman told me that he didn't want to see me for a week. One day's rest was all I could take. By the second night I was getting edgy. With all the dance halls in Brooklyn, I wandered down to Prospect Hall, the first time I had been there since the night I met Carrie. While I was at the table sipping a soft drink, one of the girls from my own neighborhood popped up at my elbow. Sue Gregory. A beautiful girl and a jolly girl. One of the most beautiful girls in Brooklyn. She always used to kid me that she was holding out for a millionaire but that she'd make an exception in my case if I could only come up with half a million.

Sue had always been a friend of Carrie's, and she was one of the few old friends Carrie's father still allowed her to see. It had been she, more than anybody else, who had filled me in on the depressing details whenever I'd bump into her on the street.

Sue and I were out on the floor dancing when, just like it had to happen, I looked up and saw Carrie entering the hall. May Wallace was with her, and that alone was enough to tell me that she had broken away from her father for the night. Sue must have felt me stiffen because she looked to the door and, without saying a word, took my elbow, guided me toward the sidelines, and walked away. I had spent ten months living this scene in my mind, and now that we were face to face I couldn't think of a thing to say.

Feeling the stares of our friends on us, we moved out to the dance floor together, which was enough in itself to send us to jail for a year. While we were dancing I told her I was going to slip out after a reasonable amount of time had passed and, if she wanted to talk, I'd be waiting two blocks away.

She came. The first thing I noticed was that the wedding ring I had bought for her was suspended from a gold chain on her neck. I knew she hadn't been wearing it in the dance hall and I could guess that she kept it in her purse and wore it only in secret. We embraced briefly and spent the next hour or so walking aimlessly through the side streets.

With her voice sometimes dropping to a whisper, she told me how her father had banished her old friends from the house and selected a whole new circle of friends for her. And then she dropped the bomb. One of his personally screened suitors was a young man named Jack Strang, the heir to the Strang warehouses. Carrie's father had arranged a match with the Strang family, and she was under heavy pressure to marry him. When she complained that she wasn't in love with him, her father was quick to let her know that in view of the highly publicized loss of her virtue she wasn't in any position to be choosy, let alone to balk at a prize catch like Jack Strang.

Rather desperately, I suggested that we elope again. I had plenty of money now, I told her. More than enough to get started. The only thing that could come out of that, she pointed out, was another fiasco. The police would be after us before the night was over, and this time we would most certainly end up in jail. I could only kick myself. First for being so stupid as to run off the way we had, and then for not having gotten married immediately, as we had planned. Then and there, I made a vow that I would never again do anything without knowing exactly what I was setting out to do ahead of time, and considering all the possible consequences.

For now, we agreed, it would be the better part of wisdom to be patient. After the probation period was over, we could meet openly and make our plans.

Just before our probation was coming to an end, I heard that she and Strang were getting married. The next Sunday I slipped into the rear pew of the church and watched the ceremony. Strang was a good-looking, slender young man, a couple of years older than me. He had very rosy cheeks but, along with it, such deep-set eyes that it gave him a frail, rather ascetic look. When they left the altar on the way out of church they passed within fifteen feet of me. Carrie looked so beautiful that it hurt, although it seemed to me that there was a vacant look behind her eyes.

I waited until everybody else had gone before I left. The sky was slate gray and the streets were completely empty. I had never felt quite so empty myself, but I swear that I wished her every happiness in the world.

She didn't have it. The reason a family like the Strangs would marry their son off to as "flawed" a woman as Carrie was that he was flawed too. He had tuberculosis. Whether his family had concealed it from Carrie's father or he had concealed it from her was something I was never able to find out.

The way I heard it was that his family had sent them to Florida right after the wedding, in the belief that he would recover. He didn't. Within six months Carrie was a widow. She had spent those six months trying to nurse her husband back to health while he was wasting away to nothing.

I learned about it from her friends after she had returned to Brooklyn. She stayed with her father through the period of mourning, and then they moved out to Avenue M, in another section of Brooklyn.

I never saw her again. Nor did I particularly want to. By that time, she was another part of my life. Soon afterward, I left Brooklyn under conditions that would have made it very foolish for me to return. I was a fugitive, wanted by the Brooklyn police on a murder charge.

Murder One

Once my probation was at an end, which means right after Carrie's marriage, I left my father's house and moved into my own apartment on Fulton Street. I was hanging out with my old friend Tommy McGovern again. We were hitting the Broadway nightclubs and dance palaces regularly and, when we were in the mood for the bizarre, Greenwich Village. Not infrequently with another former classmate from PS 10, Eddie Wilson.

Eddie Wilson was blond and maybe even better-looking than Tommy. Where he got it from I'll never know because he left school the same time I did, but he had a fancy vocabulary, an Oxford accent which he could call upon when the spirit moved him, and the manners of a duke. Put it all together with a truly angelic expression and he could charm the birds off the trees. He had gone to work as a bellhop in the Great Northern Hotel, a very fashionable hotel up on Fifty-seventh Street, which was the posh uptown district in Manhattan, and in no time at all had been promoted to bell captain.

He also turned into a natural thief once the opportunity arose. His mother once told him, "You continue to associate with Willie Sutton and you'll wind up on the gallows." My mother had been known to say the same thing about some of my other friends, but never about sweet-faced Eddie Wilson. As it turned out, his mother was the better prophet. Not long after I was off probation, a general depression hit the shipyards, and I became something that satisfied me more, an armed robber—a story I will go into shortly. Although Tommy was my closest friend, it was Eddie who, by natural predilection and coincidence, became my first real crime partner.

He was also a pool shark. Whenever Tommy and I were looking to pick him up we knew we could find him in One-arm Quigg's pool hall. Joe Quigg was a former longshoreman, a barrel-chested man with an almost grotesquely large head. Despite the fact that his left arm had been amputated, he would set the pool stick in the crook of his arm, just above the stub, and he could beat just about anybody in Brooklyn. He was also a feared rough-and-tumble fighter, which was just as well because his pool hall was a known hangout for toughs and thieves. Whenever the detectives from the Sixth Precinct were looking for anybody, Joe Quigg's was their first port of call.

On the evening of July 10, 1921, I went into Joe Quigg's to meet McGovern and Wilson. Tommy had just got a good job as an electrician at Bush Terminal and we had decided to go down to McCann's restaurant to celebrate. We waited for Wilson to finish off his game and, as we were leaving, Tommy said, "I hope you noticed how Happy Gleason was giving you the bad eye."

I had noticed that Happy Gleason was playing nine-ball on the rear table with his flunky, Tom O'Leary, but that's all I had noticed. I had made it a habit, I let them know, not to notice that Happy Gleason was alive. Eddie suggested that I had better start paying more attention or I'd find myself with my back turned to him at the wrong time.

I already knew that. *That* much attention they could be sure I would always pay.

Why they called him Happy I'll never know. I never saw him smile. His normal expression was either a sneer or a glower. Gleason was a few years older than me. A pretty strong guy and a good fighter. There had been a time when it seemed to be the ambition of everybody in Park Slope, myself included, to be a prizefighter. Every morning a mob of us would be out jogging the full four or five miles around Prospect Park, and after school we'd all be at the YMCA gym training for a mythical fight. Quite a few of the guys actually did succeed in becoming main event fighters in the neighborhood club, and a couple of them graduated to the big fight club down in Coney Island.

I was a pretty well-built kid; it was only after years on a prison diet and a long hunger strike that I became skinny. But, still, I was a pretty slick little boxer, all footwork and left jabs. My career as a future middleweight contender had come to an end with the discovery that it was more fun staying out late nights with the girls than running around a park in the morning. Happy had been careful to stay in shape; he was still one of the better fighters at the Y.

He was a bully-boy. If there had been an unpopularity award he would have won it hands down. He was always crashing the private parties that were held around the neighborhood and breaking them up by starting fights. The same thing with dances, although I must say that even without Happy there was always a fifty-fifty chance that any dance was going to break up with a fight.

Happy Gleason also had his own little gang and he used his ability as a fighter to strong-arm anybody he could. He shook down the local bookmakers and the word was around that he was a police informer. Which figured. If a shakedown artist was a stoolie for a detective down at the precinct, he was going to be protected. He'd also take money away from the neighborhood prostitute whenever she came around, and I had become a good enough student of human psychology by then to recognize that the difference between shaking down a prostitute and pimping for her was so slight that he was going to be taking her over and working a stable of his own as soon as he could get himself used to the idea.

My real trouble with him had begun six months earlier, right after New Year's when a group of us who called ourselves the Jolly 5—me, McGovern, Wilson, and two other guys—was running a dance at Acme Hall. We had worked very hard and we had a sellout. It was more than just renting the dance hall and hiring a popular band; the real work came in publicizing the affair and selling the tickets ahead of time. I was at the door taking tickets when I saw Gleason and O'Leary coming up the long, narrow flight of stairs. It was obvious that they had been drinking and that they were looking for trouble. "Just turn around and get going," I said, blocking the entrance. "You're not welcome here."

Happy insisted just as strenuously that nobody was going to keep him out. "Blow," I said. "Screw." In no time at all he did exactly what I expected him to do. He threw a punch. But he was drunk and I was sober. I caught his arm and shoved, and Happy went tumbling down the stairway, taking O'Leary along with him. I went running right down after them. If there was going to be a fight, I wanted it to take place at the bottom of the stairs, not at the top, where it might spill into the hall. Gleason looked up, saw that a couple of my associates had come out to the landing, and both he and O'Leary walked away. But not before he gave me the look that says, I'm going to get you for this, Sutton.

Everybody in the neighborhood knew that, sooner or later, we were going to have it out. Like I had said to Eddie Wilson: I might go out of my way to show him he was nothing to me, but I didn't intend to let him get behind me in an alley, either.

We left McCann's shortly before midnight. Tommy went home to get some sleep. Eddie and I stopped back at Quigg's. As we were going in I noticed—in the casual way you notice anything out of the usual—that Jerry Hughes, the neighborhood bookie, was across the street talking to a couple of guys I had never seen before. We only stayed there for a few minutes. It was so hot even that late at night that the door was kept open, and even then, the pool hall was so filled with smoke that it was sweltering. A friend of mine named Joe Collins, who worked nights at the postal telegraph, had taken a bungalow down at Coney Island about a week earlier, and he had given me a blanket invitation to come down anytime I wanted. "Let's go down and stay the night," I told Eddie. "And tomorrow we can go swimming."

Eddie wasn't interested. He headed home and I walked a few blocks in the opposite direction to catch the trolley car for Coney Island. At the station I ran into a friend, Al Noonan, and stood there talking to him for maybe five or ten minutes while I was waiting for the trolley.

Collins was off work that night. He was sitting in his bathing trunks on the porch, because even on the ocean it was too hot to sleep. Through most of the night we sat there on the porch, drinking beer and telling lies.

The next day I was awakened by a phone call from Eddie Wilson, telling me that Gleason had been gunned down outside the pool hall within minutes after we had left. Apparently, somebody had been waiting in ambush across the street. Gleason had been killed. O'Leary had been shot three times and wasn't expected to live.

He didn't have to say any more than that for me

to know that if they didn't grab the killer right away I was going to come under suspicion. Later in the afternoon he came down to the bungalow and told me that Detective Sammy Todd had been assigned to the case. A bearcat. Todd had questioned a number of people and then gone to both Eddie's house and mine, looking for us.

I did have an alibi of sorts, through Noonan and Collins, but even I could see where the timing was going to be too tight to be convincing. Sooner or later, I figured, the police would find out who had done it, and if I wasn't around to be worked over in the meantime they'd forget all about me.

There were several possibilities that I could see:

1. Jerry Hughes had hired a couple of out-of-town killers.

2. It was a routine gang murder by somebody whose territory Gleason was trying to muscle into.

3. He had been taken care of by one of the thousand-odd enemies he had made, possibly even some guy whose girl he had insulted.

That evening I called Tommy McGovern. Tommy's brother was on the police force, and so Tommy was able to supply us with the latest details. A dozen shotgun blasts had been fired. O'Leary was still alive. Sammy Todd seemed to be convinced that I was the killer, probably because he didn't have anything else to go on. And the word around the Sixth Precinct was that Sammy Todd had just lost his prize stoolie.

Now I knew I couldn't turn myself in. There were two forms of police investigations in those days. They got information from paid informers or they beat a confession out of someone. They beat you up and they kicked you all over the place and, if you were lucky, they apologized when they released you. I had no desire at all to walk in and say, "Here I am, beat the hell out of me."

Eddie Wilson felt exactly the same way, and so Tommy went out and rented an apartment for us on Fifty-second Street on the west side of New York.

A month or so later, Tommy brought us the news that we had both been indicted for murder. There still weren't any bulletins out for us, though, that was the odd thing about it. As a matter of fact, Eddie had continued to work at the Great Northern Hotel and nobody had even come to check up on him there. We could still be reasonably confident, therefore, that the police were just trying to prove they were on the job, and that the indictment would lay there and be forgotten. Just to play it safe, though, we decided to separate and make no attempt to contact each other until we could be sure that nobody except Sammy Todd was looking for us.

Eddie leased an apartment on the upper West Side, not far from his hotel, under the name of Eddie Loring. I was already working in the downtown office of the Con Edison Company under the name of Leo Holland, the name Tommy had used to rent the apartment, so I moved down to Sixteenth Street. I had got the job through an employment agency during my first week in New York. I was a repairman. I worked on all kinds of household appliances: electric irons, toasters, curling irons, percolators, waffle irons. And anything else I could get my hands on.

My immediate superior, Mr. Hubble, took such a liking to me from the first that he invited me to his home for dinner a couple of times a month. When he saw that I was such an ambitious young fellow he began to recommend various trade pamphlets and technical books that would help me in repairing the more intricate electrical systems that occasionally came into the shop. Such as . . . well, burglar alarms.

Ever anxious to improve myself, I began to spend a considerable amount of time at the library reading up on the operation and installation of even more sophisticated electrical alarm systems, for the primary purpose of learning how to circumvent them. After I had read through everything the library had to offer, I haunted the secondhand bookstores for anything I could find.

Now, it was purely by chance that the employment agency had sent me to Edison. Just as it had been purely by chance that a banking institution had been hiring school kids for summer jobs and that the shipyard had happened to have an opening for an apprentice burner. But the mind finds what the mind wants, doesn't it? A year later I was dating a lot of girls who worked in the theater, chorus girls and bit players, hardly unusual for a young guy on the loose in New York. I found the use of makeup so fascinating that I spent a great deal of time in the dressing rooms experimenting while the shows were going on. Not because I had any desire to be an actor but only because I could see how valuable the ability to alter one's appearance could be to a thief.

I had already left Edison by then. Rather abruptly and through no fault of my own. The repair shop where I worked was in back. Out in front were the demonstrators and sales people. The head buyer and top demonstrator, Mrs. Valerie Rodgers, was an especially beautiful and aloof woman. Everybody in the plant had made a play for her at one time or another, I was told, and every advance had been turned away. She was probably eight or nine years older than me —what the hell, I was only twenty—but I gave her my very best line and the air turned absolutely frigid.

Who cared? I wasn't making the Broadway beat so much any more, but that was only because I was living right on the edge of Greenwich Village. In the post-war sexual revolution, Greenwich Village had become, more than ever, the natural homing ground for the nonconforming and the uninhibited. A den of iniquity, a sink of perversion. In other words, the place to go. Once you got to be known around as a guy who lived in the neighborhood, you were accepted everywhere.

Tommy and I would usually meet at Madame Cutty's Pink Elephant, a jazz joint which catered to the homos, the lesbians, and the whole cast of the *Psychopathia Sexualis*. The place was always packed, the tables were jammed very closely together, and it was a rare night that didn't produce a fight between a couple of butch lesbians. They didn't pull hair or scratch either, they swung from the heels. I knew a few of them who would use a knife quicker than a man, and on far less provocation. One night while I was waiting for Tommy, who unaccountably had failed to show up, a young guy named Smitty, whom I had seen around several Village places, came over to my table and sat down. He was a customer's man down on Wall Street and—I don't know why I remember this—a Fordham graduate. At the moment Smitty was a little drunk and a lot unhappy about the increasing lesbian tendencies of his girl friend, Stella. The next thing I knew he was inviting me to accompany him to her apartment on Macdougal Street, which was only a few blocks away. There was always a party going on at her place, he groaned. That was another of the things that had gone wrong with them.

The party was in full swing. More people were dancing without clothes than with them, and the sexes were paired off in every possible combination and draped around the room in a remarkable combination of positions. And who did I see across the room, dancing naked with another woman, but Valerie Rodgers. The place was so crowded, the lights were so low, and she was so occupied that she didn't see me. Not that I cared one way or the other. Stella had come to the door to greet us. She was wearing an unbuttoned painter's frock, and her bra was fastened underneath her breasts in a way that served them up at you on a silver platter. It was obvious that she was drunk and it was just as obvious that if Smitty had ever intended to tell her off, that wasn't his intention any longer.

Before very long I was corralled by a lady poet who was down to her panties—not that she had enough on top to matter. While I was watching Smitty and Stella disappear into one of the bedrooms, the poetess was spouting Ezra Pound and slipping out of her panties. Being a lover of modern poetry, I took the hint and we headed for one of the other bedrooms. And damned if we didn't walk right in on Valerie. She wasn't with a woman any more. She was with a man. Performing what is sometimes called an unnatural act upon him. Although I pulled the poetess out of there as quickly as possible, Valerie had seen me. Later in the night she came over and begged me not to tell anybody at the place.

"Valerie," I said, "you have nothing to fear from me." And she didn't. She liked what she liked; that was her business. If she made it a policy to keep her business career and her sexual adventures in completely separate compartments, I could see where that was the smart thing to do. I had to tip my hat to her.

The next morning I came in to find the place in a commotion. The safe had been blown open during the night and the payroll had been stolen. A couple of city detectives took over, and for the next three days they called in the employees, one at a time, to question them. I wasn't exactly worried, but I wasn't exactly whistling a happy tune, either. If there's one thing a fugitive doesn't need it's to be involved in a police investigation. Especially when I didn't have an alibi that I could use. Fortunately, I didn't need one. I was one of the very last to be called, and as soon as I came through the door Mr. Hubble said, "Leo is a personal friend of mine. I'll vouch for him."

Nobody was arrested, and about three weeks later the company hired the Pinkerton Detective Agency. In those days, you have to understand, the Pinkertons were every bit as powerful as the police and a hell of a lot more efficient. Big, beefy men were in and out of the main office for the next couple of weeks, and several of my fellow workers began to complain that they were being followed home. I was having lunch a couple of streets away in a Charles restaurant, one of the better chains of the time, when I saw Valerie Rodgers come in, look around, and come hurrying over to my table. "Leo," she said, "don't go back to the place." She had been in the front office and from what she had been able to overhear I was in a whole lot of trouble. "I wasn't able to catch exactly why," she said, "but you've become the Pinkertons' prime suspect. They're going to call you in and question you as soon as you get back."

Before I left the restaurant I had to make up my mind whether I was going to go back and take my chances or just walk off and blow the job. If I went back and they fingerprinted me they'd probably find out that I was wanted for murder in Brooklyn. Assuming, of course, that they didn't already know. If I didn't go back, they were going to assume I had committed the robbery.

I took Valerie's advice and moved back uptown. The irony of it didn't escape me. For the second time I was running away because of a crime I hadn't committed, while the crimes I had actually committed I had gotten away with.

Because not to be too coy about this I had committed some crimes before I left Brooklyn. Three armed robberies, to be exact. In my travels around Broadway I had come in contact with a lot of thieves. One of my favorites was a jewel thief named Joe Vasquez, who would operate in only the most exclusive hotels in the city. What Vasquez would do was watch the society columns and theater pages to find out who was in town and then knock off the best-looking prospects. He fenced the stuff with the Feldman Brothers, who had a jewelry store on lower Broadway, and he had always assured me that anytime I wanted to do business with them all I'd have to do was walk in and say, "The Mexican is recommending me."

The first time I took him up on it came after I had met a guy named Ed Kinney, who was just out of prison. Kinney just happened to mention that while he had been visiting his sister in Brooklyn he had spotted a jewelry store that had a very nice diamond display in the window. "An easy take," in his opinion.

Since I would be going back to Brooklyn anyway, he suggested that I look the place over and see what I thought.

For three days I looked the place over. Kinney was working as a janitor in a run-down apartment building in upper Manhattan and when I went to see him in the little room they had given him in the basement, I came with a plan. The owner of the jewelry store came in about half an hour before the place opened so that he could remove the jewelry from his safe and put out his window displays. My plan called for me to use an heirloom watch I had to get him to open the door for me during that half hour. Kinney's job would be to follow behind me and stand guard over the owner while I was cleaning out the safe.

Early the next morning we met again in Brooklyn and he handed me a gun. Ten minutes after the owner entered I was at the door, tapping on the glass. When he came out to signal that he wasn't open for business

58

yet, I dangled the watch before him and, mouthing the words distinctly, said, "It must be repaired today. Very valuable."

Immediately he opened the door and let me in. While he was examining the watch, I kept waiting for Kinney. I went into a long explanation of what was wrong with it, and still no Kinney. Kinney was nowhere to be seen. So I went into action without him, and within a few minutes departed with my briefcase packed with jewelry.

The next day, after I had paid my call upon the Feldman Brothers, I went uptown to see what Mr. Kinney had to say for himself. His story was that just as he had been about to enter the store, a detective had recognized him, making it necessary for him to keep on walking for four or five blocks to throw the guy off the trail. By the time he was able to double back, he said, I was gone. All I had to do was ask a couple of questions, and he had to admit that what had really happened was that he had lost his nerve.

I looked at the guy and he was trembling. I looked at the room and the few odds and ends of furniture that no self-respecting junkman would have taken, and I thought to myself, No wonder he's willing to do anything to get his hands on some money. I wouldn't live in a place like this for a million dollars.

I gave him some of the money and walked out.

I kept the gun.

Using pretty much the same kind of technique, I robbed an insurance company and a shoe store. The insurance company was nothing. I just walked in, had the manager open the safe, and walked out with eighty-five hundred dollars. On the shoe store I only got a little over a thousand dollars, but I got a lot more satisfaction out of it. See, the shoe store was on a very busy section of Fulton Street, and I had to figure out a way to take the place and get out without hurting the guy. Well, right next to the store there was a building that had an exit on both sides of the lobby. Right at the back exit there was a cab stand.

I walked into the store a few minutes after the manager arrived, made him open the safe for me, and took the cash. There was a stockroom under the store.

I had him go down the stairs and then I walked out the door, into the building next door, through the lobby, out the back door, into a cab, and I was gone.

I had only been an occasional thief in Brooklyn, though. An amateur. Very shortly after I had walked away from the Edison Company, I became a professional. A professional thief is a man who wakes up every morning thinking of committing a crime the same way any other man gets up and goes to his job. For the next year and a half of my life I was part of one of the very best safecracking gangs in the country. Courtesy of Eddie Wilson.

For perhaps six months, the only word I'd had about Eddie Wilson had come from Tommy Mc-Govern. The last thing I had heard was that he was still working as captain of the bellboys at the Great Northern Hotel and was practically married to the daughter of a well-to-do Bronx doctor. Tommy and I were sitting in the Roseland ballroom shortly after I had moved back uptown when I felt a slap on my back and found myself looking into those familiar angelic features. Roseland was famous in those days for its flashy dressers, but Eddie's outfit put them all to shame. Flashy was the word all right. Before the night was over he had taken us all over town, flashing a roll that would have choked a horse. Neither Tommy nor I bought the story that he was getting rich from the stock tips he was getting from the Wall Street tycoons who stayed at his hotel, and when he asked me to meet him in the lobby the next evening I was sure of it.

"In case you were wondering," he said when I got there, "I didn't just happen to bump into you last night." He had a proposition he wanted to put to me, and he had been sure that sooner or later I would show up at Roseland. Eddie wasn't even working at the hotel any more. He had become part of a three-man gang of safecrackers. The leader, he informed me, was an absolute genius. Eddie Tate. Otherwise known as either Dr. Stadley or Dr. Tate. A master safecracker who planned everything so carefully that he had reduced the risk to practically zero. "If you're trying to think what jobs you've read about that could have been us," he said, "don't strain yourself. We only work out of state. That's one of the ways he's such a genius."

As successful as they had been, Eddie said, they could have been doing even better if they had a fourth man. Eddie had recommended me. Did I want to meet the master criminal?

The next day I was talking to Doc Tate.

The apartment was on West Eighty-seventh Street over by Riverside Drive, a very exclusive neighborhood in those days. In those three-story brick apartment buildings you could find some of the wealthiest men in the city and some of the fanciest-kept women. It was an elegant apartment Tate lived in, thickly carpeted and luxuriously decorated. The walls were lined with oil paintings. Everything about it reflected taste and culture.

Tate himself was dressed in banker's clothes, striped pants, and a frock coat. He was a tall, thick-chested man in his early forties but he moved with the grace of a dancer. (He always wore gloves when he went out, partly because he was a dandy, partly to protect his valuable hands, and partly because he suffered from periodic attacks of rheumatism, which forced us, on several occasions, to postpone going out on a job.)

He was out of Chicago, a university man with a vocabulary that absolutely dazzled me. Even though I knew I was going to put in with him before I had finished my first cocktail, we talked until dawn. What impressed me most was that he abhorred violence of any kind. Under no circumstances, he emphasized, would he permit anybody who worked with him to carry a dangerous weapon. Not even a knife. His philosophy was that it was better to allow yourself to be captured than to hurt anybody. Jail was an acceptable risk of the profession, he felt. Sooner or later you'd get out. Kill somebody and you'd be there for life.

He also believed in an even split of the loot. "We all take the same chance," he said. "We all get the same cut."

He took such pride in his work that his eyes shone while he was telling me about some of the jobs he had pulled off. The never-ending battle with the manufacturers of safes and locking devices fascinated him. He had all the latest "burglarproof" locks in his apartment. He would take the locks apart, examine them for any structural defects or weaknesses, and reassemble them. The locking devices on safes and vaults were given special study. His promise to me was that he would teach me his craft, and he had an eager student. "Anything with a hole in it," he liked to say, "can be picked." And it was true. Anything with a hole in it could be picked then, and anything with a hole in it I could still pick today. This is not going to be a primer in lock picking, but I will say this much: Despite what you see in the movies, it takes two picks to spring a lock. Doc Tate could sit there in his apartment and pick a lock open while he was talking to you. And before very long, so could I.

The fourth member of the team was Matt O'Reilly, who was his complete opposite in every way. O'Reilly had come out of the East Side slums and he was street smart. Having fallen under the influence of both Tate and Wilson, he tried very hard to use big words and to dress and act like a gentleman. He never succeeded in looking or sounding like anything except a hoodlum. But he was good-natured, completely trustworthy, and he had a dry Irish wit of his own which kind of grew on you. Everything considered, he balanced the team off perfectly.

As Wilson had said, we never worked anywhere near New York City. We'd either hit a city in upper New York, like Albany or Buffalo, or go to one of the neighboring states. Up to New England and as far west as Pittsburgh. Tate's system, the thing that made all that traveling worthwhile, was that we'd knock off as many as six or seven stores on the same street, sometimes in the same block. Preparation was the key to it. Each foray involved two weekends. On the first weekend, one member of the team would go to the designated city, register at the best hotel, and look over the main streets to see where the money was. Sometimes the advance man would have a contact in town who could tip him to the most likely prospect. Or—and this was the most valuable information you could get—the name of a place where the payroll was taken from the bank on Thursday and kept in their safe overnight.

In any event, it was the advance man's responsibility to lay out the whole job. Map the selected site, the method of entry, the type of safe involved, the protective device that would be encountered, and the estimated take. A jewelry store would usually be the prime target, and then we'd knock off a drugstore and everything else along the line. There weren't that many robberies in those days, and people were very trusting. Drugstores, for instance, were a cinch. Drugstores always did a very good business but their safes were primitive and their alarm systems nonexistent to laughable.

If we had a tip on a payroll, the four of us would come back the next Thursday. If not, we'd come in over the weekend. We always traveled separately, on different trains or buses. Each of us would register at a different hotel, and come together only to case the site in the daylight and then again when it was time to go to work. After we had cleaned out the block we'd go back to our hotels, check out at staggered intervals, and return, separately again, to New York.

The next day we'd run down to the out-of-town-newspaper stand on Times Square and buy the papers from the city we had just hit. In theory, it was to make sure we hadn't left any clues behind. The truth was that we always got a great kick out of reading our press notices.

We never ran into anything like real trouble. And when we did it turned out to be funny. In Boston, we were taking our third safe on a block up near Scollay Square when we heard somebody trying the door. Assuming that we had been seen, we made a hurried exit out the side window into an alley, which was especially dangerous because the adjoining building at the end of the alley was a police station. Just before we emerged out into the street, I looked through the side window and saw the uniformed cop at the switchboard. And I couldn't resist it. After we were safely past, I reached back and dropped my jimmy bar on the window sill to give them something to remember me by.

Well, the jimmy was found not by the police but by a reporter from one of the Boston papers. The article he wrote about the cops who couldn't find a clue "on their own doorstep" was so hilarious that I carried it around with me for years.

Averaging it out, we were each taking down fifteen hundred to two grand a month. It was so easy that it would have become boring if the safe manufacturers hadn't kept improving their product. What we were doing was known as "punching" safes. All we had to do was remove the dial with a gooseneck jimmy, drive the spindle through, and the tumblers would fall. To counter that, the manufacturers came up with a heavy back-up plate. When you tried to drive the spindle through now, the plate would stop it. The way we got around that was to drill through the safe door into each corner of the plate—not with a regular drill, understand, but with a punch drill—and just drive the plate out. You had to know exactly where the plate was, that's all. But there were other ways we were working too. By drilling quarter-inch holes into the tumbler box, for instance, we were able to insert special instruments and line up the tumblers. Once the tumblers were lined up, all you had to do was turn the handle and the safe would open. It was just a matter, again, of knowing where the tumbler box was.

I knew we were fighting a losing battle, though. The safe companies were beginning to use hardened steel, and I could see where we were going to come to a time when drills weren't going to avail if we wanted to stay in the big time. Without telling anybody, I made a big leap forward and began to study the melting points of the alloyed steels that were used in the construction of bank vaults. The way I went about it was to rent a garage, print up fake letterheads, and write to the steel companies in Pittsburgh for some samples. Every time I got a new sample, I would conduct my own experiments upon it with an acetylene torch. Everything there was to know about hardened steel I was learning. One of the best hardening agents, I discovered, was manganese. The resulting alloy proved to be completely resistant to a high-speed drill but melted quickly under my cutting torch.

To find out whether it would be possible to construct a vault that would resist the torch, I went back to the library to read everything I could find about the hardening of steel. The manufacturers, I discovered happily, had a problem that seemed to be insoluble. There's a limit to how much of a hardening agent can be used without making the steel so brittle that it can be broken with a hammer.

And all the while, of course, I was doing something else. I was preparing for the day when I would leave Doc Tate and concentrate on what I really wanted to do. Rob banks.

I had stopped idolizing Doc Tate by then, anyway. There was one thing about him I couldn't understand at all. For a man who was so fanatical about minimizing the risks, he had a very loose mouth. He would pick up some broad in a nightclub and try to impress her by telling her all about the robberies he had committed. And he just threw his money away. He'd lose huge amounts at the racetrack. He'd tip a maître d' fifty or a hundred dollars. But, you know, that isn't so unusual with thieves. What they are actually doing is trying to buy the respect they subconsciously know they have lost. And the more intelligent they are, the guiltier they feel. O'Reilly was the same way. They both worked on the philosophy that you might as well spend your money now because tomorrow you might be dead.

As for me, I was spending it on clothes, an expensive apartment—and a dancer called Daphne Morrison. My wardrobe was so extensive that it overflowed my closets. Custom-made suits at $150 a throw, tailor-made shirts. Thirty-dollar shoes and different colored spats to match the general ensemble. This was an era where the well-dressed man wore spats, silk gloves, and a slouch hat, and sported a cane. I had a luxurious apartment on West Seventy-second and Riverside Drive, and if you don't think that was the high-rent district, my neighbor was Charley Schwab, the founder of U.S. Steel. I was driving a Buick Riviera that was a palace on wheels until I traded it in for an even fancier Chrysler. Having fallen in with a crowd that was connected with the theater, I became an avid first-nighter. My apartment became a hangout for show people and nightclub entertainers, and I was entertaining lavishly.

That's where I had met Daphne Morrison. In the theater. The show she had been appearing in had just closed and she was visiting a friend in the dressing room, looking for a job. Seeing me backstage, she assumed that I was connected with the production of the show. I let her think so, and by the time she found I wasn't it was too late. Daphne was a bleached blonde with small delicate features and a marvelously erect bearing. She had come to New York from a small farming community in Wisconsin, dreaming like so many others of seeing her name up in lights. Like so many others who were waiting for their big break, she had talent but not quite enough. She could dance, and could sing well enough too, but this was the time of Ann Pennington ("The Girl with the Dimpled Knees") and Fred and Adele Astaire, and she was hardly in that class.

She didn't live with me after the first month, and that was another expense because I was paying the rent for her apartment too. There was no other way to do it, though. I had told her I was a real-estate man, and I couldn't see how she could continue to live with me without finding out how I was really making my living. Not that the constant weekend trips didn't present a problem. After a while she refused to believe that I was going out of town so often to put together real-estate deals. Especially since I was doing all that business on nonbusiness days. She knew what kind of business I was up to, she'd say. Monkey business. She became so convinced that I had another girl on the string that it got to the point where she was going to break off with me. We were scheduled to go to Pittsburgh that weekend, and she had already told me that if I disappeared again she wasn't going to be there when I came back. Doc Tate had the perfect solution. "Bring her to Pittsburgh with you," he said.

Doc had friends in Pittsburgh, he had friends everywhere. When we got to the hotel room I casually suggested that she might like to meet my business associates. Doc came up with a few of his friends, and when it was time for me to go out and steal I simply told her that we had to go attend the business conference now, but I'd try to make it as short as possible. We stayed over for a couple of extra days, and she had such a good time that whenever she'd fly into one of her jealous rages I'd say to Doc, "I've got to take Daphne to Pittsburgh." Wherever the next job happened to be, Doc would rustle up a few of his friends and we'd go through the same act.

But I'll show you how easy it is to become a victim of circumstances. And also how the best-laid plans can backfire. I was still as friendly as ever with Tommy McGovern and so naturally he had a key to my apartment. On this particular night he called to ask me what my plans were. I was going to meet Daphne, who was auditioning for a show, and take her to dinner. But, I told him, she was probably going to be very tired and I'd probably come home early. Well, he had a girl friend he wanted to bring up to the apartment. They probably wouldn't be there until quite late. That was all right with me. It was a big apartment and if they got there late enough I'd probably be asleep.

Daphne had such a bad headache when I picked her up that she didn't feel like eating. "You didn't have to wait around to keep the appointment with me," I said, feeling warm and protective toward her. "Gee, honey, you should have called and told me. I'll drive you home, you can get a good night's sleep and you'll feel better in the morning."

"I'm not sick," she snapped. "All I said was that I had a headache."

I was trying to show how considerate I could be, and she was being nasty about it. And so the more she insisted that she wasn't sick, the more insistent I became that she should go home and get some rest.

Her apartment was right off Riverside Drive, and in a matter of minutes we were practically there. "What are you trying to do," she said, "get rid of me?"

No, damnit, I wasn't trying to get rid of her. "I picked you up. We were going to go to dinner. You lost your appetite because you don't feel well. Remember?"

"But you're so insistent that I go home. Is there any reason why you don't want me to go to your apartment?"

"Oh, God, what are you suspicious of now?"

"Why should I be suspicious? We'll go down there and we'll have a drink and I'll take a headache tablet and maybe I'll feel better."

We walked in, and I was stunned to see that Tommy was already there. Not only with his girl friend but, what really stunned me, with his girl friend's girl friend. Daphne insisted that I take her home immediately. Nothing in the world was ever going to convince her that I hadn't been trying to shake her to keep a late date, and who could blame her? She gave me an ultimatum. Marry her or forget her. Well, I didn't want to get married. I liked things the way they were. So I did the next best thing. My uncle John and aunt Alice had bought a farm up in Warrensburg, New York, a few miles from Lake George. I had told Daphne about them, she had always wanted to meet them, and so I was able to pacify her by arranging to bring her up there for a couple of weeks. Doc Tate was out of action with one of his attacks of rheumatism, so it didn't even interfere with any of our plans.

We spent two idyllic weeks. We swam, we fished, we walked through the woods. She loved the farm, she loved John and Alice, she was as happy as a child. That was the trouble. A few days after we returned to New York, she broke the news that the farm in Warrensburg had reawakened so many happy memories that she was going back to Wisconsin where she knew now she belonged.

On the day I got back I was visited by Tate, Wilson, and O'Reilly. Doc was over his attack and he was raring to go. They were all raring to go. Doc had been in Scranton, Pennsylvania, over the previous weekend, casing the Rogers Brothers jewelry store, and he estimated that the take was going to come to half a million dollars. The biggest score we had ever had. The biggest score of his life. I was just as excited as everybody else until he told me the make and type of the safe. It was one of the best on the market, as much a vault really as a safe. What the manufacturer had done was to put the tumbler box inside a protective chest that no drill in the world was going to cut through. Not in anything under forty-eight hours, it wasn't.

For the first time, I told Doc about my experiments with the acetylene torch. He wasn't the least bit interested. He knew all about the construction of the safe, and he was willing to guarantee that he could take it his way. I suggested that I take my torches along, as standby equipment. He wouldn't hear of it. Wilson and O'Reilly, having grown a bit dubious themselves, were all for having me bring the torches along. What was there to lose? they kept asking.

There was, of course, plenty for Doc Tate to lose. Doc Tate was a very vain man. He was the best at what he did, and he was going to keep on doing it. He couldn't abide the idea that his methods were becoming obsolete, and so he refused to consider that it was a possibility. People do what they do, anyway. The police count on that, and the police are right. The time would come when the same thing was going to happen to me.

Forget it then, I told him. They could count me out. Wilson and O'Reilly went off by themselves to talk it over and finally decided that, despite their misgivings, they owed it to Doc to go along with him.

A week later I changed my mind and very reluctantly agreed to go too. Daphne had left the city by then and, Christ, I had to do something to get her off my mind.

To make a long story short, it was a fiasco. What made it even more galling was that after I had registered at the Hotel Casey, a short distance away, I had strolled over to the store to look the alarm system over and I could see that their stock fully justified Doc's half-million-dollar estimate.

We worked all through the night on the safe, hard, back-breaking work, and even when we realized that we were getting nowhere we were so frustrated that we kept at it until it was light outside.

On the way back to New York, I decided to tell

Tate that I was going out on my own. Eddie had already agreed to go with me, and so we split into two factions. Eddie and me; Tate and O'Reilly. The parting was completely amicable. We'd run into Tate and O'Reilly frequently around Broadway and we remained good friends. Once, when they let me know they weren't doing too well, I lent them a few thousand dollars. I got it back, too, because that's the way they were.

Years later, I learned how Tate wound up. He was trapped by the police inside a department store in Washington, D.C., and he tried to escape by diving through the big display window. He cut himself to ribbons, lost a ton of blood, and wound up in Leavenworth, the federal penitentiary.

In many ways, my year with Doc Tate was the happiest time of my life. I was young, I was successful, I had plenty of money and plenty of broads. I was making my reputation. But my apprenticeship had been served and I was eager to go into business for myself, using my own ideas and having total command of the operation.

Unhappily, I was faced with the problem so common among small businessmen about to launch themselves in a new enterprise. Capital. The Tate gang hadn't pulled any jobs for almost two months before the Scranton fiasco. The funds of the two stockholders of the new partnership were running extremely low and their love of the good life hadn't slackened. On top of that, tooling up for the new operation involved an enormous expenditure of time and money. The commercial acetylene and oxygen tanks I had in my garage were so large and unwieldy that all kinds of obvious difficulties would present themselves in trying to lug them in and out of a bank. The first thing I did, therefore, was to design a miniature version of each of them. Then I had some phony letterheads and business cards printed up for both Wilson and myself, identifying us as the president and the purchasing agent of a nonexistent construction company. Armed with these credentials, we crossed the river to New Jersey, exchanged some small talk with the sales managers of the indicated manufacturing companies about the cuddly personality of Calvin Coolidge, and contracted to have a pair of each of my prototypes made up for us. Very expensive and time consuming.

I had already found a bank in Ozone Park in Queens that looked very good to me, but in order to buy the time we needed to case it properly we were going to have to replenish our treasury. We had to live, didn't we? Most businessmen go to the bank for their working capital. I needed some money before I could go to the bank. And I had just the unwilling benefactor we were looking for sitting in the back of my mind.

While I was working at the Edison Company I had been very favorably impressed by the valuable display of diamonds and other precious gems in the window of a jewelry store a few doors from the Jefferson Market Courthouse. The plan I had concocted to remove them had the two elements that have always appealed to me most strongly. Surprise and audacity. During the day there were dozens of detectives loitering around the area, waiting to be called for their testimony, and that made it the last place anybody would expect any sane thief to hit. I had also noted that the court closed at three o'clock, after which the detectives disappeared and the traffic thinned down considerably. I was going to take it between the time the street emptied and the time the store closed.

It was no problem at all to visit the store during the night and make a paraffin impression of the lock. And even less of a problem to have a key made from the impression. Why did I need a key if I was going to pull the job while the store was still open? I'll give you a hint. The next thing I did was buy the best glass cutter that could be found.

If you still haven't figured it out, I'll give you another hint. I didn't want the key so that I could open the door. I wanted a key so that I could lock it.

The next day, after the courts had closed, Eddie sat in a car a few doors away while I pretended to examine the display in the window. As soon as the clerks' attention was diverted I walked over to the door and locked them in. Still unobserved, I took out the glass cutter, cut a square out of the window, and very carefully lifted out six trays of diamond solitaires. Wilson's timing was perfect. Just as he was driving up, I was walking over to the curb with the trays pushed up against my chest. Eddie opened the door for me, I got in, and off we went. Leaving behind nothing more than a few curious stares from the passersby.

The following morning the Feldman Brothers had the jewelry, and the cash was deposited in our safety deposit box. We were now free to turn our attention to the Ozone Park National Bank.

If there's one thing about casing a bank it's that your afternoons are your own. Spring was in the air. The baseball season had started. I had always been a great Dodger fan and they were playing the Giants at the Polo Grounds.

We were seated in our usual box, a front box on the first-base side of home plate. Eddie was wearing a diamond ring which he had held out of the Jefferson Market job, a monster of a diamond he was going to have converted into an engagement ring for the doctor's daughter from the Bronx. I couldn't help but notice that he was wearing it because every time he leaned forward and rested his hands on the iron piping it almost blinded me. Halfway through the game, I felt a tap on my shoulder. "Leo," a voice said. "Don't make any phony moves. There are three of us here surrounding you." I looked back and there sure enough were. "Just walk to the back of the stadium with your friend," he said. "We want to talk to you."

The first thing I thought about, naturally, was the diamond ring. The only thing that could connect us with the job. As soon as the guy who had been doing the talking stepped back out to the stairway to lead the way, I hissed, "Drop the ring on the ground, Ed. Get rid of it. I'll cover you while I'm putting on my coat." Having very artfully placed myself between Eddie and our three friends as I got up, I swung the coat around like a matador while I was struggling to put it on. Eddie wasn't leaving any ring behind on the grass of the Polo Grounds, though. While I was going through all those calisthenics, Eddie was casually pulling on his silk gloves. Just as casually, he strolled back to the rear of the stadium where the three guys were waiting for us. They turned out to be Pinkertons, and at first I couldn't understand what they were getting at. A million different things flashed through my mind. But then the head Pinkerton started to question me and—surprise of surprises—he isn't talking about the jewelry store, he's talking about the payroll that had been stolen from the Con Edison Company.

I admitted that I had been working there at the time. Other than that, I told him, I didn't know a thing about it.

"Well, we'll have to take you over to the precinct stationhouse and question you," he said. "Because we have some information you did this job."

I said: "You're entirely mistaken about that."

They took us downtown to the Mercer Street station. I never saw such big detectives in my life. These fellows filled the room. After we had steadfastly maintained our innocence under a barrage of questions, they booked us, fingerprinted us, and took us down to police headquarters on Mulberry Street. As soon as we got there, they put us in different rooms and interrogated us separately, which is standard police procedure. I didn't mind at all. At least, I didn't have to look at the ring on Eddie's finger any more.

For hours they questioned me and, of course, I'm still all innocent bewilderment. "Geez, I'm no rob-ber. You don't think I'm a rob-ber, do you?" I'm so shocked that a real, live detective can think such a thing about me that I can hardly get the word out. A rob-ber? Me? A crim-in-al?

Somewhere around midnight they gave up and told me they were holding me overnight. When I asked about the fellow who had been arrested with me, they said, "Oh, we let him go." I was sure it was a trick and, do you know, I was wrong. Eddie had convinced them that he came from a good family in Newport—anybody could see how suave and cultured he was—and since he was a Harvard man had undoubtedly been studying for his midterms at the time of the robbery. There was nothing to connect him with the Edison Company, of course, but he was wanted for murder in Brooklyn and he had talked them into letting him walk out of there, with a stolen ring on his finger, before the report on his fingerprints came back.

What Eddie had done was go right back to my apartment to get rid of the tanks and cutting equipment. After that, he called an attorney for me and left town, presumably to rejoin his family in time for the Newport regatta.

In the morning I was put in a lineup and then taken to a detention pen. After a while, a guy from another lineup came down and said, "Geez, I think they made you. Boy, they're all talking up there about you."

I said: "They're not going to make me, I'm innocent."

"Are you sure you haven't been arrested before in Brooklyn? They're sure talking a lot about Kings County up there."

"No, I've never been arrested in my life."

As soon as he said Brooklyn, though, I knew that I had been made.

The detective I had put on the bewildered act for came in with the news that my fingerprints matched those of Willie Sutton. "No, you don't commit crimes," he mimicked. "No, you're no rob-ber. Not much you ain't."

"Willie Sutton?" I said. "I'm not Willie Sutton."

In order to get me away from my attorney while they were waiting for the wagon to come from Brooklyn, they shipped me back to the Mercer Street station, the same place where I had convinced all those big guys I was innocent. Before we left, the lawyer said to them, "Look, don't lay a hand on him. Because if you do I'll have you in court myself."

The detective who had interrogated me put on the same hurt and bewildered air that I had. Oh, they weren't going to touch me. Heaven forbid.

As soon as they had me in the goddamn police station they began to rough me up. "You sonofabitch, you're not a robber, huh?" Whack. "You're not Willie Sutton, are you? You're no goddamn murdering little bastard." Splat.

After they'd had their fun, I was taken upstairs and all of a sudden I was face to face with Sammy Todd, my nemesis. "Yeah," he said, looking as though he could hardly wait. "That's Willie Sutton."

So finally I was taken back to Brooklyn. In New York, they had just shoved me around a little, but when Sammy Todd got me back to Brooklyn, boy, they really went to work. Todd really did believe I was guilty; no question about that. As a matter of law, flight carries a presumption of guilt, and Sammy Todd wasn't buying my explanation of why I had left at all. During the drive down he had made it clear that he was going to get a confession out of me. To show that he meant business, he no sooner had me inside the precinct than he picked me up over his head and flung me down a flight of iron stairs. If I had landed on my head I'd have been killed for sure. It was a miracle I didn't fracture my skull. Then they picked me up, Sammy Todd and his Merry Men, and gave me a terrific beating. They beat me with rubber hoses, they beat me with their fists, they kicked me. All through the night they beat me and all through the night I steadfastly maintained my innocence.

It could have been worse. I was still functioning well enough when they were finished with me to know that I had better get myself a very good trial lawyer. A good lawyer is, first of all, a lawyer who knows—and is well known in—the jurisdiction. So I hired the firm of Ruskin & Snyder. Ruskin had been the District Attorney of Kings County before he went into private practice, and Snyder had been his chief assistant.

For nine months they kept me in jail awaiting a trial. I was being charged with murder in the first degree, and Murder One was an unbailable charge. When I did finally come up on the docket, the case was transferred from the County Court to the Supreme Court, something which was rarely done at the time and only in cases that were considered extremely important.

As a man who has had both experiences, I can tell you that it's far, far easier for a guilty man to stand trial than an innocent one. When you are guilty you are depending entirely upon your legal rights; the maze of protections, legal maneuvers, and loopholes that can help you beat the rap. You have no qualms whatsoever about using them; the law says you have that right. When you are innocent you are always in a rage of indignation. You feel helpless and put upon. You are totally on the defensive. Constantly you have to fight back the desire to leap up and scream out your innocence. You can't believe that this massive grinding machinery can be doing this to you.

Tom O'Leary, who had survived a bullet in the stomach, testified that he had seen me and Wilson flee from the scene after the shooting. Another witness testified that just before I left the pool hall he had heard me say to Gleason: "I'm going to take care of you for squealing on me." And the prosecution kept implying there were other witnesses to that threat who had either disappeared or been frightened off.

Noonan and Collins both testified for me, to give me an alibi. Other friends of mine testified to the slimy character of O'Leary, which, by extension, also turned into testimony about the slimy character of Gleason. All of my witnesses, incidentally, had been tracked down by the third member of the defense team, a young lawyer from lower Manhattan named Mark Murzin, who had been engaged to do the legwork. Murzin went on to have a very distinguished career although that is not, as you will see later, why I am bringing his name up here.

Under cross-examination, O'Leary admitted that it was a dark night, that he hadn't seen anybody standing across the street until the shooting started, and that there could have been somebody concealed in one of the doorways they had passed. No matter how you looked at it, though, it was eyeball testimony from one of the victims that he had seen me do it. And my lawyers couldn't put me on the stand to let the jury hear me deny it without having the whole Carrie Wagner episode come out.

Before the case was given to the jury, Ruskin and Snyder came to me in the bullpen. "Look," they said. "You're facing the electric chair. The evidence is very strong against you. We just had a talk with Judge McMann, and the judge has advised that we talk to you and see if you'd take a plea to manslaughter in the first degree."

Do you know, I was indignant? Although I have

been a professional thief all my life, I am unable to understand exactly how an average citizen feels when he gets caught up in what are usually called the toils of the law. Even though I could understand very well that they had ample evidence to put me on trial, I had assumed somewhere in the marrow of my bones that there was some majesty to the law which was somehow able to set those kind of errors right. As strong as I knew the case against me to be, I had always believed that somewhere during the trial, somebody or something would intervene to prove that I was innocent.

Things looked very bad, my lawyers told me. My choice, as they explained it to me, was to gamble on a sentence of five to ten years against an almost sure sentence to the electric chair. "My duty as your attorney is to explain your options to you," Ruskin said. "That's all. But I believe it's also my duty to tell you that if Judge McMann didn't feel that he was going to have to sentence an innocent man to the electric chair he would never have called us in and made this kind of an offer."

I could feel the shadow of the electric chair fall over me, and the first thing that cropped into my mind was: *If I plead guilty I will be labeling all of my witnesses as perjurers.* Noonan and Collins had stretched the time of our meetings in my favor far beyond what I myself knew it to be. But that wasn't perjury; they had been asked to go far back in their memory and they had resolved every doubt in my favor. They had come into the courtroom to help me, and I would be exposing them, I thought, to possible arrest. Even with the electric chair staring me in the face, I was the kid from Irishtown again. You don't leave your friends holding the bag. And you don't cop out.

"I'm innocent," I told my lawyers. "I'm not going to plead guilty even if they send me to ten electric chairs."

The jury was out for seven hours. They filed back into the box, looking grim and somber. The judge instructed me to stand up. And then somebody noticed that my attorneys weren't in court. While we were waiting for them, I sat there stealing glances at the jury box. The jurors kept their heads down and their eyes lowered. I thought for sure I had been found guilty.

The five minutes that it took Ruskin and Snyder to come down from their office seemed like five hours. And then they were at my side, and the clerk was asking the jury whether it had reached a verdict. The foreman responded that it had.

"What is your verdict?"

Life or death was hanging in the balance.

"Not guilty."

As soon as we were out of the courtroom, Ruskin said to me, "Willie, we have always been convinced of your innocence. But from my long experience in the courtroom I have learned that justice doesn't triumph in every case. The very best verdict we expected was second-degree murder. Every time you wake up in the morning, mark it off on the calendar as a day of profit."

The First Bank

It could be argued, I suppose, that my foray against the Ozone Park National Bank had met with so many delays that somebody was trying to tell me something. I'm not as superstitious as the average thief, though. The way I looked at it, I had an investment in that bank by then, and once I was a free man again I was more determined than ever to take it. Me and Wilson both.

Within a month after my acquittal, Eddie had been arrested up in Boston in a stolen automobile and returned to Kings County. They had put him on trial immediately. This time, the witness who had testified to my hurling the threat testified that he had been pressured by Detective Todd into making statements that weren't true. Wilson got a hung jury, and they let him go.

So there we were, the old firm back in business. Almost, anyway. With all the attorneys' fees, we were in desperate need of another quick score to build up our reserves. I picked out a jewelry store on Broadway and Forty-second Street, right next to the Astor. The store had a siren over the door and silent alarms that could be set off in the adjoining stores. There were policemen on both corners and cruisers always coming around. It was the busiest block in the country and we were going to hit it at the busiest time of the day. Again, audacity. I was depending upon surprise, speed, and timing. Eddie would hold a gun on them. I would scoop the jewelry into a bag, lock the door behind us, and we'd go off in opposite directions and be lost in the crowd before anybody got around to pushing a button.

Everything went exactly as we had planned, except for one thing. Two doors from the jewelry store, I heard someone call, "Hey, Willie Sutton." Walking past me, no more than a few feet away, was Mark Murzin, the young lawyer from my defense team. I waved at him as nonchalantly as possible with my free hand, and kept going.

The evening papers gave the robbery such a big play that I decided I had better drop in on him the next day to see whether he had made the connection. Just by the way he greeted me I could see that he hadn't.

So now, at last, we were ready for Ozone Park. We cased the bank thoroughly again. The first time I had looked at the bank it had seemed to have a built-in safety factor. The bank was situated on the corner, and there were windows on both sides and a very large light over the vault that was kept on all night. Even without the light, an acetylene torch would be seen immediately by anybody passing by. There were, however, a few feet of empty space between the side of the vault and the wall, and I had seen immediately that it would be possible to erect a canvas screen and go in that way. There was also a big wooden bookcase against the wall. A regular bookcase, three shelves high, containing books on banking and finance. By moving it over three or four feet so that it would be even with the side of the vault, I could be sure that the view from the street would be blocked off completely.

The best way to get into the bank itself, I decided, was to go through the ceiling of the cellar. It took me about thirty seconds to pick the lock and go down there to look the place over. The ceiling was made of concrete and appeared to be about four or five inches thick. It would be no problem, it seemed to me, to break through and come up in one of the rear rooms of the bank.

Wilson had dumped the first set of miniature tanks, of course, but we'd had another set made up by then and I was very eager to see how the torch would perform. We couldn't afford to take a chance of being seen carrying all that equipment in at night. In the afternoon, shortly after the bank had closed, we brought the tanks and everything else into the cellar and covered it over with the canvas. The timetable called for us to come back around ten-thirty. In the evening a torrential rain hit the city. The forecast was that it was going to last through the night. Perfect weather for a burglary, you would have thought. Everybody would be off the streets. And yet, from the moment we got down into the cellar everything that could go wrong went wrong. The first thing that went was our timetable. Working by flashlight, we built a platform for me to stand on and I began to drill between the floor beams. The concrete was thicker than I had thought possible. Thicker and tougher. It was seven forty-five in the morning before we had a hole large enough for us to get through. Still time enough, if the torch worked as effectively as I expected it to.

Outside, the rain was still falling. Very gingerly I pushed the door open and peered into the bank proper. The bank was brightly illuminated and two policemen, clad in rain capes and rain hats, were standing in the doorway, chatting.

By the time they left it was almost eight o'clock.

The guard would normally be arriving in fifteen minutes, and I could only hope that the rain was going to hold him up. As quickly as possible we set up the canvas and pulled the bookcase into place. And then I ignited the torch and went to work while Eddie watched the door. It was a race against the clock. The flame cut into the steel and the molten metal began to run. Fifteen more minutes was all I needed. Ten. Within a matter of minutes, though, Wilson was calling out that two employees had just arrived and were standing in the doorway, talking.

Clearly, there was no time to cut the rest of the way into the vault and get to the money. Leaving the equipment behind, we scooted through the office door, dropped back down into the cellar, and walked, not too happily, back to the car.

An unsuccessful foray, sure. But not a disastrous one. Yet. The failure of the robbery had been due to bad luck and faulty preparation. What happened after that was so unforeseeable that it wouldn't happen again in a thousand years. Having married the doctor's daughter, Wilson was now living out on Avenue J in Brooklyn. He took the wheel and started to drive home through the rain-soaked streets. We were almost there, a good fifteen miles from the bank, when the car skidded into a Con Edison repair truck that was parked in the middle of the street. We didn't hit hard enough, fortunately, to injure any of the linemen working on the high platform. Just hard enough to damage my radiator and knock out one of my headlights. We went through the ritual of exchanging license numbers and names and continued on our way. Wilson's new home was only a few miles past my mother's house in Park Slope. From the time I had left that house, almost five years earlier, I had seen my mother only once. She had come to visit me in jail a couple of days after the beating by Sammy Todd, and the sight of my battered, swollen face had so upset her that I had made myself a promise that I was never going to disrupt her life again. I knew what I was, and I knew what kind of life I had mapped out for myself. Which meant that unless she was able to write me off, she'd be crying over me for the rest of her life.

And yet, as I doubled back toward New York and came closer and closer to my old home, I had an overwhelming desire to see her one more time. Maybe it was so that she would see me looking fit and healthy, I don't know.

The first thing she did, of course, was to sit me down and prepare a breakfast. While I was eating—I hadn't been there more than five minutes—there was a knock on the door. It was a police officer wanting to know who owned the grayish-green Buick parked outside the house. "That's my car, officer," I said, going to the door. "What's the trouble?"

No trouble. He just wanted to know how the headlight and the radiator had been damaged. Since I had nothing to hide, I told him.

"Listen," he said. "Will you come down to the police station with me and clear this up?"

What was there to clear up?

Well, an elderly couple had been killed the night before by a hit-and-run driver only two blocks away, and the witnesses had described the car as a grayish-green Buick. "You say the licenses were exchanged by your friend and the driver of the Edison truck. All you have to do is come down so we can check it out."

The police station was only a couple of blocks away. Why not? They sent for an assistant District Attorney and he went over it with me at length. Since it was my car, I had all the names and license numbers and he took them all down. "Well," he said. "You tell a straightforward story. You living there with your mother now?" And so naturally I lied and said, "Yes." Just to keep my record up of never telling an unnecessary truth to a lawman.

I should have followed that basic principle earlier. Two weeks later I got a call from Eddie's wife, telling me he had been arrested. They had traced the oxygen tank to him. How, I will never know. Neither of us had any record as bank robbers or torch men, and although he had signed for it as purchasing agent he had used an assumed name.

I told her I'd send a lawyer over to Eddie and keep in touch with her. Maybe they tapped her phone, maybe they trailed her to one of our meetings. Or maybe they just saw that Wilson and I had been tied together once before and took a shot that we still were.

Two or three days later I was looking into the window of a department store when two detectives came up and asked if I was Willie Sutton. "We've got your partner, Wilson," they said.

"What partner? Who's Wilson? I don't know any Wilson." Nor did I know anything about an attempted bank robbery. I denied everything. And it hurt me badly when I came to trial.

We were tried separately. Eddie first, because he had been arrested first. He told the judge that he believed all lawyers were crooks and wanted to handle his own defense. The jury was so impressed by his spunk, his legal acumen, and his all-around demeanor that they found him guilty. As a second offender, he was given ten years.

For my part, I hired one of the best lawyers in Queens County, Sidney Rosenthal. I was careful as always to hire a lawyer who was well connected in the jurisdiction. If any thievery was going on behind the scenes between the lawyers, I wanted to be the beneficiary of it. The courtroom thievery went the other way in the end, but I have to say for Rosenthal that he gave me my money's worth.

The reason why my denial that I knew Eddie Wilson was so damaging was that the prosecution was able to produce the statement I had made to the DA's man in Brooklyn about the automobile accident, which proved that I had been with Wilson that very morning. Until that statement was produced in court I had completely forgotten about it.

That was absolutely all they had, though: that I had been in a car with Wilson fifteen miles away from the bank and for reasons that must have had something to do with a guilty conscience had lied about it. Rosenthal seemed to be well on the way to beating it for me when the prosecution beefed their case up by coming up with a phony witness. They produced an auto-repair-shop owner named Gabbe, who testified that he had driven in from Long Island on the night of the robbery to visit a sister who lived four doors away from the bank. His testimony was that as he was pulling up to her house at eight o'clock in the evening he had been able to see us so clearly under the light over the vault that he was able to make a positive identification. What was I supposed to say? That we hadn't got there until ten-thirty, and there was no way he could have seen us because we had set up a screen?

Rosenthal tore his testimony apart anyway. "What kind of a night was it?" he asked.

"It was a dark night, but I've already said that I could see them because of the light in the bank."

"Was it raining?"

"No."

Rosenthal subpoenaed the head of the weather bureau and proved that the heaviest rain of the year had occurred on that night, and that it had started well before eight o'clock.

He got a hung jury for me, and the state offered to let me plead guilty to a misdemeanor. I turned it down. Another mistake. When I came to trial again, the case was assigned to Judge Frank Adel, who had just been appointed to fill a vacancy on the bench. Adel had been a banker all his life, and Rosenthal did everything he could think of to get the case away from him. But for all of Rosenthal's influence, he couldn't begin to match the influence of the insurance companies. In those days, they didn't have a bank robbery every day like now, and when a bank was hit the insurance people were willing to put up all kinds of money to get a conviction.

The second trial lasted only a few days. Adel had no idea what he was doing, he just overruled every objection Rosenthal made and pushed the conviction through. Gabbe not only repeated all of his earlier perjuries, even to testifying again that it hadn't rained, he perjured himself even more. Rosenthal took the stand himself and testified that he had gone to Gabbe's house to inform him that he was going to bring charges against him, and that Gabbe's sister had told him that he wasn't home. At which point Gabbe stood up and yelled, "I was at home that day, and nobody at all came to my house!"

Rosenthal, who was a very distinguished-looking man, leaped up in the witness box and shouted: "I will let no man impugn my honor! I am going to seek an indictment for perjury against this man because he has committed perjury again and again during the course of both of these trials."

It didn't do a bit of good. Who was going to bring the perjury charge against him, the District Attorney he was perjuring himself for?

On April 5, 1926, more than a year after we had left the Ozone Park National Bank, I was found guilty of burglary in the third degree and attempted grand larceny and given a sentence of from five to ten years.

From Sing Sing to Siberia

Sing Sing was the most horrible prison I have ever been in, for one very basic reason. As soon as I entered its gates I was converted from a name to a number. I was No. 84599. Nothing. Upon my arrival, my head was shaved. Then they had me strip and turned me over to an inmate who was stirring a long stick around in a tub of blue ointment that gave off the smell of disinfectant. He smeared the stuff all over my head and around my private parts; I was being deloused. From there I was taken to the state shop and given an issue of clothing. A pair of dark gray prison suits (this was back in 1926, and the striped uniforms which are still somehow associated with prisoners had already been done away with), a coat, a cap, some heavy brogans, and, although it was summer, very coarse heavy underwear. There was no such thing as summer underwear. In the summer you itched.

There was one long, dark, dreary cellblock to house the nine hundred inmates. One of those old-fashioned buildings with walls that were about ten feet thick. The windows were carved out of these massive walls, and very little sunlight penetrated into the block. The cell was so narrow that you had to walk in sideways and so small that the bed, which was more or less a flat iron latticework, was suspended from the wall on heavy chains. If you hadn't been able to lift it up during the daytime, there wouldn't have been enough room to move around in. The thing that jarred me most when I was first led into my cell was that the walls were made up of jagged rocks which were pointed at you like daggers. The door was constructed of a series of heavy steel slabs, running both horizontally and vertically—an iron latticework again—and the only ventilation we had came through the pattern of one-inch-square holes.

A small bulb in the ceiling gave off a dim light. It would become even dimmer during an execution while the current was passing through the condemned man's body.

In certain ways, though, Sing Sing was not a bad prison. One reason was purely geographic. Ossining is only about thirty-five miles from New York City, a negligible distance for visitors to travel in comparison to the state prisons at Attica, Auburn, and Dannemora. Under Warden Lewis E. Lawes, the visiting privileges were very generous and no screen was interposed between the inmate and his caller. (The visiting privileges could also be very flexible, by which I mean that if you dropped five dollars on the desk you could see anybody you wanted to.)

Technically, the prison was run under what was called the Auburn system, which meant that inmates ate at a common mess hall on long tables with everyone facing in the same direction and absolute silence being enforced. In practice, they sat across the table from each other and talked as they wished. It wasn't mandatory to eat in the mess hall, anyway, and only the most hapless, friendless, penniless inmates ever did. The inmates were permitted to receive food packages from the outside and to purchase food, meat, dairy products, and all kinds of canned foods from the commissary. The prison food was terrible. At night they might give you half a bowl of prunes, a few slices of bread, and maybe half a bowl of thin soup. For those who had their own food, there was a cookhouse with at least fifty gas ranges. Steaks would be sizzling; Italian sauces bubbling. Recipes would be exchanged. Above the mess hall, they had what was supposed to be a recreation hall but was actually the dining room. Underneath the tables were cupboard-like lockers in which you kept your cooking utensils and nonperishable foods. Small groups of friends would get together at the same tables or benches and eat together every day.

The same division between theory and reality existed wherever you looked. This was mostly due to Warden Lawes, who was easily the most famous penologist in the country. Lawes was a man of about fifty, with iron-gray hair. He was such a bitter opponent of capital punishment that he refused to attend the executions. He advocated a nonpunitive policy toward prisoners and initiated programs for rehabilitation that would probably be considered progressive even today.

Under Warden Lawes, the prison was run to a very large extent by the convicts. The governing body was called the Mutual Welfare League. There were two political parties, the Democratic party and the Cheese party, with elections held once a year. In theory, it was supposed to give the prisoners a voice in the running of the institution. In practice, it developed into a way of insuring peace by pitting the prisoners against each other. The delegates were, to all practical purposes, quasi-guards with full authority to arrest other prisoners and discipline them in whatever way they saw fit. They filled the available jobs with their friends and doled out what was left to whoever would pay the most for them. What you had was a privileged group which was able to enforce its will upon others with no interference from the prison authorities. A new inmate who came into Sing Sing without friends was in a very vulnerable position.

If it wasn't what Lawes intended, one of the

reasons was that he ran the prison pretty much in absentia, anyway. Most prisons are run by the deputy warden, and the "dep" at Sing Sing was Johnny Sheehy, a wholly corrupt individual. Sheehy was a man of such enormous girth that he waddled when he walked. He was type-cast for the part, with heavy, beefy jowls and bushy, protruding eyebrows. The clothing issue, for instance, was like it is in the army; everything they gave you was either too big or too small. If you had a little money you could have a uniform tailor-made for you in the prison, and in a lighter, more attractive shade of gray at that. The inmate paid the tailor, and the tailor paid off Sheehy. He had his hands in everything, including the payoffs that were made for jobs to the delegates of the Mutual Welfare League. There was open gambling. There were bookmaking concessions. The most notorious prisoners were the most privileged characters. Fuller and McGee, the bucket-shop operators who had fleeced the public with fraudulent stock schemes; Bridell, the labor czar who had made millions through labor extortion. If you had the money, you could buy anything in Sing Sing.

It was the outside world squeezed between the prison walls. Power counted. Money talked. Everybody who mattered got something. Sheehy didn't have to worry about a riot; not when the natural leaders had such a stake in the status quo.

And through it all, Warden Lawes sat in his ivory tower, published his books, and took his bows.

I very quickly made the right friends, and with my experience as a florist was given a job in the prison greenhouses, which were supervised by Charlie Chapin, the former editor of the *New York World* who was serving a life sentence for killing his wife. A fascinating man. Chapin had been the most famous editor in the United States, known for his toughness and his crusading fervor. It was common knowledge that he had entered into a suicide pact with his dying wife, killed her, and then lost his nerve. If he was in prison it was because he had insisted on being there. He was a privileged prisoner and nobody begrudged it to him. He had actually succeeded in making the prison grounds attractive by planting flowers, bushes, and trees, which he paid for himself. The greenhouses were filled with all kinds of songbirds: canaries, goldfinches, cardinals. He had a full staff of inmates working under him and he would regale us with tales of the crimes that had been solved by his reporters. Some of the most sensational cases of all time, including the Rosenthal murder which I had followed so avidly in my youth.

Chapin, who was already in his seventies, was the real author of the books that were making Warden Lawes so famous, including the longtime best-seller *Twenty Thousand Years in Sing Sing*. He had special living quarters in the greenhouse. He made numerous trips away from the prison, usually "under the custody" of the warden's wife, to purchase plants and shrubs and was allowed to receive his constant stream of visitors in the greenhouses. Irvin S. Cobb, the best-known newspaper columnist of the time, came up to see him often. It was a common thing for me to walk in and see him talking to actors, actresses, and newspaper people whose pictures I had been seeing in the papers all my life.

Either I had maneuvered my way into too good a job for a newcomer or had managed to incur the wrath of a league delegate in some other way. Whatever it was, I had been at Sing Sing for only three months when I was taken off the greenhouse detail and assigned to the section of the block reserved for those who were going to be transferred to another prison. There were sixteen of us assembled there, including my old buddy Eddie Wilson. I didn't think anything of it at first. Sing Sing is the receiving prison in the state system and when it gets overcrowded they have to start shipping people out. It wasn't until we were getting ready to leave that we were told we were being shipped to Dannemora in "a punishment draft." I was sure it had to be some kind of a mistake, but it wasn't. We were taken to the train in handcuffs and leg chains and guarded by a squad of officers on the long trip north. At Dannemora, which is located in the northeast corner of the state, seventeen miles below the Canadian border, we were lined up and taken before the deputy warden, Asa Granger, the worst animal I have ever come across in my life. A hulking 280-pound ape. When it came my turn, he growled, "You know what you're here for, don't you? You're here for planning and attempting to escape Sing Sing with your partner, Wilson."

He paid no attention whatsoever to my denial. "If you ever get caught in any corners around here," he bellowed, "we'll blow your head off!"

Compared to Dannemora, Sing Sing was a paradise. Surrounded by dense woods and subject to weather that could get as low as thirty degrees below zero, it was known as the Siberia of America. The whole system was built upon such brutality that before I left there I became involved in what was probably the worst and certainly the most destructive prison riot in the history of the country up to that time. The guards were all of French-Canadian descent. They were destined for work in the penal system from birth and they were the most sadistic people I ever came into contact with. The officers carried sticks with metal tips on them. You had to march everywhere in complete silence. (The whole prison was operated on a silent system, which meant that the inmates were allowed to talk only within certain specified areas.) The marching orders were given by tapping the stick on the ground. Two raps meant go. One rap meant stop. For no reason at all, you would get rapped sharply across the back. At the slightest provocation, they would pounce upon a prisoner, batter him to the ground, and beat him almost to death.

Off in the corner was a small red brick building with twenty-two cells in it. That was the isolation block. The number of prisoners who "committed suicide" there by hanging themselves was truly remarkable. Especially when you consider that everything except the clothes on their backs had been taken away from them, and no other inmates were ever permitted near the place.

Right next to the prison was the insane asylum, which was never referred to as anything except the Bughouse. Seeing that it was so handy, Granger would send the most recalcitrant of the prisoners there on the sound medical theory that anybody he couldn't bend to his will had to be crazy. The guards were the sons of the regular guards, young boys of fifteen and sixteen who were preparing for the day when they would become old enough to graduate to the prison. The stories that were told by inmates who had come back from the Bughouse were enough to make your hair curl.

One of the great delights of these kids was to goad two of the mental cases into a fight by going back and forth with made-up stories about what they had said about each other and then refuse to let them stop until one of them was unconscious or, better yet, dead. The death rate in the Bughouse was enormous. One of the men I came to know very well had been in there and he told me how they'd execute some poor raving soul by putting him on a blanket and keep tossing him in the air until they had him bouncing off the ceiling. Here too, the verdict was always suicide. "I was never a cream-puff in my life, Willie," he told me. "I always thought I was pretty tough. While I was in that bughouse I was always afraid. They were giving me injections. Experiments. I'd be sitting down and all of a sudden my knee would come up and hit my chin. One time I was in there, jerking around, and I heard one doctor saying to another, 'I probably gave him too much of the stuff.' "

Warden Harry M. Kaiser was a handsome white-haired man. As personable and charming a man as you would ever want to meet. And in his own way every bit as cruel as Granger. Relatives would go to him with the prisoners' complaints about the brutal treatment, and Kaiser was such a persuasive talker that he would spin them a tale about the vast rehabilitation program he was trying to install against the resistance of the inmates and guards, wax poetic for a while about his great dream of redeeming as many of these lost souls as possible, and send them out of there thoroughly convinced that it was their own relatives—who, after all, didn't have much of a track record for honesty—who had been lying to them.

Inside the cellblocks, the living conditions were harsh and primitive. The food was so bad that it was a wonder anybody survived. Breakfast usually consisted of unsweetened mush, bread, and imitation coffee. Supper never varied: a half bowl of soup, bread, and tea. Sunday dinner, the big treat of the week, was a slice of mountain goat, heavily veined and unappetizingly gray in color.

The cellblocks were so infested with bedbugs that we would roll up some newspaper just before we went to bed, set it afire, and hold it against the bedsprings in an effort to burn them out. Not that it did very much good. New battalions of bedbugs were always crawling through the cracks of the wall. During the winter months the cellblocks were so cold that the only thing you could do was go to bed as early as possible. The rumor, widely circulated, was that the coal was bought from a company owned by the warden's brother. The coal cars would come in, the tags would be changed, and half of them would go out again, full, to be sold again.

There was no water in the cell. Twice a day you would hold a little basin up and they would pour a little hot water into it, once in the morning and once at night. That was how you washed. You took a shower once a week, and it lasted for two minutes. They would turn on the warm water for a minute and then the cold water for a minute, and that was your bath.

For a toilet, you had a round iron bucket with a wooden cover. In the morning the prisoners would march to the shop area carrying their shit buckets, empty them into a latrine before they went to work, leave them in the bucket racks, and pick them up again when it was time to march back to the cell.

There were six shops in the work area. A weave shop, a cotton shop, a tailor shop, a shoe shop, a paint shop, and a laundry. Once you were placed on a job, that was where you were going to work through your entire time. There were no excuses tolerated; no negotiation. In the cotton shop, the air was so filled with lint that many of the prisoners developed TB. Still, it did no good at all to protest that you had a lung condition. To refuse an assigned job was considered an act of insurrection. You'd be thrown into the cooler, put on bread and water for fifteen days, and when you came out a tin sign saying KEEPLOCKED was hung on your cell. For the keeplocked, they had a squad that would empty the buckets and bring them back. You never left the cell until you were ready to accept the job you had been assigned.

I never was assigned to a job in all the time I was there. It happened like this: You marched from your cellblock according to size, with the shortest fellows in front. My height made me the sixth man in line. After I had been there for two weeks, a fellow named McNally was released after eighteen months in keeplock and when it came time for yardout, the two-hour exercise period, he was placed right in front of me. Just as we stepped through the narrow passageway that led to the yard, two knives came flashing toward McNally, one from either side. McNally dropped, I kept marching on, and the rest of the line kept marching right behind me. We were all in the yard before they saw his body lying there.

I was called down to the dep's office, shown the pictures of the two inmates who had wielded the knives, and asked if I knew them. "No," I said.

Granger demanded to know what I knew about the killing.

"I don't know anything about any killing," I said.

"You must have seen him killed. He was right in front of you."

I said: "No, I didn't see anybody killed. I know there was a lot of confusion when we came out there, but I kept walking like everybody else."

Granger just looked at me. "Sutton," he said, "we're going to hold an inquest and unless you change your story you're never going to get anything as long as you're in this prison. You had to see something."

"Well, I saw nothing."

Getting nothing didn't mean I was going to be keeplocked or put in isolation, it meant that I would get no job. And you have to do something in prison or you go crazy. I was allowed to leave my cell for yardout. Other than that, I was supposed to stay there. Actually, I was very fortunate. The guard on the south hall, where I was locking, was a fellow named Pender, who was one of the few nice people up there. Pender thought I was getting a raw deal. By the sheer accident of height, he could see, I had been placed in one of those situations where no matter what I did I was in trouble. I couldn't finger the killers—even if it hadn't gone against my code—without being killed myself. And I couldn't remain quiet without being blacklisted. Pender would let me out to walk along the gallery or to work with the porters mopping up the floor, and if any of the prison officials were coming I'd run back to my cell.

And I began to study. I sent to the International Correspondence School for a course in psychology. The course was called Key to Culture and consisted of about two dozen monthly pamphlets. A few months later I sent for a collection of the classics of literature. There were days when I spent sixteen or eighteen hours reading, never leaving my cell even to eat. The worst thing that happens in prison is that after a while your mind begins to rot. They could lock up my body but I was not going to let them lock up my mind.

I did have a chance to mix with the other inmates during yardout, and they included some of the most notorious bad men in the country, with prison terms to match. There were always people planning to escape, and supervision was very close. Once you were out of the cellblock, you were never out of the sight of both the foot patrol and the tower guards. Before you could go to the hospital, you had to have a written pass telling the time you left the shop: the doctor would write in the time he had completed treatment. When you were ready to go back. And even with that, the prisoner would usually be accompanied by a guard, coming and going. The visiting room consisted of a long table with a foot-high glass partition running across the entire length. A screw sat on an elevated chair at the end of the table where he could observe anything being passed by either the visitor or the inmate.

Occasionally someone would get over the wall, but once they were out there was nowhere to go. We were in the heart of the Adirondacks. There was only one road through the forest, the road to Plattsburgh. The only inhabited area within miles was the little town of Clinton, which was inhabited exclusively by the guards and their families, plus the few shops that were needed to service them. It was a closed society. There wasn't even a hotel there. When a wife traveled all that distance to visit her husband she would usually stay for a week, and there was no place for her to stay but in the homes of these guards. They wanted it that way. There was a standard daily rate. The only other people we ever saw was a small group of trappers who lived in small shacks in the interior of the mountains. Once a year, early in the spring, they would come in through the underbrush, a dozen of them or so, to be given the inmates' old underclothes and shoes. They were like nothing I have ever seen before or since. Their eyes were abnormally large— unbelievably large—and they moved as if they were floating on air. They'd come in silently, dressed in their old, shaggy clothing, pick up the stuff, and go back through the underbrush they had floated out of.

But no prisoner who escaped could make his way through the miles and miles of underbrush. In no time at all, they'd be hauled out of the woods, hungry and freezing.

That didn't stop others from trying. Although it never occurred to me to make any plans for escaping myself, I did get involved in helping out some of those who did. The man who kept getting me involved was a fellow named Jack Bassett, whom I had got to know because he had attended college and was one of the few other inmates who was taking courses. Bassett was a member of the prison band, which gave him a certain amount of freedom, and he could always be counted upon to round up help for anybody who was trying to escape. If it surprises you to hear they had a band at Dannemora, don't be. Believe me, they didn't have Wednesday-night concerts for the inmates. The band was there exclusively for the purpose of playing for state legislators and other visiting dignitaries. The band would be trotted out along with the inmates who worked in the administration offices, the white-shirt-and-pressed-pants boys.

They would tell the visitors how nicely we were being treated, and everybody would go home believing they had really got a chance to question a true cross-section of prisoners.

The best plan of all, I thought, was dreamed up by the leader of the band, a man named Otto who had formerly been second in command of a German liner. Another musician, named Mackey, was going to hide in the cellar underneath Otto's cell for two weeks, after which the search would presumably be abandoned and they would both go over the wall. Meanwhile, Mackey was going to have to eat, and it was Bassett who went around collecting scraps of food from about half-a-dozen of us who weren't on regular work details.

They were brought back hungry and freezing after a couple of days, too.

The most notorious gang there, the baddest of the bad men, was the Richard Reese Whittemore mob. Whittemore was a good-looking young guy, too. Put him and Eddie Wilson side by side and you'd think you had the start of a church choir. The other members of the mob were the Kraemer brothers, Jake and Leon; and Frenchy Levine. They all had thirty to forty years for robbing jewelry stores and armored cars, and Reese Whittemore also had a warrant of detention placed against him by the state of Maryland. He had killed a guard while escaping from the Baltimore penitentiary and they were very anxious to get him back. Reese Whittemore had every reason for wanting to escape. Frenchy Levine had only one. Frenchy was an ugly, bull-like man with a huge barrel chest, powerful shoulders, and a massive neck. He had married an attractive girl, much younger than himself, just before he was captured and he was crazy to get back to her. Whittemore's idea was that there was no way you could plan your way out, the only way you could get out would be to smuggle some guns in and crash your way out all down the line. Their opportunity came when Jake Kraemer somehow managed to get himself assigned to the warehouse where he would be in a position to intercept all incoming packages. The guns were going to be sent into the prison by Whittemore's girl friend, Tiger Lil.

I had got to know them quite well by that time, and it became a time of great tension for me too. I was in the cellblock waiting for my friend Johnny Feinstein to come over with the latest news. Johnny had worked for Dutch Schultz on the outside, but he had also been a jewelry thief. His M.O. was to hang around fashionable hotels, follow jewel-decked women home, and burglarize their houses. In Dannemora he was a runner, a job that allowed him to move around the prison and pick up all the latest information. This particular day, he came over, very much disturbed, and motioned for me to walk down toward the end of the gallery where we could be alone. A friend of ours named Russo, who was working in the deputy warden's office, had stopped Johnny on the way to tell him that the authorities had been tipped off to the escape plan and had knocked off the gun shipment. The man who had tipped them off, Russo had told him, was Frenchy Levine.

Now this was almost unbelievable. Frenchy had worked with some of the best mobs in the country; his reputation as a solid guy was unquestioned. This was like a bombshell exploding; we didn't know how to break the news to the others. When the call came for yardout, we almost didn't want to go. Whittemore was up on the little hill alongside the baseball diamond, playing chess, and Johnny finally went over and gave him the eye. After the game was over he got up from the table and walked off to the side with us. All the while that Johnny was passing on the information he had received from Russo, Whittemore's face remained absolutely expressionless. He listened, he nodded once, and then he went back to the table.

What we were expecting, of course, was that Whittemore and the Kraemers would be arrested, beaten up, and put into isolation for years. Nothing happened. The authorities were apparently protecting Levine and waiting for some other excuse to grab them. Nothing happened between Frenchy and the others, either. They continued to be as friendly as ever. Either they couldn't believe that Frenchy had betrayed them, or they wanted to make absolutely sure. Believe it or not, they actually got together again and arranged for Tiger Lil to send a second shipment in. And when that shipment was knocked off too, they knew.

Two more weeks went by, and then it happened. Suddenly, they had him in a circle and garlic-stained knives began to flash. One of the knives broke off in his stomach, another in his head. But Frenchy was so powerful that he broke out of the circle, went running down the hill toward a couple of guards, and collapsed at their feet.

For a week his life hung in the balance. Pounds of flesh, poisoned by the garlic, were sliced from his hulking body. The story of how he had betrayed his friends, ratted on them, circulated in the yard and still most of the people in the prison refused to believe it.

He finally recovered, that's how strong he was. And when he did, he got a commutation of sentence from the governor. Unfortunately for Frenchy, the newspapers printed why he had got it.

His days of freedom were destined to be very brief; nobody knew that better than Frenchy himself. Fully aware that there would be a contract put out on him, he took care to carry a pistol. Shortly after his release he was arrested in front of a bank on the east side of New York, charged with having a gun in his possession, and taken to the Tombs. Rather than go back to prison, where he knew he would be killed, he hanged himself in his cell.

Reese Whittemore was turned over to the Maryland authorities, tried for the murder of the guard, and hanged. Jake and Leon Kraemer remained in solitary for the rest of the time I was there. Which meant that they didn't get a chance to participate in the great Dannemora riot of 1929.

Three years and two months after my arrival at Dannemora, I became eligible to appear before the parole board. I went without any particular optimism. There was no such thing as automatic "good time" in those years, and although I had been a model prisoner I took it for granted that there were two black marks on my record. The charge that had got me sent there in the first place and my refusal to identify the murderers of McNally.

Before the day was over, I was notified that the date for my release on parole had been duly approved. It is incredible how that first glimpse of freedom can quicken the heartbeat and alter your perceptions. Suddenly you become aware of the passage of time. Of the passing seconds and minutes. The flavor returns to the flattest of foods and the color to the drabbest of objects. The world outside the prison wall becomes real again and you begin to contemplate its pleasures. My first thought wasn't of women or new clothes or fresh air. It was food. I drew up menus in my mind, and as I set the table with all of my favorite foods my mouth would actually salivate.

But through the prison the atmosphere was charging up too. The brutality had pushed the inmates past the point of no return. They just didn't care what happened to them any more. The word *riot* began to be heard. First in whispers and then as a serious proposition and finally as an inevitability. It wasn't *whether* any more; it was *when*. Inmates gathered in small groups during yardout. Riot leaders were appointed for each of the workshops. Assignments were handed out. It wasn't an escape that was being planned, understand. After the Whittemore escape plan had been discovered, the security had been tightened to make it impossible for anybody to shoot their way out. Powerful searchlights had been placed atop the walls, and machine-gun emplacements had been constructed outside the wall.

It was sheer destruction that was being planned. Destruction for the sake of destruction.

The plan was for the inmates to line up in front of their workshops as usual after breakfast for the five-minute smoking break and, upon a signal, break ranks, smash everything they could get their hands on, and then put everything that would burn to the torch.

There was no pressure on me to take part in it. On the contrary, with my parole due to take effect within a week it was made clear to me that I'd have to be a fool to take any part in it. But Eddie Wilson was one of the key men for the taking over of the weave shop, and I always had a fierce sense of loyalty toward my partner. I was hoping that the riot would somehow be postponed until after I had left, but once it started I knew that it would be very difficult for me not to make an appearance.

It was originally supposed to come off on a Sunday. For some reason or other it was called off at the last moment and pushed back a day.

On Monday morning I joined a group of cellblock porters who had assembled in the west hall to watch the inmates from the work companies leave the mess hall (the system was for them to leave in pairs) and walk past our line of vision toward the industrial area. There were about fifteen of us, maybe more, and there were some solid guys there. Marty Walsh. Pops Stewart. Quite a few others. And the more we talked about it the more we knew that we'd have to show ourselves when it began, if only as a gesture of solidarity. If you're in prison and there's going to be a riot, there comes a time when it doesn't pay not to get in it in some way.

As you were leaving the west hall you had to pass the dep's office before you could turn the corner and go down into the industrial area. Just as we were passing his office, Granger was turning the corner coming the other way. Automatically he stuck his chin out the way he always did, but as soon as he started to talk you could see that he was worried. He knew something was being planned, he told us. "You guys are smarter than them others. Some of you here, you even got a little brains. You go down there and tell them to get together a committee, and we'll talk about their grievances and see what we can do to iron this thing out."

What he was really out to do, of course, was to play for time so that he could weed the ringleaders out. This Marty Walsh said, "You had your chance to do something before now."

So Granger picked me out and said, "Sutton. You're supposed to leave here in a few days, aren't you?"

I kept my mouth shut. I didn't say one word,

and as we walked on past him he was saying, "I won't forget this."

By the time we got to the yard we expected that we would be walking right into the middle of the first wild eruption. To our amazement, the inmates were still assembled in orderly ranks in front of their shops. The guards were very much on the alert, and none of the key men—the man from each of the shops who was supposed to give the signal—had apparently been willing to be the first one to stick his neck out.

When we came walking through the doorway it was like the signal everybody had been waiting for. They knew we weren't allowed out there, and when they saw us they broke ranks and ran to their designated positions. The riot was on!

It was the most awesome, frightening thing I have ever experienced. From one second to the next, they turned into a wild-eyed, hate-crazed mob. They were out to wreck, to render asunder, to tear apart. For some of them, it was the accumulated hatred of thirty and forty years.

Into the shops they ran. They grabbed sledgehammers and smashed the machinery into small pieces. Crowbars, pickaxes, wrenches; anything they could wield. Everything that wasn't nailed down was picked up and heaved through the windows. Oil was poured across the floors and splashed across the walls and then set to the torch.

That was as far as the planning had gone. To break everything up and burn the place down. Once the buildings began to go up in flames, the maddened inmates were driven back out into the yard. They seemed to come pouring out like ants. And right into a crossfire. The yard guards, having fled for the safety of the cellblocks, had broken out rifles and were shooting through the windows. The tower guards opened up with machine-gun fire. The off-duty guards had come rushing up from Clinton and they were on top of the wall too, taking pot shots with small-arm fire. It was like a battle scene out of the Civil War. Half the buildings were burning like bonfires. Small flames were rising from all the broken furnishings and trash that had been thrown out through the windows, and the yard was quickly covered by a pall of smoke. Everybody was running helter-skelter for cover or crawling through the debris. At the first burst of gunfire, I had flattened myself against the nearest wall. A friend of mine named Chuck Reese, out of Buffalo, had just had a visit from his wife and she was supposed to visit him again that day. He was only about fifteen feet away, running right toward me, when a burst of machine-gun fire got him right in the head, three or four bullets—*splat-splat-splat*. All around him there were bodies dropping. I flattened myself even tighter against the wall, and all I could think was: Oh, God, I'm supposed to be leaving in a couple of days and they're going to carry me out in a box.

For five hours it went on. The fire departments from Clinton and Plattsburgh parked their equipment in the hills behind the wall and sent a steady stream of water into the burning building. The state troopers came from fifty miles away with riot guns. Two infantry companies were sent from the army barracks in Plattsburgh, armed with grenades and tear gas.

One by one the pockets of resistance were mopped up until there were only a couple of hundred holdouts barricaded behind a wall of mattresses in the tailor shop. They finally came filing out with their hands up after Warden Kaiser had given them a choice between surrendering or taking their chances with the army's grenades.

Officially, there were three prisoners killed and twenty wounded. Ridiculous. I personally saw more than three dead bodies and the grounds were littered with the wounded. And it didn't stop there. Once the prisoners had given up, the guards took over with a brutality that is probably unmatched in the history of American prisons. The suspected ringleaders were beaten until they were unconscious. Bones were broken. Men were crippled for life. Once the ringleaders had been taken care of, the rest of us were forced to strip and run a gauntlet through the guards. Every cell in the south hall was emptied out. Beds, buckets, everything. Nothing remained except the bare walls. And then they were filled with the beaten and broken bodies, one thrown on top of the other.

They threw people in there until there wasn't room for anybody else. And they kept them there. They made them defecate right there on the floor. Once a day they'd send some inmates around with hoses and flood the cell so that the feces and stuff would float out into the main corridor, where other inmates would come around and sweep it up.

After a couple of days, Governor Franklin D. Roosevelt came in, in a big car, circled the place once, and went out. That was his inspection. Any chance for protection from government officials disappeared two days later, when Auburn blew up. After that, the government officials were going to avert their eyes and let the prison authorities do whatever they had to do to keep things under control.

South hall remained an isolation ward. Some of the prisoners remained there for as long as five years. The officers had warned the administration that if any of them were ever released into the general population they would quit en masse. The administration was so convinced they meant it that whenever any of these prisoners' sentences were coming to an end, they would be transferred to one of the other prisons and released from there.

I was very lucky. I took a beating like everybody else but my parole saved me. And it wasn't just the parole, either. I'd had a set of picklocks on me at the time of my arrest, and a warrant of detainer had been placed on me at Dannemora for "possession of burglar's tools." Now that's the kind of charge that is normally dismissed as a matter of routine as soon as you're found guilty on the more serious charges. Somehow it had been overlooked by both the judge and my lawyer at the time of my sentencing, and some overzealous clerk had apparently run across what looked to be an open charge and whipped up a detainer. Still, it was there in my folder, and so the prison had informed the New York authorities of the date of my release and word had come back that a couple of detectives would be coming up for me. So I wasn't sent to the south hall. I was put in the east hall and waited, holding my breath, to see whether the detectives were really going to be there.

When I was taken to Granger's office, where the detectives were waiting, he warned me, "If you ever come back here, Sutton, you won't leave alive." I believed him.

During the train ride back to New York the detectives were very eager to hear about the riot. "I never really believed it was that rough in prison," one of them whistled. "Believe me, I'm going to be more careful who I send to prison from now on."

The reports in the newspapers hadn't even resembled the truth. The warden's version was that it had only been after the guards had beaten back a mass escape attempt that the prisoners had rioted. The detectives told the magistrate what had really happened, and when they were finished the judge looked at the warrant and said, "I don't know why they wasted the taxpayers' money and the time of two good detectives on this." He sentenced me to one day, credited me with a day served while I was under custody of the detectives on the train, and told me I could go. By the freak of a judicial oversight and a bureaucratic error I had been saved from a terrible beating.

Within the limitations set by the terms of my probation, I was a free man.

Willie the Actor

It was 1929 when I came out of jail, twenty-eight years old and determined to go straight. Morality still didn't have a thing to do with it. The only law I was obeying was the law of self-preservation. Under the Baumes Laws, which had gone into effect in New York while I was away, a second felony offense called for a mandatory sentence of thirty years. Not at the discretion of the judge. Mandatory.

There were two people I had corresponded with regularly. One was my old pal Tommy McGovern. Tommy had married a girl from the neighborhood after all that running around—a girl I knew very well —and settled down in Elmhurst, "out on the Island." The other was another girl from the neighborhood, Louise Leudemann, whom I hardly knew at all. The Leudemanns had lived on Thirteenth Street just down the block from us, and I had been a very good friend of her brother, Chick. Louise had been Chick's little sister, that's all. The last time I had seen her she was eleven years old. It had started with a chatty letter expressing sympathy for my conviction and carrying news about Chick and the rest of the family. I answered with a chatty letter of my own, and we started to correspond. Her father died, Chick became credit manager for a big company in the city, they moved to a garden apartment in Richmond Hill. By degrees, the letters became increasingly romantic and I had come to look forward to them as the one bright spot in my existence.

It was two weeks before I saw either of them, though. Although I had been able to tell the parole board that a job had been arranged for me with Frank Hessian, a Manhattan landscape gardener, the terms of the parole had stipulated that I live with my uncle John and aunt Alice and uncle Jim on their farm in Warrensburg. As out of character as it may have seemed, Uncle John had always dreamed of having his own farm. The blood of his Irish ancestors was in him. They grew potatoes, cherries, all kinds of produce. They had some milk cows. Among her other talents, Aunt Alice was a professional-class cook and baker. She baked fancy cakes that looked as if they came right out of the showcase; her pies, which were made from an old family recipe, were flavored by the most delicate and subtle wines. In the morning there was always fresh bread to go with the fresh eggs and the fresh air.

Altogether, it was driving me crazy. I was a full generation away from Ireland. I was a city boy.

After two weeks I came back to New York, went to the parole office on East Fifteenth Street, and told them the farm couldn't support an extra person and I no longer wanted to burden them with my presence. And so it was agreed that I would work for Hessian and live with my mother in Brooklyn.

Tommy McGovern had picked me up at Grand Central Station, and he insisted that his wife, Marie, would be very hurt if he didn't bring me home for dinner. But it was funny. Right from the beginning, there seemed to be something different about Tommy. While I was telling him about the riot, during the drive to Elmhurst, he kept agreeing that the kind of brutality that was practiced at Dannemora should not be tolerated but he was also saying things like, "Yeah, but what are you advocating, the abolition of all prisons? You got to have prisons."

As we stepped inside the house he very deliberately took off his jacket so that I would be able to see that he was carrying two .45-caliber pistols in arm holsters. "I didn't want to write it in a letter," he said, "because it's too hard to explain. I'm working for the government, Willie. I'm a narcotics agent." And, you know something? I wasn't really that surprised. Tommy had always hated drug peddlers with a passion, and I could pinpoint exactly when it had begun. One day as Tommy and I came out of his house there was an ambulance parked two doors away. A few minutes later an eighteen-year-old girl who was living in a furnished room there was carried out dead. She had committed suicide, we learned, because she was a drug addict. It was the first experience either of us had ever had with drugs; there were very little drugs around in those days. Still, I probably would have forgotten about it within the week if it hadn't made such an impact upon Tommy.

The accidents that determine your life, again. While we were waiting for Marie to come back from the market he paced back and forth, delivering a long diatribe against the gang leaders who trafficked in drugs with perfect safety. "They ought to be wiped from the face of the earth, all of them," he shouted.

"I'll never be satisfied until every drug peddler is six feet under the ground."

No sooner had we sat down to dinner than he and Marie exchanged a glance and he blurted, "How would you like to work for the government, Willie?"

All I could do was stare at him.

"You could get a lot of information for me, Willie." He didn't have to tell me that. While I was with the Tate gang I had got to know most of the mobsters around town. And, he pointed out, I had probably got to know some of the people who were involved with drugs during my stay in the can. "The government is willing to pay for that kind of information," he told me. Seventy-five dollars a week plus expenses.

"I wouldn't want to do that, Tommy," I said, trying to keep the coolness out of my voice. "If I understand you right, you're asking me to become an informer."

See? That was just the trouble. "You make it sound as if I'm asking you to commit some kind of crime. These people are worse than murderers! If you'd seen some of the things I've seen . . ."

We remained friends, Tommy and I, but it never was quite the same. I saw him rarely, and only by chance, and there was always that restraint that comes when two people are thinking along entirely different lines on something that is the most important thing in the world to one of them.

I've thought about that conversation more and more in recent years, though. In the old days a prisoner who was down for selling junk was looked upon as scum. Today, they're big deals. The big money is in drugs and respect goes where the money is. I thought of that conversation particularly when I was in the Queens County jail after my arrest in 1952 and could hear the screaming of the addicts who were taking the cold-turkey treatment in the next cells.

The next day I called on Louise Leudemann. I remembered a little girl. A gorgeous twenty-one-year-old woman met me at the door, threw her arms around me, and gave me a great big kiss. Her mother and Chick welcomed me almost as enthusiastically. My criminal record and my years as a fugitive in New York were never mentioned. It was as if I were an old friend who had moved away for a while and had finally, to their great joy and pleasure, moved back.

I had already visited Frank Hessian and was due to start work the next day. I also had a little money stashed away that I had been careful not to let my lawyers know about. Louise and I began to date. Very soon we were going out every night. To nightclubs, the theater, the best restaurants. Almost from the beginning we were talking about getting married, and within a couple of months we eloped to Elkton, Maryland. We called it an elopement, anyway. Actually, both of our families were extremely pleased.

I had a wife I was madly in love with and I was making a fairly good salary. Not as much as I had made in the defense plants, of course. And nowhere near what I had been making as a thief. We lived with her mother for a short time and then got our own little apartment nearby. Nothing like my luxurious apartment on Riverside Drive, of course. Or the fancy hotel suites Carrie and I had shared. Or Bell's beautiful little apartment in West Virginia.

Hessian's shop was on Eighty-sixth and Madison in the high-rent district, and he catered to a high-society clientele. I liked the work very much, it brought me a great deal of satisfaction and I was developing into a very good landscape gardener. I worked on the Vanderbilt home on Fifth Avenue, one of the showcases of the city, planting a lot of rhododendron bushes and laying out really magnificent flower beds. I landscaped the Carnegie townhouse which was farther up Fifth Avenue, on Ninety-first Street. Over a period of a couple of months I commuted every day to Strawberry Hill, Connecticut, where Samuel Untermyer, the lawyer, had a huge estate. Most of the first month was spent planting ten thousand tulip bulbs. Most of the second month we spent digging up trees and replanting them to reestablish an overall sense of design and symmetry.

The only shadow on our own landscape was the economy. We were married on October 21, 1929. The stock-market crash is dated from October 29, but that's in retrospect. At the time, it seems to me, it was looked upon only as the end of the wild speculation, not as the beginning of the great Depression. But as the months passed, it became more and more evident that the money was drying up. As a luxury business we were among the first to be hit. No more small jobs were coming in to Hessian, and the Unter- myer estate was the last big job we had. Somewhere in early May, Louise announced that she was preg- nant. The next week, Hessian had to let me go.

Right there, I began to think about making money in the way I knew best. Or, to be more honest about it, I began to think about what I had been thinking about all along.

As soon as I was locked up in jail, it had been only natural for me to go over the attempt to rob the Ozone Park bank and try to figure out why everything had gone so wrong. It was too easy to write it off as bad luck. "Learn from your mistakes," Doc Tate had taught me. I had badly underestimated the time it would take to break through the ceiling, that was obvious. It was also obvious that it had been a mis- take to leave the tanks behind. *Take nothing for granted.* We should have picked up and cleared out of there the moment I realized that there might not be time enough to complete the job.

But the more I relived those final minutes in the bank, trying to make it come out different, the more I began to see that there had been another possible course of action. We were inside, and those two em- ployees were outside. What had there been to prevent us from taking them both under control the moment they entered? First them and then all the others? I knew from casing the place just about when each of them could be expected to arrive. I also knew from my first job at the Title Guarantee Company that there would be a half-hour period between the time the manager arrived and the time the bank opened. Half an hour would have given us plenty of time to cut through the vault.

But wait a minute! I wouldn't have had to do even that. The manager had the combination. All I'd have had to do was order him to open it!

All very interesting. And very useful in keeping my mind active and passing the time. Unfortunately, there was one weakness to this marvelous new modus operandi that I had never been able to resolve. It simply took too long to go through a concrete floor. Even with as ideal a situation as I had found at Ozone Park, I had barely made it in time. With a thirty-year sentence hanging over me if I was caught, that made it just too risky.

And yet, banks continued to have such a strong appeal for me that I never was able to pass one without automatically, almost unconsciously, looking it over. Much in the way that a man with an entirely different kind of compulsion might take that hard, appraising look whenever he passed a pretty woman. So there I was about to pass a bank on Broadway, after another unsuccessful day at the employment agencies. It was late in the afternoon, well after the banks had closed. In much the same automatic way, I saw two guards getting out of an armored car. Saw them walk over, saw them ring the bell, and saw the door being opened almost immediately to let them in.

This is the answer, I said to myself. A uniform provided automatic entrée. Ring the bell and you could walk right in.

In that moment, everything came together. Because I had spent so much time around show-business people my mind went immediately to the theatrical-costume houses from which all kinds of uniforms could be obtained. Once I was inside the bank, I had the knowledge to dismantle the security systems. The courses I had taken in prison on the reaction of people under stress would enable me to keep everybody under control.

Only one thing was lacking. With Eddie Wilson still in jail, I needed a partner. Not just any partner, but a partner whom I could trust absolutely. While I was making the rounds, I ran into a mutual friend who let me know that Jack Bassett had been around, trying to get connected.

I have already described how Bassett was always ready to lend a helping hand to anybody who had a plan for busting out of Dannemora. I now want to explain how Bassett had got sent to Dannemora in the first place. His background was rather unusual for a thief. He came from a very good family in Buffalo, and he had been educated at the Bordentown Military Academy and Syracuse University. Somehow, however, he had always been directed toward crime, and after being picked up a couple of times he was sentenced to Sing Sing for two and a half to five years for stealing a car. At Sing Sing he became friendly with a lifer named George Stivers, who had killed a state trooper. Bassett was coming to the end of his sentence and he had been made a trusty, which gave him rather free access to the prison. He managed to get an impression of the key to Stivers's cell and have a key made up, and after the lockup he opened Stivers's cell door and together they crept up to the arsenal. Bassett hit the guard over the head with a sockful of steel filings, they grabbed a couple of rifles, and made good their escape. Each of them was given twelve years when they were recaptured—seven years for the escape and five years for the assault on the officer—and sent to Dannemora.

Now, I'd have to concede that it wasn't a very smart thing for Bassett to have done. Instead of having six months left, he had twelve years. But if you can't expect people to act logically, you can expect them to act consistently and Bassett's pattern of behavior was certainly one of unswerving loyalty to his friends.

If you couldn't trust a man like that, whom could you trust?

Jack wasn't difficult to find; he was living at the Somerset Hotel right off Times Square. Things hadn't gone well for him at all. He had married his old girl friend as soon as he got out, his wife had given birth to a premature baby, the baby had died, and between the medical bills and the inability to find work he was deep into debt. Once he had heard my idea for getting the bank to open its door to us, he was eager to put in with me. I began by having him bring his wife, Kitty, out to the house so that she could meet Louise and we could convince both of them that we were going into the realty business together.

Since I had no police record as a jewelry-store robber I wanted to test out the plan on a jewelry store. I chose M. Rosenthal and Sons, on Broadway between Fiftieth and Fifty-first, two doors south of the Capitol Theatre. Right in the middle of the kind of busy section where I liked to work. After due thought I decided to be a Western Union boy. I went to one of the smaller costume agencies, told them I was going to appear in a church play, and asked if it would be possible to rent a uniform for a very brief time. Then I went to a friend in an entirely different line of business and got some pistols.

The store, I had discovered, was opened every morning by a black porter whose name I would come to learn was Charley Lewis. It was Charley Lewis to whom I would be handing my telegram.

Now I am going to digress here for a moment to explain why my knowledge of automatic security systems was so important to me, not only when it came to knowing what to look for after I was inside the establishment but also in answer to the question of why I didn't just come by at night, make an impression of the lock, and let myself in. The Rosenthal jewelry store was protected by a Holmes burglar-alarm system, which was made by the foremost security agency of the time. At the Holmes office was a master board, resembling a switchboard, which had a separate light for each establishment under its protection. If that light went off or on at any time other than the listed times for opening and closing, the Holmes guards would be there within a matter of minutes.

A client could buy either partial or full protection. Under full protection the place was completely sealed. The doors, for instance, would have wooden lattice forms in which the electrical wiring was embedded. In the windows, the wires would be embedded in half-inch tinfoil strips. The walls had thin wooden slats, about a foot apart, running from the ceiling to the floor. Before the last man was ready to leave at night he would throw a switch which closed the electrical circuit. If any of the openings hadn't been secured—if, say, a window had inadvertently been left open—a loud buzzer would go off as soon as he closed the door.

In the morning, the procedure was reversed. The first man in walked several feet into the store and pulled the switch up, thereby disconnecting the circuit. If I had walked in and thrown the switch fifteen minutes early, the Holmes office would have been alerted that something was wrong.

At Rosenthal's, the porter arrived at about seven-thirty in the morning. After I had given him time to "take the alarm off," I walked up in my Western Union uniform and rang the bell. "I've got a telegram here for Mr. Rosenthal," I said. "You want to sign for it?" He had the door open just a crack, keeping his foot in the door to keep it from closing. In order to take the book and pencil he had to open the door a little wider, and while he was signing I pushed my way in and put my pistol against his stomach. "Back in and stand still," I ordered. "My partner will be here in a minute."

This Lewis turned out to be the coolest customer I ever came across. "I don't think you're going to get away with it," he shrugged, after I had explained the whole operation to him. "There's a policeman on each corner. There's policemen passing back and forth in front of here all the time."

"Don't worry about it," I told him. "You're going to stand in front of the window where everybody can see you until your fellow employees arrive."

As soon as Bassett came in he took a roll of picture wire out of his pocket. One end of it he tied to the porter's ankle and the other end to the leg of the showcase. There were six other people who worked in the store: a watchmaker, two salesmen, the bookkeeper, and Mr. and Mrs. Rosenthal. If everything went according to plan, we were going to be out of there before the bookkeeper and the Rosenthals arrived.

For the time being, I went behind the showcase and found four alarm buttons under the overhang. In answer to my question, Lewis told me there was a fifth one in the back room. There were also two safes there, one slightly larger than the other, and although both of them were protected by Holmes doors I could see by the general look of them that it was the larger one that was in constant use.

Lewis had already told me that it was the young salesman, Fox, who had the combination. By the time Fox arrived we had already taken the watchmaker and the other salesman under control and he was so stunned when he saw them sitting on the floor with their hands tied behind their backs that the combination went right out of his head. You know fear when you see it. The man was absolutely petrified. "If you'll give me a few more minutes I'll remember it," he kept saying. "I know it as well as I know my own name." He even made an effort at spinning the dial, just to see if his fingers wouldn't automatically go to the right places, and his hands were trembling so badly that he could hardly manage even that. "Don't you think I'd open it if I could," he pleaded. "Don't you think my life means something to me?"

From the jewelry store, Lewis called out: "I think the boy is nervous. Mr. Rosenthal has the combination. Why don't you let me call him at home and I'll get it for you."

Well, I had to think a little about that. "Okay," I said, finally. "But if you're going to be cute you're taking a very large chance. I just want you to remember that if anything happens, it's going to happen to you, not to Rosenthal or anybody else."

He was an iceberg, this fellow. I put my ear to the phone while Bassett held a gun on him. "This is me," he said. "Lewis. We have to put the display out, and Mr. Fox has forgotten the combination."

Rosenthal, who had obviously been awakened from a deep sleep, grumbled something about having to go somewhere to get it. When he came back he was still grumbling. "It's nine-seventeen, and you're telling me the store isn't open yet, Charley?"

"Well," the porter said. "Mr. Fox arrived late. Everybody oversleeps now and then."

While I was taking the combination down, Rosenthal suddenly said, "What's the matter with you, Charley? You know the combination."

Lewis tried to cover it over by saying, "No, Mr. Fox has forgotten it." I'd heard it, though, and there was no doubt in my mind that he had made the call in the hope that Rosenthal would understand that his store was being held up. Boy, I just looked at him. "I had more consideration for this man," I said after he had hung up, "than you did. Come on. You're going to open it for me. You probably open it more often than he does anyway." And I could see just by looking at the others that I was right.

Even then, he tried to get away with opening the smaller of the two safes. "Uh-uh," I told him. "The other one. I want the good stuff." I couldn't believe this guy. "Have you ever been in a robbery before?" I had to ask him. "You sure are one cool customer."

Once he had the big safe open, I pulled the drawers out and dumped the contents into a traveling bag. It was so full—$150,000 worth of precious jewelry— that I actually had to throw a few watchcases out before I could close it. Then I went back out into the store, handed the bag to Bassett, and told him to leave. I put Bassett's overcoat over my uniform, and stuffed the messenger cap into the pocket and replaced it with an ordinary cap that I had been carrying in the pocket of my jacket.

The car was parked halfway down the block on Fifty-first Street. Two minutes later, I walked out the door and locked it behind me. I hadn't taken more than three or four steps before the burglar alarm over the door was setting up a racket. That sonofagun Lewis had realized that with the door locked and the safe open the Holmes circuit would not be activated, and as quickly as that he had leaped across the floor and thrown the switch.

Everybody was looking around to see where it was coming from. The cop at Fifty-first Street was hurrying toward the store. It didn't matter, though. I had already melted into the crowd by then, and it was just a matter of turning left at the corner and walking to the car.

Even though I had run into the coolest porter in the city of New York, the over-all plan had worked to perfection.

Now that we had such a profitable test run under our belt, I was ready to try it out on a bank. I had already had letterheads printed up for the Waverly School of Art & Drama, and in no time at all I had all kinds of uniforms stored away in an apartment on Eighty-seventh Street, just off Central Park West. Immediately I came across a bank in Richmond Hill, right in my own backyard, that was so easy that I came back every morning for a full week, unable to believe what I was seeing. The door was protected by a sliding gate which was kept padlocked overnight. The manager would arrive first, at seven-thirty in the morning—which was a switch right there—unlock the padlock and slide the gate back. He would then insert the key into the keyhole and turn back to slide the gate shut before he unlocked the door. Fifteen minutes later the guard would arrive, slide the gate open, close it behind him, turn the doorknob, and walk right in. Each of the other six employees would do the same thing. In other words, the door was never locked after the manager opened it. There I was with all those uniforms hanging in my closet, and I had stumbled across the one bank where I didn't need one.

A few days later, Bassett sat behind the wheel of the car with the motor running while I stationed myself across the street. A minute after the manager entered, I slid the gate open and walked in. Nobody in sight. Toward the rear of the bank, however, there was an office. I opened the door cautiously and there he was, sitting at his desk reading a newspaper. "Who are you?" he blurted. "You can't come in here."

"I'm here," I said. "I want you to open the vault in one minute flat or they'll be reading your obituary in that newspaper tomorrow."

I was out of the place with nineteen thousand dollars before the guard arrived.

When I did get to wear a uniform it worked like a charm. To take the first bank, I dressed up as a policeman, rang the bell, and asked the porter whether I could use the toilet facilities. "Of course, officer," he said. I used the same technique to rob the Converse

Bank on the outskirts of Boston. A uniform was indeed like a badge of admission. Any uniform. Policeman, fireman, mailman, Western Union boy, carpenter; even a window washer. During the next six months, we walked in and out of banks as if we owned them. We hit jewelry stores, insurance companies, anything.

A new M.O. had hit the police files and they were completely baffled. After the Rosenthal job, notices were sent to Western Union offices all over the country asking for the name of any former employee who had left without turning in his uniform. One name came back from a small southern city and when they finally tracked the guy down they found he had been right under their nose all the time, serving time on Riker's Island for some minor crime. By then I had used a policeman's uniform enough so that the New York police department was searching its own roster, past and present. They were so sure they had a gang of rogue cops on their hands that they were shifting captains of police all over town.

After we had expanded our operations into Massachusetts and Pennsylvania, the Bankers Association sent a pamphlet to their members around the eastern states advising them to set up "precautionary security measures," something I first became aware of in the course of taking a large bank in New York. This was a bank where both the porter and the guard had a key. The porter would come in and go about his business, and the guard would come along ten or fifteen minutes later and let himself in. I had got the porter to open the door to me by posing as a postman with a special-delivery letter and Bassett was guarding him while I hid behind the door, waiting for the guard. Well, he came to the door, started to open it, and then closed it again and peered inside. And then he did it again. Opened the door a crack, peered in, looking puzzled, and closed it. Three or four times he went through the same ritual and then he shut the door firmly, turned the lock, and began to back away.

I came hurrying out just in time to see him turn

into a candy store two doors away. And also in time for him to see me. As I came dashing into the store, he was stepping into a telephone booth along the wall. I stepped in with him. "Are you going to call somebody up?" I asked, showing him my pistol.

Call somebody up just because he happened to be in a telephone booth? Nothing could have been further from his mind.

"Now you just do as you're told," I said. "We're going back into that bank, and always remember that I can shoot faster than you can run."

The next day I picked up the newspaper and learned what had caused the guard to be so hesitant. The bank had devised a system of leaving a small light on over the electric clock all night. The porter would come in, and if nothing had happened after about five minutes he'd go back and turn it off. I had seen it burning brightly in the dawn and thought nothing of it.

After that, it became a game with me to try to spot the warning signal ahead of time. The favorite was to go through a routine with the window shade. The first man in might wait five or ten minutes before he pulled it up; or he'd pull it halfway up when he came in and then pull it the rest of the way a few minutes later; or he'd pull it halfway up and the next man would come in and pull it all the way up.

At some banks, they'd leave something in the window. The first thing I noticed in looking at a bank in Massachusetts was that in the window there was a daily calendar that was turned over on its side. That's it, I said to myself. And, sure enough, within a few minutes after the guard came in he turned it up straight.

"By the way," I said to him, when the day of reckoning came. "You can go and turn the calendar in the window up straight now." I thought he was going to fall right through the floor.

The thing that really had the police so confused was that I was using so many different disguises. I would dye my hair different colors. I had sideburns which I could paste on. I had all different types of mustaches. Sometimes I'd grow them, sometimes they'd be false. If I really wanted to look distinguished I'd wear a Vandyke. I could make my eyebrows very heavy by intertwining separate little patches of hair. Also my eyelids. At times, I wore elevated shoes. I had a whole set of hollowed-out corks to alter the shape of my nose. I knew how to use cosmetics to change my complexion. I also knew how to use collodion to put a small scar on my face or a wart along the side of my nose. On the spur of the moment, I'd affect the barest hint of a lisp or accent. Never anything really conspicuous; just enough to give the victims something to focus on.

And even if I didn't alter my appearance, I'm a very average-looking sort of guy, easily lost in the crowd.

I enjoyed playing the different roles. I was always so wrapped up in any job I was planning that as soon as I put on a policeman's uniform I felt like a policeman. The car would usually be parked a block or two away, and while I was strolling to the bank I'd automatically check the doors of the shops with my eyes. From time to time someone would stop me to ask directions. On two separate occasions, motorists asked me if it would be all right to leave their car in a no-parking zone for a couple of minutes—they were just going to run in and pick something up. I lectured them severely. How could they ask a policeman for permission to violate a city ordinance? "Now if you happened to ride around the block," I told them, "I might not be here when you got back."

While I was crossing a busy intersection in Philadelphia in my uniform—this was years later—I was hailed down by a police cruiser. A captain got out and bawled the hell out of me for having a button loose on my collar. I felt just awful about it—yes, sir; you're right, sir; an absolute disgrace, sir—not because a police officer had stopped me right across from the bank I was about to rob but because I was being censured by a superior. I was a very conscientious cop right up to the time I stopped being a cop and started being a thief.

It was the same thing when I was wearing a mailman's uniform. In my mind, I was a dedicated member of the postal service on my way to deliver a special-delivery letter—neither rain nor snow nor dark of night—up to the very moment that I pushed my way inside and took out my gun.

I looked upon the gun the same way. As a prop. You can't rob a bank on charm and personality, so I had to carry one. And I can't swear that I wouldn't have used it if it had come to the crunch. Bassett and I both understood that we couldn't afford to be captured. As a three-time loser, he'd be in even worse shape than me. On the day before we were going out on the Rosenthal job he got a couple of strychnine pills from a pharmacist he knew. Just in case. Actually, I always had a strong premonition that if anything went wrong I would be shot to death rather than captured. Still, I kept that pill on me for a long time. A big green pill. Not because I had any intention of using it but because I felt that they served as a constant reminder to Bassett that he had something besides his gun he could reach for.

As far as I was concerned, I was as incapable of shooting anybody as I was of committing suicide. During my brief stay at the farm in Warrensburg, my uncle John was always trying to get me to go hunting with him. I never would. What did I want to kill a bird for, I'd tell him. I didn't have anything against them. The lesson from Doc Tate had cut that deeply. You pull the trigger the first time and maybe it would become easier the second.

My abhorrence for violence came to be so well known that by the end of my career the New York police automatically eliminated me from any robbery where it was used. And it wasn't only because of Doc Tate. Professional thieves prided themselves on not having to use violence when I was coming up. To a good jewel thief like Johnny Feinstein, part of the job was setting things up so that his victim would turn over the jewelry without offering any resistance. When you stole some jewelry only the insurance company was unhappy. If you had to hit a rich lady or her husband over the head, the police were going to come under tremendous pressure to get you. Violence not only defeated its own purpose, it meant that you hadn't done the job right. By your manner, voice, and timing—as well as your gun—you were supposed to be able to immobilize the victim psychologically.

In later years I would sometimes carry a Thompson machine gun for the same purpose. A pistol frightens people but it doesn't necessarily immobilize them, and I was always afraid that somebody was going to lose his head someday and make a grab for it. With a machine gun I never had to say a word. As soon as anybody sees a machine gun, his automatic reaction is to throw up his hands. I chose the Thompson because it was so easy to assemble that I could carry the gun itself under my coat, have the drum in my pocket, and just slip it out and slide it in.

The only possible weakness of my M.O., the thing I was most concerned about at the beginning, was that after I had entered the bank and taken everybody under control I was still going to be totally dependent upon the willingness of the manager to open the vault for me. Never once did I have the slightest problem; it always amazed me how quickly they complied. I'd hold out that psychological bribe to them, letting them believe that if it was only their own safety that was involved they'd have held out courageously, and immediately we'd be heading for the vault.

If there was the slightest question in my mind about whether my M.O. was going to be effective I would simply write the job off. Or, at least, make the necessary accommodations. There was one bank I looked over for a very long time. A small suburban bank that was just begging to be taken. The problem was that there was a policeman stationed at a school crossing on the corner. Not directly across the street, but close enough to have a good angle on the door if he happened to be looking in that direction. So I waited until the day the summer holidays started, and then I took it with ease.

By the same token, if anything happened to make my presence known to anybody outside the bank I would leave at once. It happened to me at the National City Bank in Brooklyn. A large bank, with a

121

switchboard and everything. Having estimated the take at fifty thousand dollars, I had cased the job as meticulously, inside and out, as any job in my life. They had an enormous vault in the cellar, divided into two sections. On one side was the section where the bank kept its money, and on the other side was a section where the public could rent safe-deposit boxes. As soon as I disarmed the guard and explained the situation to him, I had him open the gate and take me down there so that I could check out the alarm system. The second man to arrive every day was a sprightly old gentleman who supervised the rental section. The guard opened the door for him, and he came waltzing in, humming a happy tune, without even seeing me. "Ahhh," he said when he saw that the gate had been pulled back. "The bank is open."

I stepped behind him and whispered, "Yes, I opened it."

Because it was such a large bank, with so many employees, I had been worried that Bassett would have some trouble guarding them all. To get around that, I had decided to sit them together at a long table in front of the bank and handcuff them together. Two to a cuff. Just as I was taking the manager downstairs to the vault, Bassett let out a holler. One of the last of the employees to come in, a young kid, had slipped his handcuff and was running for the door. I shouted to Bassett to let him go, and in almost the same breath told him to go out to get the car started. I stayed behind only long enough to sit the manager down in the chair the kid had just vacated, and then I walked out and jumped into the car.

That's when I discovered that the car was stalled. In those days you had to pull the choke out to start an automobile, and if you didn't push it back in as soon as the motor caught it was no trick at all to flood the carburetor. When things go wrong . . . I looked down the street and here comes this kid, naturally, with a police officer. The only thing I could think to do was jump out of the car and stand there, looking at him. Well, this was one police officer who wasn't looking to start out the day by going for a citation. The closer he came to me, the slower he moved. By the time he reached the bank he had stopped completely. I'm standing there staring at him; he's standing there staring at me. The kid is jumping up and down, pointing. Bassett finally got the car started, I dove in, and as we drove past the officer he was just beginning to tug at his gun. We were around the corner and picking up speed by the time he had it out.

It was the only time I ever left a bank hot.

The Third Degree

I had a new fence for the jewelry. I had been getting only about fifteen percent on the worth of the stuff from the Feldman Brothers, and during my stay at Dannemora, Johnny Feinstein had told me I could do a hell of a lot better than that with Dutch Schultz if I came to him through the proper channels. Well, I had known quite a few of the people who worked for the famous Dutchman. Larry Carney, one of his chief lieutenants, in particular. While I was at Dannemora, I had also become very friendly with Solly Girsch, who was one of the Dutchman's top strongarm men.

It wasn't a question of whether I had the credentials; it was a question of whether I wanted to do business with him. I had met Dutch Schultz around New York from time to time, and like anyone else who ever knew him I disliked him intensely. Nothing I heard from his boys at Dannemora had made me change my mind. He was a vicious, pathologically suspicious killer who kept his people in line through sheer terror.

The surprising thing to me was that Dutch Schultz had become such a powerful mob leader. At the time

I went away, he had achieved a certain position as a beer dealer—meaning hijacker—in the Bronx, but you wouldn't have mentioned him in the same breath with Legs Diamond or the Rock brothers, Joe and John. And even at that, everybody knew that the Dutchman's partner, Joey Noe, was the smarter of the two and, in the real, nonbullying sense of the word, the tougher.

And then, all of a sudden, Schultz was on top. He and Noe had simply let it be known that they were taking over. You didn't like it? A rap on the door of your top henchmen, four gunmen, and a few blasts of the machine gun. When John Rock refused to bow out gracefully, the Dutchman kidnapped him, hung him up on a meathook, and, according to the grapevine, wrapped a piece of cloth saturated with a gonorrhea infection around his eyes. For fifty thousand dollars, Joe Rock was allowed to buy his brother back. Blind.

All the beer that came into New York was trucked in from the New Jersey breweries. The next thing you knew, every beer truck that crossed the state line was either owned by or paying tribute to Joey Noe and Dutch Schultz. Including Legs Diamond's trucks. Joey Noe was ambushed and killed by some unknown gunmen, meaning Legs Diamond's boys. A couple of months later, Legs Diamond was ambushed and killed by some unknown gunmen, meaning the Dutchman's revenge. Dutch Schultz had become the undisputed Beer Baron of the Bronx.

By the time I was out and ready to fence the Rosenthal jewelry, the Dutchman was riding high. He was in complete control of the Bronx, and he had a working agreement with Owney Madden and Big Bill Dwyer, who ran Manhattan. His political protection came directly from Jimmy Hines, the Democratic leader of the Bronx. Jimmy Hines operated out of the Monongahela social club, and that was the Dutchman's headquarters too. He was into everything. He had a stranglehold on the policy racket in the Bronx, and he was moving in on Harlem, where the real policy money was. When he did get control, he wasn't satisfied with the outsized odds he had against the bettors. He hired Abbadabba Berman, a human calculator, to rig it further. The policy number was figured from the pari-mutuel payoff totals of predetermined races at predetermined tracks. Abbadabba followed the horses to those tracks, and just before the final race went off he would make a final split-second calculation on the payoff price of the two favorites, match what the resulting number would be against the most heavily played numbers of that day, and, if the Schultz book was going to be hurt, thrown in a last-second bet that would change it.

Being that greedy, it wasn't any great surprise that he was the biggest fence in New York, too.

The relationship between a jewel thief and his fence is a dangerous one, because the fence has to know where the stuff came from. If it has come from out of town, he can operate on the theory that it's pretty safe and start maneuvering it right away. If it's as hot as our stuff was, he's going to have to hold it, or, if he has contacts out of town, bring in yet another partner for the privilege of selling it at a discount. The Dutchman was so big that he'd be able to put it away and let it cool off. And that was what decided me, in the end, to have Johnny Feinstein set up a meeting.

"Well," Johnny said. "He'll be at the Monongahela club tomorrow morning, that's where he conducts his business."

For whatever it's worth, Schultz's real name was Arthur Flegenheimer. None of his own people ever called him anything except "Arthur" to his face, and I never heard them refer to him as anything except "the Dutchman" behind his back.

By any name, the Dutchman was very, very interested.

I didn't have the stuff with me, needless to say, and so he made an appointment to meet me the next day in one of Bill Dwyer's West Side bistros on Forty-fourth Street off Broadway.

Here's how much I trusted him: By offering to meet me away from his home grounds, and in the Irish section of town at that, he was showing his good intentions. Which made me wonder whether he wasn't really trying to allay any suspicions I might have had that his real intention was to have me hit on the head. There was another possible motive that I could see, though. Having knocked off all the old-timers, the Dutchman was in a highly publicized shooting war with "Mad Dog" Vincent Coll, who had been one of the Dutchman's top guns while he was taking over. Just as Schultz himself had once been for Legs Diamond. Bodies were falling all over town. I could see where the Dutchman might want to show his face around to prove that he wasn't holed up in his Bronx stronghold, shivering.

I knew where he lived, and so I picked him up outside his apartment house in the Bronx and tailed him most of the way down there. Just to make sure, you know, that I was going to find the right man waiting for me. After his appraiser had looked the stuff over and given him the nod, he offered me thirty-five thousand dollars. "We figure we can get seventy-five thousand for it," he said. "Anything over that, I'll give you five or ten percent, depending."

Now, thirty-five thousand was a very good price. He wasn't carrying that kind of money on him either, and so I met him at the Monongahela club the next day. I handed over the briefcase, and Bo Weinberg, who was both his chief bodyguard and top administrator, handed me the packet of money all neatly wrapped and tied.

My relationship with him never changed. He always gave me an exceptionally good price—like from the H. L. Gross robbery a couple of weeks later— and I always distrusted him. What it was, you see, was that I had a good reputation all over town. He was scoring points with his own people, and I was supposed to go around telling everybody else what a great guy he was when you got to know him.

Dutch Schultz never did anything in his life that wasn't self-serving.

And also he would have liked to have me join his gang. What he could offer me was information from all over the country, a pool of professionals for any kind of job I wanted to pull, and legal protection. All I could tell him was that I was constitutionally incapable of operating that way. I had to plan my own capers and have total charge from beginning to end. (I didn't think it would be helpful to tell him that from everything I'd heard from Johnny Feinstein and Solly Girsch, he'd probably have me driving a beer truck in between jobs.)

But, do you know, he did force a couple of his people on me. Once. He had taken on two heist men from Chicago, John Scanlon and Nick Romano, who had come to him so highly recommended that he had put them up in the best hotel and was paying all their expenses. They had been on his payroll for months, he told me, and they still hadn't made an effort to do a piece of work. I could do him a very large favor, he emphasized, by taking them along on my next job. A favor I might have been able to refuse him. A very large favor, no.

I had been casing a bank in midtown, and I was just about ready to take it. Instead of trying to explain to them how I worked, I had them meet me for breakfast in the restaurant directly across the street from the bank so that I could map it out for them. They didn't approve of my methods at all. There was too much activity on the street, they insisted. Too much traffic. The police cruiser which passed periodically had them in a permanent sweat.

They let me know, finally, that they were going to take their objections to the Dutchman before they'd go with me, and while they were at the Monongahela the next morning explaining why the bank couldn't be taken, Bassett and I were taking it.

The Dutchman put them on the next train back to Chicago, and he never tried to move any of his people in on me again.

Bassett was a very good partner when it came to pulling off a job. He did what he was supposed to do, and he did it without a moment's hesitation. That's all I ever expected from a partner, and all I ever wanted. For his protection, as well as the Dutchman's, I never told him where I was fencing the jewelry. He never asked. What he didn't have to know, he didn't care to know. He got fifty percent of the money and he understood that he was to leave a hundred percent of the thinking to me.

Other than that, we went our separate ways. Immediately after the Rosenthal job I rented a place out in Laurelton, Long Island, and shortly after that I bought an English-style Tudor house in an exclusive section of Lynbrook. I had explained the Rosenthal money by telling Louise that I had enjoyed a fabulous day at the racetrack, and if she suspected anything— and she wasn't dumb by a long shot—she didn't say anything. As time went on, I told her the money was coming from the business. Every day I would take the eight-fifteen train to the city and catch the five-thirty home. Louise would usually be waiting at the station to pick me up, just like any other commuter's wife.

But Bassett wanted to become a playboy. He loaded up on suits from the D'Andrea Brothers on Fifth Avenue. (I had made the mistake of taking him there while I was being fitted.) He rented an apartment on West End Avenue. One automobile wasn't enough for him. He had to have two, and sometimes three. The best of everything. He'd tip a maître d' a hundred dollars and a waitress fifty, and the more his reputation as a big spender spread, the more he tried to live up to it.

Inevitably, he got himself a broad. Phyllis Cromley from Atlanta, a real tart in my book. He set her up in the apartment on Eighty-third Street and tried to keep his wife happy, and hopefully in the dark, by showering her with money. Under those conditions, it didn't matter how much we made, he was always borrowing money from me. We'd go out on a job and he'd owe me as much as five thousand dollars.

After Louise had given birth to our daughter—on September 26, 1930—we left the baby in the care of her mother and took a trip through New England. The day we got back, Kitty Bassett called me. And I could tell by the hysterical undertone in her voice that it was trouble.

I met her at a cocktail lounge on Fifth Avenue. Well, Kitty was no beauty to begin with, and she had let herself go. She was fat, she had the beginning of a double chin, and you could see that she had begun to drink. Right off the bat, she told me that she knew

Jack was cheating on her. I didn't try to tell her she was imagining things, because it was clear that she had been hearing about Jack and this woman from some friends. The only thing I could think to do was come up with a story that she might be able to accept, if she wanted to accept it badly enough. I told her that this woman, Phyllis, had a husband up in Sing Sing and that Jack was in her company so much because she had asked for his aid in helping him to escape. "I'll tell you the truth," I said. "I didn't want any part of it. I think it's crazy. But . . . well, you know Jack."

In the beginning, she found that very difficult to accept. But the thing was that she wanted to believe it. At last, she looked me straight in the eye and said, "If anybody else told me that, I wouldn't believe it. But insofar as it's you that's telling me, Willie, I will."

I went right from the cocktail lounge to the apartment on Eighty-third Street and found Phyllis there with him. "Let's take a walk, Jack," I said. "I've got something to say to you." The look Phyllis gave me was pure hate. She always did believe I was trying to break it up between them and, of course, she was right. I always figured that women were the weak link when you're stealing. If you're going to be married, you shouldn't be cheating. One of the things she had done was let me know that she was more than willing to be available to me, too. Not by anything she said in so many words, but by the way she paraded around in a loose robe when I'd have to come to the apartment to pick up something. I knew damn well that eventually we'd get in some kind of a jackpot because of her. Although, actually, the jackpot didn't come from her, it came from Kitty.

Once I had Bassett outside, I said, "Listen, Kitty is wise to you going out with this Phyllis." I told him about the phone call and the conversation I had just had with her and I said, "Jack, if we ever take a fall we have to get thirty years as second offenders. Do you realize the situation you are causing here? If Kitty should go haywire, we're cooked."

He promised me absolutely that he'd get rid of her. And he sounded so frightened that I believed him.

The very next day he informed me that he had given her some money and sent her on her way. And that's where I was stupid. It was one of those things where I pretended to myself that there was nothing more to worry about while all the time the thing continued to gnaw at my mind. What he had really done, I discovered a few weeks later, was move her to another apartment, on Fifty-seventh Street.

Now, Bassett and I were still on probation, remember. All the while we were knocking off these joints we were making monthly reports to the probation office. As far as they knew, I was still working at Hessian's and living with my mother. According to the law, I wasn't entitled to get married without the permission of my supervisor. Well, I wasn't about to take Louise up to the probation office and put her through that kind of ordeal, and I wasn't going to ask any stranger if I could please marry the woman I was in love with, either. Those rules were antiquated even then, and most of them are still in force today. You're not supposed to drink, drive a car, or hang out with prostitutes. Nobody tries to enforce those kind of regulations, they'd look too silly. I didn't have to worry anyway, because I was paying a guy off at the parole office. A guy named Brosnan. Every now and then Bassett and I would take him to lunch and give him a couple of hundred dollars. The deal was that if anything came up that we ought to know about, he'd get the word to us.

I was also keeping in very close contact with Mother, and a couple of days after I made out my November report she called to tell me that a letter had just come from the parole office. What it said was that my report had been misplaced and they wanted me to come down immediately so they could make out a new one and get it up to Albany on schedule.

Now that was kind of hard for me to believe. And a little hard for Brosnan to believe too, when we got together with him that afternoon. He had never heard of a report being lost before, he said, but there was always a chance that it could have been temporarily misplaced.

We all went back to the parole office, which was located on East Fifteenth Street right across from the big Con Edison building where I had once worked. Bassett and I waited outside, and when Brosnan came back he assured me there was absolutely nothing in my folder about a parole violation.

I still couldn't shake the feeling that I'd be walking into a trap. What I did was pay a call upon my friend Al Jantzen in his Pine Street office. Al had become an insurance broker with the Travelers Insurance Company and, while he was about it, the official bootlegger for the financial district. Al knew that I was stealing. I had been stashing money away with him regularly so that if anything happened to me he would be able to turn it over to Louise and tell her it was from an insurance policy.

"Lookit," I told him. "You go over there and tell them I'm working overtime at Hessian's and I couldn't leave or I'd lose my job. Then when you're leaving, watch and see if anyone is following you." Bassett and I were going to secrete ourselves in a doorway about a block away and we'd be watching too. I was going to be waiting for him in a restaurant down in the financial section afterward, but he was not to come unless he was absolutely sure it was safe.

He walked past us in the doorway and a few seconds later we could see that three detectives were following him. They had told him at the parole office that they didn't care whether it cost me my job or not, I had better show up before noon the next day. One of the parole officers had then walked all the way down the stairs and out of the building with him. When they got to the top of the stoop, he patted him on the shoulder and said, "Don't forget, now. Tell Willie he has to come over here tomorrow morning."

Al was a very hip guy. As soon as the officer laid his hand on his shoulder, he knew he was being pointed out to a tail. A lot had happened between that moment and the time he was telling me about it in the restaurant. When Al came to work in the morning, he parked his car on the Brooklyn side of the bridge and took the subway over to Manhattan.

This time, he took the subway uptown, and by getting off and changing trains a couple of times, he was very quickly able to shake two of the detectives. To shake the third one, he took a train all the way up to the Bronx, left the subway, walked around the corner, and went into a store and bought a pair of gloves. When he came back out, he couldn't see the guy anywhere so he took the subway all the way back to the Manhattan side of the Brooklyn Bridge. It was quite dark by then and there was practically no traffic. Just to be on the safe side, though, he stopped the one taxi that was cruising by and told him he'd give him double fare to take him across the bridge fast. "I've got my car parked there," he told him, "and I've got to get to the airport in a hurry."

As the cab took off, he looked back and saw the third detective marooned there on the corner, wildly looking around for a taxi.

I didn't have to be a genius to see that I was in serious trouble. But, you know, as much as I racked my brain I couldn't see what it could be. I was still going on the assumption, remember, that Bassett had gotten rid of Phyllis. And as far as I knew there was no parole violation listed in my file. Another thing I discovered much later was that Brosnan had come under suspicion for taking money from parolees and they were withholding information from him whenever they wanted to pick anybody up.

All night I mulled it over in my mind. They thought they had something, there could be no doubt about that, but for all I knew it could be something very trivial. If I didn't report as ordered, I'd blow the whole thing. There wasn't much doubt about that, either. When it all settled out, I could see that the only way I had any chance of not becoming a fugitive again was to go over there and see what the hell it was all about.

It was a very old building, with iron rails running up the stoop. The parole office was on the top floor. Right away I could see that my supervisor was stalling for time. It took twice as long as usual for him to make out the report and when he finally got through all the questions he began to make small talk. "I'm very sorry," I told him. "I have to leave right away. I have the truck parked down the street and I have to drive to the market and get some flowers."

"Come off it," he said. "You haven't been working at that Hessian's for a year. We know you're doing something, but what you're doing we don't know."

I said: "You're mistaken. You can come downstairs with me and I'll show you the truck."

We weren't going anywhere, he told me firmly. He had already talked to Hessian, and he knew there was no truck anywhere. "You've violated your parole. You have to be returned to Sing Sing prison." A couple of detectives were on their way over to place me under arrest.

I wasn't going to go back to Sing Sing, that I knew. There were two big, burly guys standing in the doorway directly in front of the switchboard operator, and the doorway was so narrow that they had it completely blocked off. I shrugged as if I realized that there was nothing I could do but wait, but I was ready to go the second I saw daylight. My chance came when the switchboard operator said something and one of them turned to say something back. When he moved, I moved. I was in very good shape, and I had always been athletic. I went ramming right in between them, swinging my shoulders as I went, and as heavy as they were I lifted one of them right off his feet and sent the other guy crashing into the wall.

Then I was hurtling down the stairs, taking them about twelve at a time. Just as I hit the bottom floor, I could see two men, whom I took to be the detectives, coming up the steps outside. Nonchalantly, I straightened my tie and opened the door for them. A line of cars was parked right outside, and so I continued on casually down to the corner and turned at the block where Bassett was waiting in his car.

I had got away, but I was still completely bewildered. There was no reason for them to have checked with Hessian unless they already knew I was doing something, and yet they still didn't seem to know. If that was all they did have—that I had left my job—there was a very good chance that it could be patched up with money. For the next week or so I sat perfectly still to kind of let things calm down.

And then I got another call from Kitty. Just as distraught as the first time, although, it seemed, for an entirely different reason. Jack was in trouble with the parole board, she told me, and she had to meet me somewhere so we could decide what to do. Well, under the circumstances that hardly sounded unreasonable. But, of course, I had to be very careful. "Here's what I want you to do. At eleven o'clock sharp, I want you to leave your apartment and walk down West End Avenue toward Seventy-second Street. Just keep walking and somewhere along the line I'll pick you up."

Ten minutes before eleven, I was stationed on a rooftop a few blocks away with a powerful pair of field glasses. Kitty Bassett came out of her apartment house at the appointed time and walked down West End Avenue. Shortly afterward, I was following a few blocks behind on the other side of the street. Instead of going on to Seventy-second Street, though, she turned left on Seventy-third and walked into a Childs' restaurant, which was contrary to my instructions but, considering the state of mind she was in, not *that* much contrary.

When I walked in she was seated at a table facing the door and looking very uncomfortable. I hung my overcoat on the rack and joined her, turning the chair so that I could keep one eye on the door.

She said: "I think the police are looking for Jack. I think he's going to need a lawyer, and I don't know how to go about it. I think you ought to hire one for him."

"I'll certainly do that. But why? What's he been doing?"

She didn't know. All she knew was that a detective had come up to the apartment and asked her all kinds of questions about him.

Well, that didn't sound very good. I told her to go right home, pack a bag, and check into the Plaza under the name of Helen Morrison. "I'll phone in a couple of hours to make sure you've checked in and then we'll be able to talk about getting the right lawyer." The lawyer, I assured her, would be able to find out for her what kind of trouble Jack was in.

While I was putting on my coat, watching the door every minute, a pair of detectives came out of the kitchen, pinioned my arms behind me, and placed me under arrest.

They took me down to the station on West Fifty-fourth Street, and it didn't take long for me to figure out where my troubles with the parole department had come from. Kitty, of course, had found out the truth about Jack and Phyllis. To her way of thinking, which I could fully understand, I had betrayed her by lying about the other woman. It didn't matter that it was her husband who had really betrayed her; she still wanted him and she apparently believed that if she could get me out of the way he wouldn't have enough money to be able to keep another woman. She knew we were involved in some kind of holdups because she had seen him handling a lot of jewelry one night. For her purposes, all she'd had to tell them was that I had left my job.

That jealous a woman wasn't going to be able to keep it inside of herself, of course. She had confronted Jack with it a few nights earlier, and he had walked out on her. In a jealous rage, she had called the police and told them everything she knew. Even where his autos were parked. One of them was kept in a garage on West End Avenue, just below Seventy-second Street, and the detectives had just missed him. He was driving up to his sister's house in Buffalo with Phyllis. Kitty had guessed that he might be headed there, and she had given the police the address. And just because they let him sit with Phyllis on the train while they were bringing them back, he had told them everything he knew. They didn't even lay a hand on him. He confessed to everything we had done, in detail, and to any other crimes the police wanted to clear up. Thirty-seven robberies in all. He told them everything they wanted to know about every crime and every criminal he had ever heard about.

And this was the guy I had trusted so completely. This was the guy I had loaned all kind of money to. But I could understand the psychology there, too. You can help a person only so much. Keep helping them, and they're going to build up a resentment against you.

He was already back in the city and being held incommunicado when Kitty went the rest of the way and set me up for the police.

I admitted that I had known Bassett in Dannemora and had run into him a couple of times after I'd got out. I denied that I had ever committed any crimes with him. I was then taken to police headquarters on Centre Street, where I had the shit kicked out of me.

It was a time of brutality in every police station in the country. The favorite trick was to hang you over the top of an open door by the handcuffs and pretend that you were a punching bag. New York and Chicago were the worst, and New York wasn't as bad as Chicago. In Chicago, when they took you down they didn't care whether you were dead or alive.

But first, they sent for everybody that I had robbed in New York, a large group of people. Before they were sent in they were told, "We have a lineup of men in the other room. We want you to look them over carefully and if you see the man in that lineup who robbed you, put your hand on his shoulder and don't say anything." I had been so heavily disguised that out of more than a hundred victims, only one man put his hand on my shoulder. And he didn't even hesitate. That's right. Charley Lewis, the colored porter at Rosenthal's.

They took me upstairs, handcuffed me to a chair, and began to throw questions at me. There were two captains of detectives who were more or less in charge. Captain McPhee and Captain McCoy. McPhee was the hitter, a real sadist. He and a couple of the others punched me around a little and then McCoy came in. The good guy. The psychologist. After a little chitchat, he handed me a sheaf of papers. "Read it, Willie," he said softly. "This isn't any trick. It's all there, the times, the places, and the details that only you and Bassett knew about." It was Bassett's confession. And as I read it my heart dropped right down to my shoetops.

I threw it back at him and I said: "This man, if

136

he implicates me in anything, is either insane or he's trying to cover up who his real partner is."

Well, they wouldn't go for that. The one thing Bassett hadn't been able to tell them was who our fences were, and that was what they wanted to know from me.

"What fences? I don't know anything about any fences."

Blackjacks came lashing out at me from around the whole perimeter. All around me, they were swinging and cursing. A telephone book came down on my head with such force that lights seemed to go popping all around me. When my head cleared, McCoy was ordering them to stop. He was trying to go easy on me, he pleaded, and so why didn't I make it easy on myself and get it all off my chest?

"I have nothing to get off my chest."

So they took me down two flights of stairs to the target room in the subbasement. A long narrow room, with three or four bull's-eyes at the far end, and a long wooden table just inside the door. Soundproof. They could kill you and nobody would hear you hollering. After I had been ordered to strip, my hands were cuffed behind my back and I was picked up and thrown on top of the table with my stomach sticking up. There were six detectives there under the command of McPhee. One of them held me around the neck, a couple of them held my shoulders, and two others held my feet. McPhee and the other detectives stood on opposite sides of the table and with long rubber hoses they started to beat me methodically from my private parts all the way up to my neck. Then they turned me over and beat another tattoo on my back. When they were finished my skin was completely black. I was one solid contusion, front and back. A slab of quivering pain.

And then they turned me over and started all over again. Unbearable! Every time they laid the hose on me, it felt like a red-hot sword stabbing into me. "Why don't you kill me, you bastards!" I screamed. "You'll never get me to confess." And I knew that they wouldn't. And the more they beat me the surer I became. They beat away at me for probably half an hour, and then I pretended to lapse into unconsciousness, which is almost impossible because the body stiffens in anticipation of every blow. But I suppose the body also must become desensitized when it reaches a certain level of pain, and the time came when I was able to let my mouth sag open and just lay there, inert, every time the hose came down on me.

At last they rolled me off the table and let me fall to the floor. They dragged me out of the room by both arms and deposited me in one of the two cells at the end of the dark, narrow corridor. The door clanged shut, and I could hear McPhee say, "This was only the first session. We'll have the second session a half hour from now."

Another beating was going to kill me, I had no doubt whatsoever about that. I also knew that I'd let them kill me before I'd talk. When you think of all the men who put themselves right into the electric chair because they couldn't withstand the third degree, you realize that it is impossible to say ahead of time that you can't be broken. You might think you can't, but you have to be put to the test before you can really know. I felt a great pride in myself lying there, face down in the dirt, naked and only half conscious. It was as if I had known all my life that this moment of truth was going to come and I had always been secretly afraid that I might not be able to stand up to it.

But that didn't mean I wasn't going to try to save myself. There's another part of the mind that is keyed in, at all times, to survival. I put my finger in my mouth and with my fingernail I made a small tear in the roof. The blood started to trickle down and I kept my mouth closed so that it would collect there.

Before long, they brought another guy down and put him in the other cell. I don't know whether they had him look at me or whether it was just the sight of the place that intimidated him. All they did was threaten this guy, and he must have talked for a full hour, telling them everything he had ever done. As far as I was concerned, it was all to the good. I lay there, pretending to be unconscious while my mouth filled up with blood. I heard them taking the other guy away. I heard them coming back. They opened the cell door and slapped me a couple of times across the face. As I opened my eyes, I let the blood come trickling out. And then I suddenly "came to" and let it come out in a gush. "You sonsabitches," I croaked. "You ruptured my stomach. You better get a doctor for me or I'm gonna die."

"That's what we want you to do," they said. "We're going to kill you, you sonofabitch."

They didn't, though. They didn't lay another hand on me. They dragged me back into the target room, helped me put on my clothes, and half carried me back up the stairs. The beating was over. I had beaten the bastards.

They held me for four days without booking me. I wasn't allowed to contact anybody. When they told me my wife had been arrested I didn't believe them. Why would they arrest Louise, she didn't know anything. It was true, though. She had turned all the money in the house over to them, and then she had taken them to the bank and turned over the three thousand dollars they found in my safety-vault box. For all that cooperation, they had arrested her anyway. They held her in a hotel for four days before they let her go.

I had been arrested on Tuesday. On Saturday I was brought to Captain McCoy's office. My friend. My buddy. If you don't think it works, you're kidding yourself. It didn't matter that I knew he was playing a role; when I saw him I knew I wasn't going to get hit and that tends to make you very happy to see him. He was all smiles and confidences. "I know you're innocent, Willie," he said. "But let me tell you this, it's too bad you picked Bassett as a partner because you'd have made millions of dollars. We were absolutely stumped. We didn't know where the hell to turn."

They'll do that too, the good ones. They like to keep shifting around like that to keep you off balance. He starts by telling me I'm innocent (*I'm your friend, I believe you*) and in the next breath he's telling me I'm guilty as hell but also smart as hell (*I admire you*). And maybe we can both let the whole world know how smart I am and what a rat stool pigeon that Bassett is, huh?

It wasn't until he brought in a famous Pinkerton detective to bargain with me that I discovered what I was being softened up for. Mosher, the supervisor of the eastern district. *Captain* Mosher. A heavy, jowly man with fierce eyes. All I had to do was agree to tell him who my fences were and he would get me a written guarantee from the District Attorney himself that the charge against me would be reduced to a misdemeanor, which would mean a maximum sentence of five years. That was all he wanted from me at the moment, he emphasized, an agreement. The guarantee would be placed in the hands of my lawyer, and everything I said would be said in his presence. I didn't doubt for a second that Mosher could deliver on that promise. They didn't call it plea bargaining then, but that was what it was. You did it with the insurance companies through the Pinkertons.

"I don't know any fences," I told him.

Up to that point, this lawyer of mine that he was talking about was a mere rumor. Even though Dutch Schultz had sent a lawyer down to headquarters the day I was arrested. The Dutchman had a lot of cops on his payroll, and they always tipped him off when anybody he knew was picked up. Don't think that Dutch Schultz was doing me any favors, though. All he knew was that if I talked he was in the soup, and so he was out to show me that he was going to take care of me.

The cops were out to make sure nobody was going to take care of me, that's why they hadn't booked me at Centre Street. "We don't have anybody named Willie Sutton," they told the lawyer. "Somebody's given you some bad information." For three days they kept telling him that. The law said that they had to book me after forty-eight hours or let me go. They had got around that quite easily by throwing me into a car, booking me up at Sixty-eighth Street, and running me right back. "Sutton? We don't have any Suttons around here." It wasn't until I was taken back to the Magistrates Court on Fifty-fourth Street to be arraigned that the lawyer was allowed to see me.

Following the arraignment, I was taken to the Tombs prison, where I was examined by the prison doctor, Dr. Lichtenstein. This was four days after the beating, and my body was still a solid mass of welts and bruises. Lichtenstein happened to be a good doctor, in later years he became one of the leading psychiatrists in New York. "Willie," he said, "I have been examining people coming into this prison for seventeen years and I have never seen anything like this. You tell your lawyer to subpoena me when your case comes to court. I'm going to make a complete record of this."

Dr. Lichtenstein didn't testify, but it was not because he didn't want to. Shortly after Dutch Schultz had learned that I had refused to talk he sent me a new lawyer, Judge Arthur Vitale, an ex-magistrate. Vitale came to the Tombs with his own doctor and photographer, and they couldn't testify either. Before my case came to trial, the DA had gone before the New York Supreme Court and had all the records pertaining to my beating impounded on the grounds that it was irrelevant and immaterial. The law being what it is, the ruling was correct. Since I hadn't confessed, there was no basis for introducing any evidence pertaining to a confession. "You'd have been better off if you'd have talked," Vitale told me. "With this kind of a beating you would have elicited so much sympathy from the jurors that they wouldn't care whether or not you were guilty."

The truth was that I might have been able to elicit more sympathy from the jury if I'd had a different lawyer. Not that Dutch Schultz hadn't meant well. The first thing Vitale told me was that the Dutchman was underwriting my entire defense, including the cost of an appeal if it should become necessary. And not that Vitale wasn't a good lawyer. The only thing wrong with Judge Vitale was that he was even more notorious than I was.

While Vitale had been serving as a magistrate in the Bronx, a huge banquet had been given in his honor at the Roman Gardens. The leading gangsters in the community had mingled in good fellowship and harmony with some of the foremost minions of the law, which would have been nothing to get excited

141

about except for one thing. During the height of the festivities, some masked bandits had joined the party and walked away with a lot of jewelry and money, which still wouldn't have been very serious if they hadn't also taken a service revolver from a detective who was in attendance. The departmental regulations then in force called for the immediate suspension of any police officer who'd had his gun taken away from him, and since the civic-minded mobsters in the assembly did not wish the community to lose the services of such a valuable public servant, three of the top gunmen in the city were given the assignment of recovering the revolver—and all the other loot while they were at it—a task which they accomplished with a speed and dispatch that must have been the envy of every police department in the country.

The story of the stickup at the judge's banquet, and of its rather curious aftermath, came out during the Seabury Commission's investigation into political corruption in New York City, and it had enough humor to it so that it shoved all the other stuff off the front page.

And Vitale's luck continued to run bad. The Seabury Commission investigation stemmed from the equally curious aftermath of the assassination of Arnold Rothstein, the leading underworld figure, money man, and political fixer of the day. Voluminous files, comprising the records of his activities, were seized in his apartment immediately after his death, with the result that half the politicians in the city began to check the ocean-liner schedules to Europe and South America. A compliant judge, who obviously didn't own any stock in the Cunard Line, ordered that the records be placed in the custody of a Tammany leader for safekeeping, whereupon the records were mysteriously stolen, whereupon half the politicians in the city decided that they didn't really have to take that trip to Europe for their wife's health, after all.

The investigators for the Seabury Commission did manage to dig up one record, though. It had fallen behind the desk or something. It was the record of a loan of more than nineteen thousand dollars which

Rothstein had made to Magistrate Arthur H. Vitale of the Bronx.

What with one thing and another, Judge Vitale had resigned in disgrace, and he was now working for his old friend Dutch Schultz, openly. I had been hopeful that, as a former colleague, he might be able to do some good for me with the trial judge, Cornelius Collins. I couldn't have been wronger. The judge's distaste for Vitale was so evident that it could be seen from the farthermost bleachers. He interrupted him frequently. He questioned his trial tactics. I was being tried for the Rosenthal robbery, of course, because nobody except Lewis had been able to identify me. Vitale had stated in his opening address to the jury that it was a case of mistaken identity, and every time he would try to discredit a witness's testimony the judge would break in to ask him what difference it made whether the witness was telling the truth in every detail, or even whether a robbery had taken place, if he was going to prove that I hadn't been there.

Because we *didn't* have to prove it, Vitale kept telling him. It was up to the state to prove beyond a reasonable doubt that I was.

Actually, my defense was based on establishing an alibi. And my aunt Alice was going to provide it. She had agreed to take the stand and testify that I had been visiting her up in Warrensburg that day. Well, she presented such a striking figure when she came into the courtroom that the DA wouldn't believe at first that she was a relative of mine. He was sure Vitale had hired an actress.

Not that it did any good. Lewis was as cool and impressive on the witness stand as he had been during the robbery. The others came in and testified that although they hadn't been able to identify me in the lineup they had "recognized" me, which was kind of weak as corroborative testimony. So they beefed it up by having old-man Rosenthal come to the stand (he wanted to have his insurance renewed, didn't he?) and swear that he and his wife had seen me and Bassett looking in the window just before they closed on the night before the robbery, and that as they were passing behind us outside the store they had heard me say, "That is all now."

A very observant man, considering that we hadn't been there. And even if we had, it almost defies belief that anyone could believe I'd say anything like that while the owner and his wife, whom I would have had to have seen come out of the store, were passing right behind us. But I have never been in a trial where the prosecution didn't put on that kind of phony testimony. When you talk to them about it in private, they'll tell you they only do it where they're sure the guy is guilty. And, of course, they always think the guy is guilty.

So I was convicted. During Lewis's testimony, he had said: "I never saw anybody so cool in my life. He acted as if he was at a tea party." In sentencing me, Judge Collins said: "I doubt very much that there could be a recital of a crime so daring in New York City. Right in the heart of the busiest thoroughfare in the world, in broad daylight, you went into a jewelry store and over a period of two hours, and maybe two and a half hours, with police passing . . . you forced the porter to open the safe and then you got away. Years ago when we read about holdups of that kind in the West, we marveled at it, and didn't think that in our civilization such a type of crime could exist."

I had left Dannemora in the early part of August 1929. On June 5, 1931—only twenty-two months later—I was being sent back to Sing Sing. "You are only twenty-nine years of age," Judge Collins said. "Yet I must sentence you to a period of time greater than you are years old."

Bassett had already pleaded guilty, and he had also been given thirty years. I had seen him only a couple of times after I was arrested and spoken to him only once. We had been arraigned together at the Municipal Court, and when we were taken down to the detention cell he was locked in a cell directly across from mine. I stripped off my shirt and I said, "Take a look at this. This is the result of your talking." He turned away from me and kept his face to the wall until he was taken away.

When he got to the Tombs, he feigned insanity and a lunacy commission was appointed to examine him. After he had been declared sane, he was catching so much hell from the other prisoners that he sent out a request for Vitale and tried to square himself by offering to testify on my behalf. As Vitale and I were talking it over we both realized that if he took the stand they could introduce his full confession, and whether he claimed it had been beaten out of him or not, all that information about all those robberies would get into the record. On the other hand, Vitale, who was a pretty shrewd article, could see where there might be an even greater risk in turning him down. Once Bassett saw that he wasn't going to be able to square himself, he just might decide to make a deal with the prosecution to take the stand against me. And so Vitale had let him think right to the end that we were going to call him.

When I came to Sing Sing, they were very careful to keep us separated. And then Bassett asked to see me. So they brought him over to my cell and he said, "Willie, I'll make out a sworn affidavit that you weren't with me when the Rosenthal crime was committed. I'll do anything in the world to have your sentence revoked and get you a new trial."

So I said, "All right, Jack. The only thing that surprises me is that you weren't even slapped in the face before you confessed."

PART TWO

Breaking Out

Sutton's Law

Medical students throughout the English-speaking world are taught something called Sutton's Law, my one permanent contribution, however indirect, to the good of mankind. Sutton's Law really belongs to Dr. William Dock, a very distinguished New York physician. Back around 1960, Dr. Dock, who was then a professor of medicine at Kings County Hospital, was a visiting professor at the Yale Medical School. In making the teaching rounds with the students and interns, he came across a young girl from Puerto Rico who had a liver disease that had left the Yale doctors baffled.

Taking note of where the patient came from, Dr. Dock said, just off the top of his head, "Why don't you apply Sutton's Law?" For the benefit of those students who had been wasting their youth reading books, he explained that when Willie Sutton had been asked why he robbed banks Sutton had answered, "Because that's where the money is."

The diagnostic point Dr. Dock was making was that instead of starting at the top and going through the whole routine of tests and X-rays—most of which would simply confirm that something was wrong with her liver or, even worse, force them into wasting more time checking out diseases which had the same symptoms—it wasn't a bad idea to look for the obvious, even if it was nothing more than a hunch, and take a shot at checking that out first. The girl was from Puerto Rico, he pointed out, and there was a parasitic liver disease quite common in Puerto Rico called schistosomiasis.

A tissue sample was sent to the pathologist. It

came back negative. Oh well, back to the drawing board. Except for one thing. One of the students had been so impressed by the logic of what Dr. Dock had said that he spent several hours examining the tissue under the microscope on his own and, at length, detected the tiny eggs of the schistosome that the pathologist had missed. Which made Sutton's Law even stronger. When you have a strong personal stake in your hunch, you are going to be especially diligent in pursuing it to the very end.

That would have been the end of that except that there had been two Yale physicians on that training round, Drs. Robert G. Petersdorf and Paul B. Beeson, who were working on a phenomenon called FUO, which had the whole medical profession baffled. Patients with fevers of at least 101 degrees which persisted for more than three weeks, and whose symptoms continued to puzzle their doctors for a period of time after the fever began to subside. A year later they published their medical paper, "Fevers of Unknown Origin," which is still considered a classic in its field. And it was in this paper that they popularized Sutton's Law. What they had done was collect one hundred of these cases which had eventually been diagnosed, and they discovered that although all of the cases had unusual side features, eighty percent of them could be broken down, in the final analysis, into three categories of common diseases. "Sutton's Law," they said, putting the phrase permanently into the medical vocabulary, dictated that by checking these three obvious possibilities first, in the order of their frequency, they would not only have a far better chance of making the correct diagnosis, they would be able to make the diagnosis quickly enough to save the patient's life.

Five years later, Dr. Beeson became a professor of medicine at Oxford, and when he started to explain Sutton's Law to his English students, he was very quickly informed that they had not only heard of it, they had been applying it for years.

The irony of using a bank robber's maxim as an instrument for teaching medicine is compounded, I will now confess, by the fact that I never said it. The credit belongs to some enterprising reporter who apparently felt a need to fill out his copy. I can't even remember when I first read it. It just seemed to appear one day, and then it was everywhere.

If anybody had asked me, I'd have probably said it. That's what almost anybody would say. Like Dr. Dock said, it couldn't be more obvious.

Or could it?

Why did I rob banks? Because I enjoyed it. I loved it. I was more alive when I was inside a bank, robbing it, than at any other time in my life. I enjoyed everything about it so much that one or two weeks later I'd be out looking for the next job. But to me the money was the chips, that's all. The winnings. I kept robbing banks when, by all logic, it was foolish. When it could cost me far more than I could possibly gain.

Actually, I spent far more time planning how to break out of jails, if only because I spent so much more time inside, trying to get out, than outside, trying to get in. If any enterprising reporter had ever asked me why I broke out of jail, I suppose that's what I would have said: "Because I was in." But also, you know, because there's a thrill that comes from breaking out of jail, after years of the most meticulous planning, with everybody watching you, against all the odds, that is like nothing else in the world.

Seven Doors to Freedom

The moment the door closed on my cell in Sing Sing I knew that I couldn't possibly live through my sentence. I had more than the thirty years. Having broken probation, I was going to have to serve the full six years and six months left on my previous sentence before the new one would even start.

Before I could even think of busting out of Sing Sing, though, I had to make sure I stayed there. Although Sing Sing had been completely rebuilt since I'd been there, it was still a receiving prison. I was an officially designated "desperate criminal" and that meant I was ticketed for Dannemora. That animal, Granger, had given me his word that if I ever came back I wouldn't get out of there alive. I believed him.

Since that wasn't exactly the way I wanted to get out, I sent a note to Warden Lawes, requesting an interview. "I am appealing my case," I told him. "And I have every reason to believe my conviction will be reversed. It is very important that I remain in Sing Sing so that my attorney will be able to confer with me."

Not unexpectedly, Warden Lawes reminded me how I had been sent to Dannemora the last time. And, finally, I discovered what the charge against me had been. Information had come to the deputy's office that my partner, Wilson, had been trying to get ahold of a wrench for the apparent purpose of helping us in some kind of an escape plan. "Then it could only have come from someone in the league who had something against me," I said hotly. My job in the greenhouses, I reminded him, had taken me outside the picket fence, alongside the river, every day. "If I'd had any plans for escaping I could have gone overboard anytime. Why would I go back in and then try to bust out?"

All he would promise was that he would check the records and if there seemed to be anything to what I was saying he would give me the benefit of the doubt. "Otherwise, I'll have to send you back to Dannemora."

A few days later I was assigned to the shoe shop as a bookkeeper, another very good job. The inmates were on piecework, and my job was to keep track of the slips.

Between the time I had left Sing Sing, in mid-1926, and the time I returned, in June of 1931, Sing

151

Sing had been rebuilt so completely that it didn't look like the same place. On my first tour, the whole prison had consisted of one little compound between the river and the hills. It had the look of a factory town. One long cellblock surrounded by a huddle of workshops with high-rising chimneys jutting up all around. Since then, the hills behind the old grounds had been leveled off so that the prison grounds were twice the size and set on two plateaus. The old section was now called the lower prison, and consisted, in the main, of a series of modern concrete workshops and industrial buildings.

Up above, dominating everything, was the new, massive five-story prison building. A ground floor plus four stacked tiers. The cells in these new cellblocks were much larger than before. There was modern plumbing. Each cell even had its own radio. That is, you plugged into a wall outlet and everybody got whatever happened to be coming out.

The new Sing Sing had been given an enormous amount of publicity as an "escapeproof" prison. The Sunday supplements had described how the bars, having been built from hardened steel, were not only impossible to cut through with any known kind of hacksaw but, indeed, were impervious to even a high-speed drill. The iron picket fence along the river was higher, and the rest of the prison was surrounded by a higher, thicker wall.

Under the circumstances I'd have been far happier with the old, crummy, often-condemned cellblock. It wasn't comfort I was looking for, it was a way out. Well, if you couldn't get out once you had been locked up, the only thing left was to find a way of getting out while you were outside at work.

The shoe shop was in a long, three-story concrete building, with enormous floor space, which extended almost to the river. The first chance I got, I slipped down into the cellar and, through an incredible stroke of luck, found a boarded-over space that led underground. The board wasn't even bolted down. I lifted it up and saw that it was covering a not very large square hole. When I let myself down I was in what seemed to be a very large tunnel, easily large enough to walk through. And also very dark. In order to explore it further I was going to have to come back with a flashlight when the shop was closed. Which meant over the weekend. On Saturday and Sunday, you had yardout privileges all day. From the time breakfast was over until it got dark. The only restriction was that once you left the cell you were out for the day. You couldn't go back until everybody came back.

I was also going to need a key to the side door, as I had known that sooner or later I would. The blank keys were kept in the powerhouse. Also the files. Under the casual eating arrangements at Sing Sing, the people who worked in the powerhouse ate there, and I made it a practice to join them. Given a little time, I could have had a key to every workshop in the joint.

Come Saturday, I slipped away during yardout, inserted my key, and a few seconds later I was lowering myself through the hole. It was a long tunnel, I could see, extending the full length of the grounds. Wherever I looked, there were steam pipes. Running in and out of everything the way steam pipes do. The main pipe came out of the powerhouse, which was approximately 250 feet away. Not far from where I was standing, there was an open pipe, not connected to anything. Just lying on the ground. Sixteen to eighteen inches in diameter and welded together in twenty-foot lengths. I knew where it was going as soon as I began to follow it. A new powerhouse was under construction and, as another security precaution, it was being built outside the prison, approximately 100–150 feet beyond the north wall.

You didn't have to be an engineer to realize that if there was an open pipe running out toward the new powerhouse, there would have to be a corresponding pipe coming in. And that sooner or later they were going to have to break through the wall to connect them.

If a man knew when the breakthrough was going to take place, he could secrete himself into the pipe and make his way through to the new powerhouse. The dangers were many but so were the possibilities. The first thing I had to find out was whether it was possible for a man to make his way through a sixteen-inch pipe. Preferably, for the first trial run, somebody smaller than me. Well, one of my friends in the shoe shop was a Greek kid, Tommy, who must have weighed all of ninety-five pounds. He and his buddy had come to New York from Ypsilanti, Michigan, and celebrated their arrival by robbing the Brass Rail restaurant. Instead of seeing the big city, they were seeing Sing Sing. He was a happy-go-lucky kid with a sunny personality. He worked in the storeroom, and he was always whipping back and forth as if he actually enjoyed his job.

"Will you do a favor for me, Tommy?" I asked him.

"If I don't have to murder anybody when I get to the other side," he said, after I had described what I wanted him to do. "You can count on me."

After we had dropped down into the tunnel the following Saturday, he stripped down naked except for a jockstrap. I put Vaseline all over his body, tied his ankle with a rope, and in he went. The first time he hit one of the welded joints, there was a tugging on the rope which signaled that he wanted to be pulled out. The welding job had been so sloppy that some of the molten metal had dripped through and hardened to a dagger sharpness. Poor Tommy was cut all around the shoulders. Half of the Vaseline had been rubbed off, and there was rust all over his body. I rubbed him as clean as possible with the towels I had brought with me, and he spent a long uncomfortable Saturday afternoon in yardout.

The only thing left was to try to learn the exact moment when they were going to break through the wall. There was very little activity down there during the next couple of weeks. I knew none of the inmates on the work crew. They didn't even lock in the main cellblocks, they locked in what was called the 5 Building, a separate facility. When I did nose around, I had to be very careful not to run into any of them because they could very well have turned me in to the dep. For some reason, people are under a misapprehension that everybody in prison is a stand-up guy. Far from it. You have to know exactly who you're dealing with; the rat quotient is very high.

In this regard, as in most other regards, the league was a very mixed blessing. Because the league delegates had so much authority, it was very easy to pick up equipment, such as my flashlight, and it was also a little easier to wander around. By the same token, it became that much easier to get into trouble, and with all the politicking and jealousies, there were more rats at Sing Sing per square foot than at any other prison I was ever in.

At any rate, while I was waiting around trying to find out when the great breakthrough was going to take place, it took place. Four guys did get out. They knew exactly when the ball was going to break through because one of them had been on the steam-fitting crew. Within a couple of hours they were caught a short distance away, trying to steal a rowboat to take them over to the other side.

So there went that. I was going to have to find another way, and the older a prison is the more difficult it is to escape from. For a very good reason. In a prison as old as Sing Sing, there had been hundreds of attempts to break out. Every time a prisoner had concocted a plan, the authorities had been able to strengthen the weakness he had tried to exploit.

Like trucks. Between the mess hall, the commissary system, and the workshops, there were big trucks going back and forth all day long. In building the new prison, they had closed off the old gate and put in a double gate at the eastern wall. As a truck was leaving, it had to pull up on a pit between the two locked gates and undergo a thorough search. In the pits were different detecting devices. Like mirrors to make sure that nobody was getting out on the undercarriage. The search of the truck itself was so meticulous that they even opened the hood.

One of the things they manufactured at Sing Sing was mattresses. A friend of mine, Jack Levy, tried to smuggle himself out by means of a camouflage system that permitted the mattresses to lie perfectly flat. First thing they looked for. "You know how often that's been tried?" they said when they captured him.

A year had passed, more than a year, when an old trusty passed on the information, for what it was

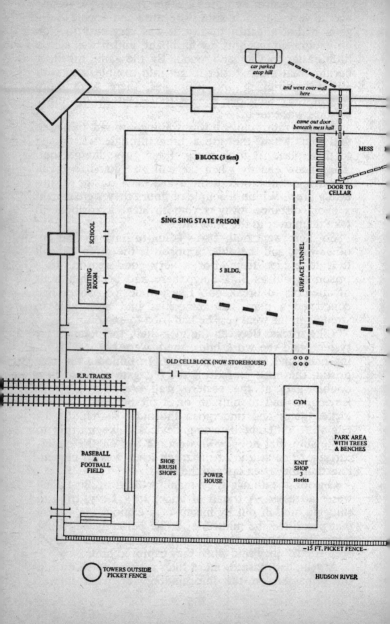

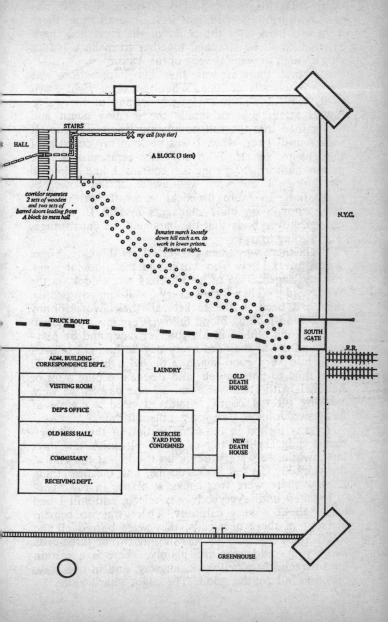

STAIRS

HALL

⊠ my cell (top tier)

A BLOCK (3 tiers)

corridor separates
2 sets of wooden
and two sets of
barred doors leading from
A block to mess hall

Inmates march loosely
down hill each a.m. to
work in lower prison.
Return at night.

N.Y.C.

TRUCK ROUTE

SOUTH
GATE

R.R.

ADM. BUILDING
CORRESPONDENCE DEPT.

LAUNDRY

OLD
DEATH
HOUSE

VISITING ROOM

DEP'S OFFICE

OLD MESS HALL

EXERCISE
YARD FOR
CONDEMNED

NEW
DEATH
HOUSE

COMMISSARY

RECEIVING DEPT.

GREENHOUSE

worth, that the tower behind A block was left unmanned during the midnight shift. And also that there were two ladders in the cellar of the mess hall, hard by, that could be strapped together to make a ladder long enough to reach the top of the wall.

My first thought was that his information was worth practically nothing. When you came right down to it, they didn't need anybody in any of the guard towers after they had made the evening count and determined that the full population was locked up. It wasn't until later, when I was back in my cell, that I thought to myself, Who says it's escapeproof? The prison authorities? From the courses I had taken in psychology I was very well aware of the power of suggestion. In more practical terms, I had used it often enough on bank managers myself. If you can convince everybody that the bars can't be cut through, who's going to try?

Right there was when I reversed my thinking. There was a guy I knew who worked in the plumber shop. Johnny Eagen. Two of his brothers ran a dock on the West Side. They were very well-known people, they had been in the rackets all their lives. Johnny was a good-looking blond fellow. Very strong. He had been a good athlete in his younger days, and by playing handball in the yard every day he had got himself back into very good shape. I played a little handball from time to time myself, and I began to play a lot of handball with Johnny Eagen. So one day as we were walking off the court, I said: "I need a couple of hacksaws, Johnny. Can you get them for me?"

Johnny locked in the same section of the cellblock that I did. The top tier of the A block. A few days later, while we were walking up the hill at the end of the workday, he fell in beside me, and the next thing I knew there were two hacksaw blades in my hand.

I waited until everybody was asleep, and still I had to go about it very carefully. There was no cement in front of these new cells; they were barred all the way across. If somebody was snoring two or three cells away you could hear him plainly. There is a certain kind of echo to a cellblock, anyway, and in one way, that was all to the good. The night guard came by every half hour or hour, depending on his mood, and the way the sound carried, I was able to hear his footsteps all the way down the gallery. After he had made his ten-thirty check I lay down in the front of the cell and very carefully . . . very slowly . . . began to saw at the corner bar. It took quite a while for the saw to begin to bite in, but once I had a notch on it, it began to go quite well. In fact, considering the way I was working, I could see that the "escapeproof" bars cut even easier than ordinary steel.

That didn't prove anything conclusively, though. Not yet. It was always possible that they had put a spinning rod inside the bar. What happens when you hit a spinning rod with a saw is that it keeps moving on you. If you have a spinning rod of hardened steel and you're never hitting the same place twice, you can see where you'd be able to spend the rest of your life trying to go through it with a hacksaw.

As it was, it took me practically the whole night to get more than halfway through and satisfy myself that there was nothing there that didn't meet the eye. Marvelous. I smoothed the cut portion over with green putty and painted it black, and now the "escapeproof" propaganda was working for me.

I wasn't the only one who was excited. Once Eagen had stuck his neck out by handing me the blades, I had told him what my theory was. As we started down the hill the next morning he could scarcely contain himself. "What the hell happened?" he hissed. "Can it be cut?"

"Yeah. It was just like cardboard. I was three quarters of the way through."

And even then he couldn't believe it.

Getting out of the cell, I cautioned him, was a far cry from getting out of the prison. I was still going to have to get from the upper tier to the lower tier of the cellblock, and out into a fifteen-foot corridor which led to the mess hall. From there, I'd have to go down into the mess-hall cellar and out into the yard. Seven doors I'd have to go through at four key intersections; three blind wooden doors, three barred gates, and, finally, the huge metal door in the cellar that opened into the yard.

But even here, the overconfidence of the jailers would be working for me. Seven doors, and not a guard at any of them.

With the old powerhouse closed down, Eagen came to my aid again by working longer hours in the plumber shop so that he could pick up the material for picklocks and keys. The first two wooden doors had Corwin locks, which is nothing more than a routine house lock. I knew the lock so well that through a process of elimination on the basic patterns, and with my burglar's touch, I could very easily narrow it down to the right key. Just in itself, that took a great deal of patience over a matter of months because while the doors weren't guarded at night, there were guards all over the place during the daytime.

The last two doors were going to be the toughest. Before I could get to them word came through that my appeal had been denied and I was faced with the possibility that I might be shipped to Dannemora at any time. The lock on the door from the mess hall to the cellar had a somewhat more sophisticated lock, and there was no trade name stamped on it to give me a clue. With time running out on me, I went to a friend of mine, a fellow named Bugsy Goldstein, who worked for one of the officers in the mess hall. Goldstein was a natural clown, and he and this officer had become very friendly. So I gave him a slab of wax and told him what I needed, and he gave me his word that he'd get it for me.

A few days later he began to fool around with this officer, and all of a sudden he grabbed his hat and his keys and went running into the bathroom. Quick like that, he took an impression of the key, slapped the wax under the washbowl, and came running back out. Well, this officer was screaming at him, that's how mad he was. He bawled the hell out of him. And all Bugsy Goldstein did was shrug his hands and say, "Well, now you know why they call me Bugsy."

I had my keys to the three wooden doors. The gates I could pick with my eyes shut. The iron door leading out into the yard I was just going to have to take my chances with. The trusty had told me that nobody was ever in the mess-hall cellar at night, and that was all I needed. A little time. If it had a hole in it, I'd open it.

I told Eagen I was ready to go, and asked him to get me some more hacksaws. And that was when he told me he wanted to go with me. There were two very good reasons why I didn't think that was such a very good idea. In the first place, he had only about two years left on his sentence. In the second, two men cutting their way out of their cells was going to vastly increase the chances of detection. Still and all, Johnny Eagen had helped me so much that he was entitled to come along if that was what he wanted.

Eagen was on the same tier but he locked on the other side of the back-to-back cells. With two of us going, the coordination had to be perfect. By the time Eagen appeared outside my cell, I had already cut through the bar and made a form under the blanket to make it look as if I were asleep. I just pulled the bar out, squeezed through, and then wrapped a hunk of tape around the bar after I had put it back in place. That's how confident I was that the guard wouldn't notice anything when he came around. Three officers were congregated on the flat of the tier directly below us, and we could hear almost everything they were saying. As stealthily as possible, we padded down the gallery to the end of the cellblock and went down the three flights of stairs. The first door was right at the bottom. It opened to the key, and the gate yielded very easily to my picklocks. Down the fifteen-foot corridor we went, through the second door and gate, and we were into the mess hall. At the other end of the mess hall, we had to go down a stairway and take two more locks at the foot of the staircase—another blind door and a gate—to get into the cellar. It was an L-shaped cellar; you had to make a sharp turn and pass through the back section where the refrigerating plant was installed in order to get to the big steel door.

Before we got to the turn, we could hear somebody moving around. An inmate was bent over a work table back there, a trusty. That was something I hadn't planned on. But, then, he hadn't exactly planned on having us drop in on him, either. I slipped up behind him and threw my arm around his neck. "You will do exactly what I tell you to do," I said. "Or I will kill you." And then I told him that it was an escape. You never know what enemies a man might have in prison, see, and I didn't want him to get any wrong ideas that it was him we were after. Once he understood what was happening, he not only showed us where the ladders were stored, he helped us to lash them together and carry them to the exit. In order to protect him, we then tied him up. Loosely. In order to protect ourselves, we made him promise to give us as much time as he felt he could before "breaking loose" and sounding the alert.

There was still the steel door to be dealt with, and it was a ponderous-looking thing. But, you know, it doesn't matter how formidable a door may look, when you put a lock into it, it's still the same lock. And it wasn't that formidable at all. A couple of manipulations of my picklocks and I had it.

Although the searchlights lit the yard up far more than I had thought possible, the towers themselves are always kept dark. They don't want anybody to be able to look up there and see what the guards are doing. We had to take the trusty's word that the rear tower was empty. The only thing I could be sure of, looking up, was that the railed catwalks surrounding the towers were empty. Since the towers on either side of it weren't that far away, we also had to count on a general lack of alertness on the part of the guards there. Sitting all night in a dark tower is a miserable job; it's more or less punishment duty, nobody wants it. With no lights, they can't read. They can't do much of anything except call in to the main office every twenty minutes or so to let them know they're still awake.

Crouching as low as we could, we pushed the ladder along the forty feet or so to the wall and, even more gingerly, raised it up to the tower. Barely breathing, I started up, expecting the machine-gun fire to start every step of the way. Up in the tower, we got lucky. Right there, hooked to the rail, was the rope which the day shift used to hoist their supplies from the ground. We weren't going to have to run the final risk of spraining an ankle or something while dropping to the ground. To make sure the rail wouldn't collapse under our weight, I wrapped the rope completely around the tower before we lowered ourselves down.

A second after I hit the ground I was scrambling up the steep hill, practically on my hands and knees. It was about a hundred yards to the road, and when we were about twenty yards away I could make out the silhouette of my Buick waiting there, exactly where it was supposed to be. At that moment, a feeling of exhilaration came over me beyond anything I had ever experienced before. A feeling of freedom and release that was so strong it was as if I could spread out my wings and fly. I felt so good that I stood up, like the King of the Hill, and looked down on the searchlights and the general panoramic view of the sleeping prison. And then I did something very childish. I shook my fist at it and I said to myself, I beat you, you bastards!

And then we were running for the car, and I could hear the motor starting up.

Louise had come up to visit me in Sing Sing a week after I arrived. I told her that if my appeal didn't come through I was sure I'd be able to buy a pardon, a thought that had been in the back of my mind from the time I'd gone back to being a criminal. Back in my early days in New York, when Al Smith was governor, everybody was doing it. Smith didn't have too much money at that stage of his career, and whenever he was out of the state it seemed as if his lieutenant governor was issuing them by the hundreds. That's the way, it seemed, they had decided to work it. During Smith's first term as governor, there were probably more pardons issued than at any other time in the history of the state.

The times had changed, Vitale told me. As who should know better than he. The Seabury Commission had frightened everybody off. Roosevelt was governor, and Roosevelt was a rich man with his eyes on the White House. Money wouldn't do it, and you couldn't buy that kind of influence from anybody else. All Vitale could suggest was that I sit tight, hope

Roosevelt became President, wait for a couple of changes in Albany, and, sooner or later, Tammany would be back in the saddle. At which point, I knew, the question would arise: How much money did I have to put up? The answer by then would be: Not enough. Not unless I was outside where I could earn it.

The first time Louise came to visit me after I learned I could cut through the bars, I instructed her to rent a cottage somewhere under an assumed name. Immediately. I then gave her a set of instructions that would enable us to meet there following my escape, instructions which began with her watching *The New York Times* personal section for my message.

Eddie Wilson was out on parole, and he came up to see me a few times while the plans were in progress. I had taken care of him while he was at Dannemora and I was on the outside making all that money with Bassett. Anything he wanted he had got, and now he was ready to do anything for me. What he could do, he said, was to be there with a car. I didn't like it. Being on parole, he couldn't get a driver's license in his own name, and a man driving around those hills at night could easily draw suspicion. If he got picked up, the police were going to wonder why he'd be taking that kind of chance. The answer would be so obvious that it would be off to Dannemora for me in the morning. Too risky. Eddie Wilson was out.

The new visiting room at Sing Sing was divided into square sections, each containing four chairs. There was no dividing screen, the whole setup had been devised to allow an inmate to sit opposite his wife and hold his children in his arms. An officer sat at an elevated desk where he would be able to observe everything without overhearing any of the conversations. The next time Louise visited me, I told her I was going to need her help. "Don't look surprised," I said. "Just keep talking as if we were talking about the mortgage payments. How far are you willing to go?"

"How far do you want me to go? All the way."

I told her I was going to need a car at a certain place at a certain time. "Can you do it?" I asked.

"I can do it."

"If there's hot pursuit, there'll be roadblocks erected on all the main roads. That means you're going to have to get a road map and find a secondary route that will get us back to New York along the back roads. And when you've found it, you're going to have to know every twist and turn of that route so perfectly that you'll be able to drive it in the dead of night without getting lost. Do you think you can do that?"

Her eyes never wavered. "I can do it."

By the time I had the keys for the Corwin locks, she had traveled back and forth often enough so that she had the alternate route down cold. So then I told her where I wanted her to be parked. "Circle in back of the prison so you're on the road there, as close as you can get. So you can actually look down and see the back of the prison. If you look out of the window when you're leaving the prison, you'll be able to see the road I mean."

The next Sunday, she came back and said, "I know exactly where you mean. I'll be there."

I told her I was going to need a full set of clothes, shoes included. And some money. A thousand dollars.

From the beginning to the end, I would never say a word about the escape until just before she was ready to leave. As her last visit was coming to an end, I said, "Look, I can make it at midnight on the twelfth. Can you be there with the car?"

"Yes."

That's when I told her that somebody else was going to be with me. "We're going to need two of everything. Make his two sizes larger than mine on everything, and it will be close enough. Have it all in a suitcase and keep the suitcase on the floor."

"I'll have it."

After I had kissed her, I said, "You know, if you're not there I can be in a lot of trouble."

She said: "I'll see you at midnight on the twelfth."

And there she was. The moment she saw us she started the motor. We jumped into the back seat, and she didn't put the lights on until the prison was out of sight. By then, Eagen and I already had our prison jackets off and were digging into the suitcase.

The way things turned out, we could have made it right down the main highway. The trusty had given us two full hours before he sounded the alarm. Still, the delay was very helpful from another standpoint. Once the prison authorities had completed their first search, they were going to assume that we'd had help. Which meant that sooner or later they were going to check on Louise. The plan therefore called for her to drop us off in the city and drive on home.

I kissed her quickly and we jumped out. "Watch the *Times* personals," I said. "It won't be long."

Eagen and I walked over to the Marseilles Hotel, on Broadway around 105th Street, and registered for the night. It was so easy that we had to sit there and laugh.

The next morning I called Bo Weinberg at the Monongahela club and made an appointment to come right over. I had called Bo because the Dutchman had sent word to me, during my trial, that he had instructed Bo to give me anything I wanted. Bo had fifteen hundred dollars from the Dutchman, and he told me I had unlimited credit.

From there I went to the West Side docks and sent out word that I wanted to see Eagen's brothers. One of them came right over. "What the hell did you come out with him for?" was the first thing he said. "He's a lush. We did everything we possibly could for him." They had put him in a good job picking up numbers on the docks, he told me, and half the time he'd be so drunk that he wouldn't show up. So they had taken him off that and opened up a speakeasy for him. "It was a hell of a nice place, we went all out for him. So, anyway, he didn't show up there half the time either. He was off somewhere on a bender. The guys he had working for him robbed him blind, and he blew that too."

There was nothing you could do for these alcoholics, he said. "Do yourself a favor and get rid of him because he'll destroy you. Everything he touches, he destroys."

He didn't seem to be a lush to me. He was the best

166

handball player at Sing Sing, and one of the best baseball and football players, too. "There comes a time when everybody gets smart to themselves," I said. "Anyway, I've got to give him a chance. I owe that much to him."

He looked at me and he said, "You're a fool." Then he turned around and walked away.

I went back to the hotel and had it out with Johnny Eagen then and there. He admitted that everything his brother had said was true. "I used to hit the sauce up a lot," he said. "But I'll give you my word. I'm not going to touch the stuff." The next morning we moved to an apartment Eddie Wilson had rented for us over in Columbus Heights, a quiet section of Brooklyn. Now, you may think it was stupid to stay together, but that wasn't the way I saw it. If we had separated, there would have been two different sets of people to protect ourselves against and we'd have to be going in and out every time we wanted to see each other. If you have a good partner, it's far safer to stay together. He's going to be as alert as you are, and you have two sets of eyes watching everything.

Besides, I wanted to keep this here Eagen under as much control as I could.

The first thing I did after we entered the apartment was disguise ourselves. Eagen had very light hair and a light complexion. By the time I finished with him, dying his hair and staining his face, his own mother wouldn't have recognized him. My own hair I dyed with peroxide. I'd been a blond before and I always looked as if I'd just got off the boat from Poland.

I had also told Eagen that he was going to have to stay in the apartment until he grew the semblance of a mustache. But I couldn't sit guard on him, I was out casing banks. We were going to need money. For the first couple of weeks, he went out only to pick up a newspaper. And then he'd be gone for a few hours and come back with the smell of liquor on his breath. Well, I had known enough alcoholics to know that the first drink was the one that killed them. When I put it to him, he admitted that he had been going over to New York to see some of his friends from the West Side. Who? Well, Owney Madden and his brother, Marty. The Maddens and the Eagens had grown up together on the West Side when Owney was fighting his way up from the bottom of the ladder. I knew Owney too, so I went over to see what he could suggest about keeping a rein on this guy.

"Well, there's something has got to be done with him," Owney told me. "Because if you don't, you're not going to have to worry about his being arrested, I can tell you that."

What the hell was that supposed to mean?

What it meant was that Johnny was screwing around with the wrong man's wife. A very tough monkey whose specialty was hijacking trucks. "If this guy ever hears about it," Owney said, "he'll put so many slugs in him he'll make him look like a sieve." All Owney could suggest was that I take him out of town for a while and see what I could do with him. And that did seem to be the only answer.

I wasn't going to leave, though, without putting the ad in the *Times* personal section that would activate the plan I had mapped out for meeting Louise. Somewhat earlier than I had intended to, to be sure, but—what the hell—as closely as I knew she was being watched, I was sure it was foolproof.

On the morning after the ad appeared, Louise got into her car and drove toward the city in the leisurely, unhurried manner of a woman who is out on a shopping trip. As she passed a designated spot along the way, I was standing in a doorway to catch a look at her tail. Immediately, I went to a pay phone and dialed Al Jantzen's office, where Wilson was waiting for my call. After he had the description of the police cars, Wilson went down to his own car and headed for the point of rendezvous.

Louise's instructions were to do her best to shake the tail after she had passed the designated spot, without varying too much from her normal route into the city. In other words, if she got lucky, fine. If not, she wasn't to do anything that would get their suspicions up. The rendezvous was a West Side garage which had both a front and a back entrance. Louis drove her car in through the front, took her parking ticket, and walked right out the back entrance and into

Wilson's car. Halfway to the cottage Louise had rented in Massapequa, Long Island, Wilson stopped off and phoned me at Jantzen's office to let me know that they were rolling free and clear.

A couple of hours later, I walked to the door of the cottage, picked Louise up, and carried her into the bedroom, as I had done on the night we were married. For one full week we had the time of our lives. We went for long drives. We swam down on the beach. There was a hotel nearby noted for its cuisine, and we dined there almost every night. We drew up rosy plans for the future. Louise, always the optimist, still believed that I would be able to buy a pardon. If I couldn't, we talked about getting out of the country, going to the South Seas or South America. As much as I knew that it was a pipe dream by then, I got caught up in it too. Although I must admit that, pipe dream or not, I never did close my mind completely to the idea that I'd be able to buy my way out, in one way or another, if I had enough money. My entire experience had been that you could buy anything in New York if you had enough money.

When the time came to leave, I stopped kidding myself. From the moment I woke up that last morning, I was in a deep state of depression. I had a two-year-old daughter who had been only two months old when I had been taken away. I longed to see her, and it was out of the question. During that equally depressing stretch at Sing Sing before I had questioned the "escapeproof" propaganda, I had frequently urged Louise to go to Nevada for a quick divorce and try to make a new life for herself and the baby. And while I most certainly hadn't brought it up again during the idyllic week, I knew in my heart that the only thing I could really do for my wife and my daughter was disappear from their lives.

Although I told Louise I would make other plans for other meetings, I knew better. She was in for a rough enough time from the police for the next day or two as it was. The chances that they would ever relax their vigilance long enough for us to get away with it again were practically nil.

As she drove away from the cottage in Massapequa

I knew absolutely that that part of my life was over and I suspected that she knew, too.

I came back and started planning to make some quick money to take Eagen out of town. Why didn't I just go to Dutch Schultz again? Easy. The Dutchman had just been indicted for neglecting to file any income-tax returns, and the news was all over the papers that he had also neglected to turn himself in. In other words, he was a fugitive. Some fugitive. For the next eighteen months, he lived in his regular apartment, showed up at the Monongahela club almost every day to conduct business, and visited his Manhattan nightclub, the Chateau Madrid, almost every night. I wouldn't have gone to the Dutchman anyway. That first fifteen hundred dollars he owed me. If I had come back a second time, I'd owe him. I wouldn't have wanted to be beholden to Dutch Schultz under any circumstances. Now that he was in such deep trouble, he would be looking to make a deal for himself and—knowing the Dutchman as I did—he wouldn't have hesitated a second to make me a part of it.

I was going to have to get the money on my own, and my first look around town had been very discouraging. Among the other things Bassett had done with his confession, he had blown my M.O. The day after I broke out of Sing Sing, the motorcycle division of the New York police was given the assignment of guarding the banks while they were being opened. Outside of every bank, I would see a motorcycle parked along the curb. Standing close by would be a cop with an unshielded holster.

They weren't going to be doing that indefinitely, I knew. But I couldn't afford to wait much longer, either.

I finally found my bank in Brooklyn. What made it such a good prospect was that there was another bank on the corner of the same block, maybe seventy-five or a hundred feet away. Things had loosened up enough so that the motorcycle cop was out in the middle of the street, directing traffic and keeping his eye on both banks. Still pretty risky, of course. But only if I entered the bank the way he was expecting. So I wasn't going to. I was going to get in at night through the roof.

That left two problems. How to get out, and where to leave the car. It would be too dangerous to leave through the front door, and too suspicious to leave a car in a commercial district overnight.

Right next to the bank was a big theater, and in the back of the theater, overlapping the bank, was a large stage entrance. I was able to walk in there, and I could see that the rear windows of the bank had bars on them. The plan was for Wilson and me to get in through the skylight by going over the roof from a building two doors away, disconnect the alarms, and cut all the bars out of one of the windows. Eagen was to bring the car around at six-thirty in the morning, park it in the street behind the bank, walk in through the stage entrance (which I would have opened for him), climb over a little fence, and come in through the window. It was going to take three men anyway, with that cop out there, because it was a big bank and the employees arrived very quickly after eight o'clock. I would take them at the door, and Wilson would take them from me immediately and bring them over to Eagen, who would be guarding the chairs.

After it was over, we would leave the same way. Out the window, over the fence, through the stage entrance, and out to the car.

Wilson and I carried off our part of it without a hitch, and settled down in the bank to spend the night. At six-thirty I went out to the stage entrance to wait for Eagen and guide him through. No Eagen. It gets to be seven o'clock, and still no Eagen. It was impossible for two men to do the job with any safety, particularly when we had no car, so when it got to be seven-thirty and Eagen hadn't shown up, I had to go back into the bank and tell Wilson that it was off. Out the window we went. Empty-handed.

Back at the apartment, we found Eagen flopped down across the bed in a drunken stupor. No thought at all that he had to get up and go rob a bank. I said to Wilson, "I owe this guy a lot of obligation because he helped me get out but I certainly don't owe him an obligation to put me back again."

We woke him up and made him take a cold shower, and then I put it to him. "Johnny, we just blew our-

171

selves a seventy-five- or hundred-grand job. And not only that, we put a lot of heat on ourselves." I said, "I'm going to give you half the money I got left. You go your way and I'll go mine."

I moved to an apartment in East New York, not far from where Wilson was living. Eagen went back to New York, and a few weeks later I picked up a newspaper and saw that he had been killed in Porky Murray's speakeasy just off Times Square. He and the hijacker's wife plus a bartender who had kept the joint open late for the wrong guy.

According to the papers, the prime suspect was the guy he had broken out of Sing Sing with, Willie Sutton.

Despite the confidence I had in my disguise, I made plans to take up residence in Philadelphia, a town which had proved to be quite hospitable by that time. And to take my new girl friend, Olga Kowalska, with me. I had met Olga within a week after my rendezvous with Louise, when I dropped into Roseland to look the crop over and saw this innocent-looking girl dancing with a good-looking young pimp who worked the dance halls to get his hands on stage-struck kids from the sticks by pretending he knew a producer who was casting for a new show. The last thing I needed was to get in any kind of a brawl, but I cut in anyway and took her away from him. And she wasn't even my type. I always liked them kind of dainty, and while Olga wasn't exactly raw-boned, she came from Russian stock and had those squared-off peasant features.

She was a singer, and not a bad one. She sang folk songs in a very wistful, appealing voice. But, like so many others, New York wasn't quite ready for her talents.

She was only about eighteen, and so naïve that she had come to New York from a little steel-mill town below Pittsburgh with hardly any money. She was so gullible that right after I had warned her not to believe what any of these sharpies who picked her up in a dance hall told her, I told her that I was a gambler and real-estate speculator with show-business connections, and she believed me. Everything I ever told her, she believed.

I took her home for a one-night stand, and she was such a sweet, defenseless girl that I became very fond of her. I liked her so much that I persuaded Herman Stark, the manager of Owney Madden's Cotton Club, to let her sing a few of her folk songs. For her opening night, I bought her a glittering evening gown and sent her to a beauty salon. Herman didn't suggest that she become a permanent feature. No agents came knocking at her door. She didn't seem to care. She was the least demanding woman I ever met in my life.

On the day we were going to leave for Philadelphia, I decided to go to Joe's Restaurant in Brooklyn, a well-known place on Montague Street not far from the courthouse. When you're a fugitive you develop such keen antennae that you become aware, automatically, when somebody's eyes settle on you overlong. While I was sitting there having breakfast, I suddenly knew that somebody was trying to make me. In due time, I let my own eyes drift across the room and saw that it was Johnny McGovern, Tommy's brother. The detective. I had practically grown up in the McGovern home. Johnny had been almost as good a friend of mine as Tommy. It had been years since Johnny had seen me, though, and as heavily disguised as I was I didn't really think he could make me unless I got up and gave something away by my gait and bearing. I shouldn't have been all that confident. In very short order, Johnny walked over to the table and sat down. "Hello, Willie," he said. "What the hell are you doing here? Every cop in town is looking for you."

"What are you doing here, John?" I asked politely.

He was appearing in court. "We got a couple of robbers coming up. They robbed a warehouse and wounded my partner. So they offered us five thousand dollars not to identify them."

I said: "Are you on the make, John?"

"You know I'm not on the make," he bristled. "If I wanted to make money I'd be out robbing banks, like you."

I was very happy to hear that. But I still wasn't sure whether he was going to take me in. So I asked him, "Do the police think I killed this Eagen?"

"Oh hell. Frankie Phillips knows you since you were a kid. Anytime there's any violence on a crime, he rules you out immediately. Inspector Sullivan too. They know you didn't do that." The way he heard it, they didn't have very many clues but he thought there was a good chance they'd be picking up somebody very shortly.

So I said, "Well, John, if you're seen talking to me you're liable to get your walking papers from the police."

He was leaving anyway, he said. He had to go to court.

We walked out of the restaurant together, and the last thing he said to me was, "You better get the hell out of town as fast as you can."

"I think you may have something there," I said, and we were on our way to Philadelphia that same afternoon.

Philadelphia, Here I Come

One of the things Bassett had done for me in blowing my M.O. was to make it impossible for me to walk into any theatrical costume agency and buy a uniform. Still, the great thing about New York is that you can get anything you want if you want it bad enough. At length, I was directed to a shop on the lower Bowery which looked like something right out of Dickens. So did its proprietor, Old Tom. A nondescript, buttoned-up sweater hung loosely on Old Tom's emaciated frame, and tufts of gray hair protruded from the side of his battered top hat. Not a very tall top hat, but still a top hat. He had thin, pasty cheeks, marvelously wrinkled, and loose dentures which chopped his words into bits and pieces. His deep, sunken eyes took on an icy glow of suspicion until I was able to identify myself to his satisfaction.

In the front of the shop, along the side of the walls, were cases of pornographic books and pictures, and racks of clothing without labels. The rear room was incredibly cluttered. He had a collection of badge molds from which he could make any kind of badge anybody could possibly want. And all manner of guns. I was particularly fascinated by a three-barreled gas gun he demonstrated for me. The craziest thing you ever saw. Three different triggers to shoot gas pellets out of each of the barrels. There was nothing he couldn't get for you, as long as it was illegal. From barbed wire to furniture. And, what I was most interested in, he could supply any kind of uniform. He got a cop's uniform for me that was perfect in every respect: the shield, the shoulder piece, even the precinct number.

Despite his ancient appearance, he was a lively old fellow and his great joy was to bargain over the price. I had a standard formula with him. Whatever price he quoted to me I would pay him one half, and how he'd snort and cackle while we were getting to it.

Wilson came up with a third man to replace Eagen whenever we needed one. Joe Perlango had been born on the East Side in the worst kind of poverty, had left school the first chance he got, married very young, and, after hustling around as a helper on produce trucks, gravitated into sticking up A & P trucks. Wilson had known him for a long time and recommended him highly. All I wanted to know was: "Will he be there on time, and will he do what he's told to do?"

He met those two requisites, I've got to give him that. I never took to him that much, though. Whenever we needed a third man I'd just leave it to Wilson to get in touch with him. For a while, we didn't need him that much because we were making all of our forays out of town. As a matter of fact, it wasn't until after I had been operating out of Philadelphia for several months that the police protection relaxed enough for us to take a whack at a New York bank.

The Corn Exchange Bank, on 110th Street between Broadway and Amsterdam Avenue, looked just about perfect to me. All the activity anybody would want. There was a subway kiosk on the Broadway corner about a hundred feet from the bank, and all through the morning hours the people came pouring out. A traffic cop was stationed at each of the corners, and because the traffic was so heavy there was no parking on the block at all. I had to use Perlango for one specific reason. A few minutes after the porter opened the bank, an iceman would drive up to the curb, take a basket of chopped ice out of his truck, put it up on his shoulder, and ring the bell. After the porter let him in, he would pack the ice around the water coolers before he came out and drove away.

The question that arose in my mind concerned not so much the iceman himself as the ice truck. If I could let him deliver his ice and go on his way, I'd be happy to. If I thought he was on to what was happening, it would be necessary to take him under control and have Perlango there to drive the truck away.

On the morning of the robbery I came strolling out of the subway in my police uniform, exchanged a fraternal wave with my colleague on the corner, and walked on. When the porter opened the door in answer to my ring, I asked him if I could use his bathroom.

Once inside, I took the gun out and said, "This is a robbery." He was so frightened that I was still trying to make him understand that nothing was going to happen to him when the iceman came along. And then I was willing for him to be frightened again. "I'll be watching you every second," I said. "If any expression appears on your face I don't like, you're in trouble."

The iceman came in, just as happy as the day is long. "Hello, officer," he chirped, and we had a pleasant little chat about the crime wave all the while he was piling the ice around the water coolers. Instead of walking out when he was finished, he turned to the porter. "Where's my envelope?"

The porter pointed to the desk. "Right over there." The iceman picked it up, looked at the name on it, nodded, and walked out. Whistling a happy tune as he went.

"What was that envelope?" I wanted to know.

"I forgot to tell you," the porter gulped. "Today is the day the iceman gets paid."

Among the first of the employees to arrive were two young girls, as cute as they could be in their summer dresses. As they came in and saw me standing behind the porter, one of them said jokingly, "Hey, look at the handsome policeman." She gave me a flirtatious little smile. "Have you locked up any robbers lately?"

"I don't lock up robbers," I said. "I only lock up bank employees."

"Well," she said. "You'll have to wait until we rob the bank."

"Okay, I'll wait. I'll even help you rob it."

They still didn't know what I was talking about until I led them around the glass partition where Wilson was standing and told them the bank was being robbed—by us—and that my partner would tell them what was expected of them.

It's funny how people act under stress. This girl was so hurt that whenever I'd come into view she would deliberately turn her back to me. "What are you so sore about?" I asked her, while we were waiting for the manager. "It's not my fault that you wouldn't believe me."

"Well," she said. "You didn't have to make a fool out of me, you know."

"Aw, come on, think of the exciting story you'll be able to tell your boyfriend tonight." Encouraged by her wan smile, I asked the girls whether they double-dated, and the ensuing discussion about their love life got to be so interesting that Wilson had to call out to me that the bank manager was arriving.

This was another of those banks where the manager and the assistant manager each had half of the combination. I took them both down to the vault and grabbed all the money in sight, and then, just as in the Rosenthal robbery, the siren over the door started going as we stepped out. I was still in the policeman's uniform, remember, and the policeman was coming down from the corner. All he had to do was call to me for help and it would have been a very interesting situation. But he went his way, and I went down the subway stairs and grabbed a train back to Washington Heights where we had left the car. The take came to something under thirty thousand dollars, which was far less than I had expected. On the other hand, it was one of the robberies I most enjoyed. You can't have everything.

The police knew it was me, of course. They always knew when it was me. Every time I did a job, it was like leaving my calling card. It didn't matter, because I went right back to Philadelphia.

I had heard many things about Philadelphia when I was a kid, none of them good. Whenever there was a strike around New York, the companies went to Philadelphia for their strikebreakers. The first time I ever heard the name, my uncle John was calling it a scab town, and to me that's what it always was. I had also heard a lot of jokes about Philadelphia being a city where they took the sidewalks in after dark. I found out different. Olga and I picked out one of those fashionable apartment houses on Chestnut and Forty-second. Switchboard, doorman, hostess, and everything. The hostess was named Marian Saunders and through her and her husband, Eddie, we discovered that there was a very lively afterhours community consisting of private clubs and speakeasies where the fight promoters, the gamblers, and the racketeers met. The night people. Boo Boo Hoff, Blinky Palermo, Frankie Carbo. And, every once in a while, Waxey Gordon. I had known Waxey when he was so poor that he'd go to the East Side Baths and steal a bar of soap. I had known him a year later when, as the first of the racket guys who had realized what Prohibition was going to mean, he opened up a couple of his own breweries in New Jersey and was riding high. And this was at a time when Meyer

Lansky was just a hot young automobile mechanic who was renting hyped-up cars to the hijackers and bootleggers. Waxey was under indictment for income-tax evasion too, but he'd be sitting there at the best table, the monarch of all he surveyed. He ended just the way I always figured he would, riding the ferry-boat to Alcatraz, penniless, discredited, and fleeing the wrath of the underworld after he had turned state's evidence and ratted on everybody. At least, Dutch Schultz went out in a blaze. The Dutchman went crazier than usual and put out a contract on Tom Dewey, whereupon the combined forces of the Mafia and the more loosely knit Jewish mobs—in short, the Syndicate—put out a contract on him.

Shortly after we got settled in Philadelphia, Wilson arrived with his new girl, Rita Reynaldo. A fashion model. A dark, willowy beauty, bright and witty. Eddie's wife had divorced him while he was in the can, and as always his taste in women was faultless. As different as Rita was from Olga, they became very close friends.

Within a few months we picked a couple of soft touches. A small bank in Ambler, one near Doyles-town, and another near Allentown.

There had also been a bank in Philadelphia that should have been a soft touch, and wasn't. And how that one galled me. In cruising around the city, I had been sure I had found exactly the bank I was looking for. The Corn Exchange Bank up on Sixtieth Street near Market. (No relation to the Corn Exchange Bank in New York, which actually didn't come off until a few months later.)

During the morning commuter hours, Sixtieth Street was a kind of terminal point and transfer station for the entire northwestern section of the city. The big two-decker buses came streaming in from every direc-tion to disgorge their passengers at the elevated sta-tion on Market and Sixtieth. Although there was a traffic officer stationed on the corner, the buses came in so fast that they would pile up, one in back of the other, and there were always people getting off to walk, which choked the approaches up even further. The whole area was positively teeming with activity.

What made it absolutely perfect was that the entrance to the bank was pretty much masked by a vestibule arrangement. In other words, before you got to the two enormous bronze doors of the bank itself, you had to push through a pair of storm doors which were metal on the bottom and glass only at the top.

I went in there and gave the place a thorough scanning while I was changing a large bill into smaller denominations, and it looked very good to me. Large enough to have a mezzanine, plenty of tellers, quite a few customers. The enormous walk-in vault in the rear, its thick door open, was lined with safe-deposit boxes.

By the time I was through casing it, I had it all down to perfection. The time schedules of the employees, the traffic conditions, the cop on the corner. I phoned Wilson to come down from New York, and he agreed with me that we could handle it without Perlango.

The next morning I came around the block wearing a postal uniform, and Wilson took his station directly across the street. It took a couple of minutes for the guard to come to the door. Apparently, he was downstairs. All the while I was waiting, the buses were piling up from the elevated station practically to the bank.

When the guard finally opened the door, I told him I had a special-delivery letter and used the same techniques as always. I handed him the book, handed him the letter, and with both of his hands fully occupied, pushed my way inside and closed the door behind me. The whole thing didn't take more than a few seconds, and yet at that key instant when I was pushing my way in, a woman stepping down off the bus happened to be in perfect position to look in through the glass window of the storm door and catch the action.

Fortunately for us, Eddie Wilson saw it all happening. Saw the look of recognition cross her face, saw her go hurrying over to the officer on the corner, saw them starting back.

I had already disarmed the guard when, suddenly, the bell rang. In addition to the pistol this guard had a very peculiar rubber blackjack, with a tear-gas bomb on the end of it. The idea seemed to be that when he hit you over the head, he'd also be triggering the tear gas to finish you off. I couldn't believe it when Wilson told me I had been seen; he actually had to argue with me. I threw a few words of caution at this watchman, and then we went slamming out the storm doors and through a side alley to the back street where we had parked the car.

I can't describe how frustrated I was. It's always the ones that don't come off that stand out in your mind, because the successful ones get to be so routine that after a while they tend to blur. Over the years, I must have taken close to a hundred banks, and the ones I see most clearly are the four I missed. The Ozone Park National Bank where we left the tanks behind, the National City Bank where the kid got out, and the Brooklyn bank when Eagen didn't show up. And the Corn Exchange Bank in Philadelphia.

There was another one, with Bassett, on the outskirts of Buffalo, when the alarm unaccountably went off just as the guard was opening the door. But that one doesn't really count. "That's just what I'm checking up on," I told the startled guard. We'd had a lot of that kind of thing lately, I said sternly, and the captain wanted it known that he didn't have the manpower to go chasing down every defective alarm.

The next morning I was back again. "You see," said the guard, "it's working just fine now."

"It sure is," I said, showing him the gun. "Let's see if we can do it right this time. You wouldn't want me to spend another night in this burg, would you?"

After all the time I'd spent at the Corn Exchange Bank, it really rankled. "Stick around for a while," I told Wilson. "I want to take another look." The next morning I went back to see what kind of security measures were being taken. What I saw, I liked. All the employees had been given a key to the outside door, and as each of them arrived they would lock it behind them before they rang the bell. Jeez, I said to myself. *They're trapping themselves inside the vestibule*. Even if they saw me standing inside when the guard opened the door for them, they could never get out to the street to warn anybody.

"Listen," I said to Wilson. "I hate to see this job go. Suppose we look around and see if we can get in there through the roof at night."

A few doors from the bank we found a vacant house where we could go into the hallway, up to the roof, and across the rooftops to the bank. Perfect. The only thing was that we were going to need Perlango to bring the car around in the morning.

Well, as it turned out, it was eleven months before I was able to go back and take it. A couple of days later, we had to rush Olga to the University Hospital with a burst appendix. For two weeks she was on the critical list, and for two weeks I stayed in the hospital in the room alongside her. When at last she was ready to leave, I told her she could have anything she wanted. "I want to visit my folks in Braddock," she said.

On the way down I had a bit of a scare thrown into me. The distance between Philadelphia and Pittsburgh is about five hundred miles and somewhere along the highway we were slowed down by a long line of cars. I figured there had been an accident up ahead, but as we inched forward I could see that a couple of troopers had set up a roadblock. The first thought to occur to me, quite naturally, was that a bank had been robbed and they were looking for contraband. I had a pistol planted in a false compartment behind the glove compartment, and while I wasn't really worried that they'd be able to find it without tearing the whole car down, I was every bit as concerned as you'd expect a fugitive to be who had got himself trapped in the middle of a roadblock.

When I got to the barrier, one of the troopers looked in through the window. "Have you got any plants in the car?" he asked.

To a thief, a plant means only one thing. A place of concealment.

"What do you mean, plant?" I said, in my most law-abiding, nonplant way.

He looked at me like I was an idiot. "You don't know what a plant is? A plant is something that grows

182

out of the ground, like a bush. Do you know what a bush is?"

Ooooooh. That kind of plant. Well, I can tell you, I heaved a sigh of relief. What had happened was that an epidemic of Japanese beetles had hit all along the eastern shore, and road blocks had been set up on the main highways to prevent the movement of potentially infested plants from state to state.

Braddock was a steel town a few miles out of Pittsburgh. The dirtiest, smokiest city I have ever seen. The whole town lived off the Carnegie plant. One immense steel mill and a bunch of small wooden houses begrimed with soot. It was never light, there was too much smoke in the air, and it was never dark because those open-hearth furnaces would light up the skies at night.

So I met Olga's people, her father, her mother, her brother. Her father had lost his leg in an accident after working in the mills all his life, but that didn't stop him. He was a bear of a man. It was a Russian and Polish community, with maybe a Hungarian thrown in here and there, and it seemed as if they had the whole town in there, dancing the mazurkas and polkas and drinking corn liquor out of ketchup bottles.

This is 1933 now, and as poor as the community had always been, the Depression was really biting in. Like poor poor people everywhere, their great hope was to hit "the number." It was all so much in the open that the numbers writer would go from door to door, like the postman, and make out the bets in triplicate. They weren't even paying anybody off. Boy, I thought, Dutch Schultz would love this.

Well, I had come driving up in a brand-new Buick, which made me a celebrity right there. My license plate had three numbers, 368, and the whole neighborhood plunged on it. The number came out, and that's when I found out what it was really like when Russians and Poles have a celebration.

Upon our return to Philadelphia, I saw that the Corn Exchange and all the other banks around Philadelphia were now following the precautionary security measures recommended by the Bankers

183

Association. And while that didn't bother me particularly in itself, it was the best possible indication that the police would have also been alerted to watch out for me.

Working out of Philadelphia, I continued to restrict my activities to the neighboring towns and states. From time to time, though, I'd make it my business to drive up to Market and Sixtieth because I felt by now I had a franchise on the Corn Exchange. It was always something; some little thing. Getting in wasn't going to be any problem. The problem was going to be getting out. In that regard, the manager was a very undependable fellow. You never knew what time he was going to arrive, except that it would be late. No sense of responsibility to the bank's stockholders or the needs of us robbers.

Well, it had to happen. I told Wilson we were going after it regardless, and on the appointed date he brought Perlango over to my apartment, the first time I had ever permitted Perlango to know where I was living. Perlango was to park the car on the rear street at seven o'clock and come around through the alley.

We got in through the roof, exactly as planned. In the morning we let Perlango in. Standing alongside the window, I can actually see the guard through the blinds as he approaches. He's still being very alert, looking both ways before he opens the storm door. Locking it behind him. He opens the big bronze doors, steps in, and there I am, sitting at the manager's desk. The way his eyes bugged out, I thought he was going to have a heart attack. "I know you," he said, when he was finally able to speak. "You held me up."

"That's right," I said. "I came back to get what I didn't get the last time I was here." For the time being, I took another pistol from him.

Well, the manager was even later than usual. It might have been eight-fifty before he came in. By that time, there were already a bunch of depositors gathered outside the storm door. Milkmen, mostly. It was the fifteenth of the month, I was told, collection day. They were stopping off at the bank to deposit their receipts.

You can't do a conscientious job of robbing a bank in anything like ten minutes. By the time we were leaving, the crowd had not only grown to alarming proportions, it was getting impatient and even unruly. "Just another couple of minutes, folks," I announced. "Due to an unavoidable delay that will be explained to you, we're a little behind time today. The management wants to convey its apologies for any inconvenience." And then the three of us passed through the crowd and went up the same alley again to the car. It was a very disappointing haul. Only $10,980.

I had planned to go to Braddock with Olga until the heat died down, and now that Perlango knew where I lived I was going to move into a new apartment before we left. "I just don't trust this guy the way you do," I told Wilson.

That was where Wilson told me that he was going to have to change his apartment, too. Broads again. The way he explained it to me, a friend of ours named Frank Capapano (a parolee from Brooklyn) had introduced him to two sisters. Eddie had dated the younger one for a while, and then he started going out with the older one. The younger one had got jealous and whether it was because of her or not, he kept getting the feeling he was being tailed. Just to be safe, he was going to put the car in a private garage when he got back, move into a new place, and then re-register the car so that it would have different plates. All of which affected my plans only because he was so jumpy that he wanted me to stay in Philadelphia until he could call and tell me everything was all right.

A few days was all it would take, he promised. A week at the most. Well, it was more than a week and as the time passed I began to have the kind of feeling I get on these things. A kind of uneasy tremor in the air. I always had these hunches, and if I had always acted on them I'd have been a lot better off. The call, when it came, didn't come from Eddie Wilson. It came from Johnny Feinstein. "Willie," he said. "I know you're leaving town today."

The meaning was so unmistakable that I only had to say one word. "Yes."

He said: "Immediately. Without delay."

Without delay, I hung up and told Olga I was leaving. "It's an emergency," I said. "I'll call you up before the day is over and let you know where I'm going to meet you."

For the time being, I was going to be traveling very light. Just me and a change of underclothing and a bag of money. The money bag was in the false bottom of a big steamer trunk we had in the bedroom. While I was down on my knees leaning over the trunk, I got a blow on my head that almost knocked me unconscious. The next thing I knew I was down on the floor with all the cops in the world on top of me.

Fourteen months after my escape from Sing Sing I was back in the hands of the law.

Wilson had been made all right, and it had nothing to do with broads. It had to do with Perlango. What I didn't know—here we go again—was that all the time that Wilson kept assuring me that he never contacted Perlango except when I wanted him for a job, they had been socializing on a regular basis in New York. Perlango and his wife; Wilson and Rita.

Despite all the money Perlango had been making with us, he had continued to live in the East Side slums, where his new car and expensive clothing had inevitably brought him to the attention of the police. So much so that an illegal tap had been placed on his phone. That morning, Wilson had picked Perlango up on his way to get his new license plates. Rita was with him. Instead of going to the motor-vehicle bureau in Brooklyn, as he had intended to, he decided at the last minute to play it even safer and go all the way up to Westchester.

Unknown to them, they were followed by a carful of detectives in an unmarked car. As Wilson was getting back into the Chrysler outside the license bureau, he saw all these guys sitting in this car and when he spotted them behind him on the way back to New York he realized that it was a tail. With the tremendous power of his hyped-up Chrysler he felt he could outrace them. He was doing pretty well, too, until he hit the city line. At the intersection of

Broadway and 241st, he had to jam on the brakes at a red light to avoid the cross-traffic. Before he could start up again, the car with the detectives had cut him off. The official police version was that Wilson had appeared to be reaching for a gun. In the fusillade of shots that followed, a bullet went into the side of Wilson's head, severing the optic nerve and leaving him permanently blind. Rita had a fingertip shot off.

Perlango, who had escaped without a scratch, was brought to police headquarters. It wouldn't have mattered if he had simply told them about our crimes, I was a fugitive anyway. But when they threatened to place his wife, who was pregnant, under arrest he capitulated completely and told them where I was living.

Six New York detectives, headed by my old friend Captain McPhee, were dispatched to Philadelphia to pick me up. One of Dutch Schultz's contacts in the police department had been able to get the word to him, and the Dutchman had passed it on to Johnny Feinstein so that he could warn me.

The warning came just too late. The six New York cops had picked up four detectives in Philadelphia, and they were already secreted in the apartment directly across the hall. They had opened the door with a pass key, shoved Olga aside, and swarmed all over me. Not only was the money grabbed out of my hand, the New York detective who was lying on top of me reached into my pocket and lifted my wallet.

The police commissioner of Philadelphia had also been in on the raid. Shooey Malone, a very well-known person in Philadelphia. I think it would be fair to say that all the people in the rackets knew Shooey Malone. At the first opportunity, I took him aside, let my eyes run to the bagful of money, and suggested we might be able to work out a way to square this. "Gee," he said sadly. "We have six New York detectives with us. We can't do any business."

Oh no? A few minutes later, the detective who had lifted my wallet took me aside, having discovered by then that there was two thousand dollars in it. "Don't say anything about the wallet," he whispered, "and I'll give you half. We'll go fifty-fifty." Okay. Sure.

"You got a deal." It goes without saying I didn't get a dime out of it. I didn't even get a pack of cigarettes from this New York detective.

In addition to my thirty-five-hundred-dollar cut from the Corn Exchange Bank, there had been thirty-five thousand of my own money in that bag. The money from the robbery went back to the bank. The other thirty-five thousand just disappeared. After the judge hit me with a sentence of twenty-five to fifty years, he asked, "Did he have any money when he was arrested?" Somebody at the prosecution table piped up, "Yeah, fifteen hundred dollars."

"All right," the judge said. "I'll fine him the fifteen hundred." And that kind of discouraged me from making an issue of it.

In fairness to Philadelphia justice, it should be said that local pride was undoubtedly a factor. The sentencing judge, Harry S. McDevitt, had announced publicly before the trial that he was going to show Willie Sutton that no out-of-state thieves were going to come into Philadelphia and rob their banks.

Ironically, when the Supreme Court eventually demanded that trial judges pay more attention to the Constitution, he became my unwitting benefactor.

Plotting

The Eastern State Penitentiary is in the heart of Philadelphia, twenty-two prime acres on Fairmount Avenue between Twentieth and Twenty-second streets. I was taken immediately to the office of the warden, Hard-Boiled Smith, a former state trooper who had come up through the ranks. Hard boiled was exactly what he was; a tough man, a rough-talking man, but by no means a brutal man. A cigar smoker. "Willie," he said. "I know you're going to try to escape from this prison. You could never convince me otherwise no matter how long you talked. I want you to know two things. One, as long as I've been warden of this here institution nobody has escaped on me yet. Two, as long as you are here you are going to be under a special watch. All the guards have been notified to be on the alert. One false move and they'll blow your fuckin' head off."

I said, "That's all right with me, I have no intention of escaping."

I was, of course, thinking of nothing else. After I had been brought to the Moyamensing jail in Philadelphia following my arrest, a state senator named Joe Nolan had come to me with a proposition. For ten thousand dollars, he said, he could have me sent back to New York.

"I haven't got ten thousand," I told him. "They've impounded all my money."

That didn't faze him. "All you have to do is give me a telephone number," he said. "I'll send somebody for it."

Senator Nolan, I could see, was a man who knew his way around. There were a couple of numbers I could have given him. As it was, I gave it a great deal of thought. For ten thousand dollars, he wasn't merely offering me a chance to serve my time in New York and then come back to be tried in Philadelphia. He was guaranteeing that somewhere in those intervening years, the charges were going to disappear.

But that was no bargain, either. I owed New York thirty-six years, plus whatever extra they tacked on for the escape, and I was always mindful that back in Dannemora this Granger was waiting for me. And, boy, that sonofabitch would have killed me in a minute.

Wherever I was, I was going to have to either escape or resign myself to dying in prison. As far as I was concerned, I was going to have a far better chance of escaping in Pennsylvania than in New York. They had me cold on the Corn Exchange Bank, of course. They had the money, they had Perlango's

189

confession, and they had a dozen witnesses from the bank. And so as much as it went against my principles to admit anything, I thought I might get lucky on the sentence by pleading guilty.

I was wrong on both counts. Judge McDevitt was out to hit me with everything he could. He found me guilty on three separate charges for a total of twenty-five to fifty years and, still not satisfied, announced: "I will see that you are indicted as a fourth offender and that you are sentenced to spend the rest of your life in prison, where you belong."

He didn't forget about me, either. The trial had taken place on February 12, 1934—Lincoln's Birthday—and a year to the day later he celebrated the Great Emancipator's birthday again by having me brought back into court, on his own volition, to try me as a habitual criminal. In order to do that, he had to find that I was a fourth felony offender, which, of course, I wasn't. Apparently nobody had ever been tried as a habitual offender in Philadelphia before, because, as unbelievable as it sounds, the prosecutor came up to me while we were waiting and told me that he didn't have the slightest idea how to proceed. "How do they go about this in New York?" he asked. "Do you know?"

McDevitt knew exactly what he was up to, though. By ruling that the attempted robbery of the Corn Exchange Bank in 1933 constituted a separate felony, he was able to remove the ten to twenty years that had already been imposed upon me for that and hit me with a life sentence on top of the fifteen to thirty years that were left.

Fortunately, I had been given enough notice so that I had been able to hire Louie McCabe, a well-known labor lawyer, to represent me. McCabe, who was a ferocious fighter, had already warned McDevitt that the whole procedure was legally invalid. As soon as the sentence was handed down, he informed him that he was going to get it thrown out in the Superior Court. Which he did. The Superior Court ruled that I was not a fourth felony offender, and threw out the life sentence and restored the original one.

But even more than that, I had never dreamed

they were going to be so goddamn watchful. That first full year had been spent in the isolation ward, and it was another six months before I was taken out and allowed to mix with the rest of the population.

If eighteen months sounds like a long time to spend in semi-isolation, it wasn't in the Pennsylvania scheme of things. The whole prison system in America began in Philadelphia, you know. It was a Quaker invention based upon rehabilitation through seclusion and religious meditation.

When the Eastern State Pen was built in 1829, it was looked upon as a revolutionary development in prison design. So much so that it became the prototype of what came to be known as the Pennsylvania system. Structurally, the design was based on the wheel concept, with seven narrow cellblocks shooting out like spokes of a wheel. The hub of the wheel was the heavily armed center from which everything was controlled. Each of the cellblocks was connected to the center through a covered passageway, and also isolated from it by a locked iron door. Viewed from above, it looked like nothing so much as a windmill, with the cellblocks appearing as paddles at the end of a thin blade.

The cells were roughly twelve by seven and a half feet, which is quite large even by modern standards, and enormous—compare it to the tiny cells in Sing Sing—by the standards of the day. But there was a reason for it. From the time one of those earlier prisoners arrived until the time he was released he was never allowed to leave his cell except when he had a visitor. He ate in his cell and he worked in his cell. In the back of each cell was a workbench equipped with some kind of machine that permitted him to learn a trade. Above the work area was a kind of corrugated roof in which there was an air slit. As Oscar Wilde once put it:

I never saw a man who looked
with such a wistful eye
upon that little tent of blue
which prisoners call the sky.

Each cell also came equipped with a Bible, and no other reading material was permitted. Presumably, the prisoner would contemplate the sins of the past and resolve to mend his ways and return to society, as they say, as a useful, functional, contributing citizen.

The theory was that while you had to protect society by locking criminals up, you were not going to rehabilitate them by having them associate with other criminals. Which does have a certain logic to it. It certainly makes more sense than taking a young kid and throwing him in with hardened criminals.

Quite literally, the prisoners were never allowed to come into contact with each other. When they were taken to the visiting room they would be given a shield to hold over their face, a masklike thing with two eye holes and a mouth slit. Inside the visiting room, they were placed in a narrow booth which, once again, shielded them from all other eyes.

Under conditions like that, five years was an exceptionally long sentence. Anything longer and they'd have been ready for either the monastery or the bughouse.

By the time I got there, of course, things had changed. There were no longer any machines in the cells, and the corrugated ceiling back there had been replaced by a slanted window which could be held open by a notched pole—making Oscar Wilde's imagery of the "tent of blue" literally true. And, of course, most of the prisoners were allowed to mix freely. Nevertheless, living conditions are permanently fixed by architecture. They had yardout, but what they still didn't have was a yard. While I was in isolation they'd take us out for an hour a day and allow us to stand in a tiny fenced-off area against the wall and breathe the air. The other prisoners would take their yardout in the little triangles of space between the cellblocks.

In what was probably an outgrowth of the original philosophy, the inmates who possessed marketable skills were permitted to purchase small shops which had been built along the original 7 cellblock and even hire other inmates to work for them. In every cellblock, as an example, there was one cell which was set aside as a barber shop. An inmate would have bought the concession for something around two hundred dollars and he was entitled to sell it to another inmate upon his discharge. The barber had to give each of the inmates in his cellblock whatever haircuts and shaves they would normally be entitled to. That was for free. If you wanted an extra haircut or shave in between, or any extras—like, say, a massage—he charged you. At the end of the month, the barber submitted the bill to the prison authorities and it was deducted from your account.

There were all kinds of concessions that could be bought. Prisoners manufactured leather belts, billfolds, picture frames, and cigarette-case coverings. Beaded bags were made of such fine workmanship that they were sold to Wanamaker's department store in Philadelphia for as much as seventy-five dollars each. I'm not sure what Wanamaker's sold them for, but the demand was so great that they took all they could get.

The inmates who owned the shops were allotted specific times to go into the state-owned craft shop, which was attached to the 10 block, and use the machines.

The most lucrative concession, by far, was run by an inmate named Benny Arnstein. Benny made those replicas of the *Mayflower* that you've seen in taverns all over the country. He'd ship them out by the truckloads. The rumor was that some of the prison officials shared in the profits. It was such a successful undertaking that the Internal Revenue Service came in and filed a claim against him for not paying his income tax. How was Benny supposed to know? Thieves don't pay income tax, that's one of the advantages. Benny had to go to jail in order to become a tax-paying citizen. He was the one prisoner in the history of the penal system, I guess, who more than paid his own way.

The guy I did some work for was Georgie Nelson. Georgie was a first-class cabinetmaker, and he had a concession for making sailships, radio-banks for kids, and about half a dozen other wooden novelty items.

Georgie and I became so friendly that he wanted to make me a partner. No chance. The dep was willing to let me help George out in his own shop, but anything that would put me in the craft shop, where I would be around tools, was out of the question.

He was right. That was exactly what I had in mind, as Georgie well knew.

When I was taken out of the segregation block after eighteen months, I was given a job as secretary to the supervisor of industries, H. Earl Gray. It was a good job and there were two reasons why it was given to me. While I was in isolation I had taken a course in typing and shorthand and I had become very good. Although I didn't have a typewriter I could practice the touch system by looking at the exercises and moving my fingers. Over and over. Sixteen or twenty hours a day. Also because the office was at the head of the 10 block, only a short distance from the center. Anytime the guard on the center wanted to look in on me, all he had to do was take a few steps.

I had to bide my time. The job allowed me a limited amount of freedom to look around. Occasionally Gray had to make a trip to Harrisburg, the state capital, and while he was away I was in a position to make the right kind of friends. Planning to escape from prison takes infinite patience. Precision work spaced over a long period of time. A plan which can be described in a paragraph may have taken two years to put together.

Within any jail there are people who are planning to escape. There are constant plans, sometimes overlapping, because these people are always looking for the best shot they can get. I was careful to avoid any entanglements with most of them. The "right" guys are not always right guys. There are always inmates who are looking to go running to the warden. Inside or outside, it's always the informers who do you in.

The first thing you have to do, then, is eliminate the rats, which is a matter of instinct. The second thing you have to eliminate are the talkers, which is nothing more than common sense. We had a couple of kids there, Jimmy Murray and Harry Flynn, whom we called The Plotters. They'd walk around looking intently at the guard towers and drawing all kinds of plans on how they were going to get out. If the wall fell down, these guys wouldn't have made a run for it. They'd have been the first ones there with mortar boards helping to put it back up.

You also have to estimate just how much risk a man will take. Among the first friends I made were some New Yorkers who had landed in Eastern State because they had robbed a bank in Hawley, Pennsylvania. Tommy Kling, Georgie Moore, Herbie Miller, and Tommy the Greek. A solid group of guys. They had a plan, which I was in on, that depended upon assembling a ladder in the print shop, which was right under the 1 tower, and making the break during yardout.

Guards are creatures of habit like the rest of us. Anytime you can count on one of them doing the same thing at the same time, you've got something. The guard on the 1 tower would bring his own sandwiches up with him, eat almost immediately, and since the wall was without toilet facilities, he would then send for a slop bucket. We were going to storm over the wall while he was taking a crap. Very, very risky. It wouldn't have been conceivable except that we were only a block away from the city.

Georgie Moore, who had originated the plan, worked in the print shop and he was going to jigger the door in a way that would allow us to get in after it had closed for the day. When it really came down to it, Georgie began to get sick. His complaints about his health grew more frequent; his voice began to take on a bit of a whine. On the day before we were ready to go, he went on sick call. When the big day arrived, he could barely drag himself out of bed. Well, when you see that someone who is that vital to the break is losing his nerve, the only thing to do is scratch it. I just didn't feel that we could depend upon him to react properly if we ran into any kind of trouble. It wasn't a question of blaming him or being sore at him or anything like that. You can't expect a man to do what he doesn't have the stomach for, that's all.

The difference between a Georgie Moore and The Plotters is that Georgie not only liked to talk about it, he'd like to help you out just to be able to say he'd been a part of it. There are a lot of Georgie Moores in prison, you'd be surprised. You can count on them for all the help they can give, just so long as they don't have to go with you.

So time went on, I looked and I listened. And I studied. There's a saying in prison: "Don't serve time, make time serve you." Everybody says it, and hardly anybody does it. Most of the people coming into jail are uneducated, unintelligent, and uninterested in improving themselves. They live for whatever diversion is fed up to them, a game of baseball, a game of football, or a motion picture. By the time they leave, they have become so dependent upon the institution to feed them, clothe them, and tell them what to do that they are unable to take care of themselves. I can almost always recognize an ex-con at a glance by a certain lifeless quality behind his eyes; something lost and vacant. Stir crazy is what the prisoners themselves call it, and it can give you the creeps.

To keep my mind active, I studied avidly. Everything. I studied abnormal psychology, which was almost a new subject at the time. I took three or four refresher courses in English. There was one period where I concentrated on the rules of grammar precisely because it is such a taxing, basically unrewarding subject that it serves as a discipline for the mind. And history. I took every high-school history course that was offered. American history, European history, ancient history. I had made myself a vow in Dannemora that I would never allow them to imprison my mind, and with books I was able to travel around the world and marvel at the variety of its customs and its peoples. "History is little else than a picture of human crimes and misfortunes," Voltaire wrote. Not quite. It is a vast morality play in which mankind's higher aspirations are forever being crushed to earth. I studied the religions of the world, went on crusades to search for the Lost Grail, smelled the foul air of the Spanish dungeons under Torquemada (that was easy), and attended the witch trials at Salem. I was spectator at the amphitheater at Rome and listened to the dying groans of the fallen gladiators.

I read Adam Smith on economics. I studied geography. Political science. The European philosophers; Spinoza, Schopenhauer, and Nietzsche. Speculative philosophers, scientific philosophers, social philosophers.

Schopenhauer said the greater intelligence a man has, the more he suffers, and that genius therefore suffers most of all. There is an interesting philosophical conflict in there that I became aware of even as I was reading it. If you are in prison, you have to devote all of your time to study in order to overcome the surroundings, and yet the more intelligent you become as the result of all that study, the more you are dooming yourself to suffer. But, then, Schopenhauer always did see life as a constant search for the lesser of two evils.

While I was looking and listening I picked up anything that came to hand. Like the six aluminum rods that were slipped to me by a guy who worked in the machine shop. Each of the rods was three and a third feet long, and while the circumference was quite small the metal itself was an eighth of an inch thick, which is very heavy for aluminum. I didn't have the slightest idea what I could do with them. All I knew was that if I screwed them all together, I'd have a twenty-foot rod which could take a lot of stress.

At that stage of the game, the question of what I was going to do with them was secondary to where I was going to hide them. That was where George Nelson and his skill as a cabinetmaker came in. In the back of my cell I had a small bare desk which had a kind of open-framed backing. George cut me three thick boards to fit across the frame. Thick enough so that George was able to hollow them out and slip the aluminum rods in, one on top of the other. He then closed up the opening by gluing on a piece of end-wood. All I was going to have to do when I wanted them was pull out the end-wood with a sharp knife—which was easy enough to get once you had made the right contacts in prison—lift up one end of the board, and the rods would come sliding out into my hand.

Three of my other good friends were Johnny Barr, Spence Waldron, and Adam the Polack. Unlike the New York crowd, they hadn't come in together; the only thing they had in common was they had a lot of time to serve and were thinking very deep thoughts about breaking out. Adam worked in the plumbing shop. He was a big guy, always pleasant but not very communicative. The kind of a guy who believes in keeping his own counsel. Being a plumber and pipe-fitter, he had to spend a great deal of time in the cellar. Being a hard-working, apparently trustworthy guy, he was allowed to go about his work without any real supervision.

There are two things everybody dreams of finding in prison. The first is a secret passageway, the second is the main sewer. In every prison I have ever been in, there is a mythical "abandoned passageway" which was supposed to have been used for runaway slaves or as a pirate hideout. (In Sing Sing there actually was an abandoned tunnel which had once been used by the New York Central Railroad. Unfortunately, everybody knew exactly where that one was; it was about fifty yards outside the prison grounds.)

The main sewer wasn't mythical at all. There has got to be a sewer system, and it has got to connect with the main sewer of the city. So what? Sheer common sense should tell you that any architect drawing up plans for a prison would make sure that the main sewer would be extremely difficult to find and, in any case, impossible to get into.

Adam's dream was to find the "abandoned passageway," and he was always digging far deeper into the dirt than the job called for in the belief that sooner or later his pick or his shovel was going to break through. Johnny Barr and I happened to be standing together near the chapel when we saw Adam come hurrying toward us in a high state of excitement. No, he told us, he hadn't found an abandoned passageway. "I found the main sewer," he said.

In the course of doing some repair work in the

cellar of the 10 block, he had come across a six-inch
pipe which broke away from the interlock and dipped
into the ground. After following it down for about a
foot, he could see, to his disappointment, that it was
leveling off. Out of habit, he had kept digging anyway
in the hope of breaking through. Instead, he had hit
a hard surface. A few more minutes and he had exposed a four-foot slab of cement. From there it had
been merely a matter of prying up the whole block of
cement with a crowbar. At first, just enough to be able
to hear a rush of water underneath; and then far
enough so that he was able to beam his flashlight
into the darkness and see the bottom of the sewer
pipe, six feet below.

For more than a hundred years, prisoners had been
dreaming of finding the main sewer, and Adam the
Polack had found it.

Having found it, what had he found? With each of
the cellblocks having its own cellar, the underground
network was an exact replica of the hub-and-spoke
design. In order to catch the refuse from all of the
buildings, Adam could tell us, the sewer would have
to run underneath the cellars in a kind of a horseshoe
until the pipe from both sides came together in a deep
basin at the base of the wall under the 1 tower.

During the day, the basin was kept dammed up by
a solid steel door. Every night, after all the inmates
had been locked in their cells, a guard would come
down, throw back a heavy grating, and crank the
door up. What we had to do was find out whether the
steel door could be raised from inside the sewer
during the daytime, preferably very early in the day
before all the water and refuse came flowing in.

I had finally found a use for the aluminum rods.

Before I could get into the sewer, I was going to
have to get into the cellar. The only direct entrance
from the yard was through a door on the 7 block, and
that door was always guarded. Never mind. Adam
was going to get me in through a ground-level window
in a little corner which was completely blocked off
from the sight of the tower guards by the craft shop.
The window was on the 11 block. The craft shop,
which was the largest shop on the grounds, was at-

tached to the 10 block. Only one half of the window was above ground level. The other half had been constructed below a grating to permit the greatest possible amount of sunlight to come slanting through. Adam was going to cut a bar out from the bottom section of the window and, when the time came, remove the padlock from the underside of the grating.

The time came at the end of the month when H. Earl Gray made the trip to Harrisburg.

Like the upper prison, every wing of the cellar radiated out from the center. It was only a matter of going out the door of the 10 block and right into the door of the 11 block. While Adam was shoveling up the dirt, I was stripping down to the buff. There were three items I was going to be carrying. I had a flashlight, which I had made watertight by taping around the button and around the screw-in caps at the top and bottom. I had a wristwatch. And when Adam was finished with his shoveling, he strapped the six aluminum rods onto my back with adhesive tape. The idea was to get near enough to the steel door to raise it perhaps six inches, just enough to allow the water to empty out of the basin. If I were able to do that, I would be able to get down into the basin itself and find out whether it was possible to force the door high enough to allow a human being to squeeze underneath and get into the sewer system outside the walls.

I was going to have to pass under the craft shop, under the 11 block, under the print shop, under the 1 block, and under a relatively small portion of the yard, a total distance of perhaps one hundred yards. I was on a tight time schedule. Adam was going to return in exactly an hour to pry open the cement block and let me out.

As I began to lower myself, I flashed the light in. It was a thirty-inch pipe constructed entirely of red brick. What I saw when the light hit the bricks was the most loathsome sight I have ever seen. I don't know how many hundreds of these waterbugs started to run around frantically. Big, ugly things, the size of giant cockroaches. There must have been thousands of them. Uggggh. I gave a shudder and dropped down on my hands and knees. Adam let the cement block drop back into place. Except for the light from the flashlight, I was in complete darkness.

I had to lie absolutely flat and propel myself along by my elbows and knees, holding the flashlight out in front of me. There wasn't very much water in the pipe at that point and, although the bottom had been smoothed by the running water over the years, it was still quite abrasive under those conditions. Above the waterline, the sewer was coated by a thick green slime, the encrustation of a hundred years. Periodically, there was a rush of water as a toilet was flushed.

The only landmarks I had in the widening circle I was traveling were the indentations at the top of the pipe that told me I was passing under another cement block. The farther I went, the deeper the water got, until it was practically up to my chin. There was everything piling up. All the solid waste matter from the toilets and sinks. Not to mention the discharges and soiled bandages from the hospital building, which was in the 3 block, only two buildings up from where I had started. As raw as my knees and elbows had been rubbed by then, it was a miracle that I didn't later die from an infection.

When I had reached the point where it would be impossible to go any farther without being over my head, I was sure that I had to be right outside the basin. With excruciating care, I screwed the aluminum rods together and pushed it forward. Nothing. I couldn't believe it. Twenty feet is a tremendous length. I flattened myself out again and pushed it forward . . . forward . . . forward, and it still didn't hit anything.

Well, the only thing left to do was submerge myself into all that slime and sludge and try to swim the rest of the way. And I couldn't. It wasn't water any more; it was gook. As hard as I tried, I just couldn't make any headway. My lungs were bursting. *I'm going to drown here in a sewer, all covered with shit.* Sheer panic. There was no room to turn around in the pipe, so I had to backtrack. The strength of desperation. As far as I could, as fast as I could. When I got back to where my head was out of the water and I was finally able to turn around, I took a deep breath, trying to fill my lungs with air. There had been little enough oxygen in the pipe all along. When I took that deep breath, my lungs seemed to be bursting. And right there, while my whole chest felt as if it were cracking, the flashlight went out. The water had got through to the battery.

I doubt if ever in your life you have been in a place where you were in total darkness. Most rooms have some light coming in from somewhere. In total darkness you lose all sense of orientation as to time or place or direction. I found myself crawling up the side of the pipe without being aware that I was leaving the water. It was only when I'd feel myself pushing onto the slimy crust at the top that I'd realize where I was and try to straighten myself out. And all the time I had to remember to keep feeling around with my fingers for the indentations at the top of the pipe that would tell me I had come to one of the cement blocks. For it had finally dawned on me somewhere along the way that those blocks were the only signposts I had. And as it dawned on me, I wasn't sure whether it was the second or the third one I had reached. I had to get back to where Adam was going to let me out, and I had not the slightest idea of the time. Right to the end I didn't know whether I was waiting under the right block. I didn't know whether I was early or whether I was late. All I knew was that if I was under the wrong opening, or if Adam had come and gone, I wouldn't be able to last very long.

I could stand up, though, and I did the only thing I could think to do. Knowing that it was stupid, knowing that I was using up both the oxygen and my strength, I put both hands against the cement and tried to push it up. All I succeeded in doing was bringing down a rain of siltlike dirt onto my head and into my eyes and mouth. My chest is raw, my knees and elbows are aching. I'm standing there, not a human being but a mass of slime, with the waste of a hundred years dripping over me, and wondering whether I'm even in the right place.

And do you know what I thought? I suddenly remembered that I had dropped the aluminum bar while I was backtracking out of the basin. If only I had held on to it, I kept telling myself, I could have used it somehow to get out of there. It didn't matter how, I'd have found a way. There was always a way! I could have beat on the cement, I could have let Adam know I was there. I could have ...

It seemed like an eternity before I heard a sound of scraping overhead. And then the indescribably beautiful sound of the crowbar grating against the concrete. I placed my hand flat on the cement and when I finally felt it move I said to myself, This is one time you should have been dead.

As Adam lifted me up, I felt as if I were rising out of the grave. Ruskin had told me after the murder trial that every day I lived I should consider profit. And, boy, I considered this to have been a profitable day. As far as I was concerned, I had escaped death twice. First by managing to turn around in the pipe when my lungs were bursting, and then in stopping under the right cement block.

Adam had some rags there to wipe me down. He was able to clean the dirt and the bugs and gook off my body, but my hair was so matted that we just clamped the cap over my head and hoped for the best. Johnny Barr was standing in the doorway of the craft shop. As soon as he saw my head pop up under the grating, he pulled the door shut. Just in case anybody happened to be walking out.

I made my way up to the 7 gallery where I was locking, went into the shower, and just let the water pour down over my head. The way I felt, I didn't think I would ever be completely clean again, not if I lived for another fifty years.

I looked at my knees and elbows, and they were already scabbing over; big, wet, ugly scabs that were to get an eighth of an inch thick later on. I was so sure that they had to be infected that I poured every kind of disinfectant I could get from the hospital into them.

A few days later I was suddenly placed under arrest and thrown in the isolation block to await a hearing before the deputy's court. Whether it was for the escape attempt I didn't know. If it was, I couldn't imagine how they could have found out about it. My first night there, the cleanup man slipped me a note and whispered, "Georgie Nelson wants you to have this."

The note read: "Say you were in my shop and that I was painting the hull of a model with red lead."

Well, I knew that Georgie always used red lead to waterproof the hulls of his boats. Beyond that, it meant not a thing to me.

Dep Martin was a tall, swarthy man with very even features. A Syrian. Like the warden, he was a strict disciplinarian, but from everything I had heard he ran a very fair court. Unlike the warden, he was usually very soft-spoken. Not this time, though. He started by glaring at me and then he snapped, "What were you doing down in the cellar?"

Already I felt a little better. His intention had apparently been to stun me by showing me he knew I had been down there, but what he was really telling me was that he didn't know anything more than that. The first thing that crossed my mind was that somebody must have seen me going in through the window and had decided, after a little thought, to see what good he could do himself.

"What the hell would I be doing in the cellar?" I said. "I don't know what you're talking about."

"I'll show you what I'm talking about." He reached down underneath the desk and brought out a pair of shoes. "Are these yours?"

One pair of prison shoes looks like any other. "Where did you get them?"

"The officer got them out of your cell."

"Then I guess they have to be mine."

He pointed to a little red spot on the toe. "That's red lead," he said. "You want to tell me where that red lead came from?"

The smudge was so small that I had to squint to see it. I let the squint remain there as an expression of bewilderment. "That's funny," I said. "It looks like red lead, all right." But, of course, I didn't have the slightest idea where it came from.

"Well I'll tell you where it came from." The expression on his face said that he had me now, and he had me good. "There's only one place where there's wet red lead in this place and that's down in the cellar." He not only knew I'd been down there, he said triumphantly, he knew how I had got there. "You sawed the bars out of the window in the alley behind the craft shop."

So that was it. They had discovered that the bar had been sawed and they had naturally gone right to my cell and found that goddamned little red spot on my shoe. "I don't know where I got it," I said. "But I certainly didn't get it from the cellar, that's a cinch. I never been down there." And then, very thoughtfully, "I think I may know where I came into contact with that red lead, though."

"Where?"

"I was helping Georgie Nelson with his boats the other day," I said. "We were, you know, painting them. Maybe I got some of it on me there."

It was perfect, and I could see that it was. The dep not only knew that I liked to help the Swede out, he happened to be very fond of Georgie himself. The dep had invented a game called Cops and Robbers, and Georgie had drawn up the design and specifications for him so that he could have it patented. Everybody knew that he would do anything in the world for George, except—of course—permit him to take me into his concession.

Immediately he picked up the phone and asked for George to be sent to him.

"What's it all about, Dep?" Georgie asked when he arrived. He was playing it perfectly, looking only moderately surprised that he had been called and not at all surprised at seeing me there. Everybody knew I had been arrested and was going up before the deputy's court.

"Was Willie helping you with your boats?"

"Oh sure. He gives me a hand every once in a while, when I ask him."

"When was he helping you last, George?"

Georgie gave it some thought, almost as if he were counting back on his fingers. "I think it was Wednesday," he said.

"I want you to tell me what you were doing at the time."

George looked up at the ceiling. After a while he said, as if he weren't all that sure of it, "I think I was painting my models."

"Well, what were you painting with? What paints were you using?"

"Well," George said. "I was painting with white enamel. I was painting with red lead. I was painting with gold leaf." And he guessed that was all.

"And you're sure it was Wednesday?"

Yes, he was sure. "If you arrest Willie, you better arrest me too. Because he was with me and whatever it is, I guess I'm guilty too."

The dep kept looking at him. "All right," he said. "You can go now, George."

I was being released from isolation, he told me. "I'm not convinced that you weren't down that cellar," he said. "Anybody else told me that, I'd have my doubts about it. Insofar as it's George . . . well, George has always been pretty truthful to me."

Georgie was waiting for me at yardout to tell me what had happened. He had happened to receive a large order for his ships, and when you get that kind of an order you have to get special permission from the dep before you can go to work on it. While he was waiting in the outer office, he had seen the guard come in with the shoes, heard the discussion about the red lead, and had immediately gone out to find Adam, Spence, and Johnny and discuss how to get word to me.

"You could have blown your shop, you dumb Swede," I said. "You could have wound up in the 'icebox' for a couple of years with me."

"A stubborn Swede." He grinned, correcting me. "Stubborn ain't dumb, Bill."

A few days later the warden sent for me. Hard-Boiled Smith wasn't dumb, either. I might be able to fool his deputy, he bellowed, but I wasn't fooling him. "Since the day you entered this prison you never stopped thinking of how you could get out of here."

Naturally, I denied it. "But," I said, "you've got

your mind made up, and I know there's nothing I can say that is going to convince you otherwise."

The warden blew out a puff from the cigar that was always in his mouth and opened the top drawer of his desk. Nothing was in there except for maybe seven or eight folded pieces of paper. That was his Sutton drawer, he told me. Every one of them was a note from an inmate informing him that I was planning an escape.

"I can't control what people trying to curry favor with you write."

"And I can't prove any of it yet, that's the only reason I haven't locked you up." But some of them he believed. "You're a pretty slick article, Willie. You stay out of trouble. You violate no rules. As far as the officers go, you wouldn't say shit if you had a mouthful." He closed the drawer, leaned back, and blew out some more smoke. "I'll let you in on a secret, Sutton. I don't worry about the trouble-makers. I worry about long-termers who you'd hardly know they were around if it wasn't that they always seem to be congregating together at yardout."

"You see the paradox there, Warden. If I stayed by myself you'd assume I was planning something and I was too slick to trust anybody. If I associate with other long-termers you're sure I'm planning to escape with them." So it didn't matter what I did, did it? He was going to think what he wanted to.

He bit down hard on his cigar. "You were in that cellar, Sutton. I don't know what you were doing there, but you were there." He let me go, but just as I was opening the door he said, "You're going to make your move before long, Slick Willie. And I only hope I'm around." I turned back and he was leaning over the desk with his cigar turned over in his hand and pointing right at me, as if he were sighting over a gun barrel. The gun barrel was pointed right between my eyes.

The message about congregating with other long-termers was impossible to miss. I was going to be watched so carefully that everybody I came into contact with would automatically become suspect. Under those circumstances, I told my friends in each of the groups that we were going to have to pull back and let things cool off. The word got back to me, in turn, that almost every rat in the joint had been delegated to watch me.

Spending more time by myself only gave me more time to think about the one thing I was most interested in. The one thing I had been thinking about now for seven years. Escape. The 7 block, where I locked, was one of the two cellblocks upon which they had built a gallery. I had been put up there, quite obviously, so that a closer watch could be kept on me. And also, I suppose, so that I'd be that much farther away from the door. But it generally happens that every time they close up one avenue they're opening up another. The way the prison was laid out, it was going to be far easier for me to go over the roof than it would have been to go out the front door.

By climbing up to the slanted window on the roof of my cell at night I was able to get a very good view of the prison yard. The searchlights swinging back and forth in a half arc from the towers. The captain of the guard flashing his light on and off to identify himself to the wall guards as he made his rounds. And what interested me most of all, the changing of the guard at midnight.

And the weather. The wall was kept so well lit that it seemed to be lighting up the surrounding streets as well as the prison yard. Except under certain conditions. I had already noted that at certain times in the summer and fall a heavy fog would come rolling into the prison. When it was really dense, the lights would become as dim and fuzzy as if they were no more than the headlights of a distantly approaching automobile. The wall you couldn't see at all. If a man could get out of his cell while the new shift was still settling in—checking into the center, arranging their gear, all the little things attendant to coming on duty—there was not the slightest doubt in my mind that he could go over the wall between the towers without being seen. I wasn't even worried about the guards in the tower. The only danger, as I saw it, would come from the guards who were coming off shift. Indeed, the fog sometimes got so heavy that

I had to consider the possibility that I might bump right into them in the yard because I hadn't been able to see them.

To play it safe, I would have to give them all the time they needed to clear the yard and be back inside the prison. A matter of four or five minutes.

And that was going to make the timing even tighter. Up where I was, the midnight bedcheck usually came five or ten minutes after midnight, too. I wasn't going to be able to use pillows and blankets to simulate a sleeping man, as I had at Sing Sing. As closely as I was being watched, I couldn't even fall asleep with the blanket over my head without the guard clanging on the bar until he had got a good look at me. I was going to have to get a dummy of some kind that looked enough like me to pass muster, that I knew. A dummy, plus a rope, plus a hook to catch on the top of the wall.

As closely as I was being watched, I was also going to have to find a place to hide them until the night of the heavy fog. A hiding place in a small cell which was searched at regular intervals while I was at work by a whole detail of guards. Impossible? Not at all. The hiding place was the easiest part of it.

I have already said that they had put me up in the gallery so that they could keep a closer eye on me, and that these things have a way of working both ways. Where the floors in the regular cellblocks were solid concrete, the gallery had a wooden floor made out of conventional tongue-and-groove boards.

I cut out a fifteen-inch square in the floor with a hacksaw blade that had been slipped to me by Georgie Nelson, and I'll tell you how I was able to do it. By cutting right along in the cracks, you are cutting right where the tongue goes into the groove and you can lift it right out. Each board was three inches wide. By attaching two narrow strips of wood across all five boards, on the underside, I had myself a cover which I could take out and put back at will.

Between the gallery floor and the first-floor ceiling, there was a space of about fifteen inches. The distance between the floor beams was about a foot. Just perfect for a secret cache.

The cover was secured to the beams by a pair of countersunk screws which I was able to camouflage with some wood dust mixed with putty. The cache was under my desk, which was against the side wall between my cot and the door of the cell. The desk still had a double rack Georgie Nelson had made for me, and by now both racks were filled with books. As confident as I was that the cache couldn't possibly be spotted, I was also playing upon the tendency of the guards, like the rest of us, to back off from any unnecessary lifting and tugging.

Once I had the cache, I was ready to work on the "dummy." The idea for making a mask had been in the back of my head, I suspect, for a long time. I had once read a magazine article about how to make a plaster cast, and it's really very easy.

I had a friend named Kliney who worked in the plastering shop. He was a first-rate plasterer, and he didn't have much time left, so he was permitted to roam around, patching up whatever needed patching. Actually, Kliney was more or less an unofficial trusty. He was also one of those guys who would do anything—as he proved again later—just to be able to say he'd been in on it. Even when it was against his own interests.

"Plaster?" he said. "I can get you all you want of it."

"A little bag is all I need, Kliney." That's all, just a little bag.

I got some Vaseline from the hospital and covered my face and neck heavily with it. And then I mixed the plaster of paris and poured it on, shoving a few straws up my nostrils so that I could breathe while it was hardening. It doesn't take very long, you know. No more than fifteen or twenty minutes.

What that gave me was a mask. A mold. What I wanted was a head. A bust.

I greased the mold thoroughly and poured in the plaster of paris to convert it back to an actual replica of my face. When I was able to take it out, I couldn't believe my eyes. It was perfect. Beyond my wildest

210

dreams. Every crease and wrinkle. Every pore of it was me. Willie, I said to myself. You missed your calling. You're a regular Michelangelo.

By the sheer coincidence that I had taken a course in painting, I already had all the paints I needed in my cell. And it really was a coincidence. I had started by enrolling in a course on cartoon drawing, and I had shown such an aptitude for it, drawing the faces of all my friends and the guards, that I had just kind of graduated to painting. With all the time I had, I wanted to make myself as lifelike as possible. The barber on the 7 block, Jimmy Lavelle, was another good friend of mine. (Lavelle was in for robbing an armored car, and he was known around for being a good fellow.) Every time I got a haircut, Jimmy would save some of my hair for me. At first I had only intended to do the half of my face that would be exposed, but I got to where I enjoyed the work so much that I did the whole thing. First, a full head of hair, and then on into the eyebrows and, even, the eyelashes.

In the meantime, I was working on the face so that it would have a true fleshlike appearance. Not too healthy-looking, with just the merest touch of color around the cheekbones. I reddened the lips, penciled wrinkles upon the brow and along the sides of the mouth, and along the shell of the ears where the blood courses close to the surface a thin tracery of veins to indicate the glow of a healthy circulation.

The eyes I didn't have to worry about. I was sleeping; my eyes were closed. A bit of heavy shadowing at the top of the eyelids and I looked as if I were having the most pleasant and peaceful of dreams.

Having gone that far, I also made a plaster cast of my hand and lower arm. Long enough so that it could be seen outside the blanket.

And all the time I was getting myself into top physical condition, doing daily calisthenics, playing handball. I was going to have to go over the roof, drop myself down, make my dash across the yard, throw the rope up high enough and accurately enough to catch the wall with the hook, and then pull myself up like a mountain climber. Escaping from a prison isn't easy work. You've got to be in shape for it.

When the foggy season came around, I took the bolts out of the steel frame of the roof window and inserted dummy bolts that could be easily removed. For three straight days the fog rolled in, but never with quite the density I felt I needed. As I was returning to my cell after yardout on the fourth day, I was pretty well convinced that this was going to be the night.

A few minutes before midnight, I removed the cover from the cache and placed the head and the hand in the bed. Then I loosened the window enough to push the rope and the hook onto the roof, curled up inside the frame, and peered into the swirling fog. The tower searchlights were barely visible. The only thing I could make out as they turned was the iron ladder rising up on the smokestack of the powerhouse.

It was midnight. Four minutes to go.

It was two minutes past, and there were about two minutes to go.

One minute . . .

And suddenly there was a shout, and the sound of scuffling and running down in the yard. And then all hell broke loose. The yard was filled with movement and shouted orders. The sirens were blasting off.

A minute later, the frame of the window was back in place, the head and the rope were back in the secret cache, and I was back in bed.

In the morning I learned that a couple of other guys had had the same idea about going over the wall on a foggy night, right after the changing of the guards. They had also realized that it would be necessary to wait long enough for the off-duty guards to clear the yard. So what had gone wrong? Well, only one of them owned a watch, and his watch had been a couple of minutes fast. They had run right into the guards coming across the yard.

The next day, Hard-Boiled Smith had his guards shake up every cell in the place. I'm not sure whether they found the false bolts first, and that's what led them into such an intense search for the cache. Anyway, they found it. I was taken into custody and placed on the isolation block for the next six months. Pearl Harbor was bombed while I was in isolation, and I didn't know a thing about it until after I was released.

The mask? The last I heard, the mask was on display in the Franklin Museum in Philadelphia. An artistic success, anyway.

A Tunnel to Holmesburg

A couple of months after I was out of isolation, a runner came up to me on the little ball field to notify me that the prison psychiatrist, Dr. Philip Q. Roche, wanted me in his office. The first thing that comes to the mind of an inmate on a thing like that—especially if he's just been in trouble—is that they're going to try to "bug" him. Many a troublesome inmate had gone that route at Dannemora, it was a going business. All the warden had to do was call in three outside doctors who received five hundred dollars, went through the motions of questioning the poor guy, and off he went to the Bughouse. Maybe the warden didn't tell them what he wanted their finding to be, but how smart did a psychiatrist have to be to know that if he decided the guy was well enough to stay outside, the warden was going to decide not to call him in the next time he was handing around the five-hundred-dollar fees.

Dr. Roche's pleasant smile put me even more on guard. He was a handsome man, a couple of years younger than me, tall, slender, and immaculately dressed. His complexion was so smooth and clear that you were immediately put in mind of expensive creams used over a long period of time. To put me even further on guard, there was something almost feminine in the way he held his cigarette holder and pursed his lips. Never was a first impression wronger.

"You've been in a lot of trouble here in the prison, haven't you?" he said.

I told him that it came with the bit. "I don't think in terms of being in trouble," I said. "But it seems to be a way of life with me."

It turned out that his personal secretary had left to get married, and with the country at war, an adequate replacement had been impossible to come by at the salary that was being offered. The job was to type up the records of his interviews with prisoners and, since Dr. Roche was only there for two or three hours a day, take care of the office while he was away.

"Why me?" I asked.

Because, he said, there was one other requirement which was more important than a mere ability to type. Absolute confidentiality. From a study of my record he had concluded that I was a man who knew how to keep his mouth shut.

Dr. Roche was one of the leading psychiatrists in Philadelphia. He had an extensive private practice, was on a number of hospital staffs, and he also taught at the University of Pennsylvania. A wealthy man in his own right, he had married a woman from an even wealthier Main Line family. But where others in his field talked about rehabilitation and then turned up their noses at the relatively low pay scale offered by the prison system, Dr. Roche put himself right on the line. In New York State, you know, a grandiose plan was put through the legislature for establishing a clinic at Sing Sing that was to take inmates from all five state prisons and several of the reformatories as well. As part of the enabling statute, the law was changed so that sex offenders would be given indeterminate sentences running from one day to life, on the expectation that they were going to be given massive treatment by six full-time psychiatrists. The whole thing fell apart—and, in fact, turned into a disaster—because the state was never able to get the psychiatrists.

Dr. Roche was different. Although he commanded as high a fee, I suppose, as anybody in the business, he had taken the criminal law as his field of expertise and so he went where the criminals were. In later years, when I was in Attica studying Supreme Court decisions, it always gave me a particular thrill to see the Supreme Court itself quoting from Dr. Roche's masterwork, *The Criminal Mind.* He had started writing that book while I was working for him, and I could recognize some of the quotes from the chapters I had typed up for him.

Dr. Roche was some man. As fragile and delicate as he looked, he had the courage of a lion. Some inmate who had gone on a rampage would be brought into the office, bound and cuffed, and the first thing Dr. Roche would do was order the guards to uncuff him and, with a wave of the hand, send them away. After the guards had left, shaking their heads, the doctor would invite the prisoner to sit down, give him a cigarette, and smile at him as one human being to another who had found themselves in a ridiculous situation. It never failed. No matter how disturbed the inmate seemed to be, he would always respond with a smile of his own.

After every interview, whether it was by appointment or on an emergency basis, Dr. Roche would walk the prisoner back to his cell himself, and the impression you always had was not of a man under guard but of two friends having a pleasant chat.

As in all prisons, the Pennsylvania system was a part of the political labyrinth in which everybody from the warden on down owed his job to a political sponsor. A man named Dr. Goddard, who was connected with the industrial department, was the political powerhouse who really ran the place. I never did find out what the "doctor" meant, but I do know that he was able to get anything he wanted, not only where the industries were involved but from the parole board and from the governor himself. Dr. Roche alone had the wealth, the position, and the personal reputation to rise above all political considerations. Since the governor's only interest was in avoiding trouble—all any administration wants from the prison system is that it remain invisible—the warden's principal interest was in security and control.

Dr. Goddard knew enough to leave Roche strictly alone, but the rough-and-tumble Warden Smith and the prissy-looking psychiatrist were at constant loggerheads. Dr. Roche never backed off an inch. Except once, and that was because I asked him to.

Since the medical people didn't work regular hours, there was a special dining room for them over on the hospital block. The first day I came to work in the office, Dr. Roche put me on the list. I lasted for exactly one meal. The warden came in, saw me sitting there, and threw a fit. I couldn't blame him, either. I was a permanent security risk. He was hardly going to allow me to walk over to the medical building and back alone every night, and he certainly wasn't about to detach a guard every night to stay with me.

My main interest, of course, was similar to that of the governor; to stay out of sight and out of trouble. And so if I didn't say a word about it to Dr. Roche . . . well, he had hired me because I knew how to keep my mouth shut, hadn't he? At least two or three months went by before, out of nowhere, he asked me how the food was over at the medical building.

"Gee," I said. "I wouldn't know about that."

"What do you mean?" he said. "I put you on the list myself."

When I told him what had happened, he uttered an oath and started to reach for the telephone. "Wait a minute, Doctor," I said. "It's all right for you to be feuding with the warden. But you're only here for a couple of hours in the morning, and he can make life miserable for me twenty-four hours a day."

Even though most of his arguments with Hard-Boiled Smith came over the pardoning of prisoners, Dr. Roche was no part of a bleeding heart. He was remarkable when it came to diagnosing inmates who were trying to fake insanity. "The only thing insane about him," he'd say, "is in thinking he'd be better off in a state mental institution than a state prison."

What an education I received. It was the doctor's practice to dictate his report into a recorder after every interview, and as a general rule I was able to wipe it out of my mind as I was typing. Some of the cases, however, were unforgettable. I don't know how many people know this, but there are pockets of Pennsylvania where voodoo plays a very important role in the community life. It was simply amazing how many of the cult members were serving life sentences for murders that had come about as a direct result of practicing their religion. They were mountain people mostly, humorless and gaunt, and, by and large, the least vicious people in the place. I was able to learn quite a bit from them about the witch doctors with their voodoo bibles and their incantations and their power to cast spells. The Pennsylvania branch of voodoo believes that it is possible to invoke an evil spirit against an enemy only by chanting an incantation over something that has come from his living body, like a fingernail paring or a strand of hair. It was surprising how often they seemed to murder an enemy while they were trying to get it—until you realized what their purpose had been from the beginning.

On the whole, I have always felt that there are as many causes for crime as there are criminals, and I found nothing in my experience with Dr. Roche to cause me to change that opinion. Except, of course, where you are dealing with a common psychosis. Like, for instance, arson. If insurance isn't involved, you will find that arson is usually motivated by a sexual aberration. We had one guy there at Eastern who was serving a long term because his thing was to have sexual intercourse while he was watching the flames. He burned down half the barns in Pennsylvania before they caught up with him.

In certain ways, I seemed to intrigue the doctor every bit as much as he intrigued me. What impressed him most, I think, was the way I had been able to educate myself in prison. Both the interest I had in any kind of knowledge and the ability I had to absorb and retain it. For reasons which are fairly obvious, books on psychiatry weren't allowed in the prison. Dr. Roche, who was hardly a stickler for rules, was able to get around that quite easily. Once he was sure that he could trust me, he added the title "library assistant" to my duties and brought in books from his personal library for me to read. From time to time, when he was in a relaxed mood he would tell me about some of his more fascinating cases—detective thrillers of the mind—and, when he was finished, assign me what could be called collateral reading. I particularly remember a long discourse he gave me on the misuses of mesmerism in its early stages which had caused it to fall into disrepute for almost a century. Although he was an accomplished hypnotist himself, he still felt that hypnosis was of dubious value in dealing with the criminal mind. Not completely useless, but, unless the practitioner understood its limitations, more time-consuming than helpful. To complete the course, he recommended that I read the book *Rebel Without a Cause,* which is not the Jimmy Dean movie but a case history by psychiatrist Robert Lindner, who details how he attempted to uncover the hidden motivations of a murderer through the use of hypnosis.

About me, he said nothing. Oh, in the early months I had caught him studying me once, but all he did was smile and mutter the one word, "Michelangelo," in obvious reference to the dummy head. Jeez, I thought, remembering that I had said the same thing. Can this guy actually read your mind? That was what was so irritating about it. When you're working with a psychiatrist, a guy who knows, you keep waiting for him to tell you the magic secret about yourself.

Finally, after I had been with him for about a year, I used a discussion we were having about rehabilitation to ask the question that had been on my mind. "Doctor," I said, "what do you think about me? Do you think there's any hope that I'd be able to go straight if I were ever released?"

Just by the way he looked at me I could tell that he had been asking himself that same question for some time. "Willie," he said, "I think that banks will always present such a challenge to you that I have serious doubts that you wouldn't try to rob one as soon as you were out on the streets."

An honest answer, I thought to myself. That's my opinion too.

Out on the streets! You'll never know how beautiful those words can sound until you've been in jail for about a dozen years. My father died while I was in Eastern State. My aunt Alice died, my uncle John died, my uncle Jim died. I had been in prison for seven years when World War II started, and I was still there when it ended. If I say I gave myself a complete education while I was at Eastern State, remember that a child who had started public school on the day I entered would have graduated. As much as I admired Dr. Roche, the day never passed that I didn't long for my freedom.

Sooner or later, in one way or another, everything you learn about a prison has a way of being of use to you. Watch:

The prison doesn't exist where there isn't a group or two working on a tunnel, and the guys involved always know about each other. There was already supposed to be a tunnel going out from the 10 block. A few of my friends were involved in it, particularly a guy named Mickey Webb. Mickey had let me know that I would be cut in on it when they were ready to go. I wasn't exactly holding my breath. To my way of thinking, they were starting from too far back. Tunnels never work, anyway. There are just too many difficulties, not the least of which is getting rid of the dirt.

I was leaving the 7 block one day, just as I had done for ten years, when I suddenly became aware of how thick those outer walls were at the end of the cellblocks. Huge granite walls, a good six feet thick. And to make my pulse beat even faster, the guy who locked in the end cell—right there on the other side of the wall—was my friend Kliney. Because, just like that, the idea had come to me that if we could remove one of those huge slabs of granite from inside the cell, at floor level, and then replace it with a dummy frame, we would have ourselves a completely protected shaft leading right into and—better yet—underneath the yard.

I approached Kliney in the yard about a week later, and I said to him, "Kliney, what do you think of a tunnel out of your cell?"

To me, the 7 block was perfect. For one thing, it was the cellblock nearest to the wall on that side of the circle. We were only going to have to dig about ninety-five feet in order to tunnel under the wall and come out on the grass lawn that sloped down between the prison and Fairmount Avenue. But that wasn't the primary reason. I was the only man in that prison, remember, who had been in the sewer, and I was very sure that the bend of the horseshoe would have to come pretty much directly under Kliney's cell. And I'll tell you why. Connected to the 7 block was a building which consisted of several small shops. Between that building and the end of the cellblock there was only a very little space, and it had been my observation in going through the sewer that all of the attached buildings had been built out just far enough so that they would cover the sewer system.

Which still wouldn't have meant that much if I hadn't known something else about the sewer to make that kind of information infinitely more valuable. I knew that it was made out of bricks. Can you see what that meant to me? It meant that once we had a tunnel started, we could dig down until we hit the sewer, take out a few of those bricks, and we would have ourselves a permanent dirt-disposal unit.

Although Kliney only had a year or two left on his sentence by this time, he was very interested. As I've said, Kliney was the kind of a guy who liked to be involved in things. I had been counting on that. Particularly with the cons who had reputations.

He thought it over for perhaps two weeks and then told me he was willing to give it a try. At the beginning there were just the two of us. In fact, until he was able to get the block out, Kliney had to do it pretty much by himself. At night. Between bed checks. And it didn't take as long as we had expected. "Geez," he told me after only a few days, "I think this is going to be a helluva lot easier than I thought." The builders hadn't used solid six-foot widths of granite, as I had somehow assumed; they had used three separate blocks, held together by mortar. "Most of the mortar is so old it's like powder," Kliney told me. "You can almost lift it out with a spoon."

After he had the first block out, the rest of it was easy. The real problem, as always, was getting rid of them. Kliney's job in the plaster shop made that comparatively easy too. For one thing, he had access to a wheelbarrow which he used to wheel bags of plaster around the prison. The blocks weren't that heavy but they were big enough to be unwieldy, and he needed my help in lifting them onto the wheelbarrow. We'd cover them over with a big burlap cloth and Kliney was able to get rid of them in a dumping grounds over in the corner of the prison grounds.

How was I able to get into his cell to help him? Ah, that was another of the reasons why Kliney's cell was so perfect. In every cellblock there were two doors. A steel, barred door leading into the center, and a regular door at the far end of the block which led directly into the yard. That was the door that was used in the normal traffic for yardout and also by the work forces leaving in the morning on their way to the shops.

Because of the small shops attached to the 7 block, there was always a certain amount of traffic in and out that door during the free hours. And a lot of visiting back and forth. I could go into his cell without being conspicuous, and the cells were so deep as the result of the workshops that had originally been built back there that even if somebody came in from the yard while we were working it would have been impossible for them to see what we were doing.

Theoretically, of course, you were always under surveillance by both the guard on duty in the center, who had an unobstructed view down the full length of the cellblock, and by the cellblock officer. The center guard could hardly see into the back of the cell, though, and the cellblock officer would usually be seated at his desk, just inside the steel door, conversing with a few inmates.

In other words, it wasn't that difficult for us to load the granite blocks onto the wheelbarrow, and it wasn't that unusual for Kliney to be seen wheeling it out of the door on the way to a job.

After all three blocks had been removed, Kliney made a thin wooden frame, filled it with plaster, and then painted the plaster and the wooden edges with the same paint he had used on the walls of the cell. To

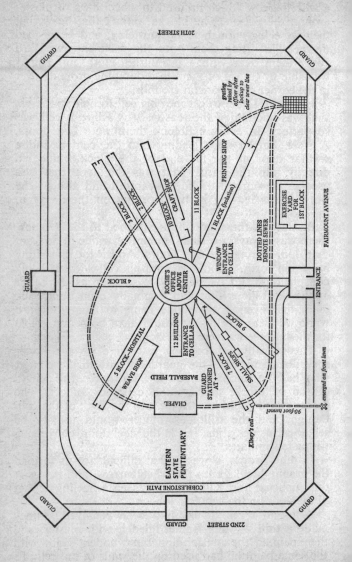

get into the tunnel once the digging began, all we had to do was lift the frame out and slip in through the open shaft.

Roche's office was on the gallery directly above the center, and since the center gallery was connected to the galleries of both the 7 block and the 5 block— the only cellblocks which had galleries—I was able to get away in the afternoon without having to pass through the center. My typing had become so good by then that I could let the recordings collect during the week and catch up on it by working all day on Saturday and Sunday.

While we were looking for the sewer, though, it was necessary to get rid of the dirt. We would take it out to the yard in small amounts, sprinkle it on the ball field, and shuffle it around with our feet until we had covered it over. Slow and dangerous work. To help us, we decided to put a couple of others in on it. The guys from the Hawley bank robbery were gone by then. Johnny Barr and the Polack thought it over for a couple of days and decided it was just too dangerous. And so we took in a couple of Philadelphians, Freddie Tenuto and Bocchi. I had got to know Tenuto because he locked in the 7 block. Bocchi was Tenuto's buddy. Both of them worked in private shops, which enabled them to get around the institution pretty easily.

Now, Tenuto was the kind of guy I normally would have stayed away from. He was known as The Accommodation Killer because he had been caught on a murder he had committed as a favor to a friend. He was a short, stocky, swarthy man, with jet-black hair and hard black eyes. A gun for hire. A man without fear. A dangerous man but, nevertheless, a man who was accustomed to taking orders. I felt that I could handle him, and I did. (It is possible that Tenuto did me the greatest disservice that was possible for any one man to do to me, and that he did it out of the mistaken belief that he was helping me. But—if he did—that came years later. We'll get to it.)

Although Bocchi was built very much along the same lines as Tenuto, his personality was entirely different. Bocchi was a good-natured fellow with mischievous eyes. Always ready to laugh and make the rest of us laugh. A good man to have working with you underground.

Within a very short time we were able to find the sewer and from there the work went much more quickly. But not that quickly. The tunnel was only a little over three feet in diameter, and for that reason alone no more than two of us could work down there at the same time. A front man, who would scoop the dirt into empty plastic bags supplied by Kliney, and a back man, who would crawl back and dump it into the sewer. We worked in our shorts. To dig, we had a shovel with the handle sawed off almost at the base, and the lack of air made the digging laborious. Even if the tunnel had been larger, it would have been very rare that all four of us could have got away at the same time. More often than not, we would be working alone.

We picked up bits and pieces of lumber wherever we could to shore the tunnel up as we went along. It wasn't a solid shoring by any means. Lumber wasn't that easy to come by. The best we could do was space it out so that in case of a cave-in only a small portion of the tunnel would collapse. For light, we strung together a complicated system of extension cords. The current came from the light socket in Kliney's cell. See, you were permitted to have a lamp in your cell, and Kliney had pulled his little table over so that it was sitting right there by the wooden frame. We just pushed the extension cord under there, tapped onto the lamp cord, and it was perfectly disguised. We had it rigged so that it could be disconnected at the base of the cell before we came back up.

It was common knowledge that the prison had been built upon what had once been farmland— Cherry Hill it had been called—and as the tunnel progressed underneath the yard we began to hit moist spots, and an occasional small puddle of water from the natural springs that were all around the area. The farther the tunnel extended, the slower it went. There was a period of perhaps ten days where we just couldn't get our hands on any scrap lumber. But finally, after something over six months, we knew we had to be very close to the wall. The work turned feverish. In short order we hit the wall and began to dig down to get underneath it. I was down there every afternoon. Kliney was beginning to look pale and haggard. He was slipping down during the night, between the hourly bed checks, even though he could only get in fifteen or twenty minutes' work at a crack.

He was down there alone during the night when he hit a main spring, and the tunnel began to fill up with water. For once, all four of us went down together the next morning to have a look. Although the tunnel wasn't completely flooded, the water was up to within a foot of the top and, as far as we knew, still rising. When we got back to Kliney's cell we were so discouraged that we were ready to seal it off and abandon the thing completely. By the time we left, however, we had decided there was nothing to lose by waiting five or six days to see whether the water might have begun to recede.

It hadn't. But it hadn't got any higher either. It had leveled off, we found, at exactly the point at which we had originally seen it. Immediately we stripped down to our shorts and went splashing in. When I got to the wall, I bent over and began to dig into the mud with my bare hands. Not so much digging it up as brushing it away and leaving it to the guy behind me to take it from there. In a couple of days we reached the bottom of the wall and began to go underneath. The wall itself was only about five feet in width, but it was a curved wall flaring out sharply at the bottom and we knew that the base was going to be considerably wider than that. It sure was. About ten feet wider. Now, fifteen feet is quite a distance. As hard as we tried to dam off the tunnel under the wall, it was impossible to keep the water from seeping in. Every time you came down there you had to clear out the mud and water again. After we were more than halfway under, it became impossible to keep it clear. Instead of having a foot of air above the water line, we were working in inches. Under those conditions, it wasn't safe to work alone.

There always had to be another man there to pull you out if anything happened. The closer we got to the outside of the wall, the slower the work progressed. There were days that it could be measured by inches.

It was a backbreaking job, and so when the word was passed that we were outside the wall we were all so excited that we went down the next day, all four of us at various times, and took turns digging upward. Either the dirt was looser out there under the grass or, with success so close at hand, we had more energy. The only difficulty was that in digging upward, the dirt kept falling into your eyes, practically blinding you. On the second day, we had a board that caught the dirt, and it went so well that on the third day we began to see the first signs of the root system of the grass. Actually, it was Tenuto and I who were working down there at the time. We went back up, got the others, and informed them it was just a matter now of punching through.

So we talked it over and came to two decisions. We were going to go in the morning. We had to make it fast because the water was undermining the hole outside the wall at such an alarming rate that we were afraid the whole thing might collapse on us.

What made it such a difficult decision was that we were going to have to go without any help from the outside. No waiting car, no change of clothing, no hideout. If the prison hadn't been so close to the city it would have been out of the question.

The other three were all from Philadelphia, and they had people, reasonably close by, to go to. Tenuto and Bocchi wanted me to go with them. They were talking about starting a bank-robbery mob under my direction, and that was the last thing I wanted. Their friends were all well-known police characters, exactly the kind of people who were rousted whenever the police needed to make a good arrest. My old apartment was only about a mile away. My best bet, it seemed to me, would be to contact Eddie Saunders.

The other decision was to put the Mickey Webb people into it. They would have put us in on their beat. We had no choice but to invite them in on ours. And that limited our options even further. There was a free period between breakfast and the time everybody left their cells to go to work. I passed the word to Mickey during yardout to tell his people to head for Kliney's cell when they left the mess hall. That's all I told them. The mess hall jutted out from the center on the other side of the 7 block and that was going to make it relatively easy.

Counting Mickey himself, there were eight of them. Very quickly, we told them exactly what the conditions were down there, and also that it was going to be every man for himself once we were out. That was it, and make up your mind right now. Every one of them was game.

I was the fourth one through. By the time I got under the wall, the grass had been punched through and I could look up and see the clear blue sky. I stood up and high behind me I could see the outside of the wall. A second later, I popped my head through, grabbed ahold of the ground, and began to pull myself up.

Not in a million years would you believe it! The Eastern State Pen, as I have already said, takes in two long blocks on Fairmount Avenue from Twentieth to Twenty-second streets, which means that Twenty-first Street ends at Fairmount. How could we have possibly known that Twenty-first and Fairmount was the end of a walking beat for two different city patrolmen? Or that both of them would have arrived there at exactly the same time to report in on the police box?

There I was, halfway out of the hole and staring right into the faces of both of them. Well, if I was stunned, they were absolutely thunderstruck. Kliney, Tenuto, and Bocchi were already out and running east along the lawn, but it had taken these two cops so long to react that they were only just beginning to draw their guns. I ran across the lawn, jumped down, and started running west on Fairmount. Wringing wet from head to foot and covered with mud. I guess I must have charisma or something. These two cops ignored everybody else and took out after me. Both

227

of them. And while they were both chasing me, everybody else was pouring out of the hole and running the other way, too.

A couple of blocks up, there was this factory with a red brick wall all around it. They were only about half a block behind me, out in the middle of the street, plenty close enough to start shooting. I'm running as fast as it's possible to run when you're squishing mud out of your shoes, and I can see the bullets taking chinks out of the brick wall. So close to me, front and back, that it was a miracle I wasn't hit.

Three blocks or so later, I turned north alongside another factory building, dove into the side entrance through a storm door, and tugged at the factory door. It was locked. The goddamn factory hadn't opened yet. All I could do was squat down in the corner so that I was below the window of the storm door and hope that the cops would run past. "He's in there," I heard someone yell. Wouldn't you know that a citizen up the street had seen me. And, the way things were going, that it would have to be a good citizen.

The cops came in with their guns pointed at me and hollering for me to come out. All right. Out I came. And I kept on coming. They kept backing up and warning me not to come any closer, and I kept coming right at them. They were scared to death, and I was so completely frustrated that I was going to take the pistol away from one of them or get shot trying. The way I felt at that moment I would have welcomed getting shot. They might very well have accommodated me, too, but just as I was about to make a leap, a police cruiser turned the corner. Not because they had been alerted but, here again, as I discovered later, by sheer accident. Just making their normal rounds.

They came jumping out of the car, and all I could think was, Oh shit. Shit, shit, shit!

By the time they had taken me down to the stationhouse there was a general alarm out all over Philadelphia. Nine of the others were captured before the morning was over. Everybody except Tenuto and Bocchi. They were picked up two months later in New York.

When the ten of us were taken back to the prison, Hard-Boiled Smith was waiting for us, livid with rage. "You sonofabitch," he screamed at me. "I ought to put a bullet in your head and give you a third eye!" If nobody else had been there I think he would have, too, because he blamed me for the whole thing. "I knew something like this had to happen," he kept roaring, stamping around. Well, I was never going to have a chance to ruin his record again, I could bank on that. And neither were any of the others. "You're never going to get out of isolation as long as you're here, none of you. You're all going to rot there!"

For the time being, though, isolation was too good for us. We were thrown into the hole, which was a narrow, windowless concrete building containing about fifteen tightly packed cells. The cell doors were made up of thick vertical bars, broken by a continuous opening, measuring about four and a half inches, which ran the entire length of the building. It was through this opening that the guard handed us our food. A cup of water and three slices of bread in the morning, a cup of water and three slices of bread at night. It was a guard who told me that the war was over in Europe. May 7, 1945; VE Day. We had started the tunnel only a couple of weeks after D Day—June 6, 1944—and had broken out on April 3, 1945. While we had been digging that tunnel, the whole war against Hitler had been fought and practically won.

By the time we were taken back to the isolation block we were all so weak we could hardly stand. And, still, it wasn't the lack of nourishment that was the worst part of it, it was the absence of tobacco. The only thing that saved us from going crazy was that one of our friends cut a hole in the thin, dislike ventilator on the roof just large enough to slip some cigarettes and matches through. One at a time. We'd smoke them down to the last quarter of an inch and then we'd grind the last bits of tobacco into the dirt. It was a risky thing for him to do because there was a high tower above the front door to the prison, overlooking everything, and it was no secret that the cigarette smuggling went on. Periodically, the holes would be plugged up. Always, somebody else would come along to make new ones.

With so many of us in there, the tower guards had undoubtedly been alerted. But still . . . I'm not sure they didn't deliberately avert their eyes. It's funny where a man's sense of compassion—which really means his sense of common humanity, doesn't it?—will show itself. The guards in the hole weren't picked because they were known to have any compassion, and yet there were a couple of times when a guard "accidentally" dropped a couple of cigarettes and a book of matches right in front of the door after he had passed the bread and water through. It wasn't something that was done very often, but I had heard of it happening before. An unexpected treat like that is not easily forgotten, and the inmates will always find ways to show their gratitude after they are back in the general population.

We weren't back in isolation more than a week when we were awakened in the early morning by a series of revolver shots. Hard-Boiled Smith had come back from a banquet, roaring drunk, and he was taking potshots at the rats which infested the old corridors. Rats, huh? We knew it wasn't rats he was thinking about when he had come bombing into the block with his gun. "I'm going to kill all these bastards who tried to ruin me," he was shouting while the guards were coaxing him out the door. "And after I've killed them, I'm going to knock their goddamn heads off!"

After Tenuto and Bocchi had been returned, we were taken out and lined up in the corridor. And then we were cuffed, marched out into a prison van, and driven to the courthouse.

Who was sitting there, waiting for us, but my old nemesis, Judge McDevitt. We had been indicted for prison breach, he informed us. "And," he said, "we'll go to trial immediately."

I said: "Your Honor, I want to make a motion for a postponement. Nobody notified me that I had been indicted. I had no prior notice that these here proceedings were going to take place."

"Motion denied."

I said: "Your Honor, I have an attorney. I want a delay to permit me to phone my attorney and apprise him of the impending procedure."

He said: "I'm appointing a lawyer. He'll represent the whole bunch of you."

I said: "I have a motion pending. I want to get my own attorney. I have that right."

His face was turning red, that's how mad he was. "Who's your attorney?" he demanded. He knew who my attorney was, all right.

"Louis McCabe."

He instructed the clerk to call McCabe's office. The clerk came back with the word that attorney McCabe was in New York. "All right," His Honor said. "Let's proceed."

I said: "I want to appear in civilian clothes, not prison garb. This here is highly prejudicial."

"Motion denied."

"Your Honor, I move at this time for a delay so we can talk to the court-appointed lawyer and consult with him."

"You've had the indictment read to you. Motion denied."

We were going to be put on trial en masse, right there in our prison clothes. I kept putting up every squawk I could think of to stall for time. And also to make a record for the appeal. "Your Honor," I said. "I have some witnesses I have to subpoena here. I want some time to call some people who will contribute to my defense."

The hatred came steaming out of him. He banged the gavel down. "Motion denied."

There was only one other thing I could think of. "Your Honor," I said. "I have a feeling this court is prejudiced against me. I want a trial by a jury of my peers."

The first twelve veniremen were seated in the jury box without a single question being asked of them. The District Attorney said, "The jury is satisfactory to the prosecution." Our lawyer didn't say anything. Which made it even, because we didn't say anything to him.

We were found guilty and sentenced on the spot.

Everybody else got either one or two years. I had been charged with instigating the escape, and so I was given ten to twenty, which was not only excessive but downright illegal. Seven years was the most the law allowed.

Back in the corridor of the prison, we had a few minutes together while we were waiting for them to uncuff us and take us back to our cells. Since we all knew that we were never going to be taken off isolation as long as Warden Smith was there, there was widespread agreement that we should go on a mass hunger strike in order to be transferred to some other prison. I wasn't so keen on it. The trouble with hunger strikes is that eventually everybody gives in, and once you have capitulated you're worse off than ever. But no, everybody kept insisting that they would never capitulate. Especially Bocchi, whose idea it had originally been. "All right," I said, at last. "We'll go on a hunger strike."

The following morning the twelve of us refused to eat breakfast. The strike was on. For nine days not a one of us had a thing except water. On the tenth day, nine of them capitulated. By the thirteenth day, nobody was left except me.

On the fourteenth day, Warden Smith came down and stood outside my cell. "You goddamn fool," he said. "What are you trying to do, commit suicide?"

I was lying on the cot with my hands folded across my chest. So weak that I felt as if I were floating.

"No," I said. "I'm conducting a scientific experiment to find out how long it's possible to survive without food."

"All your so-called friends have given up. You know that, don't you?"

"Some guys want to live forever."

"They've deserted you, you goddamn fool. You've failed. It's over."

"So why are you here?"

He said: "I can have them feed you by force, you know. That's a sonofabitch, Willie. Take my word for it."

"It would be easier to have me transferred. You never wanted me in this prison anyway. Why the hell

232

don't you send me somewhere else and get rid of me."

"You're damn right I never wanted you. I'd have got rid of you the day they brought you back if I thought anybody would have taken you."

"You can tell them I don't eat very much. Just tell them I can go weeks and weeks on nothing but water. Months."

He looked at me, and just by the way he began to shake his head I could tell that I had won. "I'm going to have all of you sent out of this prison," he said, in an entirely different voice. "Jesus, don't I pity the warden that gets you."

"Is that a promise?"

"That's a promise."

Under those conditions, I told him, I'd eat.

No, I couldn't. "You can't start eating right away," he told me. "You're in pretty bad shape here. You oughta have a look at yourself, you're skin and bones. You know, I think those friends of yours were smuggling food among themselves right from the beginning. They all look too healthy to me."

He had the guard help me over to the hospital block, where they had me swallow a large metal ball. Jeez, I couldn't see where forced feeding could have been any worse than that. I almost choked on it. The ball is on the end of the string. They keep it down there for about twenty minutes and then they pull it up again. If I remember right, it was a test for acidity. They claim that after you refrain from food for any length of time the body begins to feed on itself.

For the first few days they fed me nothing except eggnogs and things like that. But, you know, even when I was able to take food again I ate without any appetite. Not then. Not ever. All my life, I had always had a very healthy appetite. From the time of the hunger strike, I have never needed more than one meal a day.

It took a while before the transfer came through, but Hard-Boiled Smith had given his promise and eventually word filtered down that we were being distributed among the three other Pennsylvania prisons.

During all this time, not a word had come from Dr.

Roche. I couldn't say that I blamed him. Or, even, that he blamed me. He understood me about as well as I understood myself, and he was never the kind of man who expected people to act against their nature. What it was, I think, was that I had compromised his position vis-à-vis Warden Smith. At any rate, he left Eastern State shortly after I did.

Before we left, Warden Smith did come back to say goodbye. What he actually said was, "I'm glad to get rid of you sonofabitches. I'm only sorry I didn't knock your goddamn heads off." I kind of liked old Hard-Boiled. He was a fair-minded man, and he kept his word.

The five of us who were considered the most dangerous were being sent to Holmesburg, a maximum-security prison from which nobody had escaped from the day it was built in 1894. Tenuto, Kliney, me, and two of the guys from the other group, Spence Waldron and Dave Aikens.

Sixteen months after we arrived there, all five of us broke out.

Langy the Rat

The escape from Holmesburg was my masterpiece because it was impossible. Nobody had ever escaped from there before. Nobody has escaped from there since. And we had to escape from the isolation block, which at Holmesburg meant complete and total isolation. It was so impossible that the warden refused to believe that we hadn't paid off the whole night shift. He fired about a dozen of them, maybe more. Almost everybody who had either been on shift that night or had worked in the isolation block during that day. In order to fire them he had to accuse them of various derelictions of duty, but the truth of the matter was that he couldn't believe we'd have even tried to escape in the way we did unless we had greased the way ahead of time.

What made it such a masterpiece was that without a master philosophy there could have been no master plan. The master philosophy was divided into two parts:

1/The strength of the prison's security could become its greatest weakness.

2/The weakest part of the escape plan could become its greatest strength.

It was my masterpiece, in a more classical sense, in that I was able to employ so many of the basic techniques that I had been using throughout my career, both as a bank robber and as an escape artist. And, on the other hand, because the whole thing depended in the end upon having enough flexibility to break the basic rule of the criminal's code and deliberately, with cold calculation, place the success or failure of the venture—my very life, in fact—in the hands of a rat.

Holmesburg County Prison, commonly referred to among cons as The Burg, was only ten or eleven miles from the heart of Philadelphia, but, since the suburban crawl hadn't started yet, that was enough to put it out in the sticks. The prison, which had been built from the same blueprints as Eastern State, stood all by itself across from the railroad tracks and directly atop a hard granite subsurface which made tunneling impossible. The wall was higher and more massive in every way than at Eastern. The surrounding area was flat and barren.

Holmesburg had a very bad name with the public as well as the criminal community because of the so-called Oven Deaths. Some years before I got there, the leaders of a prison riot had been thrown into the Hole, one of those cement boxes which freezes you in the winter and boils you in the summer. Prison riots traditionally occur on the hottest day of the year. As hot as it was, the donkey in charge had turned up the heat on them and four of the prisoners had been literally roasted.

Because of the hue and cry that had arisen, the

governor had been forced to step in and appoint Dr. Frederick Baldi, the medical director, as the superintendent. The warden, Robert Beverly, was allowed to hold on to his job and title, because he hadn't been there that day. Dr. Baldi was in full control, though, and he never for one second let anybody forget it.

You would think that a prison which was being run by a medical man would be a model of compassion and understanding. The very opposite was true. Dr. Baldi was gung-ho all the way. A few years earlier, there had been an attempt to bust out through the front door in the prison car, which was a pretty intrepid enterprise since they had the usual double-door system, with the inspection area in between. Even though the attempt was botched completely— five of the six would-be escapees were either killed or captured before they could get into the car and the other guy was stopped before the car reached the first door—Dr. Baldi immediately moved to discourage any further attempts. A bulletproof tower was constructed about the inner gate, with sally ports for the machine guns to enable the guards to cover the entire gatehouse area and beyond.

As soon as we were brought into his office, Dr. Baldi singled me out. "Sutton," he said. "If it was me, I wouldn't let you in the front gate of this prison. You're nothing but a troublemaker, and I know you're going to try to cause trouble here. But I have my orders from Harrisburg, and I have to obey orders too. I want to tell you this: This prison has been up for a hundred years, nobody has broken out yet, and nobody is going to. Now, all the officers here have been alerted to your past record, and I guarantee you that if you cause me any trouble they'll blow your head right off your body."

So what else is new? And yet, there was something about the way it came out of Dr. Baldi, who had the look of your friendly neighborhood general practitioner, that made it sound like something out of a class-B movie. Instead of looking hurt and innocent, as I normally would have, I found myself saying, out of the side of my mouth, "The jail hasn't been built that could hold me, Warden. I'll walk out of here through the front door."

And just as I expected, he snapped back, "Go ahead and try. Just try. The last guy who tried it got his head blown off, and that's just what will happen to you."

Kliney and Aikens were assigned to one of the regular cellblocks. Tenuto, Spence Waldron, and myself were sent to the isolation block, and Baldi left us with no illusions that the assignments weren't going to be permanent.

Although Holmesburg had the same basic pattern as Eastern State, with the seven cellblocks radiating out from the hub, the nomenclature was sometimes different. The center was usually referred to as the hub, and that's exactly what it was. The guards on duty could not only see into all the wings, they were connected to every part of the prison through the most modern communications systems and devices on the market. The cellblocks were designated by letter rather than by number. The A block—which was where the 7 block was at Eastern Pen—was the isolation block.

Isolation meant exactly that. It meant that we were never to leave the block. We didn't even go to the mess hall. Our meals were brought over by a food-dispensing truck and served to us by the cellblock guard. Even with him, the security precautions weren't relaxed for a second. There was a double-locked door off the rim of the hub. Not a barred door like at Eastern, but a solid steel door with only a small round peep-hole window. Another guard would open the door for him and then lock it immediately behind him. When he was ready to leave he would call to the hub and they would do it all over again. You couldn't take the key away from him, in other words, because he never carried one.

The same thing was done when they were taking the cell count during the night. Two guards would come down from the hub, one of them would let the other one in, lock the door behind him, and open it again when he was finished. A cell check was made every half hour.

Once a day they took us out, through a somewhat smaller steel door, to the exercise yard. The cell guard didn't have a key for that door, either. When we were ready to go out, another guard would open it from the outside and then step inside and relock it. One hour later, he'd do it over again in reverse. And even there, we weren't really out of the block, we were only out in the air. A fifteen-foot wire fence ran between the A block and the adjoining block, which limited us to a small triangular area extending only about half the distance to the wall. To sum it up, we were between a wire fence and a locked door and under the direct surveillance of the cell guard and all three towers on the western side of the wall. A handball court had been built against the adjoining building. Other than that, about the only thing we could do was play a little softball.

The main security weakness at Eastern, you will remember, had been that extensive industrial setup which gave so many of the inmates freedom to move around. At Holmesburg there was no movement because there was no industry. Most of the inmates in the regular cellblocks were short-termers in for minor crimes, and the only shops were those that were needed to maintain the prison itself. The only way an inmate could make any money was to turn himself into a guinea pig for the cosmetics industry. A product which was still in the testing stage would be plastered onto the volunteer's back for several days to see whether it caused a rash or anything, a service for which he would get paid from five to twenty-five dollars. I'd have rather been back in the sewer.

There was one thing they had to let us out of the isolation block for, though. Medical treatment. A special rule had been set up for me there too, as I discovered a few days after I arrived, when I began a run a raging fever and an officer was called to take me to the medical block. The preliminary tests revealed such an extremely high blood count that the doctor ordered me right into the prison hospital. I hadn't been there for twenty minutes before Warden Beverly came storming in to order that I be taken right back to my cell. It didn't matter that I was

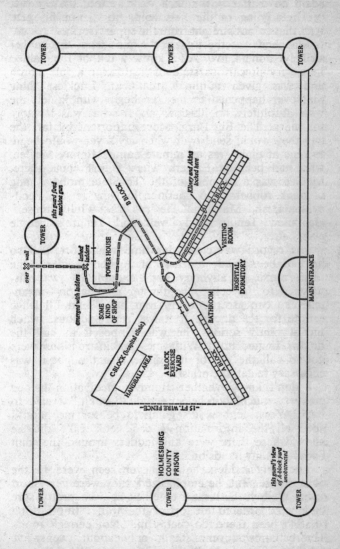

HOLMESBURG COUNTY PRISON

this guard's view
of A-block yard
unobstructed

—15 FT. WIRE FENCE—

HANDBALL AREA

A BLOCK
EXERCISE YARD

C-BLOCK (hospital clinic)

SOME
KIND
OF SHOP

emerged with ladders

scaled
ladders

over X wall

this guard fired
machine gun

POWER HOUSE

B BLOCK

A BLOCK

BATHROOM

D BLOCK

Kiley and Akins
locked here

VISITING
ROOM

HOSPITAL
DORMITORY

MAIN ENTRANCE

TOWER
TOWER
TOWER
TOWER
TOWER
TOWER
TOWER
TOWER

239

there under doctor's orders, the hospital was out of bounds for me. "He's not to be brought in here again no matter how sick he is," he told the orderly. "If he's going to die he's going to die in his cell. And that comes straight from the supervisor."

Maybe it was the lingering effects from the hunger strike, I don't know. All I know was that I remained in a very precarious state of health for a full month and was given minimal treatment. Luckiest thing that ever happened to me. To begin with, it left me with absolutely no illusions about what was in store for me at The Big Burg. More important by far, the guy they would send over when my fever would begin to rage at night was an inmate named Jimmy McGee, who had been at Eastern when I first came there. McGee was a member of the Tri-State mob, a gang of bank robbers who operated in New Jersey, Pennsylvania, and Maryland. He was from Philly himself. He knew Tenuto fairly well and Tenuto's people even better.

His record was clean, his time was short, and so he had been made a trusty and given a job as the night nurse. If anybody got sick, McGee was dispatched to the cell to administer medication—meaning take two aspirins every four hours and I'll leave a note for the doctor. If it was really serious, which meant *really* serious, he was supposed to call the doctor immediately. With me, his instructions were not to call the doctor unless he also thought it was necessary to call the priest.

I don't know whether Jimmy's medication helped me very much, but he sure did. "Lookit," I said to him. "You see how it's going to be for me here. I need all the information I can get." Like did he know where there were any ladders around the joint I could get my hands on.

The only ladders he had ever seen were in the powerhouse. But, he emphasized, they were very short ones. Well yeah, lashed together he was pretty sure they would reach the top of the wall. "But I don't see how you could do that, Bill." Not enough room. The cellar was very small, only about twenty-five or thirty feet, and although it exited into the yard, it was a side exit and you'd bump right into a small building only a few feet away.

In order to get enough room, you'd have to lay the ladders out along the alley in between the two buildings. "And that's impossible too, because now you're out in the yard between two towers and they'd see you doing it."

When you have nothing to lose, nothing's impossible. I wasn't a bit discouraged. It was only my first week in Holmesburg and I already knew where I could get a ladder. More important still, I had a pair of outside eyes. Because of the administration's preoccupation with security where I was concerned, they had—incredibly—given me access to one of the few men who could move around freely at night. The security was already beginning to turn against itself.

No, I wasn't discouraged at all.

The only thing I had to figure out was how it was going to be possible to lash two ladders together in the prison yard, march it up to the wall, and climb over without getting my head shot off.

Given everything you know about me and my M.O., the answer that came to me after a minimum of thought should be obvious.

What was the problem? I had to create a momentary confusion in the minds of the tower guards. I had to make them think I had a right to be out there doing something with a ladder.

Who is accepted with the least amount of question? That's right. A man in a uniform.

What is the uniform most likely to be accepted in a prison? That's right, a guard's uniform.

Where would I be able to get a guard's uniform? Hell, the prison was just full of them. They could be found hanging from any officer in the place. Put a gun on him and I'll bet he'd be only too happy to give it to you.

I had planned on going over the wall between two guard towers once before, remember. The plan to escape from Eastern under cover of a heavy fog. In a heavy fog, the guards would be able to make out nothing except some uniformed figures. A certain suspicion was going to be aroused in even the most trusting of breasts when I started to climb up the ladder, but if we had the guards' uniforms we'd also have the bodies they came from. If worse came to worst, we'd be able to use them as hostages.

I began to watch the weather patterns studiously. Nothing showed up like the fog that sometimes blanketed Eastern. What did show up was just as good. Maybe even better. A heavy winter snowstorm. Sure it was better. Snowstorms knock things down and put things out of order. You think of a heavy snowstorm and you think of men going out on emergency repairs. Some officers lugging a ladder to the wall was still going to cause the tower guards to stop and think, but that was just what I wanted, wasn't it. To keep them just confused enough, just uncertain enough, to make them reluctant to start shooting. To sow confusion and reap inaction. Every time you fail to do something that you are charged with doing, the easier it becomes not to do it when your suspicions are aroused again. Because now you have a vested interest in defending that decision not to have acted earlier. You *want* to believe that you had been right.

It was right there where I got the inspiration that made the whole thing go. I wouldn't lash the two ladders together in the alley. I would do it out in front of the powerhouse as if I had every right in the world to be there.

The first question that was put into their minds would be a very mild one, off at a safe distance, posing no immediate threat.

That much of it came together for me in my first couple of weeks there.

I had known from the first day that the only way out was through the steel door and into the hub. And even though the door was never kept open for more than a couple of seconds during the cell checks, I could see how it could be done. As you came into the cellblock, there was a bathroom-shower on one side and the smaller steel door leading out to the exercise yard on the other. The cells didn't begin until you were about fifteen feet in. With good reason. There's something about solid steel that fascinates security people and this one was a hell of a specimen, studded all around with big rivets. But by going for all that steel and so little window they had given up some crucial areas of visibility. The reason for all that dead space was that the guard looking down from the hub couldn't see anything until then. The night guard peering in from directly outside would be able to see a great deal more, of course, but even with him there would be a blind spot in the corner, and that's where we would be crouching.

The security was turning against itself again.

The timing would have to be perfect. We would have to strike swiftly and take over the hub before anybody could react. Even during the daytime, the hub was the stronghold. If you had control of the hub at night, you had it all.

We were going to have to know exactly what we were going to be confronted with, though, and McGee was willing to check it out for me. He was able to tell me, by degrees, that there was always a minimum of eight officers at the hub at night, including a captain. He was also able to pretty much diagram the whole communications setup for me. The only thing he never could find out for me was where they kept the guns.

None of the officers ever carried a gun, not even the captain, he could tell me that. That was security, too. If no officer has a pistol, no convict can take it away from him. Obviously, there would have to be weapons around somewhere within easy reach. At Sing Sing there was an arsenal all along the wall up on the gallery, and the gallery was always patrolled. In case of a frontal assault, they had the high ground covered. At Eastern State they had a tightly packed arsenal of rifles and guns in what could best be described as a compartmentalized vault behind the desk in the center. You could see them through a slit in the front.

The gallery of the hub was never patrolled at night, McGee told me. There was a small safe behind the captain's desk, he said, but there was no way he could find out what was kept there. My guess was that the guns would have to be somewhere on the gallery. Apparently they felt that any uprising that occurred during the night would have to take place within the cellblock. Just the kind of overconfidence I was hoping to find all along the line.

It was looking better all the time. I had always known that I was going to have to get a gun smuggled in to me. One gun against none was a very effective voting majority. The only trouble was that as much as I racked my brains, I couldn't figure out how I was going to do it.

In addition to gathering all the information that he could, McGee was also a reliable messenger to Kliney and Aikens. Whenever I wanted to talk to him all I'd have to do was complain to the night guard about a reoccurrence of my fever.

And so the summer passed. And the fall. Another winter was on us and I still hadn't figured out how I was going to get a gun smuggled in to me in isolation. But for months I had been working on an idea.

There was one person on the isolation block who came and went every day. Langy the rat. We had heard about him before we got there. Jack Lang had worked with a band of robbers. The others had all received long sentences and Langy, as a first offender, had got off cheap. Most of them were at Eastern, and I had got to know them pretty well. The story was that Langy had been picked up first and had put his finger on them.

Langy was on the isolation block not as punishment but for his own protection. In order to give him something to do, without exposing him to the rest of the prison population, they had given him an outside job. He was a painter, and they kept him busy working on the prison property outside the walls.

A rat in prison is completely ostracized. The stand-up guys despise him and those who are probably worse than him, the not inconsiderable number who had informed and hadn't been found out, are always eager to show how clean their own hands are by being harder on him than anybody else. Anybody seen talking to him is immediately set straight. All you have to hear in prison is, "Be careful of this guy . . ." and you know the guy is wrong.

That's just the way I felt. I'd see him go out every

244

morning with his pail and his brush and I'd think, I hope somebody gets that rat.

He'd come back early sometimes and since they never locked him in his cell—why bother to lock the cell of a guy you're sending out of the prison every day?—he'd wander around and help give out the food and things like that. The others would either give him the silent treatment or insult him. I gave him the silent treatment for quite a while too. But eventually I began to acknowledge that he was there. I'm generally like that with people. The same thing with cops who land in jail. A cop in jail is the loneliest man in the world. The guards hate him because he went lousy, and the cons hate him because he was a cop. I never felt that way. I always felt that a cop has a living to earn like anybody else. Even when I was in Sing Sing I took the chance of antagonizing the other inmates by talking to the rogue cops.

And there was something else that made me relent a little toward Langy. As much as I hated a professional stool pigeon, I could realize from my own experience that almost anybody would cave in under the kind of beating I took. I think you have to be abnormal to withstand such punishment. I was proud of myself for knowing I'd die before I'd talk, and how could I have been so proud of myself if I hadn't known that 999 out of 1000 couldn't have done it?

When everything is said and done, though, I began to talk to Langy because as time went by I could see that he was my only hope. He was a pleasant-spoken guy and fairly good-looking. Blond, very slimly built, gaunt at the cheeks. And vivid blue eyes. That's what I usually look at first, the eyes. For some reason, I've done that all my life. I don't know what I look for, even, but I get an initial impression and I've been right often enough to trust my instincts. With Langy it was hard to tell. There was an almost squirrel-like alertness about him which undoubtedly came out of fear but made him look more like a rat than ever.

So anyway, Langy would come over to my door and talk to me because I gave him a little consideration. And it developed in my mind during the course of these talks that this guy would do anything to prove that he was no rat. He swore to me that two of his partners had been arrested before he had and, being seasoned criminals who knew what the score was, they had been smart enough to make deals for themselves and then take advantage of the short sentence he had received as a first offender to make everybody else think it was him. "I don't know," I'd say. "They're giving you all this protection. . . ."

His story could have been true. It probably wasn't. But I was willing to let him convince me that it was true. My talking to him was a very big concession, and don't think that Tenuto and Spence Waldron didn't let me know about it. But I kept my own counsel. He was cultivating me because he knew that I could put the stamp of approval on him, and I was cultivating him because I had to be as sure as possible before I put the question to him. I guess we all want something. Langy wanted self-respect; I wanted a gun.

Before I went the final step, I drew him out by mentioning that he didn't seem to have too much money. I said, "Listen, if you need any, I figure to be able to give you something." I'd help him out, see, and then maybe he could help me out sometime.

He didn't want any part of money. "I don't have to get paid to help people if I could do something for them," he said. "What do you think I am?"

I said to him, "Well, would you help people out of prison if you had an opportunity?"

He sure would.

So I put it on him. "Would you help me out by bringing in a pistol?"

He thought for quite a while and then he said, "You know, it would be very easy for me to do that. You know, I carry a paint can out every day and a paint brush. Nobody searches me or anything. I don't think I'd have any difficulty at all."

"Well," I said. "I'll need a gun and I'll need some hacksaw blades."

"I'll bring them in for you," he said. He sounded almost grateful.

Tenuto and Waldron weren't. "Don't have anything to do with him," they said. "The rat sonofabitch will run right to the authorities. They'll set you up and blow your head off."

That was the risk. "I think I know a little about human nature with all the time I've done and all the people I've met. It might be a hell of a chance I've taken, but what the hell is left? We're buried here." And anyway, if anything happened the building was going to fall on me, not on them or anybody else.

It was now a matter of having somebody plant the pistol where Langy could pick it up. Before we had got around to that, one of those coincidences turned up that I thought was going to be very helpful. I got a surprise visit from Georgie Moore of the old Hawley mob, who had signed in as my brother. Georgie was hanging around with a bank robber named Chick Walsh and another guy. This Walsh had quite a reputation too. They had just taken a payroll out in Queens and they were looking at a couple of banks. Georgie, who knew me pretty well, wanted to know what I thought my chances were of busting out and joining them.

I said: "I'm going to be out of here in thirty days. Where are you living?"

He was living on Fifty-second Street over near Eighth Avenue.

"You're in the hottest place in New York." I groaned. "You got to get out of there. Get out of midtown. Don't do anything until I get out. Don't take any more crazy chances like coming here and saying you're my brother. You'll hear from me."

Well, it took more than the thirty days before we got the snowfall we were looking for. As far as Georgie was concerned, it didn't matter. When I got out, he was back in. I was thinking that the midtown address would be too hot for me. It also was too hot for Georgie. He took his time about moving out, the police had a lead on the payroll robbery, and they got thirty years apiece. (Years later, when we were all at Attica, I got both Walsh and Moore out on legal technicalities, which is another story entirely.)

In the meantime, we had laid the plans for planting the gun. Langy had started to paint the warden's house, and while the job was being done the warden had moved out. Langy drew us a little diagram of the area. Off to the side of the house there were three mailboxes set in a row, and Langy's idea was to pile a mound of dirt behind the concrete post of the middle one as a marker. All our outside man would have to do was shove the gun and the blades into it, and all Langy would then have to do was empty out his paint bucket before he left the job and he'd be able to scoop it up, dirt and all, on his way home.

Our outside man turned out to be Spence Waldron's girl friend. It could have been anybody, she just happened to come in to visit him. Spence had her cruise by the place in her automobile, and when she came back the next week she told him she had located it. We had already agreed that if she gave the word he was to tell her to plant the stuff five days later.

I tell you there were a million thoughts running through my mind. Spence and Freddie still didn't trust Langy. As far as they were concerned, it was just too pat that the warden should have vacated his house at that particular time. But I was absolutely determined to get out of that prison or get killed as quickly as I could.

Nevertheless, it wasn't until the day the gun was going to be planted that I called him over and said, "They're supposed to be there."

If they were there, he said with confidence, he'd get them.

The longest day of my life. Boy, I counted the minutes and I counted the hours until Langy came through the door that night, carrying his pail. He walked right by me and across to his cell. A few minutes later he came out and said to me, "I got 'em." He had decided at the last minute that it would be taking an unnecessary risk to come back into the prison with a pailful of dirt. Instead, he had wrapped the gun and the hacksaw blades tightly in cellophane and left enough paint in the can to cover them over.

"All right," I murmured. "I'll pick 'em up a little later."

Freddie locked on the same side that I did, but Waldron was up about four cells on the other side of the corridor. At the first opportunity I nodded my head to him and mouthed: "He's . . . got . . . them. He's . . . brought . . . them . . . in."

Spence just shook his head. Grimly.

Later on, I got them from Langy and I wrapped them up in cloth and hid it all under my mattress. Half a dozen blades and the pistol. Chambers filled. Now I figured if this guy is going to set me up they will probably come bouncing into my cell and knock my brains out. I waited that night and nothing happened. All through the following day. Nothing happened. The three of us waited. Langy knew nothing about our plan, remember. If the knockoff was going to come it would have to come right in the cell.

After a week, Tenuto arranged to have one of his brothers visit him so that he could explain to him that we needed a car to get out of there.

On the morning of February 10, 1947, it began to snow. It snowed very hard through the day and we all decided we were going to make the attempt that night. We had already cut our bars and put them back in place with putty and paint. (The cell guard, Greenwood, who wasn't a bad guy, got fired over that. According to the book, it was his duty to check the bars daily by running a hammer over them. That was the excuse that was used, anyway. He had never done it once from the day we got there. The over-confidence in their security again.)

At 1:00 A.M., the guard came in from the hub for his semihourly check, went up and down with his flashlight, and then went back to the hub.

That was our signal to get up and get dressed. Five minutes before the next check was due, we pulled out the bars and crept up to the steel door. I gave the pistol to Tenuto. We crouched down and waited. We were wearing our black prison pants and blue shirts, and thin blue windbreakers. I was also wearing a baseball cap which one of the other inmates on isolation had given me to keep the sun out of my eyes while I was playing handball.

Both the cellblock and the hub were kept dimly lit at that time of night. We could hear the two guards coming down from the hub. We could hear the key grate in the lock. As the door swung open we flung ourselves through. The plan was for Spence and me to bull both guards back with our first charge so that Tenuto could shoot through the gap and cover the five officers and the captain in the hub before they could make a move. It worked very nearly to perfection. One of the guards did manage to grab the side of the door and try to slam it shut, but it was purely a reflex action. Tenuto was already through and gone. All he succeeded in doing was jamming one of his own fingers very badly.

Five of the six guards in the hub were grouped around the desk, and the sight of Tenuto charging down at them, waving a gun, completely immobilized them. It would have immobilized me, too. Tenuto was a menacing enough figure even without a gun. Immediately, he ordered the captain to stand up and get in line with the others. Spence and I already had our two guys well under control. Stunned as they were, they had no idea whether we had a gun or not. I barked at them as if I had one, and they acted as if they were taking my word for it.

When we had them all together, we ordered them to line up in the exact center of the rotunda, away from everything. While they were obeying, there was a tapping on the door from the hospital block. It was Jimmy McGee, and he was there by sheer accident. He didn't have the slightest idea we were going that night. In order to protect him, we threatened him with all kinds of unpleasant things if he didn't do exactly as he was told and then ordered him to join the others.

The first thing Tenuto had done upon reaching the desk was grab the ring of keys from the wall. Now that everything was under control, he handed me the gun and went down to D block to get Kliney and Aikens. The captain looked positively sick and I could very easily guess why. He had been transferred from Eastern for bringing contraband in to a few of the inmates, and you could see him thinking who was going to be picked out as the prime suspect for bringing in that gun.

The question of what we were going to do about

Jimmy McGee was resolved quite neatly. To get to the powerhouse we had to go through the B block, and we locked him in one of the empty cells along the way.

Lying against the wall of the cellar, just as McGee had said, were the two ladders. Each of them about twenty-one feet in length. A spool of copper wire was in the bench drawer, just where he had told me. So were the hook and the rope.

Before we went out, I picked out the guard who was closest to me in size and ordered him to take off his coat and hat. Tenuto and Waldron did the same. Those three, plus two of the others, were then locked inside the little utility room. That left two guards and the captain. I told them that they were going to lead us out into the yard. "I'm going to give you your instructions," I said, "and you had better listen very carefully. If anything goes wrong we're taking you with us as hostages. If any shooting starts, you're going to be the first ones up the ladder." I didn't want to take them with us unless it was absolutely essential. I did want them to feel so relieved when we started up the ladder without them that they'd be more pleased about seeing us disappear than worried about our getting away.

Following my instructions, they carried the ladders out into the yard; the two guards out in front, the captain holding up the rear. The three of us in uniform walked directly behind the captain. Kliney and Aikens were to remain in the cellar for one minute before joining us.

There must have been a foot of snow on the ground, and it was still snowing very hard. Large snowflakes floating down softly. Not really very cold, but visibility every bit as poor as I could have hoped for. We turned the corner of the powerhouse and went all the way around to the front entrance before I handed the copper wire to the two guards and told them to lash the ladders together. As soon as the others joined us, Tenuto and Kliney bent down with them to make certain that the wire was being wound tight. The wall was only about thirty feet away, and while we weren't directly opposite the closest tower we weren't at very much of an angle from it either. Given the poor visibility and the dark background provided by the powerhouse, I felt that everything was going according to plan as far as the tower guards were concerned.

As far as the ladder was concerned, I had a worry that went well beyond how well the lashing job was done. One of McGee's most recent bits of information was that the back wall was five or six feet higher than it was out front, with much of that extra height being in the form of an overhang. In other words, a good foot and a half had been added to the flat surface at the top of the wall to provide a footwalk.

If the ladder failed to reach the overhang, there was going to be absolutely no way of getting over.

We were about to find out. The three guards were ordered to take the ladder in a straight line to the wall, walking neither away from the tower nor toward it. We stayed very close to them, all in a bunch. It wasn't until the ladder was being raised that the wall guard swung the searchlight toward us and shouted, "What's going on down there?"

"It's all right," I shouted back. "It's an emergency."

Immediately, he opened up with his machine gun, a long rat-tat-tatting blast that kicked the snow up all around our legs. "Tell him it's all right," I hissed to the captain, pushing him in front of me.

"It's all right," he shouted. "Don't shoot. We've got emergency repairs."

The guard recognized the captain's voice. There was no more shooting. And that wasn't all I had to be grateful for. Although I couldn't see to the top of the wall, I could tell by the angle at which the ladder set that it had reached above the overhang. Up we went, all five of us, one right in back of the other. I went first because I had the hook and the rope. Tenuto went last because before I started up I handed him the gun. The hook fit nicely around the overhang; I swung down the rope and dropped into the deep snow.

Now, we had always anticipated that if we succeeded in getting over the wall, the shooting would start. Although the machine gun couldn't be turned around, every guard carried an automatic rifle inside the tower. All he would have to do was step out, wheel around the railed platform encircling the tower, and start firing at us. We were slogging and scrambling through the snow in fairly close formation because the only thing on our minds was getting to the car. If anybody had just shot in our general direction there would have been a very good chance of his hitting somebody.

Incredibly, there was not a shot.

There can be no question that the psychological master plan directed at the tower guard worked to perfection. As a matter of fact, we got a bonus when the captain was forced to identify himself. The tower guard had challenged us, and the captain had said it was okay. He was in the clear.

I'd love to know what happened in the yard after we were gone because, even more incredibly, nobody came after us.

I could understand why the officers in the yard wouldn't yell out immediately. They couldn't see the top of the wall, remember, and when you're not sure what is happening you always assume the worst. I have a feeling they felt Tenuto's gun on them long after he was over and gone. The tower guards could see us as we were going over, though, and no matter what the captain had said, the thought would have to enter their minds that this was an escape. They couldn't really make out what was happening in the yard, though. If no alarm was being sounded, they would have to be thinking at some level of consciousness that there still must be some prisoners in the group below. It would be better for them to continue to believe that nothing was happening than to leave the protection of the tower and become sitting targets.

Sooner or later somebody would have to do something. Maybe a tower guard finally yelled, "What the hell is going on? What is this emergency supposed to be, anyway?"

The captain says, "For chrissake, how could you let them just drop over the wall without doing anything?"

The guard yells back, "You told me. You told

me, you sonofabitch. Hey, you ain't going to put this on me."

. Now, the captain is thinking of protecting his ass. "They had a gun on me, you donkey! Any idiot should have been able to figure that out." The guard is just as interested in protecting his ass. "Not when they were up on the wall they didn't. Why didn't you say something then?" It had to be something like that. Once we were out, I had expected that the officers would be climbing up the ladder, grabbing the rifles from the tower guards, and charging through the snow after us themselves. If they had, they would have got us. Because when we got to the designated spot, two blocks from the tracks, the car wasn't there.

We were standing there with the snow halfway up to our knees. On the road, nothing was moving. We still would have been picked up within the hour if we had found it necessary to walk out of there. But when things are breaking right, they keep breaking right. Off in the distance we could barely make out a car coming toward us. Just as it was reaching us the sirens began to go. What would be the only thing out in a driving snowstorm that early in the morning? A milk-delivery truck. The snow was so high on the road that all we had to do was step aboard, show him the gun, and tell him how much we would appreciate a ride into the city.

Even though the snow seemed to be tapering off somewhat, we didn't see another vehicle during the whole drive in. It was all virgin snow. There was not a track anywhere except those that we left behind.

Shortly after we started out, we threw the uniform coats and hats out into the snow. Spence reached back for a bottle of milk and as soon as he took a swig we all realized how thirsty we were. So I had to get cute and tell Spence to pay the man. "He's doing us this big favor," I said between gulps. "You wouldn't want him to think we were thieves?" All Spence had was a five-dollar bill. I had a couple of hundred dollars on me, but the bills were folded tightly at the bottom of a matchbox and covered over with the matches. It had been sitting like that in my cell for weeks. I took the five-dollar bill from Spence, passed it over to the milkwagon driver, and told him grandly to keep the change.

Freddie's brother owned a restaurant on Frankford Avenue, on the near side of the city, and that's where we were headed. As soon as we were close enough we had the milkwagon driver stop, threatened him with dire consequences if he said a word to anybody, and told him to turn around and go all the way back to where he had picked us up before he set out again on his route. He was so frightened that I'm sure he would have done exactly as he was told if he hadn't happened to run right into a police cruiser a few blocks away.

Where we were, nobody was out and not a car was moving. There had been a little traffic during the morning, though, because we could see the tire tracks. To keep from leaving footprints in the snow, we walked along the tire tracks for as long as we could, and when they began to be covered over we stayed close to the gutter. Freddie's brother lived in a house that was connected to the back of his restaurant. Alongside the house and the restaurant, running the full block from the back street to Frankford Avenue, was a rather large empty lot which was enclosed on the other three sides by an eight-foot wooden fence. The only way to get to the rear entrance of the house was through a gate at the corner of the lot. The house was dark. Freddie rang the bell, and after a little delay his brother came out in a bathrobe. My impression was that he had only half suspected that we would be trying to break out in that kind of a storm. At any rate, he wasn't overjoyed to see us, which I could understand, because we weren't overjoyed to be there. The first thing the Philadelphia police were going to do when the bulletin came through was send some cops to the homes of all of Tenuto's relatives. Without wasting time on any preliminaries, Freddie asked him for some clothes and some money.

"Wait here," his brother said. "I'll get it together and be right back."

While we were standing there on the porch, freezing, Spence Waldron took out a cigarette and asked me for a match. Without thinking, I handed him the matchbox. He struck a flame and, just then, two cops came bursting into the lot with their pistols drawn, shouting, "Freeze! Freeze!"

One second they were yelling "Freeze!"—we were already freezing, dammit—and the next second we were all diving across the open lot toward Frankford Avenue with bullets flying all around us. Boy, we vaulted the fence like five acrobats and scattered in five different directions. It must have been a very old, weatherbeaten fence, because when I got a few blocks away and was able to think straight again I found that I was clutching a hunk of it in my hand. Old and weatherbeaten, like I said, except for a smooth round indentation at the bottom where a bullet had gone through. I threw it away from me and kept cutting through different streets, putting distance between myself and the restaurant while following a random course that would be impossible to track.

I'm trying to make a little time, and I see some headlights shining and I figure it must be another cop car because I had to assume that an alert had come over on their radio. The only thing I could think to do was get away through the backyards. I ran into the driveway alongside a private home and when I got to the rear of the house I found myself face to face with a big wall. I was trapped. All I could do was duck into a little corner behind the house. I could see the headlights turn into the driveway and come to a stop just before the car got to the back of the house. They were so close that I could hear one cop say to the other, "Oh, he's not in there. Let's go." To this day I am positive that they had seen me go in there and knew right where I was. The only thing they didn't know was whether I had a pistol, and so I think that discretion won out over valor. They backed out and went cruising along their way.

Not only didn't I have a pistol, I didn't have any money. Because, if you remember, I had handed the matchbox to Spence Waldron just before the cry of "Freeze!" had wiped everything else out of my mind.

After the police car pulled away, I saw nobody. I seemed to be the only person out in all of Philadelphia. All the houses in the neighborhood had attached garages, but I finally spotted one car parked in a driveway. I got in, huddled down in the back seat, and waited for daylight. Very early, the homeowners began to come out to shovel off their sidewalks. Pretty soon a few hardy souls began to straggle by on their way to work. I knew Philadelphia well enough to know that they were walking toward an elevated station a few blocks away, part of the same system that went to Sixtieth and Market, the scene of the Corn Exchange Bank. I started after them, becoming in my mind another burgher on my way to work. But not for long. My fellow burghers had a dime for carfare. I was broke. I was also very cold because it was one of those choppy, icy winds. If it had been a normal commuting day I might have been able to lose myself in the crush. But the crowd was sparse, and for aesthetic reasons alone I wasn't going to be captured trying to duck under a turnstile because I didn't have a goddamn dime. Not after all I had gone through to get there.

To get to the center of the city I was going to have to walk. It was a long, cold walk. But I trudged along, in my thin jacket and baseball cap, trying to look like a man who had a job to go to but was in no hurry to get there. By the time I reached the city it was close to noon, and I was close to pneumonia.

When I entered the outskirts of the business area there were plenty of people around, although traffic was still almost completely immobilized. I was on a street of old houses and small places of business. The first chance I got, I stepped into a small hallway to warm myself.

By the time I came out the afternoon papers were out. I could see my name in the headlines of the papers outside a small variety store. There was nobody around, the door of the store was closed, and so I just picked up a paper as I passed and kept going. The whole story was there. Pictures and everything. Kliney, Spence Waldron, and Aikens had been captured within a few blocks of the lot. Only Tenuto and I were at large.

The original plan had been for me to stay with Tenuto until the heat died down and then go our separate ways to New York. There were other people I could contact. There were the Saunderses, of course. I knew Frankie Carbo and Boo Boo Hoff and Blinky Palermo and that whole crew of ex-bootleggers who were running the fight game and the rackets. Lavelle, the barber, was from Philadelphia. He had corresponded with me after he got out of Eastern State Pen, and I knew he'd do anything to help me. Under the circumstances, it seemed the better part of wisdom to me to get out of Philadelphia as quickly as I could. The whole town was loaded.

Since I knew Philadelphia like the palm of my hand, I knew where all the police booths were along Roosevelt Boulevard, the main artery out of the city. As a matter of elementary caution, I traveled along the back streets until I was sure I was beyond the booths. It was still snowing lightly. As I cut back onto Roosevelt, I hailed down a car that had come driving along. "Well," the driver said. "I'm going to Princeton. I'll take you that far."

Good enough. I get in the car with him and off in the distance I see there is one last booth that we still have to pass. These are only traffic booths, mind you, to keep the policemen out of the cold, but the officer comes out of the booth as we're approaching and signals for us to stop. The driver turns the window down, the cop looks in, and we're eyeball to eyeball. I'm sitting there in my baseball cap and windbreaker, looking right at him as if the last thing in the world I can possibly be is an escaped convict.

"Princeton, huh?" he says to this gentleman I'm riding with. "The roads are pretty bad down there, so you better drive careful."

There weren't many other cars on the highway, but there were some. Along the way, we must have passed at least a dozen going the other way. The driver, who had kept conversation at a minimum, let me off in the middle of town and told me I could pick up the highway again about a mile away. But there weren't many people out, and no cars heading out at all. So I figured, Jesus, I'd better get the hell out of town because this here is very dangerous. I started walking, looking back, and there was nothing. Not a car. Not a smell of a car. Boy, it looked as if there were a blight on the town.

I hit the highway and kept walking and it started to become dark and then it did become dark and then it became real dark. With the snow piled as high as it was, it became impossible to tell where the road began and ended. From time to time, I'd find myself stepping off into a gulley. A wind came up, an icy wind, and suddenly I was shivering. A chill to the bone. I was going to have to find some shelter fast and, as if it were an answer to my prayers, I saw the outline of this small little building off at a distance on the side. Like a barn or something.

When I started toward it I was in snow above my knees. To get to this building, I had to practically wade all the way. And then—what a disappointment. It wasn't a barn, but a kind of square wooden storage shack. The door was off and a siding was out, and the wind came whistling in, carrying a swirl of snow with it. No matter where I tried to huddle down, I couldn't get away from it. It was as if I were in a wind tunnel.

To keep from freezing to death I spent the night walking back and forth, something I had never done in prison. My mind raced like a madman's. Planning the future. While I was waiting for the heat to die down I was going to reconstruct myself completely. Alter my appearance, change my personality, lose my identity. I could remember reading about an Alabama doctor named Dr. Brandywine—how could you forget that name—who had been indicted for removing the fingerprints of an ex-con who had been paroled from Alcatraz. As I recalled the operation, the flesh had been sliced from the ex-con's fingertips and the raw fingers taped between his ribs for two weeks. The result had been fingers which were entirely devoid of prints, a circumstance which, while highly suspicious to the authorities, had nevertheless made it impossible for them to establish the man's identity according to the standards demanded by the law. I would find a doctor of my own choosing to perform this operation on me. I would have a nose job. I would design a new set of teeth that would alter the whole construction of my face.

I spent the whole night scheming on how I was going to reconstruct myself, and never thought of Dr. Brandywine and his no-print fingerprints again until the very moment of writing this.

As soon as it was light enough, I went back to the road and started walking. In a very short time I looked back and saw a big tractor-trailer chugging along with plumes of smoke coming out of its diesel. I waved my arms at the driver and pointed my thumb toward New York. He stopped.

I couldn't believe how stiff my legs were as I mounted the high step to the cab. Or how good the warmth of the cab felt when I closed the door. To make it perfect, he was going all the way to New York. "How are you going?" I asked him. "Through the tunnel?" No, he was going over the George Washington Bridge. Either way, it was going to my final danger point. I had escaped about five times in little more than twenty-four hours. It could all come to nothing if they had set up roadblocks at the approaches to New York.

One good omen was how remarkably unsuspicious the truck driver seemed to be about finding me in the middle of nowhere. "Do you live around here?" he asked. And that's all he asked. I told him I had been heading for New York to work for my brother-in-law who was a foreman in a dress house when I had got stopped by the storm. He wasn't even listening. He wanted to talk about himself. I learned that he had been driving a truck for twenty years; that the vibrations from the truck had given him kidney trouble, which was the occupational disease of truck drivers; that he was away from home more often than he was home; that he was married and had two sons; that his older son was in college and that neither of them were going to be truck drivers, what with the bad kidneys and everything. And then he began to talk about his activities with the Teamsters Union. He was a self-starting, nonstop talker. All I had to do was grunt every once in a while.

Finally, we were driving into the approach to the George Washington Bridge. As usual, there were a lot of cops around. The trailer rolled up to the booth.

The driver paid the toll, started up again, and headed toward New York. A good thirty-six hours after we had burst through the steel door at Holmesburg I was finally . . . finally home free.

As soon as we hit the 179th Street turnoff into the Bronx, I got out. I knew that Tommy Kling was living on Forty-fourth Street. I also knew that he was working again for Mickey Bowers on the West Side docks.

I walked all the way from 179th to 125th. New York being New York, there were a lot of people around. At 125th Street, I saw a guy stop at the top of the subway kiosk to light a cigarette. So I said, "Lookit, I've got a job over in Brooklyn. Do you have any spare change on you? I just found out that I left my pocketbook at home."

He looked at me the way you'd expect somebody to look at a guy wearing a little jacket and a baseball cap, and reached into his pocket and handed me a quarter.

I got off at Fiftieth Street and cut across to the docks. Tommy knew some people, see? I knew these people too. Mickey Bowers was a former bank robber himself, and he had done time in Trenton. I knew his brother Harold, and I knew his partner, Johnny O'Keefe, and I knew his brother-in-law, Artie McClellan, even better. Artie had worked for Mickey quite a while, taking the numbers and doing a little shylocking on the side.

Tommy was working on one of the luxury piers. I walked in and I asked, "Is Kling around?" And they said, "Yeah, he's up on the roof sunning himself."

Well, in a way he was. Tommy had more or less of a sinecure there. He didn't actually do any work, but he was on the payroll and he used to be put down for overtime and all of that stuff. Where Kling was concerned, Mickey Bowers had one thing in mind: that Kling was a good man to have around in case of trouble.

When Tommy saw me he nearly fell off the pier. Immediately he grabbed his coat and took me down to his place on Forty-fourth Street. Naturally, we stopped to pick up all the newspapers on the way so that I could read all the accounts of this fabulous escape.

The first things I needed were some clothes and some money. No sooner said than done. Tommy went out and came back with his arms full of clothes, and also with four or five hundred dollars from Mickey Bowers and Johnny O'Keefe. Like I said, I knew these people all my life.

Mickey had sent word back that he wanted me to come up to his home in Westchester and hide out for as long as I wanted. He had a fabulous place up there, Tommy told me. An estate. This guy was making all kinds of money on the rackets.

That was something to think about. I couldn't go out on the streets, I couldn't rent an apartment, and I certainly couldn't continue to live with Tommy for more than a week. They would be checking very carefully into all my past friendships and associations, and sooner or later they would be getting around to him.

The way I saw it, I was going to have to find someplace away from anything or anybody who could remotely be connected with me. Just disappear completely for about a month. The best solution, I finally decided, was to get a job in a hospital or someplace like that, the kind of menial job that provided full maintenance as part of the salary.

There was an employment agency over on Joralemon Street in Brooklyn, just below my old neighborhood, which was operated by the Catholic charities. A well-known agency with a wide range of employment. The man who interviewed me told me that he had a place in Staten Island called the Farm Colony, which he described as a home for indigent people. Before he called to find out if they had an opening he wanted to warn me that it wasn't near St. George or any of the big places on Staten Island. It was in New Springville, out in the middle of the island. "More or less out in the country," he said.

Absolutely perfect for me, of course. And anyway, I didn't know one part of Staten Island from the other. I had been brought up just across the river, a ferry ride away, but I had never taken that ferry ride in my life. To me, Staten Island was a world apart.

PART THREE

The Fugitive

Visiting Prisoner

Tommy Kling and Herbie Miller had escaped from the New Jersey Reformatory before teaming up with the rest of the gang that had robbed the bank in Hawley, and after their parole came through at Eastern State both of them had been sent back to Trenton to finish their sentences. Tommy had only served a year, but Herbie was still in. Before I went into hiding at the Farm Colony I had decided to call the prison at Trenton to ask about the visiting hours for Herbie Miller. That's when I found out that Herbie Miller wasn't his real name. It's a funny thing in prison. More often than not, an inmate will be known by his alias even to the guards, although in the office records he will naturally be listed by his legitimate name, followed by his aliases. After a long delay the guy came back from looking it up in the book and says, "You mean Bill Conway."

Kling thought I was insane. "What the hell do you want to see him for?"

"I want to see him." I didn't know why I wanted to see him. "I want to talk to him. What the hell is this about his name being Bill Conway?"

I had cut my mustache pencil-thin and I was parting my hair different, and I'm figuring this is the last place anybody's going to be expecting to see me. So I go over there and I'm ushered into the PK's office. That's the principal keeper, which is another name for the deputy warden. This PK there had only one good leg, he'd had polio or something when he was young, and they said he was the devil incarnate. He looks at me. "Who did you say you wanted to see?"

"I want to see my brother, Bill Conway."

He looks through the cards. "You his brother?"

"Certainly I'm his brother. I wouldn't be here unless I was his brother. I'm on my way to Philadelphia. I'm a salesman."

He says, "Where do you live?" I knew where Herbie lived. Up in the Bronx.

"How many brothers and sisters you have?" From talks I'd had with Herbie I had the answer to that one too.

"What's your mother's name?" There's where he caught me. When I didn't answer immediately, he says to me, "You know you're lying. You're not his brother. If you admit you're lying I'll let you go in to see him."

I says, "All right, he's a friend of mine. I haven't seen him in a long time." I'd heard a lot about Trenton anyway, so I took out twenty dollars and he says, "Put that away . . . put that away." What I hadn't heard was that they had a big investigation going on there. A lot of graft and brutality had already been uncovered, plus a huge opium traffic. "For chrissake," he says. "Put that away."

In order to get to the visiting room, I had to go through three gates, and every time I'd hear them lock behind me I'd think, Jeez, if anything happens here, I'm dead. You know?

There was no contact between visitors and inmates at Trenton. You sat on one side of a window, he sat on the other, and you talked over a phone. Herbie saw me and he went white. "You shouldn't have come," he said.

I said, "Since when is your name Bill Conway?"

"Holy Christ," he says. "This place is tight as a drum. . . ."

On the way out I wanted to give the guy at the gate twenty dollars. Boy, he wouldn't take anything. Before this investigation, they'd take the wallet out of your pocket.

Over the River to the Poorhouse

A home for the indigent, I had been told. It was, I discovered, the poorhouse. An institution for the abandoned aged. The jail which they would never leave.

But, do you know, it wasn't like that. Given the understanding that it was a place of infirmity and personal tragedy, it was also one of the lovely experiences of my life. I came to lay low for a month at the most, and I stayed for two and a half years. And even then I wouldn't have left if it hadn't become necessary.

The lesson is that any institution which is run by a dedicated, committed individual will be a great institution. Miss Loretta Bisset, the nursing supervisor, was the woman who had told the employment agency to send me over. I found a very handsome woman, probably in her fifties, with pure white hair which seemed all at odds with her clear, youthful complexion and extraordinarily rosy cheeks. "I will explain your duties to you as a hospital helper," she said. Clean, mop, and polish. In other words, I was a porter. She gave me some meal tickets to cover the rest of the month and assigned me to a room in what was more or less a dormitory. My fellow workers were, by and large, alcoholics. The maintenance people as well as the porters. As soon as they were paid they would go out and get drunk and you wouldn't see them again until they were broke and reasonably sobered up. They were Miss Bisset's charges too. She would fire them, they would swear that it was never going to happen again, and she would allow them to talk her into rehiring them. Over and over and over. In a very real sense they were casualties too. Ambulatory but helpless. While it was true that she would have found it difficult to find people to replace them, it was even more true that they couldn't have held a job any place else for much more than a week.

The name I was using, incidentally, was Eddie Lynch. I had appropriated the name of my boyhood buddy. I was sent to building 27. The following morning I reported to Miss Chadwick, the head nurse for our building. A redheaded lady, just this side of middle-age, with the kind of features that told you she had been a beauty in her younger days. When she told me what my duties were I figured I would last there about two hours. I was saying to myself, If I was to do all these things she's telling me to do, I'd have to build another building.

My opinion of her changed very quickly. By making such demands upon us she was establishing the principle that there was nothing we could do for these people that would be too good. She was a living saint. Her commitment to these old people went every bit as deep as Miss Bisset's, and maybe deeper. She loved them and they loved her.

I grew to love many of them myself. They had one woman there, Rebecca, who was ninety-six years old, and every time I looked at her I thought of the painting of Whistler's mother. A very well-loved woman. As old as she was, she would always be helping people.

There was another woman who was about eighty years old and still looked as regal as a queen. I became very friendly with this woman because she wrote poetry, which she would sometimes sell to one of the poetry magazines for five or ten dollars, and she always liked to have my opinion on whether they were good enough to send out. The way she had got to the poorhouse was tragic. Her husband, a prominent Park Avenue psychiatrist, had left her well over a million dollars and she had given her power of attorney over to her son, who had graduated from Yale University. Without telling her, he began to speculate in the market, lost every dollar she had, and committed suicide.

Until the very end when she began to grow a little feeble, she was a very independent and compelling woman.

There were countless cases of mothers and fathers who had turned their homes over to their children and had then been shipped off to the Farm Colony when because of age or infirmity they had become a burden. The members of the family would come driving up every once in a while and leave a little fruit or something behind. Whatever it was, the patients were always very eager to pass it around the ward. It was a way of demonstrating that they had somebody who cared enough to visit them.

I often thought of a case I had read of in the papers where the judge had commented, "How is it that this one woman could raise ten children and ten children can't support one woman." The relatives of these people shunned their responsibilities. There was one woman in particular, Miss Collins. She had been a nurse herself in younger days and I used to take very good care of her because she was a very nice person. She had a brother who was a stockbroker, and he would come to visit her occasionally in a big limousine. It cost him thirty dollars a month to have the state take care of her. That was the most anybody had to pay. If they couldn't afford to pay, there was no charge at all.

The Farm Colony itself was a huge place, with a lot of trees and walkways. The grounds covered 104 acres and altogether there were fifty-two buildings. Quite a large space had been set aside for a cemetery, and they were all very conscious of dying. Some of them were in their nineties. You can never realize how terrible diseases like chronic arthritis can be in the elderly until you've seen old women who have suffered all the ills and sorrows their sex is heir to crying under the intensity of the pain.

Each patient had his or her own cubicle. A bed, a locker, and a chair, maybe a wheelchair. Many of them had religious symbols on the locker or wall. In the evening, just prior to the time they were going to bed, I used to walk behind these buildings and I could look in through the windows and see them there, and I had the impression that every one of them was in a period of meditation, reflecting back on their younger days when there was a purpose to their lives.

Many of them were alone as death was approaching. They had nobody. They would ask me if I would be around when they died, and I would always promise that I would. Sometimes they would be in comas and wouldn't know what was happening but I was always scrupulous about keeping my word. It gives you a great insight into life to sit there and watch life ebbing out of a fellow human being. Because you can tell. Some of them were very gentle and they accepted it without any great fuss. The clock was running down, that's all. Others would fight with every breath they had.

Most of them didn't know what to make of this porter, Eddie Lynch. After I went off duty I would clean myself up and dress very nicely, which was hardly the norm for the porters or, even, the craftsmen who worked on the maintenance crew. In their minds, I became whatever it was they were looking for. Whatever their problem was I was going to solve it. And like old people everywhere they were full of complaints. "I know who you are," one of my favorite old ladies said to me. "You're an SS person."

I asked her what an SS person was.

"You're here from the Secret Service. You're an investigator from the city department."

Nothing I could say could convince her otherwise. "Oh, that's all right," she'd say with a smile. "I know you can't tell me."

It wasn't only my affection for the patients that kept me there so long. There was also Nora Mahoney nurse's aide who worked in the same ward. Every morning after I had finished cleaning the place up I would wheel a few of the nonambulatory older women out on the front lawn. Nora, who was a very dedicated person, would always be there too. She was an angel in the eyes of the patients. And in mine. A very comely woman, I had thought to myself the first time I saw her. In many ways she reminded me of my mother. She had come over from Ireland, she had a rich brogue, and she was very religious. They even had the same first name.

I became very deeply involved with Nora Mahoney. In fact, I fell in love with her.

And so in more ways than one, the Farm Colony had become a safe refuge for me. In many ways, it could be said that I was happy. Whatever that is supposed to mean. The tyranny of words. There is a word in the dictionary that says *happiness*. Therefore we expect something called happiness to fall on us. To me, happiness is something that comes in bits and pieces. A transient form of satisfaction. Moments so rare that you can look back through your entire life and remember them.

There is a big difference between happiness and contentment. To the degree that happiness can be defined as nothing more than the absence of suffering, there is—no question about it—a certain happiness in waking up in the morning and realizing that you are not in prison.

After I had been there for three or four months I began to see Tommy Kling on my days off. Sometimes I'd go into the city; sometimes he'd come over to Staten Island. When a couple of bank robbers get together, there's only one subject of conversation. They begin to plan on how to get some money.

There were quite a few tempting banks right there on Staten Island, and we were within easy reach of Jersey. On weekdays, I was going to Trenton and Newark and Elizabeth, after work, to look the banks over. On weekends I'd be casing banks or pulling jobs with Kling. Come Monday, I'd be back on the job with my mop and pail.

The real danger, and I had always been aware of this, wasn't in the job but in the aftermath. Publicity. The papers wouldn't identify them all as Willie Sutton jobs as long as they stayed small, but I always had enough respect for the New York police to realize that they would very quickly begin to put it together. Every once in a while, though, the papers would identify something as a Willie Sutton job, as often as not on banks I had nothing to do with. And, on occasion, my picture would appear above the story. At last it happened. Kling, De Venuta, and I had pulled a job in Trenton and I had melted back into the Farm Colony. I was walking through the corridor a few days later when I heard somebody say, "Hello, Willie Sutton."

I turned around, and it was a nurse's aide I had tried to date a couple of times without success. The best-looking young woman there. I looked at her as if I were completely bewildered. "What did you call me?"

She was holding a copy of the *New York Daily News* and she turned it around so that I'd be able to see it. "I'm calling you Willie Sutton. Here's your picture in the paper."

It was an old picture and I was wearing a different kind of mustache. "You kidding me?" I said. "You think I'd be working in this dump at ninety dollars a month if I was this person?"

Under the picture they had a full rundown of my criminal record, the escapes, and the fact that I was on the FBI Most Wanted List. The whole bit. I made a rueful grimace. "I wish I had his money, though. I sure wouldn't be working here long."

I could see a little doubt creep into her eyes. Her eyes went from my face to the paper and then she said, "Oh, I know that's not you. I was just kidding. But there sure is a resemblance there, isn't there?"

"Perhaps so," I said. "They say everybody has a double."

Well, as I walked away I said to myself, Goodbye, Farm Colony. She would be showing the photograph to others, I was sure, and they were going to confirm her original opinion. That same afternoon I told Nora Mahoney I was going to leave the Farm Colony so that I could begin to look for a better job. "Why don't you come and live with me?" she said.

Nora lived in a little house in the town of Westerleigh about a mile away. She had worked there as a cook and housekeeper when she first arrived in the country and she had saved enough money, she now informed me, so that she had only recently bought the place. The only difficulty was that she already had a couple of boarders, a woman named Rose Nortin, who worked on the night shift at the Farm Colony, and Mrs. Nortin's fifteen-year-old son.

Nora had to ask Rose Nortin to find another place, and I had to wait a couple of weeks until she was finally able to find a furnished apartment.

I would be safe there, I knew. Nora, who was a very moral person, didn't want any of her friends to know that a man was living with her. Rose Nortin, the only person who did know, worked in an entirely different part of the Farm Colony and paid very little attention to the papers, anyway.

Nora herself was such an honest person that if the word ever did get around the Farm Colony that Eddie Lynch was really Willie Sutton, I had no doubt at all that she would immediately come and confront me with it.

For nine months I lived with Nora Mahoney, paying board and spending a great deal of my time fixing up the house. I also began to spend a few days at a time over in New York with Tommy Kling. And all the time it was a race against time, because I was very much aware that the day would come when she too would see a picture in the paper and ask the same question.

I have always been generous with the money I got from stealing. One way or another, most thieves give their money away. Perhaps, as Oscar Wilde said about hypocrisy, it is the tribute vice pays to virtue. I have never gone the big-tip, racetrack route, myself. I always felt I planned my jobs so well and dedicated myself to their execution so completely that I deserved everything I earned. But, as self-serving as I know this sounds, I have always had a strong urge to help people in trouble. Going all the way back to the early days when I would see the poor people coming in to the Guarantee Trust with their quarters and fifty-cent pieces in their hands to make their insurance payments. That's burial money for poor people. As Eddie Lynch, I was able to indulge all my fantasies in philanthropy. My friend Al Jantzen got in bad trouble. He had gambled away thousands of dollars of the premiums he had collected from his accounts, and his books were about to be audited. Well, Al was still holding a lot of my money because Louise had remarried and remarried very well. I told Al to take what he needed to square himself and forget about it.

One of my old ladies was terribly upset one day. An operation was needed to save her grandson's eyesight, and they didn't have the money. A thousand dollars. I knew the kid. His mother had brought him around often to visit his grandmother. I left the money in an envelope on her table while she was sleeping, and when she told me in the morning that it had to be me because I was the only person she had told, I just looked at her as if she was crazy. What, did she think I went around giving a thousand dollars away to everybody who happened to need an operation?

There was a little restaurant near St. George, more like a coffeehouse really, where I'd meet Tommy Kling or Al Jantzen or some of my other friends from New York. While I was waiting, I'd talk to the guy who owned it, exchanging the time of day. How were the Dodgers doing, that kind of thing. So one day he told me he was closing for good because the rent was due the next day and he didn't have it. I gave him more than enough to keep the place going. I knew there was no chance I was ever going to get it back. It was a flat-out gift to a guy I hardly knew.

With Nora Mahoney, I had to be more careful. Her great dream was to go back to Ireland for a visit. The only way I was going to be able to swing it was to tell her I had a big real-estate deal in the works and get her used to the idea, by degrees, that if it came through we were going to celebrate by going to Ireland together.

It was the Brink's job, in January 1950, that really blew my cover, and it didn't bear the remotest resemblance to my M.O. Five guys breaking in, in the evening, in Halloween masks. But somebody had told the police they had seen me in Boston, and my picture was all over the papers again.

I held my breath and got Nora all excited by telling her that my real-estate deal was just about set and that it was only a matter now of waiting for the bank loan to be approved. I didn't tell her that it was the Manufacturers Trust in Sunnyside, nor that the loan was going to be made on such an informal, nonreturnable basis.

Nora always got home around four o'clock. The day after I had come back with the money, I was preparing afternoon tea. It isn't only the English who have tea around that time, you know, the Irish do it too. The moment she stepped through the door I knew she had found out. My picture had been on the front page, along with the story of the robbery, and it was all over the Farm Colony that the Eddie Lynch who used to work there as a porter had really been Willie Sutton the bank robber.

The best I could come up with was that I had a half brother who was the black sheep of the family and had been in trouble all of his life. I piled on details about the times I had been arrested and the jobs I had lost because of what seemed to be a very close resemblance, and as much as she was struggling to believe me I could see that it was just too much for her to swallow.

So finally I said, "Listen, I'm going to go over to New York and I'll bring back the proof to you." I didn't know how long it was going to take, I told her, but I was going to have such irrefutable proof, like pictures of us together when we were kids and things like that, that she would have no choice but to believe me.

I went upstairs to pack a few things (there went another wardrobe), and when I came downstairs again I peeled off about seven hundred dollars, put it down on the table, and called in that I was leaving something to tide her over until I returned. Nora was in such a state of shock that I doubt whether she even heard me. I was so upset myself that I left my car in the garage and went to the ferry by bus. If anybody had passed on their suspicions to the police, one of the first things the police would have done was run a registration check on Edward Lynch.

By the next day I was calm enough to become convinced that I was running too scared. Whatever anybody might suspect at the Farm Colony, I couldn't imagine them informing on me to the police unless they were absolutely sure. Except for Rose Nortin, none of them even knew I was still living in Staten Island, let alone that I was living with Nora Mahoney.

In the morning I stained my face, dyed my hair, and went back to get the car. It was a very close thing. A few days later the police moved in on Nora Mahoney. Even though she told them everything she knew and voluntarily turned the money I had left on the table over to them, they took her to the women's jail in Jefferson Market, a hellhole, and held her as a material witness.

Rose Nortin was the one who had informed. What had made the police so suspicious that Nora knew more than she was telling them was that she had picked up her passport for the trip to Ireland only a couple of days before the robbery of the Manufacturers Trust.

The crimes we commit two by two, I read somewhere, we pay for one by one. Very true.

The crimes we commit alone are paid for, and paid for dearly, by those whose lives we touch the closest. Even truer.

The Finger of Fate

I am the master of my fate;
I am the captain of my soul
　　　　—W. E. Henley
　　　　(1849-1903)

Baloney
　　　　—W. F. Sutton

I was captured five years and one week after the break from Holmesburg, and then convicted of the

Manufacturers Trust robbery, because of a series of accidents, coincidences, and flukes so precisely timed and interwoven that it was as if some Scriptwriter in the Sky had set out to write a scenario too improbable for anybody to believe.

And, on top of everything, it came about at a time when I felt safer than I had in years. After putting it off and putting it off, I had finally got myself a nose job. It's very difficult for a fugitive to put himself in a position where he is helpless and at the mercy of strangers. Even though Tommy had been telling me from the first that he knew a doctor who could be trusted. He had dealt with this doctor for years, it seemed, first in selling him some stuff, like powerful microscopes, that had been pilfered from the docks and then in going to him to have his skull sewed up after somebody had opened it with a baling hook during a dockside brawl.

I have always maintained, as you know, that every lawbreaker's motivation turns on his own life, and Tommy's doctor illustrated the point perfectly. Back in his younger days, a drug addict had come to his office in terrible condition pleading for something that would help him. The doctor had given him something to make him comfortable, refused to accept any money, and sent him on his way. A few minutes later, the police were in his office. The addict had been trailed, and the police took the doctor down to headquarters and subjected him to a long, bullying interrogation before they let him go. That one experience with injustice had left him with such a hatred for all law-enforcement people that it had become the ruling passion of his life.

Tommy's doctor would understand very well why somebody like Tommy would bring a friend around to have his looks changed and—maybe it was only my imagination—I had a feeling from the beginning that he recognized me. As it turned out, he didn't do nose jobs anyway. What he did offer to do was to give me a letter to a Park Avenue specialist who was a close friend of his.

There was no reason why a doctor I was coming to on a referral should be suspicious. With all the fighting I had done in my younger days I had a nose that could definitely be improved upon. The Park Avenue doctor read the letter, asked me whether I could arrange my affairs to have the operation immediately, and sent me to a photographer right around the corner. All photographers study their subjects carefully, I suppose. This one looked me over far more intently than I liked before he sat me down, rolled his camera practically into my nose, and took his pictures.

When I went back the next day, the doctor told me to go to a private hospital on 110th Street, facing Central Park, about a block west of Fifth Avenue. I took two rooms. One room for me and the adjoining room for Tommy. The operation might be routine but the situation wasn't. I couldn't shake the feeling that the photographer had recognized me. If he had, I could only hope that he valued the doctor's business more than the chance to send me back to jail.

The next morning, I was prepared for the operating room just as if I were going to have an abdominal operation. The full battery of tests, the shaving of the pubic area, and, just before they wheeled me in, a tetanus shot. I didn't know whether that was routine procedure for a nose job or whether I was on the record for something else; the only thing I did know was that I wasn't going to ask.

Nobody had given me the slightest information about what was going to happen, either. I had anticipated that I would be given a general anesthetic. Instead, they just sprayed some ethyl chloride or something on my nose to freeze it. There were two doctors there, my guy and an assistant. The Park Avenue doctor got what seemed to be a chisel and started to whack away at the bone on both sides of my nose. It didn't exactly hurt, but I was never in any doubt as to exactly where he was working, either. Every time he gave the chisel another tap with his hammer it echoed all the way up to my head.

After the operation he pulled my nostrils together at the bottom, put some kind of a rubber guard around it, and bandaged it all together. A few days later I was discharged from the hospital with instructions to return to the doctor's office in a week to have the stitches removed.

The very next day my picture was in the paper. The Long Island Railroad train to Babylon had been stopped and searched because of a false tip that Willie Sutton was aboard, a situation which had become rather routine for the police.

I gave it a lot of thought. When the day of my appointment rolled around, and I could feel the edges of the stitches coming out, I made up my mind. I said, "Lookit, Tommy. I want you to take these stitches out."

He didn't want to. In the worst way, he didn't want to. "You're liable to get blood poisoning or something," he moaned. "Jesus, I can't do anything like that."

I handed him a pair of tweezers and told him I'd take my chances. It was a terrible ordeal. They hadn't sewed it up with catgut, as I had more or less taken for granted. They had used a silverlike wire. The nose was still unbelievably sensitive. The pain was so excruciating that tears were pouring out of both eyes.

Eventually, however, he managed to take them all out. The nose was a little bit swollen and I still had a couple of black eyes, but in a couple of days I was able to look into the mirror and see that quite a bit of the bone had been removed. "How do I look?" I asked Tommy.

Tommy was practically jumping up and down. "Oh gee. Boy. Nobody will recognize you now."

"It didn't change me that much. Changed me a little, but, Jesus, Tommy, not that much."

"No, you'd be surprised," he said. "It made a big change in you."

It was an improvement all right. Generally, I'm able to see what I'm looking at without kidding myself, but, well, I guess I wanted to be convinced. If it hadn't made *that* big of a change, I did believe that it had made enough of a change. And that could very well have made me a bit too confident.

Confidence: a very good thing to have if you're up at bat with the bases loaded in the ninth inning and a very bad thing to have if you're a fugitive. If you set out to draw the ideal profile for a fugitive, you'd find yourself describing the classic paranoiac. What, after all, is a paranoiac? He is a man who is perpetually on the alert, whose guard is always up. He feels "they" are out to get him and, since he isn't exactly sure who "they" are, he has to see everything, hear everything, protect himself against everybody. The only difference with a fugitive is that there is nothing imaginary about it. They *are* out to get him. The police, the FBI, the law, the government. The massed power and resources of the state. He had damned well better see everything, hear everything, protect himself against everybody.

I was either paranoiac enough or realistic enough so that I had two apartments. An apartment on Fifty-seventh and Madison in Manhattan, where I lived, and a cheap furnished room on Dean Street in Brooklyn, where I slept. As far as I was concerned, my reasoning could not have been more realistic. If the police got a tip on me and picked me right up, there was nothing I could do about it anyway. The chances were, however, that they'd want to have a look at me first, and the New York police had a very effective technique for tailing people. They would assign as many as six vehicles to a subject, including commercial trucks, and pass the guy back and forth so deftly that it was impossible for him to detect that he was under surveillance.

The Dean Street apartment was only a block away from the subway station. (It was also only three blocks from the Bergen Street police station, but that made it more safe, not less. Who was going to think I'd be living right under their noses?) When I left in the morning, that one block was all I had to watch. If anything made me suspicious, there were a few stations I had picked out along the way, small stations that were never very crowded, where I could get off and take a look around.

You might think that having two apartments would give me two sets of neighbors, and therefore twice as many people who might recognize me. Quite the contrary. If I had spent all my time holed up in one apartment, the neighbors might have started to wonder about me. By having two apartments I was able to keep regular hours. To the people around me on Dean Street, where I was known as John Mahoney, I worked the day shift. To the people at Fifty-seventh, who knew me as Arthur Buckley, I worked nights.

The Dean Street address was only a mile from where I was born. Two blocks south of Atlantic Avenue and just east of Fourth Avenue. It had been the heart of the Italian section while I was growing up, and it was now a tightly packed Puerto Rican enclave. Few of the other tenants in my rooming house even spoke English. What would they know about Willie Sutton? I was able to study Spanish and test it out on the landlady, a marvelous seventy-year-old blind woman, without a worry in the world.

Dean Street was not only where I slept, it was my hideout. Not even Kling knew the address. He knew that I had a place in Brooklyn. That's all that he knew. And if Kling was a little disturbed with me about that, I had far more reason to be a little disturbed about him.

When I left Nora Mahoney's house I lived briefly with Kling. We went to New England and Pennsylvania again to take small banks near Providence and Jenkintown, and then for the next four months I took a trip through the Midwest—Detroit, Chicago, and Cleveland—with the thought of plying my trade in new territory. Throughout my career I had been contacted by out-of-town people through the grapevine, and being a fugitive only made the contacts more involved and expensive. This time, I had been the one to initiate the contacts by buying an underworld maildrop, which is routine procedure, and sending the word out. In each city, I had discovered that there was a tipster involved, and with each of the tipsters there had been something in his background to give me pause. In Detroit, where it was a bank that was supposed to have a lot of payrolls in it, the tip had come from a former private investigator who had had his ticket taken away. As soon as I was told that he was going to be using his share of the loot to buy his license back and open up his own agency, I had to consider the strong possibility that the currency he was going to use to buy his license back was me.

All I got out of it was a good vacation, and upon my return to New York, Kling began to tell me a woeful tale of what had been happening to him while I was away. Tommy had already left the docks by then. With the investigations that were going to result in the appointment of the Waterfront Commission going on, a lot of retired cops were being brought in to replace the ex-cons, and although Tommy was perfectly safe in his sinecure he just couldn't stand it. While he was still on the docks, though, he had become very friendly with a checker whose name was Bill Bradley. At least, that was the name he went by. Actually, he had come into the country illegally and had been given that name when they put him to work. The Coast Guard, which was handling that part of the investigation, was demanding that everybody produce a birth certificate, and naturally Bradley didn't have one. Tommy had brought his problem to me just before I left for Detroit, and I had been able to pick up a number of blank baptismal papers from the Mary of Christians Church with the church seal and everything.

Well, in return for this great favor, Bradley had introduced Tommy to a friend of his, a lawyer named Maxwell Van Why. This isn't an Abbott & Costello routine, that was his real name. Van Why had been just full of suggestions about how Tommy could invest his money. For openers, he had induced Tommy to invest in a tavern up on Forty-sixth and Eighth Avenue, in the Times Square area. He had then talked him into buying one of those three-story brownstone buildings down on Waverly Place with the general idea of converting it into a collection of one- and two-room apartments. Which was, in fact, exactly the kind of thing that was being done in that neighborhood at the time.

Altogether, Tommy had invested more than twenty-five thousand dollars with this Van Why, which just happened to be all the money he had in the world, and for some reason he had become very suspicious of him. As soon as I saw the tavern I could understand why. Every prostitute in the Times Square area dropped in and used it, which meant that every cop in the city knew about it. I mean, I knew the location from way back. A real hot spot. I got out of there real quick. "Jeez," I told Tommy. "Take whatever you can get, just get rid of it. Only I wouldn't let this Van Why do it, I'd get another lawyer."

It wasn't the location that bothered Tommy, the location was what he liked about it. A real action spot. He had already told me that he had met a broad in the tavern. Clara. The one true love of his life. Every time there was a pause in the conversation he'd be off and telling me what a wonderful cook she was and what a raving beauty and how I was going to have to come over and have dinner with them.

No, the only thing that had given Tommy second thoughts was that old bills were coming in all the time. Including the bill for a jukebox which had been bought, on credit, about two weeks before the title passed. What about the contract? I asked. Wasn't there anything in there that made the previous owner liable for debts that had already been incurred?

What contract? Tommy wanted to know. All he had done was turn the money over to Van Why.

Kling wasn't too bright. He was one of about ten children who had been raised in Bayonne, New Jersey, in such grinding poverty that he had gone many times without shoes. Because of that, he had developed a classic shoe fetish. Tommy didn't care how he lived, and he'd just as soon go in and buy a suit off the rack, but he always had a closetful of shoes. The most expensive shoes that could be bought. (His brother had become a fire captain in Bayonne, and if you ask me why one brother becomes a thief and another serves society, all I can tell you, having seen any number of these cases, is that I don't know.)

I took a look at the Waverly Place property and I had to admit that it looked very good. Too good. I decided I had better check up on Van Why and the property both. Finding that the sale had not yet been recorded at the Hall of Records, I called up the law firm that was listed as representing the property and asked whether they could tell me who was handling it for the new owners.

I had, it seemed, been misinformed. Not only hadn't the property been sold, it couldn't be sold. The apartment building was part of a large estate, the will was being contested, and from the way it looked the whole estate was going to be tied up in litigation for years.

In tracking down the tavern, I found that the title had passed to Tommy, all right. Better that it shouldn't have. He had bought a piece of property on which the government had placed a lien for unpaid income taxes.

In buying the tavern for him, Van Why had let him pay full price on a property that was half owned by the government. As far as the Waverly Place building was concerned, he had just shown him a house and pocketed the money. For the first, he could be disbarred. For the second, he could be put in jail.

Tommy had an even better idea. Tommy was so mad he was ready to kill him. Now, when a guy like Tommy Kling says he's going to kill somebody, it isn't just a figure of speech. He means he is going to take a gun and kill him. And probably Bill Bradley too, when he got around to thinking about it. I didn't think it would be a very good idea for Tommy Kling to kill anybody. I thought it would be an especially bad idea for him to kill anybody who could be so easily traced back to him. Tommy was quite incensed with me about that. He was particularly incensed, he let me know, because it had been my fault that he had got involved with Van Why in the first place.

My fault?

"Your fault, Bill. If you hadn't left town you'd have never let me do it."

I called Van Why, identified myself as a close friend and financial adviser to Tommy Kling, and impressed upon him the urgency of an immediate meeting.

He had an office on Seventh Avenue below Fourteenth Street. He also had an apartment around Garrett Street, on the fringes of the Village. A very nice apartment, facing the park. He had his little daughter there with him, a beautiful child of about six, and he was very insistent that she remain in the room. He didn't even try to deny anything. "I was in a jam," he said. "I was stuck." He had used the funds of a woman client for a personal investment, and she had suddenly demanded her money. "Tommy came along at an opportune time for me," he said. "The money was all tied up. But in my mind I was more or less borrowing it from him, with every intention of paying him back with full interest." In fact, he said, he expected to have the money in a week. Two weeks at the outside.

Tommy wasn't going to shoot him any more; he was going to kill him with his bare hands. Jeez, he was mad. I sent the little girl into the next room and before Tommy could do anything, pulled my own pistol out of my belt and told Van Why I was going to kill him. Well, Van Why was so frightened that he practically got down on his knees and begged for more time. He had all this money that was going to come in. Boy, was he sincere. There's nothing like a pistol to make a lawyer sincere. This one was so sincerely frightened that for a minute or two there he almost had me believing him. He was a very good talker, this man was. A virtuoso. "Right here and now," he told Tommy, "I want to make an appointment to meet you at the Robert Treat Hotel in Newark next Thursday. There will be another lawyer there who is going to turn a vast sum of money over to me from the investment I told you about, and I want you to be right there so that I can pay you immediately."

I could only hope that Tommy believed him more than I did. "Lookit," I said when we got outside. "Don't ever do anything to this fellow because then you'll never get your money. It will be gone forever."

To keep him happy I promised that I would come over on Sunday to meet his lovely lady and partake of one of her gourmet meals. So I go over there and, boy, I got the surprise of my life. I won't say she was the ugliest woman in the whole world, all I can say is that she was as ugly as anybody has a right to be. And built kind of low and square like a miniature tank. Jeez, I thought to myself, this broad has got to be some cook.

We were going to have roast beef, Kling beamed. And, boy, was I in for a treat. While we were waiting, she's showing me all the things Tommy has bought for her. A couple of fur coats. Some evening gowns. Jewels. And, of course, a whole closetful of shoes. Well, it came time to have dinner and we sat down to one of the worst meals I ever tasted in my life. Roast beef, burned to a cinder. Jeez, I'm thinking now, this broad has got to be some lay. She must know something these other broads haven't even heard of yet.

I ate as much of it as I possibly could. I had to. Tommy was watching every mouthful. "Very tasty," I said, licking my lips. "I only wish I hadn't lost my appetite in prison."

"I thought it might have been a little overdone," he said. You could see that he was very concerned.

No, no. Exactly the way I used to like it when my digestive tract was still functioning. Crisp. Nothing I disliked more than to bite into a good slice of beef and find it was all red and juicy.

And this is the same guy who had always kidded Georgie Moore back at Eastern State for being such a sucker for the broads.

She was an out-and-out prostitute, this girl, no wonder he had found her at his tavern. She knew every hooker in town by her first name, and every hooker in town knew her. She would disappear for a few days and Tommy would go hunting all over town until he found her and brought her back. It had been to keep her from running off again that he had tried to borrow the money from De Venuta while I was out of town. "Can you imagine that guy asking me for two grand so he can blow it on that two-dollar whore of his," De Venuta asked me. "I heard she once took on ten guys in an hour. Made herself two and a half dollars on the whole deal."

Thieves have always had an affinity for prostitutes. They're around, they're available, and they're disposable. And maybe underneath all the rationalization most thieves believe it's as good as they deserve. For my own part, I had resolved after Nora Mahoney was taken into custody that I was never going to get involved with any woman on anything resembling a permanent basis again. A decent woman was going to end up in trouble. A prostitute couldn't be trusted.

Like anybody else who is involved in an illegal enterprise, they are allowed to operate in return for information. In addition to which they can hardly be expected to stand up under threats or a good slapping around. That reduced the field to whorehouses, an occasional street prostitute, and, when my luck was in, an occasional pickup.

I was in the public library on Fifth Avenue one day rereading Schopenhauer's *Studies in Pessimism,* which gives a clue to my frame of mind, when this really attractive young woman sat down across from me. She looked at me, I looked at her, and I thought, Schopenhauer, old friend, we'll talk about it some other time. She accepted my invitation to lunch in a low, seductive voice, which carried the promise of pleasures, suspected and unsuspected alike. I took her to the fanciest restaurant in the neighborhood and visited her in her Chelsea apartment that night. During lunch she had skillfully parried all personal questions. When I admired the apartment and asked what she did for a living, she purred, "I am a maker of dreams. I am the inventor of love." I had found myself a poetess in the public library, right? Like hell I had. I had found another prostitute.

Even in the library, they picked me out and headed right for me.

It was a prostitute who provided the last flukish twist to the scenario of my capture.

After my nose had got back into reasonable shape, it seemed like an excellent idea for everybody concerned that we get back to work. I began to case a place over at Eighth Avenue and Fourteenth Street, one of those scenic corners where there were three banks. The one I selected was a branch of the Manufacturers Trust, not for any sentimental reason but only because it was the biggest and the busiest. The butchers from the wholesale meat markets on Tenth Avenue would come down in their white aprons to bank their receipts. The Transit Authority deposited such vast amounts that the money was carried in by the boxload. There were a remarkable number of small, confusing things about the operation that made the surveillance more interesting than usual. But also more complicated. For one thing, the porter lived somewhere in the building and opened the bank every morning from the inside. Since it was only a one-and-a-half-story marble edifice, it took a while before I was able to discover that he lived in a penthouse apartment. Or, at any rate, an apartment that had been built for him up on the roof. It also became obvious that some kind of massive internal investigation was taking place. Hordes of bank examiners would come marching in at closing time, and I could stand across the street and look up into the mezzanine and see them working away until midnight.

The real problem for me, however, was an armored car which arrived every morning to pick up a payroll during that crucial half hour between the time the vault was sprung and the time the doors were opened to the public. Due to the heavy traffic in that area during that hour, the time of their arrival could fluctuate by as much as ten minutes. My job, as anybody who has been paying attention should be able to see, was to figure out a way to tie up the traffic at a couple of key intersections along their route. An interesting project. All kinds of possibilities leaped to my mind. In the end, however, it was going to depend entirely upon the terrain. The targets of opportunity. The first thing I had to do, therefore, was trail them for a while to get their route and schedule down.

Not infrequently, I would detour to Central Park on my way back to Fifty-seventh Street, to feed the pigeons. I was sitting on a park bench during this period, doing exactly that, when a young girl sat down beside me and started to hum softly to herself. I asked what the song was, and we struck up a conversation. Her name was Mary Margaret Moore, and she had only recently come over from Ireland. Actually, she was half-Irish and half-Arab. And all-dumb. But quite pretty. She had the biggest eyes and the smallest mouth I had ever seen, and a marvelous little-girl smile to go with her little-girl brain. She lived in a small hotel on Ninety-first Street on the other side of the park. Another of those once-elegant neighborhoods that had deteriorated while I was away. The hotel now had a reputation as a hustlers' paradise, and she wasn't staying there by mistake.

Still, she was very good at her work, and after the first time she refused to take any money from me, which was great for my ego and not so great for those resolutions of nonattachment. The second or third time I took her out I did one of those things that are so dumb that after it's over you say to yourself, Did I really do that? I don't *believe* I could have done that. I took her home to Dean Street. Oh, I was pretty careful about it. I had the cabdriver drop us at the plaza across Atlantic Avenue, took the long way around to the house, and, to make sure she didn't see the address, put my arm around her and romanced her as we were going in and, again, as we were going out.

From that time on, I knew I was going to have to get rid of her. What brought it to a head, though, was something else entirely. I had begun to notice that one of her eyes seemed to look a little larger than the other one at times; not larger really but kind of bulging out. The first time I mentioned it she just laughed it off: "Oh, that's the eye I keep open when I'm making love." Finally there came a night when it was so bad that it distorted her whole appearance. And she was no longer in a mood to laugh about it. She had cancer in the eye, she told me. The doctor had warned her that if she didn't go into the hospital to have it operated on very soon it was going to spread to the other eye and blind her. After I left her, I went from tavern to tavern just trying to see how drunk I could get, that's how shaken I was. I had made another date to meet her for dinner in a couple of days—what else could I do?—but I knew even while I was making it that I was then going to make another date to see her that night and not show up. The coward's way out, that's right.

As luck would have it, I was meeting Kling that same afternoon. Clara, the gourmet cook, had disappeared again and so the three of us had dinner together and for some reason or other took the Circle Line boat around Manhattan on a sightseeing trip. Now, Tommy had shown a distinct interest in Mary all during dinner, far more than he should have under the circumstances. When he learned that I didn't intend to keep the date he had heard me make with her, he gallantly offered to keep it for me.

Jeez, here's a guy who had just been taken for everything he had by one tramp, and he can't wait to hook up with another one. "Well," I said, without enthusiasm. "You know where she's going to be."

And so Tommy started dating her. Off with the old and on with the new. Mary continued to live at the hotel, though, and it seemed that every time I'd see Tommy he'd tell me he had been out with her the night before and she wanted to see me. I didn't want to see her. Just the thought of that eye gave me the shivers.

So now you've got the background: I had things worked out so that I was ready to hit the bank anytime now, and I kept urging Tommy to get rid of her before she came to know too much about us. Van Why was still handing him those stories of imminent wealth and paying him back not a dollar. And, to complete the picture, one other thing: In order to trail the armored car, I had bought a new Chevrolet. I had bought it in the city under the name of Charles Gordon and, in case I should be stopped for anything in my own neighborhood, I had given an address on Pacific Street, which was the next street over. Instead of having De Venuta steal a car, I was toying with the idea of using the Chevy, putting the plates from one of the junked cars on it, and, depending on how it went, either dumping the car after the robbery or putting the original plates back on and holding on to it.

That's how everything stood on the morning of February 18, 1952. I had an appointment to pick Tommy up at Union Square, a few blocks from where he was living. Tommy was going to see Van Why again, and with the job so near at hand I felt it would be an excellent idea for me to be there. Just as I was ready to leave, there was a knock on the door. It was a Western Union boy with a telegram from Mary asking me to meet her the following day. Either she had seen the address the night I brought her back with me or she had remembered the location well enough to come back and find it. Damn! Damn, damn, damn. I jammed the telegram into my jacket pocket.

I didn't know it yet but the clock was ticking.

I walked out onto Dean Street and tried to start the car. Nothing. The battery had gone dead. Never happened to me before in my life. Not even with a junk car. There was a service station right around the corner on Third Avenue where I knew I could get a rental, but when I got there I was told that the mechanic who handled the batteries hadn't come in yet. "First time in ten years he's been late," the attendant told me. He couldn't drive the tow truck around and give me enough of a charge to get started, because there was nobody else there to take care of the station. The only thing he could suggest was that I come back in about an hour.

Well, I couldn't wait an hour. I was already late, and there was no way for me to get in touch with Kling. It wasn't that important, anyway. It was only a fifteen-minute ride to Union Square by subway, and we were probably better off without a car in the city, anyway.

The first thing Tommy said to me when I got there was, "Where's your car?" He wasn't going to meet Van Why in his New York apartment this time. It seemed that Van Why also had a home out on Long Island, and Tommy was going to see him there. That's why he had asked me to come along, his own car was in the garage and he needed a ride. "Jesus," he said. "I wish you'd go back and get the battery put in because I really think he's got some money for me this time." For just a moment or so I balked. As sure as Tommy was that Van Why wouldn't dare to have him come out and meet his wife if he didn't have the money, that's how sure I was that he didn't have the money and would never have the money. But, what the hell, I could be wrong too.

I walked back through the park to the BMT subway entrance and as I was going down the stairs I could hear the rumbling of an approaching train. I ran for it, got through the turnstile, and just managed to grab the door and squeeze through as it was closing. Of all the unforeseeable and unpredictable things that happened that day, this is the one my mind keeps going back to. If only I had missed that train. If only I hadn't run. If only I hadn't had a dime in my pocket. If only one out of any number of things hadn't happened that day, I wouldn't have been on that train and whether I was eventually caught or not, Arnold Schuster would probably be alive today.

Although the train was quite crowded I was able to find a seat in the corner where I could easily observe everybody else in the car while appearing to be reading my newspaper. At DeKalb Avenue, the first stop after we got to Brooklyn, a mob of people pushed in, so many that several of them had to stand. From DeKalb it was less than half a mile to Pacific Street, the shortest stop on the line. A ride of perhaps thirty seconds. Arnold Schuster, who had been shopping in downtown Brooklyn, had got on the train at DeKalb. Schuster was a twenty-four-year-old Coast Guard veteran who worked as a pants-presser in his father's tailor shop. He also seemed to have been something of a crime-story buff. On the wall, alongside the presser, he had tacked an FBI flyer that had been sent out on me; six pictures with five different kinds of mustaches drawn in. Including the pencil mustache I was wearing at the time. He had been looking at that flyer every day for two years, but still . . . How he could have made me during those few seconds, without my noticing, is something I will never understand.

As I was emerging up onto the street, I decided that I would be able to save time, in the event that the mechanic still hadn't arrived, by taking the battery out of the car myself, carrying it over to the service station, and picking up a new one.

While I was bent over the car with the hood up, a police cruiser pulled up and, out of the side of my eyes, I could see both officers get out and come up behind me. "Who owns this car?" one of them asked.

"I own the car." I grunted, without looking up. "Why?"

"Do you have a registration?"

"Of course I have a registration." I reached into

my pocket, handed it to him over my shoulder, and continued to loosen the bolts.

"All right, Mr. Gordon," he said at last. "Thank you." Perfectly satisfied, he handed the registration back to me. Now, anytime a couple of cops come up to you, you have to be concerned. And anytime they get back into their car and drive away, you breathe a sigh of relief. But that was the extent of it. When I got to the garage with the battery, the mechanic was there. I had already signed for the rental and was just preparing to take it back when another cruiser drove up. Out of it came a plainclothes detective. The first thing he wanted to know was what I was doing with the battery.

"I'm renting it," I said. "I've got a car around the corner and my battery went dead on me."

Detective Weiner, the guy doing the talking, asked to see both my registration and operating license. That was all right. I had made myself out a license for Charles Gordon. "This certainly looks genuine in all respects," he said. "The thing is that we've had a lot of cars stolen around this neighborhood lately. Would you mind coming back to the station with me so we can check on this license a little further to make sure it's genuine?"

"Sure," I said. Glad to. Why would an honest citizen like me object to a policeman doing his job?

What had happened was this: Schuster had followed me off the train, and because my mind was on the battery I hadn't been as alert as I should have been. Immediately, he had run around the corner and hailed down the cruiser. "I know you're going to think I'm crazy," he said. "But I just saw Willie Sutton. He's right around the corner fixing a car." Those were the two officers who had asked me for the registration.

Now, the police were plagued by people who had "just seen Willie Sutton." Anytime a couple of drunks wanted to have some fun they would say, "Hey, let's call up the cops and tell them Willie Sutton is here." Guys who looked like me, or vaguely like me, or not at all like me, were being turned in all the time. There was the seaman who had been pulled off the

Staten Island ferry. He was the spittin' image of me, no question about that. He was also only five feet tall.

The owner of a dry-cleaning store in Harlem once called in with the tip that I had left a couple of suits to be cleaned and was going to pick them up that night. A messenger picked the suits up, the police followed him, called for reinforcements, surrounded the house, and battered the door down. In the room they found a man who looked like me, plus a gun, plus a set of burglar's tools. Turned out that it was a guy named "A Thousand Keys" Adler who was also on their Wanted List. And a four-time loser at that.

Listen, while I had been casing the Manufacturers Trust Bank on Fourteenth Street, only a couple of weeks earlier, a guy came past me on his way to the Longshoreman's Union office across the street who was such a dead ringer for me that I thought to myself, Boy, when this bank goes, this guy is going to be in a whole lot of trouble.

When they weren't getting tips from people who had seen me, they were getting tips about jobs I was about to pull. It had become such a joke that the two patrolmen went back to the station and said, grinning, "Well, we almost caught Willie Sutton again, but he turned out to be a guy named Gordon." And then something inexplicable happened. When Detective Weiner heard the story, he said, "Let's go back and take another look." Why? One possible explanation is that before he had been promoted to third-class detective, Weiner had been a squad-car patrolman in Manhattan where he was in the habit of stopping off at a Chevrolet agency on his beat to visit a friend. "What are you hanging around here for?" his friend would always ask. "Why don't you go out and catch Willie Sutton?" Now do you want another coincidence? When Weiner began to put together the case, after I had been identified, he checked out the bill of sale on the goddamn Chevrolet that had started it all and found that it had been purchased at the Spielman Chevrolet Agency, the same agency he had visited so often, and had been sold to me—that's right—by his buddy, the same guy who had put the name of Willie Sutton so strongly in his mind to begin with.

The police station was only a block and a half away from the service station. I had a pistol on me, and I wasn't even worried about that. It was in a holster which was attached to a narrow leather belt that went around my waist in such a way that the gun was kept well concealed. I had made it myself. My theory was that if an ordinary citizen suddenly identified me I could use it to frighten him off.

The police treated me very courteously. They asked me as a routine part of the interrogation whether I was wanted by the police. "Of course not," I answered routinely. "I've never been arrested in my life."

But they took my fingerprints anyway and left me sitting in a room with Weiner. And left me sitting, and left me sitting, and left me sitting. That's when I had to consider the probability that the prints were going to be identified. There was nobody in the room except the two of us. If I had pulled my gun I could have easily taken him unawares. But, I don't know, I just didn't have the energy any more. It suddenly came upon me that I was tired of being on the lam. It suddenly came on me that I really didn't care that much whether they made me or not.

When the cops started to come to the door and look in I knew that it was over. You could see it in their eyes: *So that's Willie Sutton.* In due time, the captain came in with a couple of other detectives and told me to stand up so they could frisk me. "Ho-boy," one of the detectives said when he came up with the pistol. "Look what this fellow had on him." Poor Weiner, I thought he was going to drop right through the floor. They really had some fun with him. There he had been, practically glued to me for half an hour, and it had never occurred to him to see whether I was packing a gun. It was all done in great good nature, though. These cops were elated. They were jubilant.

They had arrested the notorious Willie Sutton.

As much as they kidded Weiner for not finding the gun, there was none of this "you dirty sonofabitch" stuff directed at me for carrying it. Because, you know, an awful lot of cops in New York liked me by then. They knew that I had never harmed anybody. And, anyway, there was undoubtedly a notation in my file that it would be a waste of time to knock me around. By the time I was taken to the Queens Courthouse late in the afternoon, we were getting along so well that they were saying, "Come on, Willie. Why don't you be a good guy and clear up a couple of sheets for us. What the hell, you're gone anyway. You've got life piled on top of life."

"What are you talking about?" I said. "I never committed any crimes."

By that time, the little Bergen Street precinct had been turned into a circus. As soon as the word was flashed to headquarters, Police Commissioner George P. Monaghan had come racing over from Manhattan, along with the chief inspector and the chief of detectives. Miles McDonald, the District Attorney of Kings County, must have been in court or something, because he didn't get there until five minutes later. By then, the place was flooded with detectives. Another five minutes, and it was flooded with newspapermen.

"Well, we've got Willie," Monaghan announced. "We've got Willie Sutton." It was the culmination, he crowed, of one of the greatest manhunts in the history of the New York police department. "Sutton was the most sought-after criminal in the United States. We've caught the Babe Ruth of bank robbers."

After Monaghan had finished taking his bows, I was handcuffed to Detective Weiner and brought out to play Meet the Press. As I stepped into the room I was almost blinded by the photographers' lights. Stage directions were shouted at me from everywhere. Look up. Look down. Over here, Willie. Hold up your wrists so we can get the cuffs. Just one more time. With Weiner and the two cops; without Weiner and the cops.

When the photographers were finished with me, the reporters took over.

"Did you pull the Brink's job in Boston, Willie?"

"No, but I'll probably be blamed for it."

295

"What is it like to be a fugitive?"

"It's like taking a long lead off first base with a nervous pitcher trying to pick you off."

"What about the cops? Did you ever talk to them while they were looking for you?"

"I kept away from cops. I walked around them. Softly."

"How come you had all that money on you? Were you afraid if you put it in the bank somebody might come along and hold it up?" (Laughter.)

They had found three thousand dollars on me when I was arrested and another seventy-seven hundred or so in my room. And you know, of course, how they found the room. The telegram in my jacket addressed to John Mahoney of 340 Dean Street. They'd found it very quickly anyway, though. The car was parked right in front of the door. The telegram did something that was far more damaging than that. It got me convicted of the Queens Manufacturers Trust robbery. Although she had only signed it with her first name, it was easy enough to track her down. She had called the telegram in from her hotel, and all the police had to do was check with the telegram office to get her full name and her address. With all the excitement, it was two days before they got around to it. Better that they had done it immediately.

She identified my picture, she told them she had been hanging around with me and Tommy Kling, she told them where Tommy lived, and she agreed to take them there.

Now we're back to the split-second timing again. Having heard that I was arrested, Kling and De Venuta had been laying low, being particularly careful not to contact each other. Two days having gone by without a mention of either of them, De Venuta had decided that it would be safe to go to Tommy's basement apartment on Eighteenth Street and talk things over.

Within a matter of minutes after Mary had brought the police there, who comes knock-knock-knocking on the door, carrying his little grocery-store bag with the tuna-fish sandwiches, but Venuta.

"Who the hell are you?" the police want to know. Oh, Venuta says, he was just a guy who had happened to meet Mr. Kling on the subway train a week or so ago and he had decided to bring over a couple of sandwiches to renew the acquaintance.

"You'd better come along with us too," said the police.

Now here's the significance of all this. Although I had been identified right after the robbery, my two accomplices hadn't been. If it hadn't been for Mary's telegram, Tommy would have been just another name on a long list of ex-cons I was known to be friendly with. De Venuta they didn't know about at all. And De Venuta was the key.

The police hustled them down to the nearest precinct, on East Seventeenth Street, and brought Hoffman, the bank manager, in to see whether he could identify them. He couldn't. So they let Sands, his assistant, look at them both through an open door first, and when he couldn't identify them either, they told him they were going to have a lineup in the morning and they wanted him to walk in and place his hand on both of their shoulders just to see how they reacted. Now, De Venuta was in no jeopardy at all. He had a perfect alibi. He could prove by the company's records—and a stamped time card—that he had been working at the time of the robbery. But when Sands placed his hand on his shoulder, he became so panicky that they were somehow able to talk him into making a full confession. In return for the promise of a suspended sentence, he agreed to return the money and testify against Tommy and me at the trial. He could have walked out with the money and his self-respect if he had kept his mouth shut. But he elected to do it the hard way.

So if you guessed back at the beginning that it was Tommy who betrayed me, you can see how wrong you were. The only reason Venuta could make that kind of deal was because he knew that whether he ratted on us or not, neither Tommy nor I would ever rat on him. He was only confessing to that one job. The police had even allowed him to specify in his confession that it was the only one we had ever pulled together. All we had to do was tell them about one of the others—and he had committed robberies with us in three other states—and they'd have had him nailed as a four-time offender.

One final coincidence. Two days after the trial ended, Maxwell Van Why was locked up in the Queens County House of Detention, the same jail where Tommy and I were being held. He had been arrested on the complaint of a woman client that he had taken money from her under false pretenses on a real-estate deal.

Now if only she had opened her mouth two months earlier . . .

Who Killed Arnold Schuster?

I was Willie Sutton, "the escape artist," and when you get a good legend going you can forget about common sense. It didn't matter that I hadn't tried to escape when I was sitting in the police station with a gun in my belt and only one detective guarding me. I was heavily manacled, put into a van all by myself— I never was to travel anywhere without being locked up in the van alone—and whipped through the streets to the Queens courthouse behind an escort of police cars. Except for a few minutes when I was put in a lineup that was being formed for Mr. Hoffman, I was kept in handcuffs all the time. They weren't even taken off then until I pointed out that if you had one man out of fifteen in handcuffs, it just might give him a hint.

While I was being arraigned the next day, I was surrounded by a double rank of armed bluecoats. Not to mention the burly bailiff who held my belt from behind to make sure I didn't flap my wings and go flying out the window. Not that it would have done me any good unless I was also able to snap my fingers and turn myself into a puff of smoke. Somebody counted thirty-two cops who had been assigned to security in and around the building.

The courthouse and the jail were in adjoining buildings. Before I was put into a cell, they examined me from head to foot to satisfy themselves I hadn't secreted anything on my person that could be used as a picklock. They gave me an anal examination. They examined my bridgework. They ran a fine-tooth comb through my hair. They searched between my toes. They had already evacuated a whole wing of the jail, and I was placed in the cell under a twenty-four-hour watch. By which I mean that a guard sat at a desk outside the cell where he could see me at all times. Like a death watch. And still they weren't satisfied. After they had locked me in, they took a big, heavy chain, wrapped it around a couple of bars of my cell and a couple of bars in the next cell, and put the world's biggest padlock on it.

They took my belt away from me. The metal thingamajig on the buckle. They took the metal drinking cup out of the cell. If I wanted to brush my teeth, I had to ask the guard for the brush and the toothpaste. Same thing with soap. No metal or points there, but if I did get ahold of something metallic or pointy it could be hidden in the soap. If I wanted to write a letter, the guard would hand me a pen and take it back again as soon as I was finished. Although my shoes had been meticulously examined during the original search, they decided to take them away from me too. Just in case, you know, the guard blinked his eyes and I managed to open the door, remove the padlock and the chains, and hit him over the head with one of them. When I was taken to Brooklyn eight days later to be arraigned on the charge of possession of firearms, I had to make the trip in a pair of bedroom slippers. I was almost fifty-two years old, you understand. Every cop there could have given me a ten-yard lead and caught me before I'd gone fifteen.

Tommy Kling was being arraigned on the gun charge at the same time and even though Tommy was going to stand trial in Queens for the Manufacturers Trust robbery with me, the judge decided to keep us separated. "That combination in one institution might be rather volatile," he said. Tommy was remanded back to the Tombs in Manhattan and I was whisked back to Queens.

I had been brought to Brooklyn in the van under a heavy escort with the sirens going. All that had done was attract a crowd which cheered me lustily as I was brought in and even more lustily when I was brought out. Nor was it only because I was being looked on as a hometown boy who had made good. The same thing had happened outside the courthouse in Queens. "Make a run for it, Willie," a bunch of college kids had yelled as I was being brought in. "We're with you."

In the course of sentencing me on the "possession of firearms" charge, Judge Louis Goldstein said bitterly, "Sutton managed for several days to bask in a kind of bizarre public adulation. There actually was applause for him in the theaters when his picture was shown." Notes were constantly being sent to me inside the jail to let me know that I was being looked upon as something of a folk hero, particularly up in Harlem. That really had me puzzled for a while. There was a Negro guard who was assigned to the floor I was on, and although there was no earthly reason why he had to come into my wing while he was making his rounds, he would come by every day and tell me that he could hardly walk through the streets of Harlem on his way home without being stopped on almost every streetcorner and asked, "How is Willie doing? Take good care of him."

I had the glimmering of an idea that it had something to do with my being an outsider. A thorn in the side of the authorities. Every once in a while I actually outwitted the bastards, you know. But words like *power structure, the Establishment,* and *rip-off* weren't part of the political vocabulary yet. Not in my wildest dreams had I ever looked upon bank robbery as a revolutionary act, and busting out of jail had no social significance to me whatsoever. Hell, I was a professional thief. I wasn't trying to make the world better for anybody except myself.

The notes wouldn't have been delivered to me at all, I'm sure, if it hadn't been for the very pleasant relationship I had developed with the warden of the Queens County House of Detention, Marvin Klein. Every night, Warden Klein would visit me, and if he had come to reassure himself that I hadn't evaporated into the winter air, he would stay to talk about all kinds of things. The books that had been found in my Dean Street room had attracted a great deal of attention. In addition to three very practical books (*First Aid and Emergency Treatment, A Business of Your Own,* and the Spanish grammar), my library had consisted of *Peace of Soul* by Bishop Fulton Sheen, *Peace of Mind* by Rabbi Joshua Loth Liebman, *You Can Change the World* by Reverend James Keller, *In Search* by Meyer Levin, and *The Basic Writings of Sigmund Freud.* Warden Klein had introduced himself by handing me a list of the best books that were available in the jail library. The one I chose, I distinctly remember, was Dos Passos's trilogy, *U.S.A.*

In a way it was funny. Although our conversations began with him asking how a man with my interests had become a thief, he was such an unusually humane and intelligent man for his line of work that in short order I was asking how a man like him had become a warden. A very interesting story. Having lost his job during the Depression, and given up hope of finding another, he had taken to getting up in the morning, walking to Central Park, sitting around on a bench for a while, and going back home. One morning he had unaccountably turned around and walked downtown instead. For miles and miles. In a complete daze. When he came to, he had found himself in front of the Municipal Building in a section of the city he had never been in before. He went in to use their men's room, saw a long line of men, and was told that they were waiting to fill out applications to become prison guards. Eventually he was called and assigned to Riker's Island, and, being so superior to the work he was doing, he had risen very quickly through the ranks. So there it was again. The accidents that determine your life.

Under the circumstances, Klein did what he could for me. He had a radio put on the guard's desk and instructed him to tune in to whatever programs I wanted. He'd have a sandwich or two sent in to me late at night. And he had a good sense of humor. As he was leaving he would invariably say to the guard, "Just remember, it's against the rules to let Willie try on your uniform." Kiddingly, on purpose.

The laughter stopped on the night of March 8, when Warden Klein woke me out of a sound sleep to tell me, "Schuster is dead."

The first words out of my mouth were, "What was it, an automobile accident?"

"No," he said. "He was shot." A gunman had jumped out of an alley a few blocks from his home and pumped four bullets into him.

"Oh my God," I said. "That sinks me."

The warden had awakened me because he couldn't wait until morning to bring me the unhappy tidings. All the big brass from the police department and the DA's office were downstairs, he told me, waiting to question me about it.

"Holy Jesus, Warden. I don't know anything about this."

Whether I talked to them or not, he said emphatically, was entirely up to me. I could refuse to see them or, if I wanted, he would send for my lawyer. "I don't want to influence you in any way," he said. "But if I were you I wouldn't put myself in the position of refusing to cooperate. If you want, I can tell them you're willing to talk to two or three of them and they can pass on what you have to say to all of the others."

That's what I did. A captain came up with a couple of inspectors. "Willie," they said. "What's this all about?" Knowing how scrupulous I had always been about avoiding violence, they were every bit as bewildered as I was.

"Jesus, I don't know. I'd like to know myself. Up to now there was a chance of beating this. I can't possibly get any consideration after this. This here trial becomes a mockery."

They knew it as well as I did.

With the murder of Arnold Schuster, the public's attitude toward me turned completely around. They had viewed me as a little guy who had outwitted the authorities without hurting anybody, and there was now a young man, a Coast Guard veteran, who had been gunned down in the street, gangster-style, because he had tried to be a good citizen. I could understand their attitude very well. I felt the same way. Even as I had said, "That sinks me," my heart had gone out to that poor kid whose life was over because he had happened to see me on a train.

Even the security had a different flavor to it. Ten days after the murder, we went to trial in a courtroom which had become an armed camp. A heavy police guard was posted all around the courthouse, and a cruiser circled the building constantly. Policemen were posted in every door and every window. Two detectives guarded the office of the jail on a twenty-four-hour basis, presumably to thwart any attempt to rescue me. I myself was always brought from my cell manacled to a guard and surrounded by a protective shield of others. While I was in the courtroom, the guard sat directly behind me, inside the rail, never taking his eyes off me.

The courtroom was on the third floor. Except for me, the elevator never stopped there. Everybody else had to get off at either the second or fourth floor and take the stairs. At the landing, they were confronted by a picket fence of guards and policemen. Those who had come to the third floor for some other reason had to state their business and identify themselves. If they were there to attend the trial, they were frisked before they were allowed to enter the courtroom. And that included the judge and the witnesses, who were being kept under guard at all times, and the jury, which was being sequestered. Juries were very rarely sequestered in those days, even in a murder trial, and when the judge had informed them they were going to be locked up a few loud groans could be heard in the jury box.

I turned to my lawyer and said, loud enough for them to hear, "Tell them I'll trade my time for theirs."

Although Arnold Schuster's name was never mentioned, his ghost hung over the entire proceedings. When the prosecutor said, in his summation: "He isn't a Robin Hood, he's just a hood," it had an entirely different meaning than it otherwise would have. It affected the sentence I received for the robbery itself and, to an even greater extent, the possession-of-firearms charge. A second pistol had been found in my Dean Street apartment, and not only was I sentenced to from fifteen years to life on *each* of the gun counts, the judge emphasized that the sentences were not to run concurrently, as was the practice, but consecutively. "If Sutton were not the miserable character that he is," Judge Goldstein said, "the chain of circumstances which led up to the death of the Schuster boy never would have happened. . . . These sentences ought to be sufficient to insure that Sutton is sealed off for life in a place where he can no longer bring misery and death, either directly or indirectly, to the public.

"I only regret that the law prevents me from sentencing him to death," he snapped. "There isn't a vestige left in him worth a damn. Take him out. Get rid of him."

Arnold Schuster haunts me. He haunted me for purely selfish reasons while I was at Attica, but, above and beyond that, there is a wrenching philosophical point involved. I had been born thirty years before Schuster, and the fact of my being born, and being who I was, had resulted in his death. Throughout my career I had plotted and planned my jobs to make sure that I would not have to hurt anybody, and now, after it was over and I was sitting in jail, a good-looking, promising young man had been killed because of me.

The laughter of the gods.

To make it even more ironic, the name of Arnold Schuster hadn't even been mentioned until three days after my capture. Having seen the patrolmen return to their cruiser after questioning me and drive away, he had gone back down the subway and continued his briefly interrupted journey to Borough Park. It wasn't until he turned on the news that night that he learned I had been arrested. And also that the cops were taking all the credit.

The official police version was that the patrolmen in the squad car had spotted me as they were driving down Dean Street and immediately whipped out the picture of me that all New York policemen were instructed to carry—tear sheets, actually, from the issue of the police magazine that had carried the full story of my career. Their version was that one of them had kept watch over me and tracked me to the gas station while the other had gone back to the police station to get Weiner.

In making the announcement of "the best collar in recent history," Police Commissioner Monaghan had thrown his arms around each of them and promoted them to first-class detectives on the spot. Mayor Impelliteri was so overjoyed, or perhaps so eager to get in on the publicity, that a special commendation ceremony was scheduled at City Hall.

At that, Schuster might very well have let the whole thing go if the morning newspapers hadn't carried the little item that because they were police officers doing their job they wouldn't be eligible for the seventy thousand dollars worth of reward money that was out on me. Schuster promptly called the Bergen Station to assert his claim and was told that I had been removed to Queens and that he should talk to somebody there. When Queens gave him the runaround too, he hired a lawyer. The lawyer called Commissioner Monaghan direct, and when the Commissioner emerged from their subsequent meeting it was to announce, with some embarrassment, that the failure to mention the part Arnold Schuster had played in my capture had been a regrettable oversight. The ceremony at City Hall was abruptly canceled. The promotions stood.

Unfortunately, the lawyer had considerably less success when it came to collecting the reward money. There wasn't any. A pure newspaper concoction. The only thing Schuster was eligible for, by stretching a point, was a standing fifty-dollar reward which the state of New York offered for information leading to the recapture of an escaped convict.

Still, Schuster had become a minor celebrity. He made a few television appearances on interview shows and game shows. A watch company got into the act by presenting him with its "good-citizenship award"—which was one of their watches. To balance that, he was subjected to a flood of threatening letters and phone calls. The family took them for exactly what they were: not serious enough to require police protection but annoying enough so that they disconnected their phone.

On the night of March 8, he left his father's shop and began to walk home, a distance of about a mile. There was a party on in the neighborhood that night, and he was going to change his clothes before he went. Along the way, he bumped into four friends who were on their way to the same party and he stopped for five or ten minutes to chat with them. It was then nine o'clock.

He was ten doors from his house when the killer, who had apparently been lying in wait for him in a darkened driveway, stepped out and pumped four bullets into him. One bullet hit him in the lower abdomen, one passed through the bridge of his nose, a third entered behind the left ear and pierced his brain, a fourth singed his scalp. The first bullet had apparently hit him in the abdomen and the others had plowed into him as he was falling. He was dead when he hit the sidewalk.

After the first incorrect reports had been straightened out, it seemed that nobody had heard the shots, or at least wanted to admit that they had. The shooting had taken place directly in front of a doctor's home. A woman came across the body as she was walking down the street; she ran to ring the doctor's doorbell, and it was the doctor who examined the body and called the police. Ten doors away, Schuster's mother, father, and sixteen-year-old brother were watching television when a bulletin broke into the program. They ran into the street, and there he was. A grisly scene. It had fallen to the brother to officially identify the body.

"That sinks me," I had said. To sink me further,

the automatic suspect as far as the newspapers were concerned was Freddie Tenuto. Why not? All they had to do was look through their files and see that the guy who had escaped with me from Holmesburg was known as The Accommodation Killer, and they were writing nonsense about "the code of the Underworld." To tie us even closer, they were able to quote unnamed police officials as identifying Tenuto as "the fourth member of the gang, and the only one still at large." To clinch it, there was a tip from a bartender that he had seen Tenuto about seven miles from where Schuster was murdered. A tip that would have been even more convincing if his description hadn't been so completely at variance with what Tenuto really looked like.

I didn't believe it for a second. To begin with, Tenuto and I weren't friends. We had been thrown together in a common enterprise, that's all. And that had been five years ago. In the second place, the "code of the Underworld" is a romantic myth. Generally speaking, thieves act out of the most primal instincts. Such as self-preservation and private revenge. An organized gang will try to eliminate a witness before he can testify against them, sure. An individual will take care of a partner who squealed on him, particularly in prison where there isn't much to do except brood about it and he hasn't got that much to lose anyway. But that's as far as it goes. If there is any "code of the Underworld," it is that you do not knock off ordinary citizens or newspapermen. To knock off a citizen is the surest way to bring the heat down on everybody, and when the heat is on you can be sure that your fellow criminals will be the first to turn you in. The law of self-preservation again.

Beyond all that, Tenuto would be aware that killing Schuster would be the worst thing he could do to me. He was a professional. I couldn't imagine anybody doing anything so dumb except some punk hoodlum who thought he'd be making a name for himself.

I could only hope that the police would find him and, in effect, clear me of any responsibility. Two hundred detectives were assigned to the case. Every police-woman on the force was assigned to interviewing the housewives in the neighborhood, on the theory that they might be more willing to give information to a woman than to a man. In the first week of April, only a few days after the trial ended, the murder weapon was found in an empty lot five blocks from where Schuster had been shot. The police very quickly established that the gun had been stolen from a U.S. Army shipment consigned to Japan. It was a .38-caliber Smith & Wesson Chief's Special that had been designed for extremely rapid fire. Before the night was over, they had fanned out through Brooklyn and arrested everybody who had been working on the pier at the time the shipment disappeared. Nine longshoremen were promptly indicted and held in a hotel on high bail.

A month later, the man who had made the actual sale of the stolen revolvers cracked, and a worldwide alarm was sent out for one John "Chappy" Mazziotta, a longtime hoodlum and bookmaker who, it developed, had disappeared from sight the day after Schuster was killed.

One interesting footnote: Shortly after the longshoremen were arrested, Anthony Anastasia, the Brooklyn dock boss, called a work stoppage as a protest against "local newspapers" which, he insisted, were trying to link him to the murder by suggesting that the gun which had killed Schuster had come from the pier under his control. Anthony Anastasia was the brother of Albert Anastasia, who was known as the Underworld Executioner and, also, as the undisputed ruler of the Brooklyn docks.

Mazziotta was never seen nor heard of again. The search for him went on for years, throughout the country and, indeed, throughout the world. The New York police followed tips that took them as far as Australia. I understand that more money was spent on the investigation than on any other murder in the history of the New York police department. From everything that I have heard, the file is larger, in sheer bulk, than for any other investigation in the department's history, too.

Tenuto was never seen again either, although his name popped up from time to time for a couple of years. There was a *Readers' Digest* article about him, part of a series on the most-wanted men on the FBI list, in which he was identified as a prime suspect in the Schuster murder. There was even a CBS-TV show, a video version of the old Gangbusters radio program, which left little doubt that he was the murderer of Arnold Schuster.

I had an interest in having the real murderer discovered that went far beyond idle curiosity. With the new rulings coming out of the U.S. Supreme Court I could see where I had a chance of getting out on a series of technicalities. I could also see that while the technicalities could get me halfway out the door, it was going to take a sympathetic judge—which meant a sympathetic public—to take me the rest of the way. Which meant that I was going to have to sit back and wait until I had been completely cleared of any complicity in the murder of Arnold Schuster.

And then, in October 1963, there was a sudden, unexpected break in the case. In the course of his testimony before the U.S. Senate Investigating Committee, Joseph Valachi, the Mafia songbird, stated—almost as an aside—that Schuster's murder had been ordered by Albert Anastasia. According to Valachi, the Executioner had become so incensed at seeing Schuster being awarded the "good citizenship" watch that he had turned to the four henchmen who had been watching the news program with him and said, "I can't stand squealers. Hit him!" Only one of the henchmen was named, the one who had done the killing. A fellow named Frederick Tenuto.

After all that time, the one man who could be tied to me in the eyes of the public had been positively identified.

But an astonishing thing happened. As I read the newspaper reports, there was nothing, anywhere, to connect Frederick Tenuto to me. *The New York Times,* which had a whole file of clips nailing us to each other, merely wrote that according to Valachi, Anastasia had "ordered a thug, Frederick Tenuto, to kill Arnold Schuster." That's all. An otherwise unidentified thug. Even in the definitive book *The Valachi Papers,* which came out four years later, all

Peter Maas wrote was: "To cover himself, Anastasia then had Schuster's killer, one Frederick Tenuto, murdered in turn. At the time Tenuto was being sought by the FBI for breaking out of prison. His body has never been found." That's all. One Frederick Tenuto who had broken out of prison.

The only way I can possibly explain it is through something I have seen good trial lawyers do when they are trying to divert the jury's attention away from the true meaning of a particularly damning bit of evidence. They call it "misdirection"—the magician's sleight-of-hand. So much information had come pouring out of Valachi over a two-day period that it became impossible to pick out anything except the highlights. In addition to that, the story of the Schuster killing had been brought up by Valachi only as a way of illustrating how unpredictable and savage Albert Anastasia had been. ("Albert A." had got *his* six years earlier while sitting in the barber chair at the Park-Sheraton.) Everybody's attention was focused so completely upon the psychopathic killer who had ordered the murder, and the almost offhand way ("murder by whim") in which it had been done that the man who had followed the orders practically disappeared from sight.

On top of everything else, Valachi had been tying law-enforcement people into the mob, and that had given everybody connected with the law a vested interest in knocking him down. The headline in *The New York Times* on the day Valachi delivered his version of the Schuster murder was "Police Deride Valachi Data as Stale Rumor and Gossip," and the story itself was filled with quotes from "spokesmen from the DA's office," "ranking police officials," "a leading attorney," and "a longtime Supreme Court justice," all of whom were anxious to get it on the record—while remaining off the record themselves— that Valachi either didn't know what he was talking about or, contrariwise, hadn't been saying anything they didn't already know anyway.

And there was this about it, too. Taken on its own terms, we have still another of those incredible coincidences. The guy who happens to be with Anastasia when Schuster comes on the screen just happens to be the one other guy who had made good on the escape from Holmesburg. It's not only a coincidence, it changes the story. It isn't that much of a whim any more, is it? What Anastasia would have been saying to Tenuto, regardless of how he said it, was, "Hey, I know you busted out of the can with this guy, and now you're the last one left. I'm going to be a good fellow about this and let you kill this guy who squealed to the cops on him." And now you've got to explain why, having given him permission, Anastasia then turns around and has him killed. It's getting too damn complicated for a guy who is writing to a deadline, even if Tenuto's name had rung a little bell, and with so many leading Mafia figures to check back on, "one Frederick Tenuto" is the last envelope the guy on the rewrite desk is going to pull.

How would I explain it? Not the way Valachi explained it, certainly. Although a great deal of what Valachi was saying rang true, much of it had obviously come to him secondhand. The gossip of the trade. The same kind of stories I'd heard mob guys gabbing about all my life. Racket guys are guys who always want you to think they know the score. They're called "the wise guys" these days, I notice, and it's the perfect description for them. I can easily imagine that when Anthony Anastasia called that strike, somebody said, "If Tony's calling his guys out, you know who told him, don't you?" And I can just hear another wise guy saying, "Yeah. Albert A. probably saw the sonofabitch getting that watch on TV, and he says, 'Hit the Jew bastard.' " And saying it with the kind of knowing smirk that lets everybody know he's heard Albert A. say the same thing a hundred times himself. After it has been repeated a couple of times, the "probably" goes and it is being stated as a fact.

Valachi could have easily remembered hearing something about it, the guy seemed to have total recall, and there was no way he couldn't have known that Tenuto had once been the prime suspect. Either the two memories had come together in his mind as the same story or, if he had simply wanted to make his story sound more authentic to the authorities, what better way than to offer confirmation for what he has reason to believe the police already suspect.

But that's nothing more than conjecture on how Valachi could have got ahold of the story if there was nothing to it. I could just as easily make out a case the other way by forgetting about Valachi and trying to figure out what was in it for Anastasia.

It has become an accepted part of the folklore that Anastasia ordered the murder out of a sudden whim. Why? Because Valachi said so? What makes a hood like Valachi so smart all of a sudden? Look, Valachi was terrified of Anastasia. The Schuster story came to light while he was explaining how terrified he was upon learning that Anastasia was going to preside at "a table" that had been called to hear a complaint that had been placed against Valachi by his partner. And yet, by Valachi's own testimony, the ruling that Anastasia eventually handed down was a very nice mixture of fairness and diplomacy.

The first thing you have to do, then, is look at Albert Anastasia for what he really was, not what Valachi, with his limited mentality, thought he was. The streets are filled with guys who will murder anybody you want for two hundred dollars. Anastasia didn't rise to the top because he was more willing to kill than the others, but because he was smarter than the other killers. So let's state some basic principles:

1 / Anastasia would have known exactly what he was doing to me. What did he care? I didn't mean anything to him.

2 / Anastasia wasn't going to kill anybody unless he was going to derive some benefit from it. "I can't stand squealers," Anastasia had said. And at the time he sure couldn't. The investigation was going on that was going to result in the formation of the Waterfront Commission with complete authority to clean everybody with a criminal record off the docks. Anastasia, in his murderous, calculating way, could very well have been looking for a way to get the message across to his people that anybody who did any squealing was going to die.

3 / Tenuto wouldn't have just happened to be there.

312

If Anastasia was using Tenuto to do the job, it was because he had sent for him. That means that he wanted somebody disposable. Somebody he could use and blow away without thinking twice about it. In other words, somebody outside his immediate organization. The story about the Holmesburg escape had been all over the papers at the time of my capture, and so Tenuto would have come immediately into his mind. "That guy Sutton escaped with," you can almost hear him say. "Wasn't he around here for a while. Find out where he is and tell him Albert's got a job for him." What's Tenuto going to say to him, no?

It's a nice scenario. It explains all the things that are otherwise unexplainable and it ties up all the loose ends. But is it true? I don't know. A couple of years later, the FBI came to Attica and asked to talk to me about Tenuto. Normally, I would have refused to see them. In fact, when the dep brought me into the visitors' room and I saw who it was, I was furious at him. That's all anybody has to hear in prison, that you're talking to the FBI. In this instance, though, there was nothing I could tell them and every chance that I might be able to learn something. I did. "We closed the file on Tenuto," they told me. A few days later I read that a Mafia loanshark and enforcer named Kayo Konisberg had led the police to a New Jersey chicken farm which had served as a Mafia graveyard. Whether Tenuto's body was found there or not doesn't matter. If Konisberg knew that much, he would have known where all the Mafia bodies were buried.

The police obviously believe that Tenuto was executed. Since they have let the record stand about the Anastasia story, I have to assume that they have also come to believe the Valachi testimony, in its broad outlines, and perhaps have even confirmed it. I tend to believe it more than I disbelieve it. I also tend more toward Mazziotta as the trigger man than toward Tenuto. Why? Because I can't imagine as experienced a killer as Tenuto throwing the murder gun where it could be found.

So why won't they tell us? The New York police have that massive file, and the FBI summaries would certainly be part of it. The public has paid for it all. Why don't they tell us once and for all whether they do or do not know who killed Arnold Schuster?

A Question of Guilt

A few days after I had been arrested, the guard at the Queens County House of Detention handed me my clothes and told me that my daughter was in the visiting room waiting to see me. I tell you, it sent me into a spin. The last time I had seen Jeanie she had been a little five-year-old girl, no more than a dim outline seen through the heavy mesh screen in the visiting room at the Eastern State Penitentiary. As a baby she had been a redhead—a Sutton trait—but that didn't mean she still was. She would be a full-grown woman now, almost twenty-two years old. A woman with a complaint against me that could never be answered.

I longed to see her and I was afraid to face her.

"How about my tie?" I asked the guard.

The visiting room was at the bottom of the stairs. Up ahead, manning the desk at the entrance to the jail, was a captain and a complement of guards. I held up my wrists and asked my guard to take the handcuffs off. Twice. "Take them off, or take me back to the cell," I said finally. "I'm certainly not going in there this way."

Well, he took them off but not before he had passed the buck to the captain, and the captain had put in a call to the warden. The solution was that the guard would stand within arm's reach of me all through the visit.

The visiting room was brightly lit, but it was cut in

314

half by a wall of glass which was segmented into narrow booths by a series of steel dividers. Jeanie was standing in the middle of the room, on the other side of the glass. For the first time in sixteen years I looked upon the face of my daughter. I thought she was the most beautiful woman I had ever seen. Her hair was still red—a light shade of auburn—and arranged in an upsweep of neat, lacquered waves. She had taken care to have her hair done before she came to see me, and that told me all I had to know.

The guard directed me to one of the center booths. Jeanie stood immobile for a few seconds, then walked very slowly into the other side of the booth. There were no chairs. We both had to stand and converse through the glass window. It was, after all, a jail not a prison. They wanted the visitors to move in and out fast. Her eyes were as large as saucers as she studied my face. Then she smiled shyly and whispered, "Dad . . . At last I know what you look like."

The only reason she hadn't been in to see me earlier, she said, was because it had been necessary to get the personal approval of the District Attorney. Once she had been able to prove to him that she was really my daughter, he had set this special hour aside for her in the evening, as much for her protection as for reasons of security.

At the time of my escape from Sing Sing, I had instructed Louise to destroy all of my pictures. As the restraints began to wear away, Jeanie told me how she had cut every picture she could find of me out of the newspapers as she was growing up so that she would know what I looked like. And how every morning for the past five years she had been studying the faces of men on the subway in the belief that she would be able to recognize me.

Her eyes positively sparkled when I told her I had been doing the very same thing in the belief that, somehow, I would be able to recognize her.

Shortly after the escape from Holmesburg, a story had made the rounds that I had died from wounds that had been received in an armed robbery and been buried up in the mountains of Pennsylvania. She had never believed it, she told me proudly. She had always *felt* that I was close by. "This is the most wonderful day in my life," she said, at last. "Tell me that you love me."

The guard at my elbow was forgotten as I told her what she meant to me. And then it was my turn to find out everything I could about her. Well, she was married and she had an eighteen-month-old daughter, Christine. "That's right," she beamed, "you're a grandfather." Her grandmother, Louise's mother, lived with her and took care of the baby while she was out to work. Al Jantzen had told me that Louise had remarried and that from everything he had been able to learn had married well. Jeanie confirmed it. Her mother's new husband was an engineer whose work took him all over the world, but they were still very close and corresponded regularly.

Throughout the visit, she expressed complete confidence that I would be released someday and we would be able to pick up the pieces. I didn't have the heart to disillusion her. After she left, with the promise that she would come to see me as often as they would let her, I went back to the cell and poured out all the things I hadn't been able to say in a long letter. She had come with a girl friend who had been waiting outside to drive her home, and I had warned her to make sure that no reporter followed them. I had learned from my sister, Helen, who had visited me earlier, that my mother had had a very bad experience with the press on the day I was arrested. Some reporters had come to her house and pushed their way in, with one photographer practically knocking her down as he shoved his camera into her face.

Because I wanted to spare Jeanie that, I asked her in the letter not to come to the jail again or, even, to attend the trial. I had made no effort to see her in the five years I was a fugitive, I pointed out, because I was determined to do nothing that would disrupt her life any further. It had not been an easy decision to make then, I wrote, and it was an even more difficult decision to make now.

As much as I want to see you, the only thing I

may ever be able to do for you and for my granddaughter is not to see you until after all this publicity dies down. Believe me, it is for the best. You may be thinking that you don't care what other people will say. But I will care. You will care what they say to Christine while she is growing up, and the time will come when you will hate me for that. It is even possible that you could lose your job. Your love is the only thing I have in the world. I do not want to lose it. Your visit made me very happy. I will write you a letter every night, and you can write me whenever you wish. The time will certainly come when I will win my release and we can see each other, without a guard listening in, every day.

I did not, of course, believe that for a second.

I ended by writing that Warden Klein would see to it that my letters were mailed and that if anything came up of an emergency nature she should contact me through my lawyer.

The most painful moment of the trial came when they called Nora Mahoney as one of their last witnesses, and I saw her come walking into the courtroom, a frightened little woman in strange and frightening surroundings. "This woman is an angel," I told my lawyer. "Under no circumstances are you to cross-examine her. I want you to give her every protection you can, regardless of how it affects the case."

As Nora took the stand her eyes darted nervously around the room. When they finally settled upon me she smiled tentatively and then, almost as an act of defiance, waved at me. She turned out to be some witness, but not for them. They were putting her on to establish that I had departed her home hastily shortly after the bank robbery and left the seven hundred dollars behind. To lay the foundation, they had to ask her how she had met me, and she leaped upon the question to tell the jury of my many kindnesses toward her and the other employees and of the generosity and concern I had shown toward the patients.

When Miss Bisset was put on the stand immediately

afterward to establish the period of time I had worked at the Farm Colony, my lawyer did cross-examine her and she was more than willing to substantiate everything Nora had said.

The two top prosecutors in the DA's office had been assigned to the case, James McGrattan and William Kerwick. I knew Kerwick. In his younger days he had been a defense attorney and he had represented Eddie Wilson in the Gleason murder trial. As often as not, he would visit me in the detention pen which adjoined the courtroom and we would sit there and talk about the good old days. "Whewwww!" he said. "If we put on a few more witnesses like that, they'll send you out of here with a medal."

"I got a winner this time, Bill," I said jokingly. "Tell McGrattan you want to quit and join the defense team."

"I wish I could believe it, Willie." But, he said, the state had spent an enormous amount of money to get a conviction, and they were going to get it. "You might have beat it at that if Schuster hadn't been killed," he admitted. "There's no way you can minimize the effect that's going to have on the jury, and if you ever tell anybody I said that I'll deny it."

My lawyer was George Washington Herz, and I'll tell you how I got him. When I was brought before Judge Peter T. Farrell the day after I was arrested, he asked me whether I had the money to hire a lawyer. "I have the funds, Your Honor," I said. "But they are being withheld by the police department at the moment." Herz just happened to be sitting in the courtroom, and Judge Farrell called him up and appointed him, temporarily, to represent me on the plea. Not that it mattered. All that happens in an arraignment is that you plead not guilty, and I had been doing that, without any help, all my life.

I asked my guards about him while I was being taken back to jail and discovered that George Washington Herz was a very well-known attorney in Queens. He had run for the District Attorney's office a few months earlier and lost by only four hundred votes. What that meant to me was that he was a member in good standing at the Queens County Courthouse, one of the family. Just happened to be sitting there, my eye. Lawyers have to get publicity the best way they can, and the Willie Sutton trial was going to be the most publicized trial to hit Queens since the Judd-Gray murder trial of the twenties. If George Washington Herz hadn't been called by Judge Farrell himself, he most certainly had been alerted by the clerk.

That afternoon, he came to the jail and I hired him. Having hired him, I lied to him. "I want you to know one thing," I said. "I didn't have a thing to do with that job they're trying me on here. Everything else they've accused me of, everything I was ever sent up for, sure, I was guilty. I did those and a hundred more they never heard about. But on this one, Mr. Herz, they're framing me."

Hadn't I ever heard about how you're supposed to tell your lawyer the whole truth and nothing but the truth? Sure I had. Who do you think started that except the lawyers themselves. I don't hire a lawyer to see how easy I can make life for him. All I'm interested in is having him beat the rap for me. Never mind what lawyers say, *if they think you're innocent they'll fight harder for you.* That's human nature.

Once I was convinced that he believed wholeheartedly in my innocence, if not my purity, I lied to him about my net worth. Most criminals are like babies when it comes to dealing with their attorney. The lawyer asks how much money they can raise, and the guy is so eager to prove what a successful thief he was that he gives him an honest count. Win or lose, the thief ends up broke and the lawyer ends up on the Riviera. I could have had Herz for nothing. I knew that. Actually, he wasn't even a criminal lawyer, primarily. He was a trial lawyer who specialized in corporation work. He had to hire a real criminal lawyer, James F. McArdle, as his cocounsel. I wanted to pay him, though, as a kind of final proof of my innocence, and so I told him I could raise ten thousand dollars. (The police had never found out about the Fifty-seventh Street apartment, and I had a

319

few thousand there. For the rest of it, I gave him a letter to Al Jantzen, who was still holding a substantial sum of money for me.) And I'll say this for him. He gave me a good run for my money. He really went all out to try to win that case for me.

Now that brings up another question. Why did I bother to fight it? I already owed the states of New York and Pennsylvania more time than I could possibly serve. In addition to that, they had caught me with a loaded pistol in my belt, and that automatically made me a fourth offender. Two reasons. My basic creed had always been never to admit anything they couldn't prove on me. I had escaped from prison, and they had recaptured me. Fine. Until they got a guilty verdict out of twelve jurors on the Manufacturers Trust job, I was still ahead of them on that one. That wasn't my rule, it was theirs. If I can get out of it, I have a right to get out of it. The other reason was that I had nothing to lose and, just possibly, something to gain. Never mind that I had all those other sentences against me. One way or another I knew that I wasn't going to be sitting still, and if it came to a legal attack, the less convictions I had against me the better off I was going to be.

To my way of thinking, the question should be put the other way around. Why did they go to the trouble and expense of bringing me to trial when they had about a hundred years against me anyway? With the massive security measures that were set up during the trial it must have cost them about a million dollars, almost as much as I had robbed from society during all the time I had operated. For the publicity, that's why. The District Attorneys want to become judges, and the judges are always looking toward the federal bench. I knew I was letting them exploit me, but what the hell, I also knew where I was going and I was in no hurry to get there.

One thing you have to say about a highly publicized trial is that you meet more interesting people than you are ever going to meet hiding in a one-room walkup or walking around a prison yard. The two most interesting people at the trial were Erle Stanley Gardner, the creator of "Perry Mason," and Meyer Berger, who was covering the trial for *The New York Times*. Gardner was doing a series on me for *Look* magazine, and he had interviewed me in the attorney's room, before the trial, in the presence of Herz and McArdle. He didn't really interview me, he was more interested, I gathered, in sizing me up. He told me about his work with the Court of Last Resort, a very successful organization he had founded to investigate the cases of possibly innocent people who had been sent to prison. We discussed certain aspects of the forthcoming trial while his secretary sat beside him, taking notes. She remained at his side all through the trial, and he was constantly dictating to her. It turned out that he had a lot of theories about me, most of them ridiculous. He wanted to "solve" me, the way Perry Mason solved all his cases, and he had been writing novels for so long that anything that looked interesting automatically became a plot device. In examining the records, for instance, he turned up a coincidence that he found absolutely fascinating. Most of my escapes and some of the robberies had taken place on the tenth of the month. Therefore, he decided, I had to believe that ten was my lucky number. It was all news to me, of course. Since escapes depend on any number of things over which you have very little control, most particularly the weather, he would have been far better off, I could have told him, studying the magical effects of number ten on the Gulf Stream.

Meyer Berger was something else entirely. He was supposed to be the reporter's reporter, the best all-around newsman in the country. And he sure didn't disappoint me. His day-by-day deadline reporting was so accurate, so remarkably well organized, and so incredibly well written that I came to look upon him with awe. In one minor regard, he came to look upon me with a certain amount of respect too. Right from the beginning, I had been taking the direct testimony of the state's witnesses down in shorthand and transcribing it for Herz overnight. Meyer was so sure that it was an act we were putting on to impress the jury that Herz turned my whole morning's work over to him during a recess and challenged him to have the court reporter check it against his own notes.

"I hate to say it," the court reporter told him. "But his are better than mine."

After that, Berger became so friendly with us that we were always sending little notes and wisecracks back and forth. For some reason that nobody was quite able to figure out, the state put a ballistics expert on the stand to testify that a couple of empty cartridges found in Kling's car had come from the automatic gun that had been found in his room. It came in the middle of the afternoon when everybody was inclined to doze off anyway, it had not a thing to do with the robbery of the Manufacturers Trust, and the cross-examination by Tommy's co-counsel became so technical and so repetitive that even the judge was fighting off sleep. After about an hour, Meyer sent a little limerick over to our table:

> They're boresome, these endless ballistics
> Intended only for mystics
> They ain't worth a button
> To Tom Kling or Sutton,
> Just jargon, and useless linguistics

During the trial a bitter argument broke out over the impounded money, which had supposedly been in the ground for twenty years. No matter how McGrattan tried, he could not get it into evidence. Finally Herz resolved it by magnanimously offering the money into evidence himself. Whereupon I whipped off a bit of doggerel of my own and passed it back to Meyer:

> My money that went to the jury
> Has caused me quite some fury.
> Tell me, is it a fact
> Will it come back intact?
> I tell you, I don't feel so sure-y

I had sent it to him along with a note assigning him to keep his eyes on the jurors and submit a report to me in triplicate if he should hear any rumor that they were skipping town. He didn't do that, he did something better. He had it printed in a special box in the *Times,* which is more than poets of a somewhat greater stature can boast.

By the end of the trial we had established such a close rapport through those notes that he presented me with a leather-bound history of the Roman Empire from his personal library.

George Washington Herz was a theatrical figure who dominated the courtroom. He would prowl around the well of the bar as he questioned witnesses; thundering and whispering, gesturing expansively, never still for a second. He had a way of crouching lower and lower as he shot his questions out until his fingers would be touching the floor like a sprinter waiting for the starter's gun to go off. At other times he would charge the witness stand like a fullback bucking the line. Whenever he was taking a witness through any movements he would act out the whole scene. It wasn't all histrionics, though. He did such a great job for me that if it hadn't been for De Venuta we would have won on a directed verdict, even McGrattan admitted that.

James Weston, the guard, put us in business right away when, to McGrattan's consternation, he backed away from making a positive identification. "He looks like him," Weston said. "But I can't positively say it's him." And that was as far as McGrattan could get the man I had spent all that time with, the only man I had been alone with, to go.

George Washington Herz cast a broad smile across the jury box when the witness was turned over to him. "No questions," he purred.

Hoffman, we weren't worried about. It didn't matter that he had identified me from my rogues' gallery photos immediately after the robbery and had walked into the lineup room after my arrest and very confidently placed his hand on my shoulder; we had a witness who we knew was going to destroy his credibility. An attorney named James T. McDonald, who had campaigned for District Attorney Quinn in his race against Herz. McDonald had been sitting in the lobby, waiting to talk to Quinn about becoming an assistant DA when Hoffman was brought in. The attorney and the banker knew each other, and so while they were waiting for me to arrive, Hoffman went over to talk to him. As the news of my arrival circulated through the lobby about twenty minutes later, they walked down the corridor and joined the crowd which had gathered outside the door of the room where I was seated between two huge detectives. "Which one is Willie?" Hoffman asked McDonald.

McDonald had to tell him I was the little one in the middle.

Knowing that he was going to be able to impeach him with McDonald's testimony, Herz had set him up good. A couple of weeks before the trial, he had taken an attorney from his firm (not McArdle) to the Manufacturers Trust, asked to see Mr. Hoffman, and spoken to him about taking out a mortgage. In answer to Herz's first question, Mr. Hoffman rated his memory as not less than perfect. It was because of his excellent memory for faces, he said proudly, that he had been appointed manager of the bank.

Q Do you recall my visiting you at the bank a few weeks ago?

A Yes.

Q Was I alone?

A No, you were with another man.

Q Do you see the other man in court?

A Yes.

Q Where is he?

"Right there," Hoffman said, indicating James F. McArdle.

"We spoke to you about twenty minutes?"

"Yes."

"Take another look at Mr. McArdle and tell me whether you are positive he was the man with me."

"Yes, I am positive."

Herz had the other lawyer stand up, and Mr. Hoffman was forced to retract his earlier identification.

From there, Herz took him through his trip to the courthouse on the night of my arrest. He was absolutely certain, Hoffman testified, that he hadn't spoken to anybody while he was waiting for me to arrive.

   Q Did you see Sutton anytime prior to the lineup in another room seated between two detectives?

   A No.

   Q Did you go to an opened door with another gentleman you had been seated next to and ask that other gentleman, "Which one is Sutton?"

   A No.

After McDonald had testified as a defense witness on the last day of the trial, Herz tried to have Hoffman recalled to the stand. Somehow the state was unable to produce him.

It was in the cross-examination of the assistant manager, Sands, that Herz really hit the top of his form. We hadn't expected Sands to identify me. We had thought he was being put on the stand for the sole purpose of identifying Tommy Kling. We knew that he had been given a chance to examine Kling and De Venuta surreptitiously at the police station. That information had been supplied to Tommy's lawyers by the DA's office. What Herz had been able to discover through his own contacts was that Sands had also been brought to the courthouse while I was being arraigned and had been unable to identify me. Having failed to identify any of us at first look, he took the stand and positively identified all three of us. By the luck of the draw, the direct examination ended late in the afternoon and so Herz had an opportunity to plan his cross-examination overnight.

It turned out to be a very rainy day, and as Herz lifted himself up and strolled, very slowly, towards Sands, the courtroom became so quiet that you could hear the rain beating on the window. "You know my name?" he asked, as his opening question.

Sands's eyes opened wide. "Yes."

"My first name?"

"George Washington."

I was as startled as everybody else in the courtroom until I saw what he was doing. If Sands knew that much about my lawyer, it could only be because he had been reading everything written about the upcoming trial and would therefore have seen my picture in the paper many, many times since the day he had been unable to identify me.

Before he was through with him, Herz had completely impeached him. As always, I had taken down Sands's direct testimony the previous afternoon and as I had turned it over to Herz that morning he had told me that he wanted me to take the cross-examination too. "No matter what happens," he said, "keep your head down and keep writing."

I had been scribbling away for about fifteen minutes when suddenly he pointed at me and thundered, "Look at Sutton. Take a good look at him. Can you see his entire face? Can you see his full face? His face is presently obscured, is it not? Didn't you notice during the entire time you were on the witness stand that he was in that exact position, taking notes?"

The witness, somewhat disconcerted by the quick change of subject, said very carefully, "I noticed he was taking notes."

"At no time did you have an opportunity to get a full view of Mr. Sutton's face—is that right?"

"I can't say."

"You can't recall," Herz boomed triumphantly, "that at any time you had a full view of Sutton's face —is that right?"

The witness nodded and murmured something unintelligible. And that's when Herz turned it completely around and got him to admit that he had, in fact, been able to get a very good look at me when he was brought to the arraignment by a couple of detectives.

A short time later, he forced him to admit that he had seen De Venuta's name and picture in the newspapers before the identification, too: that he had not been able to identify him in the police station on the day of the arrest and that he still couldn't make a positive identification on his "independent recollection alone." "Describe him," he ordered, and after Sands had described him quite accurately, he started to take one of his charges at him, came to a sudden halt, wheeled around, and shouted, "Bring out De Venuta."

It was the first time Kling or I had seen Venuta

since the arrest, and I stared very hard at him, trying to get him to look at me. He wouldn't. But, do you know, I still didn't think he was going to testify against us. Not even then.

The first inkling we had that we might be in trouble came when De Venuta was sent to the Bronx County jail, more popularly known as the Singing School because that's where they always sent the canaries. If I wasn't as worried as I should have been, it was because the police always try to make crime partners think the other one is talking. That's routine procedure. The detective who arrested Tommy had told him they knew where he was living only because I had fingered him, he admitted that from the witness stand. "I don't believe it," Tommy had told him. "If you brought him here and he told me that himself I still wouldn't believe it."

Even after Herz told me that De Venuta had made a statement implicating Tommy and me I refused to believe it. He had such a good reputation and he came from such a good family that I was sure that even if he had implicated himself he would never have brought us into it. Up until the moment that he began to spill his guts, I was sure that when he got on the stand he was going to retract his confession and claim that it had been beaten out of him.

Retract, hell! He testified to the whole thing: the planning, the stealing of the car, the intimate details of the robbery itself, and the meeting in Kling's room afterward to split the money. I was taking it all down in shorthand, as usual, and so it wasn't until McGrattan had him step down from the witness stand and identify me by placing his hand on my shoulder that I came anywhere near catching his eyes. And, do you know, I felt a little sorry for him. He had never ratted on anybody before, and I don't imagine that can be an easy thing for anybody to do the first time.

Although Herz and Kling's lawyer, John F. X. Sheridan, both worked him over pretty good, it's almost impossible to shake that kind of testimony. The best they could do was try to embarrass him. Like when Sheridan asked him whether there wasn't any "baloney" or "cheese" in the sandwiches he had taken to Kling's house the night they were arrested. Baloney meaning a pack of lies, and cheese being so intimately connected with rats.

It always gets back to the same thing. Human beings are unpredictable, and criminals are the most unpredictable of human beings. Perlango, I could understand. He was married and his wife was pregnant. With De Venuta, as with Bassett, it defies all logical explanation. Bassett didn't even make a deal for himself; Venuta made a deal he didn't have to make. A month after our trial was over, he was allowed to plead guilty in a separate proceeding but only after Judge Farrell had exacted a statement from the DA's office that nothing in the way of special consideration had been promised by the court. Two months later, when he returned to the court to be sentenced, Farrell gave him a suspended sentence.

A lot of good it did him. From the moment Venuta had begun to talk, the other inmates of the Bronx County jail gave him a terrible time. After he was through paying his lawyer, he had to sell both of his delicatessens in order to pay back the insurance company. His brother refused to have anything at all to do with him. He was marked lousy in the only world he knew. The last thing I heard of him, he was arrested for stealing a couple of cans of meat from a supermarket. He was broke, he wept, and he needed the meat to feed his children.

For ourselves, Tommy and I were still hoping for a disagreement when the case was given over to the jury. Judge Farrell had conducted a very fair trial. He had always looked at me, I felt, in a very kindly, sympathetic way. In his charge to the jury, he had stressed as strongly as we could have asked him to that they could not return a guilty verdict on the basis of De Venuta's testimony alone. The charge was completed at seven-thirty in the evening. Just before midnight we heard that the jury had sent for coffee, which lifted our spirits tremendously since it had been our feeling from the beginning that if they were going to find me guilty because of Schuster they would do it very quickly. When we were brought back into the courtroom at 1:00 A.M. and told that the jury wanted to have Sands's testimony read to them again, our spirits soared. Herz's information was that there were two strong holdouts; one of them being a telephone worker whom we had been very dubious about accepting because, according to the conventional wisdom on jury selection, people who work for the telephone company, like people who work for the government, are supposed to make good jurors for the state.

Sometime after five o'clock, they sent word to Judge Farrell requesting permission to go back to the hotel because one of the jurors was feeling ill. If he had acceded to that request, if he had allowed them to break for seven or eight hours, we would have got the hung jury—I'm sure of that. Here where we needed him, Farrell did us in. Not only did he ask them to go back and deliberate a while longer, he emphasized that it had been a very expensive trial and that he would like them to come to some kind of verdict.

He wanted a verdict, they gave him a verdict. Fast. At six o'clock, they came back with a verdict of guilty and went home.

From there, it was just a matter of adding up the time. In sentencing me to the two consecutive terms on the Sullivan Law, Judge Goldstein had stipulated that they were not to begin until I had completed the 29 years left on the sentence I had been serving at the time of my escape from Sing Sing. That gave me 59 years minimum. Three weeks later, Judge Farrell imposed a sentence of 30 years to life on the Queens conviction. When I survived that, I could begin to serve the 37–70 years I owed the state of Pennsylvania—plus whatever might be added for the escape. At a minimum, I had 126 years to serve. At a maximum, it was 3 lifetimes plus 99.

"Theoretically at least," Judge Goldstein had observed, "Sutton could do several lifetimes in jail. I trust that this time the prison authorities will insure that he will be deposited in a cell secure enough to withstand the machinations of his evil genius."

Judge Goldstein had been wrong in one regard. I hadn't been serving the 30-year hit on the Rosenthal robbery when I escaped, I had been serving out the time I owed on the parole violation. On that one, I still had six years left. The first thing the parole board did when I got to Attica was sit me down and tell me I was going to have to serve every day of it. That gave me a minimum of 132 years and a maximum of 3 lifetimes plus 105.

Minimum or maximum, high or low, it seemed like an excellent idea to start machinating. It took a long while, but when I finally found the way to open the cell, Judge Goldstein will be happy to know, it was with a key that had been placed in my hands by the law itself. I had finally found a couple of partners I could trust. The first was a young woman lawyer, Katherine Spyros Bitses, who had been a rather inconspicuous part of Kling's defense team. The other was the Supreme Court of the U.S. of A.

PART FOUR

The Fourth Escape

The Affirm-the-Order, No-Opinion Blues

I got the Affirm the Order
No Opinion blues
The Appellate courts won't tell me why I lose
I wrote a brief like Darrow
And I cited Blackstone's law
But the Judges thought that Blackstone
Was a General in some war
I got the Affirm the Order
No Opinion blues
The phrases that they use have me confused
I'm going to write the Court Supreme
And I'll ask them what they mean
By their Affirm the Order
No Opinion ruse.
>   —Words and music by W. F. Sutton
>   (circa 1966)

The song went on and on, the verses were endless. But then so were the writs that were being sung about. Despite the look of it, "The Affirm-the-Order, No-Opinion Blues" is not a complaint against the judges; it is the lament of the unschooled inmate who, having taken note of the revolution being wrought by the Supreme Court, has been whipping in his briefs for a habeas corpus hearing based upon his wholly erroneous interpretations of the new rulings. What the revolution did, to oversimplify this somewhat, was to permit prisoners who had been convicted in *state* courts to come into the *federal* courts, via the use of a habeas corpus, wherever they could claim that a Constitutional right had been abridged.

To make sure these claims were heard, the Supreme Court made it mandatory for the federal district judges (and, by extension, all judges, everywhere) to accept the application and rule on it, not just turn it down out-of-hand, as they had been doing in about ninety-five percent of the cases. And that meant all writs. Whether it was a legal brief perfectly drawn by a prestigious law firm or an illiterate plea scrawled on a sheet of paper by the prisoner himself.

As you can imagine, the writs hit the fan. So much so that Justice Felix Frankfurter was moved to remark, "We would like to help those who have valid questions of law to place before the Court, but we have now reached the point where we do not know what points of law are being contested."

When the flood of writs reached such proportions that the judges no longer had time to explain to every prisoner why he didn't know what he was talking about, they began to send back the petitions with the simple notation, "Affirm the Order, no Opinion." The inmates would then stand around and bitch and moan, coming up with all kinds of reasons why the goddamn judge hadn't given their petition the attention it so obviously merited.

1 / The judge was so busy that he hadn't bothered to read it.

2 / The judge didn't know the law.

3 / The judge had been afraid that if he granted the petition and eventually had to let the petitioner go, a lot of other, obviously less deserving prisoners would also have to be let go.

And so they would whip up another writ and send it on to the next highest court, hoping to get a favorable ruling from there or, at the very least, an explanation.

For in rewriting the trial procedures and the rules of evidence, the Supreme Court was also doing something else. By giving every prisoner hope, they were changing the prison system.

Attica

I knew Attica was going to blow. I came out saying that it was only a matter of time. It wasn't only the black revolution and the legal revolution. It was everything. What you had there was a maximum-security prison which held two thousand prisoners, many of them long-termers, and provided jobs for only about two hundred of them. You couldn't even blame the administration. By state law, anything manufactured inside a prison can only be sold to other state agencies, and that kind of limited the possibilities. The only thing remotely resembling an industry was the metal shop, which specialized in ashcans and file cabinets. "The farmers," a forty-man company that worked the huge farmland area owned by the prison, had the best jobs. They, at least, got out of the place from four in the morning until six at night. Throw in the usual jobs involved in institutional maintenance and you still had close to ninety percent of the inmates who were assigned to what were known, quite accurately, as "Idle Companies."

With nothing to do, it isn't the big things that bring on a riot. It is the small, everyday indignities. They do things that defy belief. The one thing they had up there, for instance, was a good mess. Among seasoned cons, Attica had the reputation for being the best feeding prison in the state—especially in the summer, when the farmers were harvesting the corn and tomato crops. So they ran you in and out of there in twenty minutes. It was cafeteria-style eating: you picked up your tray and went down the line. The rule was that you could take as much as you wanted, but that anything you took you had to finish. If you didn't, you were arrested and sent before the warden's court.

They had all kinds of minor infractions like that, that would lose you part of your "good time." Routinely, you earned three months off your sentence a year. For these little niggling offenses you could lose ten days on up.

They'd let you buy instant coffee or canned soups at the commissary and then arrest you for rigging up a "dropper"—a heating device which was made by attaching a couple of wires to a carbon rod. In other words, they sell you the stuff and then they punish you for doing the only thing you can do with it. They didn't have to catch you in the act, either; the mere possession of a dropper was an infraction in itself. Since the cells were searched periodically, the inmates would usually strap them along their inner thighs. Where else? Every once in a while a company of men would be stopped and patted down. Some of the screws would let it go with nothing more than a crack about increasing the dosage of saltpeter. Most of them would turn you in, and that could cost you some of your good time and also some of your privileges.

They had a grading system for privileges. If you were in A grade, you were entitled to receive packages from your relatives, you were allowed a visit every week, and you could make the allotted purchases at the commissary. If you were dropped down into grade B, all those privileges were cut in half. If you went into C grade for committing a second infraction within the same six months, you lost all commissary privileges except for tobacco, weren't allowed to receive packages from outside, and could get only one visit every month. D grade was forget it.

The relatives were supposed to be notified by letter whenever an inmate lost any of his visiting privileges, and sometimes the letter wouldn't get there in time. You can imagine how great it would make a prisoner feel to learn that his mother had been denied the right to see him after she had made the long trip to Buffalo, because he had tried to heat up a can of Campbell's chicken noodle soup that he had bought in the prison commissary.

I wouldn't be at all surprised, if you could get to the bottom of it, if every riot in history wasn't really brought about by a lack of medical attention. The prisons of America are filled with hypochondriacs; the prison system manufactures them. After a few years in the can, the inmates develop all kinds of neuroses and psychoses. The doctor throws them a couple of pills, and the next day they're back in the hospital line to complain about something else. (Inside or outside, it's amazing how many people have to take some kind of a pill in order to feel healthy.) Pretty soon the doctor begins to look upon everybody who isn't carried in on a stretcher as either a faker or a guy who is trying to steal a little time to meet his friends in the line. To get rid of the "obvious" malingerers, he'll sometimes even give them a dose of castor oil. There's a big difference, though, between a malingerer and a hypochondriac. The hypochondriac is just as sure he's sick as anybody else. Probably surer. In no time at all, he becomes convinced that they're out to kill him.

There are others who really are sick, and when they find that nothing is being done for them it causes tremendous resentment and hostility. ("They don't care whether I live or die . . . I'm no better than a dog to these people.")

At Attica, there was one doctor to take care of everybody. He'd have had to be the best doctor in the world to separate the legitimately ill from the hypochondriac from the out-and-out faker, and the best doctors in the world are not to be found within the prison system.

There was also a psychiatrist who came in on a per-diem basis; generally one day a week. When you consider that thirty percent of the inmates there were probably psychotic to some degree or other, you can see how much help he was.

336

The first night after I had been assigned to a permanent cell at Attica, I was awakened by the most godawful groaning I had ever heard. A horrifying sound, the sound of a soul in torment. The next thing I knew, the guard was entering the next cell and shaking the inmate in there until he was awake.

The cell was occupied by a big black man they called Tennessee. Ten or twelve years earlier, when he couldn't have been much more than twenty years old, Tennessee had come home early because of a wildcat strike in the steel-processing mill where he worked and found his wife in bed with another man. Driven absolutely berserk by the sight, he had whipped out a knife and decapitated her. When the police arrived, they found her head sitting in the middle of the table and Tennessee sitting there in a chair, explaining patiently and lovingly why she shouldn't ever do that kind of thing to him again.

As regular as clockwork, that same terrible groaning would come from his cell every night. Every night the guard would come over and shake him awake, and then he'd roll over and go back to sleep.

It seemed that Tennessee was having this recurring dream. . . .

I'm not saying that Tennessee was a typical case. He didn't belong in prison at all, anybody could see that. Most of the other psychotics were far more dangerous potentially because they were ready to erupt into violence at any time.

The place had almost blown in 1965, at a time when every prison in the state was in turmoil, and I was the Great Compromiser who prevented it. I got involved through an inmate named John Murphy, who was the closest thing to an official trusty I ever saw. Murphy had spent time in Elmira as a young fellow, and shortly after he got out a guy he had met in there asked him to pick up a package in Brooklyn. John's story was that he didn't have the slightest idea that it was ransom money. The jury didn't believe him. There had been a kidnapping, and John was in for life. He had been there for about thirty years and he was well liked by everybody on both sides.

When he wasn't acting as a go-between for some prisoner, he was the prison tailor, outfitting the guys going out of prison. He got a commute before I got out, and the last I heard of him he was running a classy tailor shop.

I had free access to all groups because I was helping everybody with their writs, and with C block about to erupt, John asked me to go over there with him, tell them that Commissioner Paul D. McGinnis was on his way, and try to convince them to hold off until they had heard what McGinnis had to say.

Attica is divided into four separate and distinct blocks (A, B, C, D) which are really four prisons with four separate and distinct exercise yards. Four squares within a larger square. On the day I arrived, the order had gone over the intercom that I was never to be allowed to pass through a locked door unless accompanied by a guard. Just to be sure, my picture was posted over the timeclocks in the other blocks so the guards there would be able to see what I looked like every time they punched in and out.

The checkpoint you have to pass through at the very center of the prison to get from one tunnel to any other is known as Times Square. "You know the rules around here," the guard told Murphy. "Willie is never allowed to go through a locked gate."

Murphy had to tell him to call the warden for permission before I could go through and try to prevent the prison from exploding.

I got the key guys together and made the point that having waited this long it would be ridiculous not to wait a few more hours and hear what the commissioner was willing to offer. I told them what had happened in the 1929 Dannemora riot, and explained that violence was like a forest fire, very easy to start and almost impossible to stop. "You can't win anything with violence," I said. "Because regardless of whether they agree with you or not they're not going to give in to violence."

Well, it took a little while to convince them. The radicals and the hotheads wanted to start breaking things up immediately. The Black Muslims were at the peak of their power, and they had a separate thing going about having their own food and their own ministers. Some of the old-timers who weren't so radical felt they already knew what the commissioner was going to say, because they had been hearing the same promises for years.

Talking to the entire population over the intercom, the commissioner explained that he was already attempting to institute a lot of reforms based upon petitions that had been presented by prisoners in the past. Substantial improvements would be forthcoming, he promised. It was going to take a little more time, that's all.

Most of the inmates were sure it was just another snow job, and maybe they were right. When the agitation began to boil up again a few months later, stronger than ever, Murphy came to my cell again to tell me that the commissioner was coming down to meet with a delegation of prisoners. I had been appointed, he told me, as the spokesman for A block.

"By who?" I wanted to know.

"By me."

"Oh no," I said. I didn't want to be singled out as leader on this. If anything happened, I could see where the authorities were going to be looking at me the same way Granger had when the riot broke out at Dannemora.

But Murphy kept pleading with me, and I finally agreed to go down to the warden's office with him and the other two delegates. Right from the beginning, McGinnis talked directly to me. He had been in the prison system during the Dannemora riot, too, he wanted me to know, and so he was sure I agreed with him that we had to do everything possible to stop anything that could lead to that kind of bloodbath.

I had walked in there determined to keep my mouth shut, but with nobody else saying a word, I found myself doing all the talking. Denying all the while that I was a spokesman for anybody. Dannemora had gone up, I reminded him, because the inmates were without hope. And while I was willing to concede that Attica was nowhere near as bad as Dannemora,

I emphasized to him as strongly as I could that prisoners weren't anywhere near as willing to accept that kind of inhumanity and brutality any more.

We were in there for over an hour, and I have to say that he was a powerful advocate. He pledged his word—absolutely—that if he were given just a little more time, most of the grievances would be taken care of. I believed he was sincere then, and I still believe it. Running a prison system has to be the most thankless job in the world. Although all government agencies are tied up in red tape, the prison system—as he pointed out—was ten times worse than any of the others. Nobody ever wants to divert any extra money toward it. The prisoners are stacked up inside like cordwood, and all anybody wants to do is forget about them.

Well, there were four of us who had the equally thankless job of going back into the exercise yards and telling the prisoners to wait some more. What troubled the key men most of all was that all the other prisons in New York had conducted sit-down strikes by then, and we hadn't done anything. They felt very strongly that when ex-cons got together in future years, the guys who had served time in Attica would have a very bad name.

I said, "All right, but do it orderly. Reach a point where you get enough publicity to let the other prisoners know we're with them, and then quit."

Word went out to all the prisoners not to leave their cells the following day, and the strike was about ninety percent successful. Around noon, when I heard that the news of the strike was being broadcast over the radio, I sent word to the key people that the purpose had been accomplished. The longer they tried to extend the strike, I had warned them, the greater the risk that they were going to lose control over it. "A prison riot is like a war in which only one side has guns," I had told them. "Don't ever forget that."

The following morning about ninety percent of them came out of their cells. The few diehards didn't hold out for more than another day or two.

But, do you know, I never went through Times

Square during all my efforts to keep things cool that the guard didn't call up to the warden's office to make sure that it was all right to unlock the gate.

I had arrived at Attica after two weeks in isolation at Sing Sing, leg-manacled to a prisoner who had been thrown into the shipment with me at the last moment for the sole purpose of supplying the leg for the other half of the manacle. Although the poor guy was being taken all the way up to Attica and then back down to Greenhaven, he took it in the spirit of adventure. There's two detectives across from us practically sitting in our laps, and the first chance he got he whispered, "Willie, if you have a chance I'll do everything I can to push you out the window."

After another two weeks in segregation I was taken before Deputy Walter Wilkins, a little shrimp of a man who was known as The Shadow because he was always lurking in dark corners trying to catch you for something. Wilkins stared at me sternly from behind an enormous desk and when that didn't reduce me to a quivering heap he tucked his chin down into his neck and, deepening his voice to give it the ring of authority, proceeded to read off the record of my escapes and convictions. Once that had been accomplished, he looked up at the ceiling and pursed his lips in the manner of a man who is pondering some momentous decision.

"Willie," he said to me, at last. "Every warden in this country will think I'm crazy. In any other prison in the country the warden would make you serve out your time in isolation, we both know that. But do you know what I'm going to do with you?" His voice became a hush, as if he were overawed by what he was saying. "I'm going to give you a job."

"But you're going to watch me," I said. "All the time."

Well, of course he was going to watch me. What did I think he was crazy or something? "If you ever escaped from here I'd lose my job and the warden would lose his job. Every minute you're in this place we're going to watch you."

"Dep," I sighed, "let me tell you about my experience with the warden at Eastern State Pen. A very tough warden, but a very fair warden." I told him the whole story about how Hard-Boiled Smith had pulled out the desk drawer to show me all the notes from the rats and stool pigeons, and how he had then assured me that he wasn't going to put me in isolation until he could actually prove something. "Deputy Wilkins," I said, "the only defense I have in any prison is in the intelligence of the top personnel. If you don't feel the same as Warden Smith, then I'd rather stay in isolation. I will save myself a lot of trouble and I will save you a lot of trouble."

He absolutely promised me. "I know there are those who think of me as a hard man," he said, tucking his chin down into his Adam's apple. "But you'll also find me a fair one. I can tell you that I never make a promise that I don't intend to keep."

I said, "Thank you very much."

I was assigned to the laundry and relocated on A block, 6 company, cell 1. The end cell on the ground floor of the three-tiered cellblock.

An officer stood outside a heavily barred door from where he could operate a lock box and open the cell doors. All of the doors together or any individual door separately. In front of the cell was a large window that covered almost the entire wall from top to bottom in such a way that a guard could stand outside the door and see the entire cell reflected there. A special security detail had been set up so that there would always be a guard available to escort me wherever I had to go. As a final precaution, my cell was examined every day by a succession of guards who were required to submit a written statement to the effect that nothing in the way of contraband had been found.

The laundry was a maximum-security shop manned almost entirely by long-term prisoners. One of my duties was to touch up the warden's shirts with a hand iron after they had been pressed by machine. The pay was five cents a day before we got a hundred-percent raise to a whole dime.

The inmate who operated the pressing machine was

Jimmy Callahan, an ex-air force colonel who was serving a life sentence for killing a state trooper. Colonel Callahan had been sent home from overseas on special leave to see his dying wife, and after he buried her he bought some civilian clothes, packed a duffel bag, and went out into the woods in the dead of winter to become a hermit. It was an area of hunting lodges, and when the owners began to come up over the weekends to find their food missing they notified a pair of state troopers. Caught red-handed inside one of the lodges, Callahan fired through the window and killed one of them. The largest manhunt in the history of the state of New York was mounted, with thousands of hunters and scores of bloodhounds joining the troopers. Every road was blocked. But Jimmy Callahan had been trained by the air force in the techniques of survival. By doubling around so that he was always in back of the nearest bloodhounds, sometimes only a few feet in back of them, he broke out of the trap and headed west. He was all the way to Nevada before he stopped running. Having pulled off such a miraculous escape, and removed himself three thousand miles, he had also done something very dumb. He had brought along a newspaper clipping about the search and it was spotted by the manager of a rooming house within hours after he checked in.

I got along with Jimmy Callahan so well that the next thing I knew he was transferred to another job. Same thing in yardout. Anytime I became friendly enough with anybody to talk to them for a second time, they were transferred right out of A block. So I stayed in my cell during yardout and read. After about a week, Wilkins came up to my cell. The Shadow Knows. And The Shadow wanted me to know that I wasn't fooling him any. I was staying in the cell as part of some devilish plan I had concocted for escaping.

"I'm staying in the cell," I told him, "because you've made my position here untenable. It's got so I feel I'm jeopardizing everybody I talk to."

The dep promised that it wouldn't happen any more, and I was able to go out and get some air.

A short time afterward, however, I was taken out of the laundry along with about a dozen other inmates and taken back to my cell to await a hearing in the warden's court. Over the next two days, all the others went before the court and every one of them went right back to work. Finally, Wilkins sent for me. "Willie," he said, "I'm very sorry, but I'm going to have to put you in isolation. Now, don't jump to conclusions. It's not my fault and it's not the warden's fault. The order comes from Albany. That's all I can tell you because that's all I know."

I couldn't believe it. I had been arrested and I was going to be punished, and nobody was going to tell me why? I was used to not being able to face my accuser in prison. Was he telling me now that I wasn't going to be told what I was being accused of?

That's what he was telling me.

The isolation tier was on the top floor of a completely segregated area. The only way you could get there was in an elevator which was guarded top and bottom. After I had been there for a day the officer in charge told me, "You're the first one ever sent up here *assigned* to isolation. Everybody else has come up sentenced to do a certain amount of time and then they get out. You're going to spend the rest of your sentence here." They were going to allow me commissary privileges and writing privileges, he said, and so the only advice he could give me was to write to the warden and ask whether I was ever going to get out.

"I've got a better idea," I said. "I'm going to write to the Commissioner of Corrections in Albany."

It seemed to me to be a very strange thing, I wrote, when neither the warden nor the deputy warden would assume responsibility for punishing me. "So evidently you are going to have to take the responsibility, and I want to know why I am being isolated." There was no answer.

Four months later, I got a visit from Warden Walter B. Martin. *Doctor* Martin, a psychiatrist. It was the second time he had called on me. He had come to see me early in my incarceration to tell me he was going to grant me every possible privilege and concession, and all I was going to have to do in return was "keep in touch" with him. In short, he wanted me to become his personal informer. All I did was look at him. In addition to which, he added hastily, he would recommend that I be released on parole as soon as the opportune moment arose. I still didn't say a word. I just kept looking until he turned around and walked out.

This time he had come up to let me know that I was being taken out of isolation. He didn't know why Albany had ordered me in. He didn't know why Albany was ordering me out.

Somebody knew. Shortly after I got out, a fellow inmate in the laundry slipped me a clipping from Zeltner's "Over the River" column in the *Daily News*. A fellow named Augie, who had been in Attica a number of years for a contract murder, had been bought back to Brooklyn to testify against his partner. When he got there and discovered that the DA wasn't offering him any deal for his testimony, he tried to do himself some good by telling him that Willie Sutton had succeeded in having a couple of pistols smuggled into Attica for a mass bust-out.

During the four months they had me in isolation they had ripped my cell apart, dug up the ground all around the laundry, sifted through the coal piles, and lifted, turned up, or gone through every nook and corner where it would be remotely possible to hide a couple of guns.

They still weren't letting me go anywhere without a guard, though. Not even to church. In the history of the penal system of the United States I must have been the only prisoner who was never allowed to go to church without a guard at his side. Not that I did, of course. After the first week or so, I had simply stopped going. You see, a lot of prisoners go to church in order to pass notes to their friends from the other blocks. Unless they could arrange to meet in the hospital line, church was the only place in Attica where two friends who were locking in different blocks could ever expect to see each other. There was already one guard assigned to the church to keep an eye on things. If I kept bringing another one in, I was going to make myself about as popular as Lucifer. From time to time, Father Gene, the Catholic chaplain, would ask me why I wasn't attending services, and when I would answer by asking him why he wasn't backing my protest he would say, "Well, I can't interfere with prison policy, Bill. There have to be rules and regulations."

"In the footsteps of the Master," I'd mutter.

After many years had passed, I was called down to the dep's office, always a matter of some concern to me. This time, he smiled at me beatifically and asked whether I had noticed the change that had come over him.

"No," I said.

"Haven't you noticed the peaceful expression on my face during the last month?"

"No," I said, squinting.

"Willie," he said, looking peaceful. "For years my wife has been after me to read the Bible and for years I resisted. She finally got me to do it, thank the Lord, and do you know I'm a much better person for it. I read a chapter or two every morning before I leave for work, and I'm in such a happy frame of mind these days that I find I can dispense justice in the true spirit of Christian humility and charity when I hold court."

He was looking at me so intently that I was sure I was about to have some justice distributed upon me over some new note that had been slipped to him. But no. "Willie," he said earnestly, "why don't you go to church? It will change your whole outlook. It will bring you to peace with yourself and with your surroundings."

I told him I would be very happy to go to church if he would take the guard away.

He said, "Willie, as long as you are in this institution you are going to have a guard with you because we just can't trust you."

"Yeah, but what about all this Christian humility and forgiveness you've been telling me about here? What about your reading the Bible and being fair and all that?"

That kind of hurt him. "Well, Willie," he said.

"You have to keep in mind that if you were in any other prison you'd be far worse off than you are here."

"I would?" Did he want to tell me how?

"Well, for one thing you wouldn't have a job."

"You want to know something," I said, "I'm not so crazy about the job."

All he had been trying to do, he sighed, was help me to become a better person. "For your own good," he said as I was leaving, "I'll pray for you to stop fighting me."

"Dep," I said, "you haven't changed a bit. For your own good, I'll pray that you keep reading."

Next to me, the most closely guarded prisoner in Attica was Joe Gallo. Although for an entirely different reason. Gallo was out of the Bensonhurst section of Brooklyn. Crazy Joe, they had always called him. He had put together a mob of about twenty or thirty people and gone to war with the Brooklyn Mafia boss, Joe Profaci. Gallo believed that the old guys should step aside and give the younger fellows a chance to advance themselves; if he had been a politician instead of a gangster they'd have called him a great reformer. With the Mafia showing no particular willingness to be reformed, Gallo and a few of his partners kidnapped four of the Mafia chieftains, stuck them in a hotel room, and threatened to kill them unless they agreed to elevate him and his boys in the ranks and give them a bigger slice of the melon. When it was put to them like that, they readily agreed. *Sure, Joe. It's a wonder we didn't think of it ourselves. Thanks for calling it to our attention.* As soon as they were back on the street, of course, the shooting war started.

Well, in Attica there were a lot of regular faction people from out of Buffalo, Rochester, and Syracuse, and as soon as Gallo came in several guards were assigned to keep a very close eye on him.

In certain ways, he was one of the most generous fellows I ever saw. He would walk around the yard and if he saw somebody playing handball in prison shoes he would find out their shoe size, send out for a pair of sneakers, and just drop them in the guy's cell without saying a word. He was always doing things like that.

You were allowed to receive a fifteen-pound package from your family once a month, and a forty-pound package on the big holidays. Joe spread his delicacies around indiscriminately. To anybody who happened to be around. He was always trying to push stuff on me and I never accepted anything from him because I don't like to be the beneficiary of somebody else's largess. As generous as he was, I found one great fault in him. Right from the beginning he had sought me out, and as we'd walk around the yard together he'd tell me all about this here war they had going on outside, mentioning a lot of different names and incidents. I was always very conscious of the fact that when you know too much something can happen to you. So one day when he began to tell me about certain people he had shoved into Sheepshead Bay, I said to him, "Joe, Jesus, don't tell me that stuff. That's one thing I don't want to hear."

He turned around and said, "Jesus, if I can't trust you, who the hell am I going to trust in this goddamn place?"

I said, "For my own protection you shouldn't talk about these things."

The thing about Joey Gallo was that he was absolutely without fear himself. I've seen a lot of people who could control their fear. I had met that test myself. With Joe it was something else entirely. More like a glandular deficiency. He was always having fights forced on him by these little faceless people who never did anything in their lives, and were trying to build up their reputation. Even knowing that they were going to lose, the fact that they could say they'd had a fight with Joe Gallo was enough for them. Look, people want recognition so much that there's some of them who have walked to the electric chair happy in the belief that they have finally become the center of attention.

Joe wasn't a very big person, either. He was short

and chunky. He would win because he would resort to anything. He would bite you on the head. He would chew off your ear or poke your eye out. You couldn't beat him because there was nothing he wouldn't do to win.

Not if you faced him head to head, you couldn't. Joe locked up in the gallery and from time to time they'll open the door of the cell to let them sweep out or go out for a bath. Joe happened to be stooping over his bed looking for something, and one of the other inmates sneaked in and clubbed him from behind. Knocked him unconscious. Gallo found out who it was and the next time he passed the guy's cell he said in front of everybody, "For doing that, I'll have your whole family wiped out." The next day they sent the guy down to Greenhaven, and a month later his brother was walking into his house in Green Point and got shot right in the head. Whether there was any connection I don't know, I can only put two and two together. Joe had two brothers out there. He had Blast and he had Larry.

Another thing about him was that he was always walking around with Mao's Little Red Book or one of those other revolutionary tracts. He was actually studying to become a revolutionary, and he was always trying to get me to read them, too.

"I work alone," I'd tell him. "You get your revolution and what are you going to do with bank robbers?"

"There'd be no banks."

"To hell with your revolution then, Joe."

"Well, there'd be banks but they'd belong to the people and you'd only be robbing from yourself."

"What do you mean 'the people,' Joe?"

"Everybody. All the people in the country."

That didn't sound so bad. I'd only be robbing maybe a penny on a million dollars from myself. "Hold a seat for me, Joe," I'd say. "I'll think about it."

Whether he was crazy or not I don't know, but he sure did drive the authorities crazy. There was one summer where he decided to become a painter. An artist. He'd come walking to yardout every day in his bare feet, and he'd have a big straw hat on, one

349

of those extra-big hats that horses used to wear years ago with the space cut out for their ears. We had another guy there doing yoga exercises in the yard. He'd get himself into some hopeless position and stay there staring at the sky for maybe an hour without moving. Joey would set up his canvas nearby, take his paintbrush and start daubing at the thing, and pretty soon there'd be a whole mob of art critics standing around watching him. He kind of liked that, I think.

There were a lot of guys who would have liked to get him for an entirely different reason. The blacks and Puerto Ricans had become the majority in prison by then, and Joe, who obviously saw the Negroes as potential allies when he got back outside, went out of his way to become very friendly with them. Crossing the color line isn't an easy thing to do in prison. Joe was able to do it by backing a group of colored gamblers. If there's one thing they'll never stop in any prison it's gambling, and Joe, of course, had a lot of money in back of him.

Racial feelings were running high anyway, because the administration was trying to integrate the place, and hardly anybody on either side wanted to be integrated. The symbol of the whole thing became the barber shop. They had a beautiful barber shop up there. Half the barbers were colored and half were white. The way it had always worked, the white inmates would line up for the white barbers, and the colored for the colored. In the battle for civil rights, some of the colored militants protested that it was a form of discrimination and so the administration put out an order that there was going to be only one line and everybody would have to take whichever barber came up. Racial feelings aside, the dehumanizing thing about prison is that you're told what you have to do about everything. Half the guys there hadn't been aware that they'd been making a choice about their barber before, but, boy, all of a sudden the prison was filled with civil libertarians screaming about the sacred barber-client relationship.

Joe Gallo became a civil libertarian the other way around. Joe would get into line and insist upon going to a Negro barber, and that didn't endear him to the white population at all. Nor did it endear him to the administration, which had all the trouble it wanted without Crazy Joe coming along to foul things up beyond recognition. Didn't bother Joe. While the administration was going crazy trying to find a way to integrate the place without starting a riot, Joe went into court with a suit that charged them with violating his civil rights by preventing him from associating with Negroes.

He was always at odds with the administration. The dep was always having him locked up in his cell for some minor infraction, and Gallo always treated the dep as if he were a gnat. While the dep would be walking through the block on inspection, he'd say, "What's the matter with you that you can't stay out of trouble? You're not outside now, you know. You have to obey the rules and regulations like everybody else."

Joe would turn around and say, "Well, I don't believe in obeying rules and regulations," and they'd be off on a big argument which would always wind up with Joe saying, "You know I'm going to win out, Dep, no matter how many times you lock me up. And you know why I'm going to win? Because I've got more money than you." That was Joe Gallo's favorite saying: I've got more money than you, so I'll win.

"Some revolutionary you are," I'd tell him. "You never found that in Mao's Red Book."

"Chairman Mao says all power comes out of the barrel of a gun," he'd say. "Same thing."

"What do you mean same thing? It isn't the same thing just because you say it's the same thing." And anyway, since when did Joe Gallo have to go to China to find out about the power of a gun?

"Read the book," he'd say. "It explains everything."

Jeez, between Joe Gallo interpreting Mao to me and the functional illiterates spouting legal jargon all over the yard, it's a wonder they didn't drive me crazy there.

I was still reading all the time. *War and Peace,* by Tolstoi, *Crime and Punishment,* by Dostoevski, the *Decline and Fall of the Roman Empire, Pepys' Diary, Atlas Shrugged.* I like big books because you could get your teeth into them; lose yourself in another world. There was one period where I went through all the French authors. Balzac, Hugo, Zola, Voltaire, Proust, Dumas. I even took a course in French although, not to give anybody the wrong impression, I never got to the point where I attempted to read anything in the original. My favorite of them all, I think, was *The Wandering Jew* by Eugene Sue, the best novel in terms of plot I have ever read. It was twelve hundred pages long, and when I was finished I turned back to the first page and started over. *The Wandering Jew* is no more about Jews than John O'Hara's *Appointment in Samarra* is about Arabia. For years, it was on the Catholic Church's forbidden list because it is about the old Jesuit society. Very briefly, seven people are supposed to meet in Paris to divide an immense fortune that has been willed to them. One of them is a Jesuit priest, and since he had renounced all worldly goods his share will be going to the Jesuit society. The Church fathers therefore send one of their number to keep the others away through the use of violence, and when he fails, another high official is sent out to destroy them through their passions. An anticlerical book (the Church enriches itself off the sins of the laity) with a profoundly religious theme: You cannot destroy a human being by destroying his body; to really destroy him you must attack him at the point where he is morally weak.

There was another period where the old Shakespeare-Bacon controversy flared up among the literati. Essentially, the controversy breaks down to whether an unschooled boy from Stratford-on-Avon could have written the master works of the English language or whether it didn't have to be a well-born Englishman, like Lord Bacon, who had gone to all the right schools and knew from personal experience what life was like inside Queen Elizabeth's court. After I had gone through all the arguments, pro and con, I did the obvious thing. I reread a little Shakespeare and then I sent for the works of Lord Bacon. No similarity at all in style that I could see. The literati should have presented their evidence to the police. Any good cop could have told them that if the styles were different, the authors were different. I accept completely the argument that genius is where you find it. To me, the ludicrous notions are, one, that Lord Bacon, or anybody else, could have knocked off the greatest plays ever written in his spare time, and two, that having had the ability to do it he wouldn't have known their worth and claimed the credit.

If I had been the warden the first thing I would have done would have been to make me a teacher. They had an institutional school there on the grounds run by a civilian educator. Not just a converted room like you find in most prisons but a very nice-looking building alongside the administration building. All prisons are filled with illiterates, and the main purpose of the school, in theory, was to teach them how to read and write. The teaching staff, however, consisted entirely of inmates—the white-shirt-and-pressed-pants boys again. Their main duty was to have their pictures taken and tell visitors about all the great things that were being done.

The best they ever did for anybody while I was up there, they gave them a Dale Carnegie course. As for the rest of it, from what I heard, they just sat around and talked about what they were going to do when they got out.

After two or three years had gone by I asked Wilkins for permission to teach and, not at all to my surprise, got turned down cold. "That's out of bounds for you," he said flatly. "You'll never get that close to the gate for as long as you're here."

I also think, you know, that he suspected I was trying to build up some credits to place before a parole board someday. Of course I was. But I also felt I could do a lot of good. If any of these kids had seen me as a glamorous figure, I could have set them straight in a hurry. From the time I had gone to prison for the first time in April 1926 until the time

I came to Attica in May 1952, I had spent less than ten years outside prison walls. More than six of them as a fugitive. What it was more than anything else, I'm sure, was that he was afraid that if anything happened with either me or anybody who had been attending my class, somebody up above would yell, "What? You put Willie Sutton in charge of a bunch of prisoners?" He personally had nothing to gain and everything to lose, and so what did he care whether some of the inmates might be helped? The old bureaucratic game of protecting his rear.

So, I got my own students. Mostly they were kids who worked near me in the laundry, which meant that they also locked in the same cellblock. See, we all had our own tables there in the laundry, and certain people will always congregate in certain spots during a break. I had a real big table with two big windows right in back of me, the best place there. I started with one kid—a Polish immigrant—while we were sitting around, some of the others began to listen in, and pretty soon they wanted to know something, too.

I taught them English and history mostly, although by talking about the books I was reading I was also giving them a smattering of philosophy. Just so long as I stayed within the physical areas that had been prescribed for me, Wilkins didn't mind. Why should he? As long as my mind was occupied in teaching, he could be sure it wasn't occupied in planning to escape.

It wasn't any coincidence that I was sitting right alongside Joey Gallo when out of the clear blue sky I was offered a sure-shot proposition for an escape. And it wasn't any coincidence that it came to me on Independence Day, either. The Fourth of July is the holiday everybody looks forward to at Attica, because it is the one day in the year when the gates between the four separate exercise yards are thrown open and the inmates are allowed to mix and intermingle. The tables are put together in the yard so that as many as twenty or twenty-four friends can sit together. The tables are laden with the delicacies which the inmates have been saving from the packages sent by their families. Gallons of ice cream, roasted chicken, imported cheeses, and pastries are piled everywhere. The chaplains make the rounds, taking a snack from each of the tables and telling everybody to behave themselves.

Through it all the guards stand around looking alert and edgy, although any inmate who was dumb enough to ruin things for everybody else would have had far more than the prison authorities to worry about.

On this particular Independence Day I was sitting between Joey Gallo and Jimmy Ryan, the rogue cop who had led a gang of armed robbers, when I saw Joe Curtin coming across the yard and headed my way. Joe was an ex-pug and all-around heist man who walked with a slight limp from having had his heel shot off in an Oklahoma alley while he was trying to outrun a bullet.

He came up to me and he said, "Willie, you want to take a walk?" Which means only one thing in that setting. It means he has something to say to me, and he wants to say it where no one else can hear. Joe Curtin was a runner. Although he locked on one of the other cellblocks, he had an institutional pass that permitted him to pass through any gate, into any of the cellblocks. I had come to know him pretty well. I trusted him. He had served a considerable amount of time in prisons all over the country and he was highly regarded by everyone who knew him. When he was sure we were out of earshot of any guard he asked me whether I was interested in a proposition. A proposition means only one thing to me, too. "What do you have?" I said.

He said: "There's a key man on my block can get you out for five grand and have you dropped five miles away from the prison." The only thing about it was that I would have to get from the laundry at a specified time, on my own, and without being seen. That was going to be difficult, as he very well knew. After ten years, I still wasn't allowed to buy my own commissary. And do you want to know why? Because the garage was close by the commissary and they didn't want me anywhere near that garage. Alone among the prisoners, I would have to submit my list to the officer on the cellblock and have him go over and get it for me.

Nevertheless, I told him that I was listening.

The key man was a guard. "All I can tell you for now is that it's a sure thing and you're the only one he'll do business with." And one other thing. "He also told me to tell you that you are associating with someone who is no good. He didn't tell me who the wrongo is, but he is in a position to know, so you better be careful."

Now, that I didn't like. I was hanging around with all solid guys. Guys who I knew to be as right as day. "That kind of remark casts doubt on all my associates," I told Joe. "Tell him I have to have a name. I can't see where anything like this is true, but if it is I'd be in a lot of danger here."

The next morning Curtin dropped in to the laundry on the pretext that a few sheets and pillowcases were missing from the bundles that had been sent to his block. "Before I can tell you who it is," he said, "I've got to get your solemn promise that absolutely no harm will come to him. If you can't give me your word on that, Bill, I was told to forget I ever opened my mouth."

With the understanding that I'd be free to expose him to my friends for the sole purpose of allowing them to protect themselves, I gave my word.

It was a guy named Peltz, and the name meant so little to me at first that I couldn't place him. And then it rang a bell. He had been working in the laundry for a few months, a scrawny little guy who worked back in the mangler. He seemed like such a misfit, such a loner, that when he had first come onto the laundry block, I'd thrown him a pint of ice cream or a pack of cigarettes or something when the officer came back with my commissary. Just out of the generosity of my heart because I could see the poor guy never bought anything himself and I figured that he was broke.

Even at that, I still wouldn't have been able to remember his name if the dep hadn't come by one day to ask me how well I knew him. When I told him I had never even spoken to the guy, he merely said, "I thought so," and walked away.

"Peltz," I said to Curtin. "How does he get in on the thing?"

"All right," Curtin said. "This Peltz dropped three notes in the warden's box of the cellblock stating that you were planning to escape." He had written that he was ready to furnish all the details in exchange for a promise that the warden would intercede with the parole board to have him released. Now this was a guy, I later learned, who had been arrested originally for stealing an automobile and had come back on a violation of parole to serve an unexpired term of eighteen months. For those lousy few months he was ready to turn rat on the only guy in the whole prison who had probably ever shown him a minute's kindness.

"It means nothing," I said. "Let me hear about the proposition."

"It's a truck." If I could leave the laundry and get over to the garage area within an indicated period of time, I would be put aboard a waiting truck which would immediately whisk me out of the prison.

"Jeez," I said. "These trucks are searched pretty thoroughly." At Attica, like in most modern prisons, all the trucks enter and leave through "locked gates," with the open pit and the mirrors and everything else.

But Joe explained that this guard had a way of fixing up this particular truck so that there was no way I could be discovered. Whether it was a secret compartment or an arrangement with the gate guards he didn't know. What he did know was that this guard could be trusted.

I thought it over and I said, "I'll have to give this a lot of consideration."

All I had to do was sit back and wait to be delivered like a parcel-post package. Yet, I hesitated.

Somehow the idea of being delivered by parcel post held very little appeal to me. And, anyway, I had to ask myself, delivered to what? A few more years of hiding out in a furnished room somewhere?

On the other hand, if I were to reject the proposition out of hand, I would be resigning myself to spending the rest of my life in prison. That appealed to me even less.

I sent a letter off to Jeanie, conveying a sense of urgency, and within a matter of days she was waiting for me in the visitors' room. As soon as I was sure we wouldn't be overheard, I laid out the situation for her and told her that before I came to any final decision I wanted to know what she thought.

The first thing she said was, "If you do it, it means that I'll never see you again." She hadn't said yes and she hadn't said no, but she had left me with no doubt whatsoever about how she felt. "At least," she said, "I can see you up here and talk to you. And I couldn't do that for so many years. I wish you would think this over very carefully, Dad."

"If I don't take this opportunity, Jeanie, it means I'm going to die in this prison."

And she said: "You've helped so many people get out on the law. Why can't you do anything for yourself?"

Just between you and me, I had been toying with that idea myself.

The Jailhouse Lawyer

When most people talk about the *Brown* decision,
they are talking about *Brown* v. *Board of Education*
in 1954. When prisoners talk about the *Brown* decision, they are talking about *Brown* v. *Allen*, an
entirely different case that came out of North Carolina
a year earlier. Although they are both such land-
mark decisions that even a lot of prisoners think
they're the same case. The 1953 Brown was a Negro
who had been sentenced to death in North Carolina
on a rape conviction. He had appealed the conviction
on two Constitutional grounds: first that Negroes had
been systematically eliminated from the jury, and also
that his confession had been coerced. Unlike the
school-aged Brown, he didn't win his case, he lost it.
The significance was wholly procedural. The Supreme
Court had already refused to hear the case on a direct
appeal after he had lost all the way through the state
courts, and in accordance with the generally accepted
principle that once around the circuit was enough,
that should have been the end of it. As indeed it
seemed to be. The Federal District Court refused to
accept his petition for a habeas corpus hearing on the
merits of his claim and the Circuit Court of Appeals
promptly affirmed that ruling. Brown's lawyers had
then pushed the habeas corpus petition up to the
Supreme Court, and in a complete break with established legal precedent the Supreme Court agreed to
hear it. It didn't matter to every other prisoner in a

state prison that once the Supreme Court had gone into the merits of Brown's contention they found against him, what mattered was that the Supreme Court was establishing the principle that the federal courts should, in effect, review state convictions *via* the habeas route wherever a Constitutional issue was involved.

The *Brown* decision came down within months after I had arrived at Attica, and as new liberal rulings, brought on for the most part as a result of *Brown* writs, continued to come down I began to buy law books and send away for the full transcripts of the key decisions. As Jeanie had said, I had already helped quite a few of the inmates get out.

It wasn't until 1963, however, that the rulings on *Noia* and *Gideon* kicked off the four-year revolution that completely rewrote the books. There were other extremely important decisions but to me *Noia* and *Gideon* were the most important because they established the groundwork and set the philosophy—and were certainly the decisions that most directly affected me. So if I tell you a little more than you think you want to know about those two decisions, bear with me.

Way back in 1942, Charles Noia and his two partners were sentenced to life after confessing to a felony-murder. His two confederates appealed through the state courts on the grounds that the confessions had been coerced and they lost everywhere, but in 1955 one of the partners went back into the federal courts on a *Brown* writ and had his conviction set aside at the Circuit-court level. Once that had been done, the other partner was able to get his conviction overturned on a straight appeal at the state level. The message was getting through.

Now here is the important thing: Unlike his partners, Noia hadn't filed an appeal within the prescribed thirty days. Or, for that matter, ever. Fourteen years after he had been convicted, he went into the King's County Court, the lowest court in the hierarchy, and damned if the County court judge didn't set his conviction aside, too.

The state of New York promptly appealed, and by the time it got to the Supreme Court—having been reversed and rereversed through five other courts over a period of another seven years—the issue had been refined down to a very precise legal issue. The state had conceded that the confession had been coerced. Noia had testified that he hadn't appealed at the time of his conviction because he didn't want to impose an undue financial burden on his family and because he feared the death sentence if he were reconvicted. The question that came to the Court was this: Does a conscious and knowing failure of a state prisoner to "seek his remedies" within the state system prevent him from asserting a Constitutional right forever after?

For 175 years, the answer had been that it did. In *Fay* v. *Noia*, 372 U.S. 391 (1963), the Supreme Court said that maybe it did once but it sure as hell wasn't going to any longer. In its decision, the Supreme Court did several things that were of great interest to me. The most important, from a purely legal point of view, was that they had wiped out the time-honored doctrine of "independent adequate state grounds" which had continued to keep cases out of the federal court system even after the *Brown* decision. The most important from a philosophical and psychological point of view was that the Court had not only rejected the government's argument that Noia had made "an intelligent and understanding waiver" of his rights in preferring the life sentence to the risk of ending up in the electric chair, it turned the argument on its head by ruling that his fear of the electric chair had made it impossible for him to make an "intelligent and understanding" waiver.

Okay. If that's what they wanted to say. In one way, you could say that they had ducked the issue by quibbling over the meaning of words. But that's what the law always comes down to, doesn't it? A quibble over words. After the quibble was over and done with they were saying *that you cannot waive a Constitutional right even if you want to*, and in the decisions that followed they extended that doctrine further and further, without any pretense and without any quibble, until they had said, in effect, that nobody else could waive it for you. Not your lawyer. Not the judge. Nobody.

No case was ever dead, it was as simple as that.

The more I studied *Noia*, the clearer it became to me that it wasn't the legal issue that was being ruled on, it was the entire system of criminal justice. The U.S. Supreme Court was saying that the state courts had been so remiss in protecting the rights of defendants that the Supreme Court was now taking over and appointing the federal courts as overseers of every trial—past, present, and future—no matter how much they had to strain the language to do it. They were, it seemed to me, putting all trial judges on notice that they had better concern themselves with human rights from now on instead of property rights or they were going to be reversed and reversed and reversed.

Never again would a judge say, "I'm sorry I can't sentence him to death. Take him away. Get rid of him."

All I had to do was find a way to get back into the courts, and even with my hundred-odd years I had a chance. I had a chance because everybody had a chance.

And I already had a way. On the very same day—March 18, 1963—the Supreme Court had ruled in *Gideon* that a lawyer must be provided for any defendant in a criminal case. And I hadn't had a lawyer in my Philadelphia trial. It didn't matter that I hadn't wanted one. It didn't even matter that I had pleaded guilty because they had caught me cold. If you hadn't had a lawyer you hadn't had a trial. Period. All I had to do was send in my brief and I could knock off that conviction. And also the conviction for the prison breach at Eastern State Pen, where I had not been permitted to wait for my own lawyer despite my repeated requests for an adjournment.

Okay. So what? Considering all the time I had in New York, what good was it going to do me to knock out a couple of sentences in Philadelphia that I wasn't going to live long enough to serve anyway?

Plenty of good.

Every conviction is tied to every other conviction in the sense that you can't be a fourth offender without those three other offenses on your record. The moment I reversed the Philadelphia conviction I wouldn't be a fourth offender any more, and that meant I would be able to go into the courts of New York and ask to be resentenced as a third offender. But, again, so what? The mandatory thirty-years-to-life sentences would be out, sure. But I'd still be faced with a sentence of from ten to thirty years for the robbery and from five to ten for the guns. And I'd still have the indictments for the escapes from Sing Sing and Holmesburg hanging over me.

Never mind. I had a philosophy. I had a plan. If a reversal on one case could be used to knock down the sentence on another one, then why couldn't I continue on down the line, using one case to knock over another until I had knocked them all out. It was as if I had come alive again. The blood came pounding back into my veins. I was back in business, plotting and scheming. I bought every law book I could get my hands on. I sent away to the West Publishing Company in St. Paul and the Bureau of Documents in Washington, D.C., for the complete transcript of every decision that seemed at all important. My cell became a law library. I couldn't wait to get out of the laundry every day so that I could run back and study.

And slowly but surely a master plan was formed in my mind.

1 / I was not only going to ask to be resentenced as a third offender in Queens, I was going to make a two-pronged attack on the conviction itself. In 1964 the Supreme Court overturned the *Sheppard* verdict because of the pretrial publicity after Dr. Sheppard had been released from jail by a Federal District Court judge. There were major differences between his situation and mine. Nevertheless, it was a legitimate basis for an appeal. I also had a feeling I could make a pretty good case that in telling the jury how expensive the trial had been, Judge Farrell had re-

minded them of the extraordinary security measures that were being taken because of the murder of Arnold Schuster, and that by bringing Arnold Schuster back into their minds he had prejudiced the verdict. As proven by the swiftness with which they had come back with it.

2 / If I could get rid of the Philadelphia conviction through *Gideon* and shake the Queens conviction through *Sheppard,* I'd still have the Kings County conviction on the possession of the gun. With the mandatory fourth-offense element out of it, the routine sentence would be from five to ten years, which should get me out in about three years.

3 / I was still doing time on the Rosenthal conviction, which had been imposed in 1931, and there was not a thing I could find to attack that conviction. Not directly, anyway. Indirectly, yes. I could see where I had a technicality on my first offense, the Ozone Park National Bank back in 1926. Follow this now: I had been indicted in the Supreme Court of Queens, but the trial had taken place in the county court and there had been no valid order transferring the indictment. A minor technicality, you might think. A mere oversight. Probably it was. Nobody paid much attention to that kind of thing back in 1926. But things had changed. A decision had come out of Buffalo that when a trial was transferred from a higher court to a lower court, the order of transfer had to be signed by a judge from the higher court in order to make it valid. The Buffalo conviction had been thrown out because the order had been issued by the clerk of courts. On the very next morning, I had a letter on the way to the clerk of courts in Queens to find out who had signed the order for my transfer. A letter came back that they couldn't find any order of transfer.

The dominoes were falling. I had been sentenced for the Rosenthal robbery as a second offender. With the Ozone Park robbery invalidated, I would have to be resentenced as a first offender. A different ball game entirely. On the maximum sentence that could be imposed I would already have served more than the full time.

4 / The indictment for the Sing Sing escape could be attacked on the same basis. They owed me the six years I had served on an illegal sentence. I'd swap them even up. Why be a sorehead about it?

5 / The same thing applied to the indictment for beating Holmesburg. I had served illegal sentences for both the original conviction and the Eastern State escape. The bastards owed *me* twelve years. All they could get me on, that I could see, was assault and battery on the officer who had opened the door to the cellblock that night and stealing a couple of hats and jackets.

Listen, you lie in bed late at night and try to figure these things out, and they sound awfully good to you. By the time I fell asleep on that particular night I could see where I was going to establish some new law on that one.

And who knows, maybe I would have. As long as the Supreme Court stayed in business, there was always a chance they would have ruled that an escape from an illegal sentence couldn't be punished. What they did come up with was even better.

6 / In 1966, the final piece of the mosaic fell into place when the Supreme Court ruled, in *Ewell,* that detainers did not constitute an adequate reason to deprive the accused of his Sixth Amendment rights to a speedy trial. That, in fact, by forcing a prisoner to finish one sentence before he went on trial for another the government was not only impairing his ability to defend himself but depriving him of any incentive to rehabilitate himself.

In 1966, the indictment on me for Sing Sing was thirty-four years old, and the indictment for Holmesburg was nineteen years old.

At the very worst, I had some points. Some good points. The Catch 22 was that by the time I had bounced them all through the courts I'd be the oldest, as well as the most experienced, litigant ever to walk out of an American prison as a free man.

I was going to have to find some way to tie them all together and then, by playing directly to the new sympathetic attitude toward prisoners, get a judge to say, "Yeah, Willie, I guess you do have a lot of points there. You're not a bad fellow, you never hurt anybody. We'll just suspend sentence on the whole package and save us all a lot of trouble."

If there had still been that "make a run for it, Willie, we're with you" attitude toward me, I could see where they'd have been in a mood to do exactly that. What the attitude toward me was now I didn't know. The Valachi testimony had come in October 1963, just as the Legal Revolution was getting under way, and I still didn't have the least idea whether it was going to help me or hurt me.

Through it all I had been continuing my growing legal practice. I wasn't studying blindly, you know. After I had walked a couple of guys out by drawing up the appropriate writs, everybody had begun to come to me for help. Boy, I'll bet I got a couple of dozen people out of there. They didn't have to be people I knew, either. More than half of them were Negroes and Puerto Ricans. For two very good reasons. They had become the overwhelming majority in prison by then, and they had the most open-and-shut cases. See, mostly they had been represented by the Legal Aid Society, which gets so loaded down with cases that they have to run their clients through on the plea-bargaining treadmill. A lot of them would come in and tell me that the Legal Aid lawyer had advised them to plead guilty on a reduced charge, and since the alternative had been to remain in jail for anywhere up to five years while they were waiting for their trial to come up, they had pleaded guilty even though they hadn't done it.

There are innocent people in prison, don't kid yourself. There aren't that many of them, don't kid yourself about that either. "That isn't the issue," I would tell them. If they really wanted to go back and claim they were innocent, they were only complicating things. The first thing I'd want to know on a plea-bargained conviction was: Did you ever have the legal definition of *guilt* explained to you? You see, if a man pleads guilty because he hasn't been made aware that the state doesn't have all the elements that are needed to present a legal case in a courtroom—like, say, a corroborative witness—he has been denied due process. I know that may not be very palatable to most people but you have to look at it this way: Another guy who had done the same thing and had the money to hire a good lawyer would have been out on bail the next morning, and the case would never have got into court.

The Legal Aid lawyers aren't the word offenders, either. All things considered, they do the best they can. The worst offenders are the "dirty shirts"—the ambulance chasers of the courtroom—who have some guard or jail official on the payroll to steer them to a number of prospects in every day's haul. They tell all their "clients" they'll be able to get them off cheap if they plead guilty, charge them fifty or a hundred dollars, and make their living off the volume. They wouldn't know how to actually try a case if their life depended on it.

And then there is the good lawyer who gets "grabbed" by the judge because he happens to walk into the courtroom at the wrong time. Some of them will do a conscientious job. A lot of them don't want to spend the time it would take to fight it in a courtroom. Not for the fee they're going to get as a court-appointed lawyer. "Listen," they say. "You've got a tough case here. This is a bitch. Lucky for you I've got a connection in the District Attorney's office." Same as with the dirty shirts: Take a plea and I'll get you off cheap.

We had a few regular lawyers at Attica, and they were watched very closely because the authorities didn't want them giving advice. One of them was Burton Pugash, who had hired a couple of thugs to throw lye into the face of his girl friend; another was Jack Molinas, the great basketball player who had been involved in the betting scandals. It wasn't that the authorities cared whether the prisoner got out, they had more prisoners than they knew what to do with. Their only concern was that once the papers went in, people started to be subpoenaed, and every time a prisoner was called into court two guards had to be detached to go along with him.

In all my years in prison I had done my best to stay out of trouble. I had now become the one thing that the administration disliked more than anything else, the jailhouse lawyer. A troublemaker.

If you made out a writ for another inmate you were subject to being called before the warden's court and having some of your good time taken away. So here's what I would do. I would listen to what anybody had to say, and if I decided to make out a writ for him I would write it up in my cell and pass it on back to him through somebody else. Since they were constantly frisking me and searching my cell, I started to make out writs for myself and leave them around to be found. A couple of times they got so mad when they thought they had me, only to find out I was working on my own writ, that they arrested me for "using a typewriter after hours."

Although they never actually caught me with another inmate's writ in my hand but once, I was arrested fifteen or sixteen times. I was always told that the next time I'd go into isolation. It was always the next time, though, because they knew they were on such shaky grounds that they didn't actually come right out and forbid it. The rule was that before one inmate could make out any legal papers for another inmate he had to get permission from the warden. And whenever you went to the warden's office for permission you were turned down. Catch 22. They didn't forbid it, you just couldn't do it. (After I had left, the Supreme Court finally got around to ruling that of course one inmate had a right to help another secure his rights.)

The one time I got caught I had been trying to help out a friend of mine who was supposed to get the information I needed to me through another friend by putting it inside a newspaper. One of the guards saw the newspaper being passed between them and when it was handed to me as I was coming in from the yard the guard was waiting. "What's in the newspaper?" he asked.

"Nothing," I said. "Just a newspaper."

He held out his hand. "Let me have it." Just a newspaper, huh?

Luckily for me, the dep was away and the captain who was holding court was in a good mood. As soon as I walked in, he said, "What is it, another writ, Willie? All right, you lose two days. Be more careful next time, willya?"

I had a practice of a size many a lawyer would have envied, and the best thing about it was that, unlike real lawyers, I could pick my clients. I had a right to make up my own mind. I wouldn't help a rapist, a drug peddler, or a psychopathic killer. But there were an awful lot of kids up in Attica, who had either killed or maimed somebody during a gang fight. To me, these kids were victims of circumstances. They had set out with their friends one night, just like the poor kids they had come up against, and all of a sudden something that had started out as a lark wasn't funny any more. And I think the average citizen would have been astonished if he had known how many kids were sent to prison not so long ago for stealing a car for a joy ride. If they came from the wrong jurisdiction, they could get a godawful ten years slapped on them for that. Anybody could see that unless something was done for them they were going to leave prison a helluva lot worse than they had come in.

It was an education for me. I'd sit down with these people and they'd tell me their stories and over and over again I'd think back on how right Dr. Philip Roche had been in saying that we spend our lives living out our childhood fantasies. There was this kid Bill Liss, from out of Buffalo, who worked in the laundry with me. He had been a roofer on the outside, a hard-working kid all his life. I really liked him. I sat him down and taught him English, and it was like a revelation to him. "Boy," he'd say. "If I had a teacher like you in school I would have learned this so easy." He was a good-looking young fellow, tall, blond, and blue-eyed. He was also the "Buffalo Strangler."

That's what he was up for, anyway. He had made a full confession and then tried to withdraw it during his trial. His lawyer had claimed that it was coerced.

But, still, his lawyer hadn't pleaded him innocent. He had pleaded insanity. Bill's story was that they had tricked him into confessing by making false promises to him. He didn't claim that he was smart, he'd say. Only that he was innocent.

In between the English lessons, he told me the story of his life. He was an illegitimate child who had been brought up in various institutions where they had worked him like an animal in the fields. When he was about fifteen, his mother visited him to tell him she was happily married, that her husband didn't know about him, and that she intended to keep it that way. She had come to see him after all those years to tell him that she was leaving the state and she wanted him to consider her dead.

He used to have these blackouts, he told me. He'd be somewhere across town in a bar or dance hall and the next thing he knew he would be waking up in the morning in his own bed. Immediately he would jump up and get dressed so that he could go back to the other side of town and get his car and when he got downstairs he'd find it parked right in front of the house.

To talk to this kid you'd think he was the gentlest, kindest person who ever lived. And from his own lips he began to tell me about the dark deeds he had done and was unable to understand. One night while he was with a prostitute in a whorehouse he had suddenly begun to choke her. Somehow, she had been able to reach under her pillow, come out with a knife, and stick it into his chest. Somehow, he had managed to grab his clothes and stagger to a hospital where he told them that he had been attacked by a pair of muggers.

Another time he had tried to strangle a prostitute he had brought to his room. This one was able to break away and go running out into the street, naked.

But he had never actually succeeded in strangling any of them, he'd say. What had happened, he was sure, was that one of them had reported him to the police, and that's why they had decided to pin the unsolved stranglings on him. He asked me a number of times to look his case over and see whether I could find some kind of technicality for him. And finally I did. I had him send for the minutes of his trial, and he'd slip me a few pages before I went into my cell at night, and I'd slip them back to him in the morning. When I had finished reading it I knew two things; I knew that he was the Buffalo Strangler and I knew that I could put him back out on the street.

The story started five years before he was convicted, when the body of the first victim was found at the bottom of a cliff, so badly broken that it was obvious that she had been thrown off from the top. Bill Liss had been identified as one of the men she had been seen talking to in a bar earlier in the evening, but he had been able to convince the police that it was a case of mistaken identity by giving them the name of the girl he had actually been out with that night.

Over the next five years there were a series of stranglings always following the same pattern. The meeting with the mysterious stranger in a bar or tavern, the strangled body at the foot of a cliff or the edge of the woods. The last victim was a WAC whose frozen body had been found near the Niagara Gorge. In tracing her activities of the previous night, the police discovered that she had been seen in a tavern with a guy named Bill Liss. And, of course, the name rang a bell. A bulletin went out to pick him up, his picture was all over the newspapers, and after a couple of days had passed he walked into the police station, expressing his bewilderment and protesting his innocence.

In the intervening five years Bill had married and had a child. How long his wife had managed to live with him I don't recall, although it couldn't have been very long because, of course, he had a deep hatred for all women. At any rate, they brought his wife and child in, along with his wife's parents, and between them they convinced him that if he would tell the truth he would be given psychiatric treatment and no criminal charges would be brought against him. So he made a full confession to the police, repeated it to a psychiatrist, and they brought him to trial anyway.

The prosecutor was able to attack the insanity plea by showing how cleverly Liss had set up his alibi for the first murder. He had met the victim in the tavern, strangled her in his apartment, left to keep the date with his girl friend, and then returned to the apartment and disposed of the body. Hardly an overwhelming impulse, but carefully planned ahead of time and covered up afterward. Which probably wasn't true. My guess is that it had been exactly that, an accidental meeting and an overwhelming impulse, with everything that happened afterward dictated by the circumstance of the fortuitous date. It's even possible that his hatred for women erupted when it did *because* of the date he had that night with a "decent" girl.

His lawyer had tried to have the confession thrown out by citing a Connecticut case where in precisely the same circumstances—it paralleled Bill's case exactly—the District Court had ruled that you could hardly call that kind of a confession voluntary. It got to the Supreme Court too early, though—in 1961—and although the Court did order a new trial, they ducked the main issue and did it on other, highly technical grounds.

But things had changed. Liss was quite right in feeling that I might be able to find something for him. There were three recent Supreme Court decisions on which I felt I could spring him. *Lynumn* v. *Illinois, Massiah* v. *United States,* and *Escobedo* v. *Illinois.*

In *Lynumn,* the Court had held that any promise of reward which induced or helped to induce an accused to confess would render the confession inadmissible. The only difference between a psychological bribe and a rubber hose, the Court had said, was that the psychological technique was probably more effective. In *Massiah,* the prosecutor had induced the accused's partner to cooperate with the government and had then sent him back, all wired up, to discuss the crime with him and bug his "confession." The Supreme

Court had called that an infringement of his right to counsel. In *Escobedo,* the Court had ruled that the moment the purpose of an interrogation became to elicit a confession; that is, the moment the subject ceased to be a mere suspect and was believed to be the guilty party, he must be informed of his right to have a lawyer present. Although Escobedo had made a voluntary confession, the Court ruled that he too had been denied his right to counsel.

Like *Lynumn,* Liss had been induced to confess on the promise of a reward. Like *Massiah,* the prosecutor had sent someone to him whom he felt he could trust. Like *Escobedo,* he had been thought to be the guilty party and had been encouraged to make a voluntary confession without being told that he was entitled to consult an attorney.

I figured I could cite them all and let the Supreme Court take its pick. I even had my brief drafted.

And then I looked at Bill and I said to myself, Suppose this fellow was released and met my own daughter on the street, what would happen there? Well, he would be meeting somebody else's daughter. As much as I wanted to see whether I could kick a case into the Supreme Court and maybe even make some new law up there, I couldn't do it. He shouldn't have been in jail to begin with, he should have been in a mental hospital. But he was better off in jail, away from women, than out in the street. I knew that much. Mama had seen to that a long time ago.

The revolution in the law continued on through 1966, and I did get a couple of cases into the Supreme Court. I was still reading decisions, always looking for something that might help me, when on August 23, 1966, my plans underwent an abrupt change. I had gone marching to the laundry as usual with my company. Just as we arrived I was hit with such an excruciating pain in both my legs that it took my breath away. I couldn't move, it was so bad. I just doubled over and sank to the floor. They got me to the prison hospital in a wheelchair, and after I had been given a couple of needles and X-rayed I was told that the main artery leading to my heart was so far gone that I had almost no circulation in my legs.

An operation was going to have to be performed at once, and since they didn't feel I could stand the trip to Sing Sing, where they had the hospital facilities, they sent me to the Buffalo General Hospital, thirty-eight miles away, as a private patient. Before I left, Father Gene was called in to administer the last rites of the Church, just in case I couldn't make it to Buffalo.

Now I am going to show once and for all how asinine they could get about security. I'm sixty-five years old, and I have just been given the last rites of the church because my aorta is about to fall out of me. My legs are so useless that they have to haul me down to the prison van in a stretcher. And don't you think they handcuffed me to the side of the stretcher and sent me to the hospital accompanied by two burly guards. They were still afraid that it was some kind of a trick, you know? I'll bet if I had died they'd have sent two guards down into the grave with me to make sure I didn't get better all of a sudden.

I have to say this for them, though. They hired the best surgeon in Buffalo for me, Dr. Paul A. Fernbach. Fernbach had them shoot some colored liquid into my bloodstream, took one look at the fluoroscope, and told me that he was going to operate in the morning. Eight inches of artery were going to be taken out and replaced by plastic tubing, a relatively new procedure. "Ten years ago," he said, "I'd have been sitting here telling you to put your affairs in order, because you'd have only had a week or two to live."

"Doctor," I said. "Your fee is being paid by the state, is that right?"

Yes, that was right.

"Well, I owe your client about a hundred years. If you let me beat them out of what they've got coming to them, they might decide to beat you out of what you've got coming to you."

He would do his very best, he told me gravely, not to bring either of us to such a sorry state.

He had to cut me from my collarbone to my pelvis

374

and when he sewed me up again I was stitched from top to bottom like a zipper. Five days later, they wheeled me out of the intensive-care unit and back to my own room. Sure enough, my guards were waiting for me. Well, as long as they were there they might as well make themselves useful. It was the first time I had been out of an oxygen mask since the operation, and I asked them to please open the window so that I could get some air. I was still being fed intravenously, mind you, I still had an oxygen tank standing alongside my bed, and I still couldn't move without feeling the retention stitches grab at me. Nevertheless, they held a great debate before one of them finally went over and opened it about six inches. Just enough for me to get some air; not enough for me to take a flying leap out the window. We were, after all, only on the third floor.

Coming in, I had thought I'd be out of the hospital in about a week. I had to stay closer to a month. There was one thing, though, that greatly encouraged me. When the news got out that I was in the hospital, I received a tremendous amount of mail. Get-well cards poured in by the thousands. Messages came from people who wanted me to know they were praying for me. One of them was signed in great big letters: The Boys and Girls from the Fifth Grade. Many older people had masses said for me. Most of the cards and letters I didn't see until after I had returned to Attica because all of my mail was supposed to be sent back to the prison to be processed. It was only through a male nurse named Riley that I was able to see some of it and learn about the rest. In all the time I was there, this Riley went all out to take care of me. He shaved me, he cut my hair, and he did everything humanly possible to make me comfortable. From time to time, he would reach under his shirt and give me about a dozen letters and tell me to read them whenever I got a chance and then return them. What bugged me was that he looked familiar and I couldn't place him. I couldn't even get him to tell me his first name. "Just call me Riley, everybody calls me Riley." On the day I was leaving, I finally found out what it was. He had a brother in Attica. "Will you get word to him that I'll be up next week?" he asked me. "Tell him the only reason I haven't been up lately is because I've been very busy here."

I had a final meeting with Dr. Fernbach, too. And it was so hilarious, to me at least, that I almost split a gut. The doctor was a big, rather heavy man with iron-gray hair and bushy, arching eyebrows. He looked more like a piano mover than a surgeon. He had come in the day before I was leaving, looking rather uncomfortable, and asked the guards if they would leave us alone for a couple of minutes. As soon as they were out of the room, he cleared his throat, pulled at his nose, and said, "Willie, I have noted in our conversations that you are a man with wide-ranging interests. Perhaps you have become aware of the adoration with which the young look upon a group of long-haired but not unattractive young Englishmen known as the Beatles. A craze that has all the earmarks of a true phenomenon. Journalists and academicians alike have pondered the question of what turns a normal human being into a devout and devoted fan. A fan being perhaps best defined as one who identifies his or her own condition in life with someone in the public eye. Do you follow me? Good. The question I would like you to answer for me, Willie, is what makes a person who is reasonably normal in all other respects into a fan?"

"If I was wise enough to be able to answer that," I said, "why would I be going out robbing banks?"

"Well, the reason I thought you might," he said, "is that my daughter is a great fan of yours. Every day when I return from the hospital she inquires about your progress." In fact, he said, as his eyes began to twinkle, he wouldn't dare to go home tomorrow and tell her I had left unless he was also able to hand her the letter from me that he had been promising.

I was only too happy to write her a letter, of course. But, I warned him, twinkling a little myself, we were going to have to beat the censors. Anything I wrote, like anything I received, was supposed to pass through the mail check back at Attica. "Now here's the plan," I whispered.

On that final morning, Dr. Fernbach entered the room like an arch-conspirator, being so darned casual and cheery that if he had been entering the country every customs agent within miles would have made a beeline for him. He reached under the blanket to examine my toes and ankles with his fine, firm surgeon's hands, and as he began to flex my knee I slipped the letter into his hand. He fumbled it, of course. Fumbled it and bumbled around for it and broke into a sweat. And then almost tripped over himself as he was turning away from the guards so that he could slip it into his pocket.

Great hands for a heart surgeon but, boy, wouldn't he have made a terrible thief.

The operation had been a success in more ways than one. During my hospital stay I had discovered that there was still a certain amount of goodwill for me around the country, after all. And I couldn't see how either the judiciary or the police authorities could worry that a sixty-five-year-old man who had just been sliced in half and fitted with a home-made aorta could pose any kind of a threat to the peace and security of the Federal Reserve System. It seemed to me, as I rode the prison van back to Attica, that it was only a matter now of becoming healthy enough to make my move.

The Angel on My Shoulder

Katherine Spyros Bitses was a very unusual woman, and an even more unusual lawyer. She had been a young girl at the time of the trial, only a couple of years out of law school. Her job had been to take the testimony of the state's witnesses down in shorthand for Sheridan, just as I had been doing for Herz, look for places for him to hit on cross-examination, and get him to the courtroom on time.

Sheridan had promised Tommy that he was going to appeal his conviction, even though as a court-appointed attorney he was under no obligation to. When Tommy hadn't heard anything after a couple of years, he wrote to ask when his case was coming up on the appeal calendar. Turned out that the answer was never. Sheridan hadn't filed any notice of appeal, and Katherine, who had heard him make that promise, was terribly upset. Now understand that Katherine had come to work for Sheridan practically out of law school, after a brief stint in a Wall Street firm. He was considered to be the top criminal lawyer in Queens and she admired him tremendously. As much as she admired him, she left his firm determined to do whatever could be done for Kling, at that late date, herself. Not too long afterward she went into practice for herself, opening up a storefront office in her old neighborhood and serving as a community lawyer.

In the course of working on Tommy's case she came up to Attica to find out whether I could supply any new evidence. "Listen, Katherine," I said, "Kling is innocent." Tommy hadn't been in it at all, I told her. The third man, I said, had been a friend of Venuta's whom he had been trying to protect. "A guy named Longo," I said, grabbing onto the name of a mobster who had recently been killed upstate. "Longo, that's the only name I ever knew him by. I'd have liked to have said something at the trial, Katherine, but you can see that there was no way I could have cleared Tommy without incriminating myself. Tommy understood that."

I wrote up a nine-page affidavit, using the kind of flowery language that showed the influence of all the judicial decisions I had been reading. "I planned all the details meticulously," I wrote, "and decided to contact De Venuta to discover whether his enthusiasm was equal to my own." Venuta had then brought in Longo, "a friend or relative who was the third man in our fiscal transaction."

As for Kling, "His health was so greatly impaired that it would have been extremely hazardous for anyone to seek his services in such a strenuous profession as bank robbery. Kling's only crime was in knowing me, for that is the only basis upon which his present misfortune rests. To perpetuate the injustice would be akin to placing 'truth forever on the scaffold, and wrong forever on the throne.' It is my fervent wish that those responsible for the tragedy that has resulted in Kling's imprisonment will never experience one moment of his grief and sorrow."

Now, that kind of affidavit is pretty useless after the two of you have been convicted. If you were a judge, would you take the word of somebody who has nothing to lose by telling you something that might help a friend? What I was trying to do was put it to De Venuta to see whether things had been going bad enough on the outside so that he might want to make a comeback. Toward that end, I asked him to come forward with the truth "and thereby save a lot of probing into the concealed factors which had they been uncovered at the time of the trial would have prevented a miscarriage of justice."

Was I willing to come to Queens and testify? Katherine asked me. Of course I was. I even offered to take a lie-detector test, knowing that the court would never permit it. "You're not thinking of trying to escape, are you?" she asked me suddenly.

"Katherine," I said. "If I stop thinking of escaping you'll know I'm dead."

Escaping was exactly what I had in mind, of course, although not that way. I was interested in doing what I could to help my old pal Tommy, and I was even more interested in having a fighter like Katherine Bitses on my side. "Katherine," I said before she left. "Do you think there's anything you can do for me?"

She gave me a look that said: Willie, God Almighty couldn't help you.

But that was all right. I knew there was nothing that could be done for me yet. I had only been trying to put the thought into her mind.

Her motion for a new trial based upon my "confession" didn't excite the judge at all. Although she did manage to get Kling's sentence reduced to that of a third offender in a companion motion based upon the fact that one of Tommy's felony convictions in New Jersey had been for breaking and entering, which should really only have been a high misdemeanor.

Soon thereafter Kling's case was taken over by the Legal Aid, which fought for him for fourteen years. It was on Katherine's testimony in Federal Court that Kling was finally sent back to Queens for a new trial. He was released in February 1969, and died a few months later.

Over the years, she visited me in Attica usually during the summer as she was passing through on her vacation. Her visit lasted three days and I'd ask her advice about some of the writs I was making out for the other inmates. We'd talk about my case. After the decisions began to roll in, in 1963, we stopped discussing everybody else and began to discuss me. So finally I had a professional lawyer to consult. Very frequently she would temper my enthusiasm. She couldn't see, for instance, where the *Sheppard* decision was going to do anything for me. With *Sheppard,* a newspaper had demanded that he be brought to trial and the jury hadn't been locked up. And even if that weren't true, Herz hadn't asked for a change of venue or run out his challenges in order to establish that any jury we got had to be "infected with prejudice." I couldn't blame Herz for that. He had no more way of knowing that publicity was going to become an issue than I'd had of knowing, pre-*Miranda,* that the smartest thing I could have done in any of my arrests was to see how fast I could confess.

It was Katherine's feeling that the best approach to take after the Philadelphia convictions were knocked out was to make a straightforward bid for clemency in New York on the general idea that I had already spent more than thirty years in prison and nothing was going to be gained by having me serve out the rest of my life.

Well, I couldn't see much hope for selling anybody on that. Nor could I see that anything would be gained by demanding that the authorities make the result of their investigation of the Schuster murder public. We really went to the mat on that one. "The Schuster case is going to haunt you for the rest of your life," she kept saying. "When you can't duck something, you have to hit it head-on. The only way we're ever going to pull the teeth out of it is by forcing them to put up or shut up. Even if we have to go into court to do it." Intellectually, I did come to see the logic of attempting to overcome the Schuster factor by going on the offensive. Emotionally, I could never overcome the feeling that the less said about Schuster the better.

Katherine also had a theory on the best time for me to make my move, strategically, that turned out to be a major contribution to the course that was eventually taken. When you are paroled from one sentence for the purpose of allowing you to begin another, the sentencing judge can be brought back into the picture. It is the one time you are entitled to go back into court with any motions you may wish to make.

I still hadn't begun to serve my time on the Manufacturers Trust robbery. (I don't think I ever did serve a day on it, and if you can't understand how I could be in doubt about anything like that, stick around.) I had started to serve the Rosenthal sentence in 1954, after the parole board had reversed itself and let me out of the parole violation at the end of eighteen months. With all my "good time" figured in, I was going to be eligible for parole early in 1968. There was a great deal to be said, Katherine felt, for holding back until then so that I could combine the motion to be resentenced as a third offender with the over-all plea for clemency. The psychology being that since Judge Farrell would have to rule in my favor on the first part of it, he just might find himself in a frame of mind to go all the way.

I liked the idea of throwing it back into Judge Farrell's lap for another reason. With trial judges undergoing such a battering, I could see where he might very well prefer to let me go on a tea-and-sympathy plea than to run the risk of having the Supreme Court of the U.S. of A. rule, in a highly publicized decision, that he had prejudiced my rights by turning down the jury's request to retire for the night and then having them come back with the verdict he had asked for within half an hour.

That was where the situation stood in August 1966, when I went into the Buffalo General Hospital for the operation. My recovery, after I returned to Attica, was very slow. You just don't snap back from that kind of an operation at the age of sixty-five. To be absolutely truthful, I have always believed that I died on that operating table. I had that feeling when I first recovered consciousness in the intensive-care room, and I became absolutely sure of it on the day I left. While they had been getting me ready for the operating room, one of the nurses told me she was going to give me a copy of the medical records of the operation for my memory book. She never did, and just before I left I asked her why. "Willie," she said. "If you ever read that medical record you would have had a relapse. You're leaving. Just be thankful for that."

I came out of the hospital weighing only a little over

a hundred pounds and looking about a hundred years old. For the year and a half that I remained at Attica, waiting to become eligible to send my application to the parole board, I remained so weak and frail that anytime I had to lift anything, no matter how light, somebody else would have to do it for me.

The parole board meets in every prison in the state for three days every month to consider the applications. At Attica, it's on the ninth, tenth, and eleventh. Shortly after the beginning of 1968, I received my notice that I was scheduled to appear before the board on February 11 in regard to beginning the sentence for the Manufacturers Trust robbery.

A charade. The way an inmate conducts himself during the interview has very little to do with determining whether or not he's going to be paroled. The decision has already been made in Albany months earlier, half politics and half bureaucratic roulette. They don't even bother to go through any particular pretense. Forty or fifty men a day are run in and out on an assembly line, two or three minutes apart. Nevertheless, it is the most important two or three minutes in any prisoner's life—the product they are dealing with here is freedom—and the applicants line the benches in the corridor outside the room, chain smoking to cover their nervousness.

While there is never anything automatic about parole, the situation I was in—ending one sentence for the purpose of starting an even longer one—is as close to automatic as it's possible to get. Bearing that in mind, I had decided to go in and ask for more. "Gentlemen," I said. "I certainly expect to receive your favorable consideration and secure your permission to begin my 1952 sentence." I pointed out to them that I had been in Attica for fifteen years, was almost sixty-seven years old, and still owed the state of Pennsylvania something like sixty years. "It is obvious, considering the precarious state of my health, that it will be impossible for me to serve more than a few years. Under the circumstances, I would appreciate knowing what you can do for me to have my other sentences reduced."

There was nothing they could do about it, they said. "The only remedy you have, Willie, is through the courts."

That evening, I received the notice that I was being granted parole as of April 19 for the purpose of allowing me to serve my new sentence concurrently with the remainder of the old one. The time had come, at last, for me to make my move, and I knew exactly how I intended to go about it.

Katherine Bitses had not been up to Attica since my operation. Or, for that matter, for perhaps a year before that. We had been in correspondence from time to time, though, and now that we were ready to go back into Judge Farrell's court, I sent her a letter, giving her all the pertinent information. She wrote me she would write Warden Mancusi immediately for permission to visit me in Attica. When several weeks went by and she hadn't been cleared through the Warden's office, I became impatient and I sat down, wrote out a letter myself, and sent it off to Judge Farrell.

My letter was divided into parts. In the first part, I explained why I should be resentenced as a third offender rather than a fourth offender. In the second part, I described my operation and the precarious state of my health and asked him to apply the time I had already spent in Attica toward the new sentence and then reduce the sentence to time served.

I was not only asking him to let me go, I was offering him a formula that would permit him to do it.

Two weeks later I was called to the warden's office and told that Judge Farrell had ordered that I be brought to the Queens County Courthouse to argue my motion. (It was the same court with the same jurisdiction but as the result of a reorganization that had taken place in the New York judiciary it was now called the Supreme Court.)

You ought to know by now how the prison authorities reacted to that. If I had figured out a way of getting myself out of the prison, I had to have some devious plan in the works. Call out the security people! I wasn't on A block any more, incidentally, because nobody was in A block. Due to Governor

Rockefeller's newly instituted policy for treating drug addicts in hospitals instead of confining them to prisons, the population at Attica had been reduced so drastically that A block had been completely vacated.

On the night before my departure I was taken off D block, where the laundry company had been transferred, and placed back in my old cell. For that one night, I was the only prisoner there. Just me and a lot of empty cells and my two guards.

As dawn was breaking on the distant horizon, I was spirited out of the prison by four correction officers and driven to the railroad station at Batavia, seventeen miles away, to be placed upon the train to New York.

In anticipation of my arrival, a whole section of Grand Central terminal had been cordoned off. The high brass and gold braid of the city's police and correction departments were all over the place, supervising the security and planning the strategy.

Strategy: In order to foil any masked bandits or old Indian fighters who might be lying in wait along the route to rescue me, the Commissioner of Corrections ordered that I be taken to the Bronx House of Detention instead of to Queens. Once I got there my clothes were taken away from me and I was given a jail uniform, something that is never done with a prisoner who is going to appear in court. The strategy here was that in case I was taken away from them while I was being transferred I would be easily identifiable. Naturally, I objected. Fortunately, my old friend Warden Klein had been transferred to the Bronx and as soon as he came down to pay me a visit he said, "For crissake, what idiot had this brainstorm?" and ordered them to give me back my clothes.

The next day I was whipped through the streets of New York by the usual motorcycle escort and, upon my arrival at the courthouse, whisked down to the cellar, a kind of dark, dank catacomb such as I hadn't seen since Cap McPhee and his squad of sluggers had taken me down to the target room to beat a tattoo on me. A maze of tunnels going every whichway. Every time we reached a twist or turn where two tunnels came together, a couple of the guards would peel off and take up their position as sentries. It was like being trapped in the middle of a Freudian dream. It seemed to me that we walked forever before we reached a little cell at the far end of one of the passageways, away from everything.

Between the train ride and the shuttling back and forth and the tension, what little strength I had left had been drained right out of me. I lay down on the bunk, closed my eyes, and drifted off to sleep. The next thing I knew I heard a familiar voice bellowing, "I said open that door or I'll find somebody who will! I'm going to talk to my client and I'm not going to talk to him through bars."

Katherine had been sitting in Judge Farrell's courtroom upstairs waiting for the calendar to be called in one of her other cases when one of the other lawyers sat down alongside her and said, "I see your boy is downstairs."

She couldn't imagine what he was talking about.

"Willie Sutton," he told her. "Didn't you see all the policemen on the roof?"

Katherine went up to the Bench to find out what I was doing there, and when Farrell told her about the letter he had received from me she had asked for permission to leave the courtroom.

When I saw her there outside the cell, bellowing away, tears came to my eyes, I swear it. I put my hand out through the bars. "Katherine," I said. "You're my favorite person in the whole world." Now this is fifteen years after the trial, and Katherine Spyros Bitses was no longer a little slip of a Greek girl. She was a veteran criminal lawyer, and she wasn't about to let anybody keep her out of the cell. "You've got forty-four million guards here on a sick old man," she yelled. "What's the matter with you?"

It took a phone call to the warden but, finally, they let her in. I must have looked as bad as I felt because she hadn't been in there more than a minute before she started to cry. "Don't worry," she kept saying. "You're going to come out. I'll get you out, Willie, but you have to stay alive or how can I help you? How can I help you if you're not here to help me?"

I looked at her and it was as if I were reading her mind. During one of our long talks at Attica she had told me how she had nursed her father for a year and a half while he was dying from cancer, and how a little of her had died with him. And how he had said to her at the end, "What's going to happen to you when I'm not around to help you when you need me?"

My God, I thought, remembering that this was the first time she had seen me since the operation. I look as bad to her as her father must have looked when he was dying. With me, she's giving herself another chance to cheat death. And then I thought, because who wouldn't think it in the situation I was in, My God, what an ally to have. She'll never give up.

Her last words as she left the cell were, "I have an angel on my shoulder, Willie, and the angel tells me this time you're going to walk out of here a free man."

Later in the day, after court had adjourned, Katherine met with Judge Farrell in his chambers and told him she was going to handle the motions. Now here is where I got the first of the two bonuses that were to be handed to me that day. Katherine could talk to Farrell. At the time she got out of law school, Farrell had been urging all the young women lawyers in his jurisdiction to get into criminal law. To get right down in the pit with the men and slug it out with them. Katherine had been one of the first to take him up on it, and it had been Farrell who had recommended her to Sheridan.

Beyond that, I had already discovered that I had not been mistaken in believing that Judge Farrell had been looking at me with sympathy through the trial. Shortly after Katherine had left the cell to go back to the courtroom, I had been visited by John F. Kreppein, the Chief Probation Officer of Queens County. An imposing figure of a man with a great shock of white hair. Kreppein had a national reputation as a progressive thinker in the field of rehabilitation and he had come to let me know that I was going to have his wholehearted support. After my arrest in 1952, I now discovered, he had urged Judge Farrell to suspend my sentence in the event I was found guilty. It had been his belief that I had been rehabilitated during my final two years as a fugitive (I didn't have the heart to tell him I had been planning another bank robbery at the time of my arrest) and that by expressing those sentiments from the Bench, Judge Farrell just might set off an irresistible wave of sentiment to have me freed.

By giving me a new life while I still had some productive years ahead of me, Kreppein quite obviously believed that I could become a kind of walking advertisement for his approach to probation.

Judge Farrell had been giving it very serious thought, apparently, before it had all gone out the window with the murder of Arnold Schuster. The Chief Probation Officer and the senior judge always have a very close relationship, and Farrell had remembered those talks well enough so that while Kreppein had been visiting him in his chambers a few days earlier he had slid my letter across the desk and asked, "What do you think I should do about this?"

"Get him down here," Kreppein had said. "And let's see what we can do about it."

He had come to my cell to tell me that he was not only with us but that he was ready to advise us and to work behind the scene to help me in any way he could. Before Katherine had met with Farrell the three of us had got together in my cell to devise our strategy.

The first business on hand was the motion on the resentencing. Judge Farrell agreed to hear the motion that I should be sentenced as a third offender and to delay the actual imposition of the sentence—which would have automatically sent me back to Attica—until Katherine had been given a chance to remove the detainers that had been placed against me for the Holmesburg escape. Once we were shed of the detainers we would come back into his court for sentencing and, at that time, make the plea for a suspended sentence based upon my health. "If you can do it legally, I'll go along with you," he told Katherine. "I'll give you all the time you need."

When it came to the question of the gun sentences in Brooklyn, he was willing to do even more than that. Although the gun charges had been wholly subsidiary to the robbery charge (and for the purposes of sentencing me as a fourth offender had been treated as the same charge) Judge Goldstein had made such a ringing pronunciamento on how the world would benefit from my death that it would have been very difficult for him to show me any consideration. But Judge Goldstein was no longer on the bench. His place on what was now called the Kings County Supreme Court had been taken by Hyman Barshay, and Farrell was sure that if he made a personal phone call to Barshay and explained what was happening, Barshay would be willing, as a matter of courtesy, to hold the resentencing in abeyance too.

Suddenly we had a new battle plan, combining elements of my original plan with this very promising new situation. The Queens conviction, which I had always looked upon as the toughest nut to crack, had, to all intents and purposes, already toppled. The Philadelphia reversal would be automatic. That's what I thought. Military men say that the battle plan disappears as soon as the troops hit the beach and the bullets begin to fly, and this one was no exception.

On April 5, we went into Farrell's court and had the fourth-offender sentence set aside by showing that I had not had counsel in Philadelphia. The date for resentencing was set for May 24.

On April 15, Judge Barshay set aside the life sentences on the two gun charges and announced that I would be resentenced on May 27.

In both courts, the District Attorneys agreed that the Philadelphia conviction was invalid but announced that they would oppose anything less than the maximum sentence as a third offender if only because of an alleged lack of cooperation with the police on the murder of Schuster.

That was the future. The present was Philadelphia, and I was in mortal fear that if they ever got their hands on me they'd never let me go. Katherine didn't want to go into court there either, if she could help it, because she had already learned more than she wanted to know about Philadelphia justice. In order to prove that I hadn't had a lawyer, we had obviously needed a transcript of the trial. The word from the county clerk was that no record seemed to exist. No minutes, no exhibits, no nothing. Sorry about that. If we hadn't been able to dig up a *Philadelphia Inquirer* story containing the flat statement that I had represented myself, we would have had no evidence to present to Farrell and Barshay.

We took a shot at trying to get the detainer quashed by a federal district judge in New York by arguing that since our plea was going to be based on Constitutional grounds and since both the detainer and I were presently domiciled in New York he was clearly entitled to accept jurisdiction. The judge wouldn't go for it. The place was Philadelphia, he told her, and before she could go into the federal courts there she was going to have to exhaust her state remedies.

As Katherine was leaving the courthouse with the assistant DA who had been sent up from Philadelphia, she told him that, judge or no judge, she was going into the District Court in Philadelphia with another approach.

"Why are you so reluctant to come into our court?" he wanted to know. "What do you think we are down there?"

Nothing very nice. "In other words, I don't believe we can get an honest hearing."

The assistant DA was visibly hurt. She was thinking of the old days. "We have a good office now. A fine office." He was willing to personally guarantee her that she'd be given all the help and cooperation she needed. She wouldn't even have to hire a member of the Pennsylvania bar to sponsor her to the court. All she would have to do was send in the papers, file a notice of appearance on the day of the hearing, and he personally would make the motion to admit her to practice.

She sent the papers into the Chief Clerk, and after three weeks and countless telephone calls to find out why we hadn't been given a hearing date, she was told the papers had been lost. She took the next train to Philadelphia and stood over them until they were found. A week or so later, all her papers were returned to her with the memorandum that since she wasn't a member of the Pennsylvania bar she couldn't file any papers. There went a month right there. Katherine took the train to Philadelphia, walked into the Public Defender's office (which in Philadelphia is called the Defender Association), and told them that we had no money and, boy, did we need help.

On August 27, she and the Public Defender went into the Court of Common Pleas with the same DA who had promised all that cooperation and understanding, and the first thing he did was stand up and say, "Your Honor, I want the court to know that two additional detainers have been placed against Mr. Sutton." One for the 1934 conviction and the other for the escape from Eastern State. He had filed them only three or four days earlier.

They had shifted courts on her at the last minute to bring the hearing in front of Judge Charles L. Guerin, an aging jurist. Our motion was to quash the detainer on the grounds that the indictment on which it was based was no longer valid because I had been denied my right to a speedy trial, and in this regard she got the assistant DA to enter into a stipulation that there was nothing in the record whatsoever to indicate that I had been advised of my right to a speedy trial at the time the detainer was lodged against me. On the merits of the case, that should have ended it right there. For half an hour she argued the case, laying particular stress upon the fact that our motion for resentencing was going to be heard in New York in another week and that if we were able to go in with a clean slate she had every reason to believe I would be given special consideration. From beginning to end, Judge Guerin never looked at her.

After the arguments were over, he said, "The petition is dismissed," and, still not bothering to look at her, called the next case. Didn't even go through the motions of taking it under advisement for twenty-four hours. Didn't bother to tell her why it was being dismissed.

Katherine had to come right back to New York. In anticipation of our glorious victory in Philadelphia, she had scheduled a hearing in Westchester County the next day to get rid of the indictment for the escape from Sing Sing before we went back into Farrell's court. When I heard what had happened in Philadelphia I didn't see why we should bother.

It wasn't all that bad, she insisted. The Public Defender had been so outraged at what he had seen that he and his organization had assumed full responsibility for appealing Guerin's ruling to the Superior Court. "We'll win the appeal," she told me. "Don't worry. The angel on my shoulder says so."

Yeah, and how long did the angel say it was going to take before they heard it. Six months?

It wasn't only the delay that had me so discouraged. I had always believed that we had to win every time out in order to build up a momentum that would carry us through. And right away I had been knocked out of the box. I hadn't only been knocked out of the box, I had been knocked out of the federal courts. They had jammed us into the Philadelphia courts on all three cases.

And then there was the effect it was going to have on Judge Farrell. Farrell had said he'd go along with us, sure, but how long could we expect him to hold the sentencing in abeyance? And, more to the point, convince Barshay to hold it in abeyance, too?

Katherine had already discussed the impracticability of prosecuting a thirty-six-year-old indictment with the Westchester DA, and he had agreed to take a guilty plea on a misdemeanor and recommend a suspended sentence. So I went. "Well, Willie," the judge said. "I'm certainly not going to load you up with any more time. You have done enough and probably will do more."

He sentenced me to one year and promptly suspended sentence. Well . . . at least I had finally won one.

It was a long time before I won another.

There were two separate steps that had to be taken on the appeal from Guerin's ruling. Before the Pennsylvania Superior Court heard the appeal, the Public Defender's office was going to have to get them to agree to hear it. Technically, the denial of a motion to quash an indictment can't be appealed unless some overriding issue is present. Somehow I felt that my freedom was an overriding issue.

On March 20, 1969, the Superior Court split down the middle, three to three, which meant that our appeal from Guerin's quashing had been quashed. It wasn't really a defeat, Katherine insisted. The dissenting opinion by the three-man "minority" was so strong that neither she nor the Public Defender had any doubt that it was going to carry the day for us in the more liberal Supreme Court, the state's highest court of appeals.

And what was that going to take, another six months? "I'll be dead by then."

"There's an old Greek saying," she said. " 'Before you draw your last breath, don't say die.' My father used to say that."

"There was an old Greek general who said one more such victory and we'll be entirely undone."

"One more such client," she groaned, "and I'll wind up in the booby hatch. I know a Greek lawyer who just said that."

I had to smile. "Is that what the angel on your shoulder is telling you now?"

"I have enough faith for both of us. So, be discouraged if you want to and see if I care."

And do you know, when I got to read the dissenting opinion I could see that she was right. The opinion, written by Judge Sidney Hoffman, amounted to nothing less than a powerful brief for the defense. According to Pennsylvania law, there were three overriding issues on which a motion to quash an indictment could be appealed. To prevent a great injustice; where basic human rights were involved; or where an issue of great public importance was presented. Judge Hoffman, who became my favorite jurist on the spot, stated flatly that in this case all three issues were present.

"For seventeen years," he wrote, "the Commonwealth has consciously chosen not to prosecute even though it has had the power to do so. This delay [Sutton] claims has denied him his basic right to speedy trial which now has the collateral effect of preventing his release on parole in New York. To quash the appeal at this time will result in interminable, vexatious and unfair delay."

Since "a dramatic Constitutional issue," had been raised, he said, "the speedy determination of the questions raised is in the public interest."

Having decided that the issue should be ruled upon, he then went ahead on his own, ruled on it, and found in our favor.

The key question was whether the right to a speedy trial extended to a prisoner who was being held in another jurisdiction. During all the time I had been reading Supreme Court decisions in Attica, that question had been very much up in the air. Judge Hoffman said that since there was an extradition agreement between New York and Pennsylvania, it did. Nor did it matter, he said, that I had never requested to come to trial. It hadn't been up to me to ask for it, it had been "the duty" of the state to provide it for me.

I have only been able to give the flavor of the dissenting opinion here. It wasn't an opinion; it was a howl of outrage. The only thing you could wonder about after reading it was not whether a more liberal Supreme Court was going to agree with it but how those other three donkeys on the Superior Court could have ignored it.

On June 6, 1969, the Supreme Court allowed the appeal and set the hearing for the middle of November. By agreeing to hear it, they were telling us, as far as we were concerned, that we would win it. The Public Defender lawyers promptly asked that, in view of my failing health and uncertain life expectancy, they should move it up to September. Their argument was that since the issue was my right to a speedy trial, they really ought to give us a speedy hearing so that we could go back to New York for a speedy resolution of the long-delayed resentencings. They were very good, those Public Defender lawyers, and thank God their petition was turned down. I'll give you a couple of hints:

We had a second case in the Philadelphia courts by then, involving the two new detainers, and both cases came to court on the same day. Not necessarily by coincidence.

After I had recovered from the disaster in Judge Guerin's court, it became very clear to Katherine and me that we had better sit down and decide what we were going to do about those other two detainers to make sure we didn't get all tangled up in the appeals courts with them, too.

Well, if we knew anything at all it was that in order to get anything done in Philadelphia you needed influence. Far more influence than the Public Defender's office could bring to bear. Katherine racked her brains to think of somebody who could give us a seat in the influence game, and I've got to give her all the credit in the world because here was where she really began to operate. I had always thought I had a lot of guts. I had always given myself a certain amount of credit for gall. Next to Katherine I was just a nice little boy. The question we were asking ourselves was: Who in the city of Philadelphia would be concerned enough about justice to want to help us, and also have enough clout to do something about it?

Suddenly she snapped her fingers. "The Catholic Church."

"Aw come on, Katherine . . ." If it had been anybody but Katherine, I would have felt that she was being sacrilegious.

"No, you're a good Catholic boy. Who should be more interested in seeing that you got a chance to rehabilitate yourself?" We weren't trying to subvert justice, after all. We were only trying to get in on it.

She went right to Cardinal Cooke's office in New

York and explained the situation to the cardinal's assistant. What she was after was a letter to Cardinal Krol of Philadelphia. She got it.

"All double talk," I told her when she came back from Philadelphia without any specific promise. "We'll get no help from that quarter."

"Don't write off the Church, Willie. The angel on my shoulder is getting awfully angry. And, if my angel gets angry, it's going to write you off. With the Church looking over their shoulder, maybe they'll stop kicking us around." The next best bet seemed to be to find one of those prestigious Philadelphia law firms whose members would have attended the same schools and belonged to the same clubs as the top people in the District Attorney's office. Easier said than done when you don't have the money to walk through the front door. Where did we go, and who did we see, and what the hell were we talking about?

The contact, when it finally came, came out of nowhere. An independent moving-picture producer who called Katherine to ask about making a movie of my life when I was set free. When Katherine told her that with all the trouble we were having in Philadelphia freedom was not exactly around the corner, the producer suggested, somewhat timidly, that her own lawyer had a good friend at one of Philadelphia's best-known law firms, and that if Katherine thought it would do any good . . .

The law firm was Dilworth, Paxson, Kalish, Kahn & Levy, one of the most prestigious firms in Philadelphia. Dilworth was a former mayor. Levy was our contact.

The Dilworth firm was so dignified that it had never stooped to the criminal law before. All Katherine had to do was go to Philadelphia and convince them that they should change their policy so that they could represent me, gratis, for the good of the American legal system and the good name of Philadelphia.

Levy was not only willing, he was downright eager. It wasn't until I finally met him myself, more than a year later, that I found out why. Levy had been an FBI man at the time of my escape, and he had been given the assignment of working undercover to try to find me. He had failed to track me down, and he was now offering to help me break out through the courts. How could anybody find any fault with a man like that?

By that time we had our strategy all worked out and we saw no reason not to urge it on them. There were actual convictions to attack this time and we had decided to attack them through the writ of habeas corpus. Two good reasons.

1 / We couldn't go in on a straight appeal because Pennsylvania had a postconviction act which said you had to be domiciled within the state.

2 / By the nature of my legal studies and activities at Attica, the writ of habeas corpus was what I knew best. That's what I thought, anyway. Almost all the writs I had made out in prison had gone to the federal courts under a procedure where all I'd had to do was whip them in. Applying for a writ in a state court, in the peculiar situation I was in, turned out to be an entirely different ball game. The technical problems were so enormous that working them out required the same concentration and attention to detail that had been required in planning an actual escape.

There were two principal hurdles that had to be overcome. A writ of habeas is always directed against the person who has physical control over the petitioner's body and therefore has the power to produce his body in court. Usually, it's a warden or a sheriff.

I was under the physical control of the warden of the Queens County House of Detention, and we couldn't come up with so much as the smell of an idea of how a Philadelphia judge was going to be able to enforce a writ against a warden in New York. Katherine hit the law books to see if she could find anything we could offer as a precedent, and the only thing she could come up with was a federal case. The Bureau of Immigration and Naturalization had put a detainer on an alien being held in a state prison, and the court had ruled that the detainer had given the bureau enough control over his body to entitle him to put a writ against them in a federal court. Not the same thing by a long shot. Nobody had ever questioned the right of a state prisoner to go into the federal court or the power of a federal judge to execute a writ in any of the individual states. But it was enough. It gave us something to cite in our brief and, of equal importance, a principle to work on.

I knew it was going to be worth pursuing because, as I have said, I was an expert on the writ of habeas corpus. It is the Great Writ, the Writ of Freedom. It comes out of the common law as the procedure to be used for righting great wrongs and, therefore, gives a judge as much latitude as he wants to take. And right there, it seemed to me, was where the very weakness of our position was—once again—going to work to my advantage. Any judge who issued the writ, under such admittedly questionable jurisdiction, was going to be a judge with an overriding interest in guarding the rights of the individual.

We had to make out a case that Philadelphia had "technical control" over me. All right. Hadn't they asserted their control over my body by filing a detainer which demanded that I be turned over to them when my sentence expired? We had been making the argument all along, had we not, that it was only the detainers from Philadelphia that were keeping the New York court from paroling me? Looking at my situation realistically, if it weren't for those detainers I wouldn't be in jail at all, and if I wouldn't have been in jail otherwise, then it was Philadelphia that was keeping me there. What more control over my body could anyone ask?

The other great stumbling block was that when you apply for a writ of habeas you are asking that your body be produced in court. That's what *habeas corpus* means. "Produce the body." Wild horses couldn't have dragged me to Philadelphia. I wanted to "produce the body" procedurally while keeping my actual body in New York.

All right. We weren't claiming that I was being held incommunicado or anything like that. We were asking that I be permitted to come into court for the purpose of showing that my Constitutional rights had been violated in both of the trials. I wanted the court to produce "the body of evidence" that would show I hadn't had an attorney at either trial, and the state already had that.

Which answered the question of whom the writ would be directed against. The District Attorney had "technical control" over my body because it was his office that had filed the detainers, and he had actual control over the evidence. Good enough.

They didn't need me there to prove that, and I had an excellent reason for not being there. I was too sick to come. Which was the second part of our plea, anyway.

Good, hell. It was perfect.

And need I say that when the Dilworth firm came into the case, the transcript of the 1934 trial was miraculously discovered.

Katherine had to go to work to convince the Dilworth people that it could be done. They weren't criminal lawyers, remember, and after they had checked out the legal points involved they were pretty well convinced that she couldn't be much of a criminal lawyer either.

Immediately after the Superior Court ruling came down in June, Katherine went to Philadelphia with her associate, Joan Harnes, and held a meeting with the battery of young lawyers who had become involved in the case. What you were really saying with the writ, she had been telling them, was, "Look at what they did here, Judge. This is lousy." Get it before the right judge, she had been telling them, and he'd find a way.

They read Judge Hoffman's dissent, and they were convinced. Early in July, the word came to us that Judge Edmund Spaeth, Jr., of the Court of Common Pleas, was going to be hearing the petition. "Spaeth," Katherine said, with approval. "I think that's the judge I was supposed to go before the last time before they switched me." Between the two of them, the writ and the Philadelphia firm had apparently found the right man.

Through the summer, Katherine and Joan Harnes were going to Philadelphia almost every day. True to his promise to help us, behind the scenes, wherever he could, Kreppein was also making the trip frequently. When the hearing on our petition was held in mid-August, Kreppein testified—just as he had in the Superior Court hearing—that I had been rehabilitated years ago, that I was very ill, and that he had recommended to Judge Farrell that he suspend my sentence at the resentencing. It was his opinion, Kreppein testified, that Judge Farrell was merely waiting to find out what Pennsylvania was going to do before he took action.

I had three sets of lawyers working for me gratis. Kreppein was spending his own money. Katherine had already spent a small fortune. A couple of days before the hearing on the writ, she decided it might help to have my longtime spiritual adviser at Attica, Father Gene, take the stand and testify to the good works I had done in prison: my attempts to teach the kids English and history, my efforts to act as a conciliator between the inmates and the authorities during times of tension, that kind of thing. My spiritual adviser said, "Sure, will you send me a hundred dollars for my plane fare and twenty-five for the hotel."

Father Gene was still walking in the steps of the Master. "Forget it, brother," Katherine thought. "I'll do without you."

The hearing was on our petition for a writ, and the District Attorney fought it hard on the jurisdictional issue. On September 26, Judge Spaeth turned all their objections down and issued the writ. His ruling, like Judge Hoffman's, was everything we had asked for and more.

"Everything we asked for" means that he could have taken the original memo Katherine sent to the Dilworth firm and used it as an outline. He cited the "alien" case Katherine had dug up as his authority for ruling that the DA had taken me into technical custody. He used Kreppein's testimony to support my claim that it was Philadelphia rather than New York that was holding me in jail, although he did feel constrained, in that regard, to admit that "here the court is not acting within the bounds of the statute" or even upon the history of the writ but "upon its suitable employment in maintaining the balance of the nice, clear, and true between the state and the accused."

The writ had found the right man, all right.

The commonwealth was given ten days to file its answer, which meant they were being instructed to defend the Constitutionality of the 1934 and 1945 proceedings.

We now had two cases coming up in Pennsylvania courts for final disposition, and for the life of me I couldn't see how we could do anything but win on both of them.

The Philadelphia lawyers and the District Attorney got together to see what could be worked out. Normally, a habeas proceeding moves very swiftly once the writ has been issued; however, since the District Attorney was then caught up in a re-election campaign, it seemed to make sense to hold off until after Election Day. There was no real sense of urgency as far as I was concerned, since I was going to have to wait until the middle of November for the State Supreme Court to hold its hearing, anyway.

The election was on November 4. On October 31, I was struck with crippling pains in my left leg, followed by a terrifying shortness of breath. An ambulance was called to rush me to Kings County Hospital, where I was immediately put into bed with an oxygen mask. There was almost no circulation in the leg again and this time the condition was complicated by what was diagnosed as chronic emphysema. Without the oxygen mask, I had great difficulty in breathing.

But, do you know, sometimes I have to wonder about myself. The first time Katherine visited me she tried to cheer me up by saying, "It's okay to play sick if you want to. Just don't overdo it, huh, or you'll fool your friends too."

I gave her a wink. "You want me to play sick? I'll be the sickest man you ever saw."

The next time she came I made sure the oxygen mask was on and that I was looking as close to death's door as, you might say, is humanly possible. "Do me a favor," she wailed. "Don't die until I can get you out of prison. Please don't die on me yet." I whipped off the oxygen mask, swung out of bed, and limped out to the porch so that I could light up a couple of cigarettes. One for me and one for her.

"Willie the Actor," she said, shaking her head. "Right to the end you've got to be Willie the Actor."

Christmas in New York

On Monday, November 10, 1969, it all began to come together. The preliminary diagnosis on the lack of circulation in my leg had been that the plastic aorta had dropped to the point where it was pressing against the clamps and tubes. What they were going to have to do, if that was the case, was cut me open behind the scar and reroute it. I would have put the odds on my surviving another operation like that at no better than ten to one. Late in the morning, the doctor came in with the happy news that they now felt they could get the job done with an operation that simply bypassed several inches of clogged artery in the leg itself. He was going to operate on Thursday, November 13.

The operation wasn't what I had on my mind that morning, though. On the previous Friday, Katherine had informed me that a representative from the DA's office was going to come to New York with Stephen J. Harmelin, the young attorney from the Dilworth firm who was handling my case, to meet with her and Kreppein in Judge Farrell's chambers. The negotiations were coming to some kind of a climax, and Katherine had been given to understand that they were ready to offer us something good.

They were. The Supreme Court was going to be hearing the appeal on the Holmesburg detainer on Friday, November 14, and the DA's man admitted, quite frankly, that they didn't think they could possibly win and they were afraid that the publicity attendant on Willie Sutton beating them in the appeals court would bring on such a flood of writs that their courts would be inundated. Given the choice between having the courts let me go on the legal issues or letting me go themselves on a bargained plea, they infinitely preferred to let me go themselves. The deal they were offering was this: If we would withdraw the appeal in the Supreme Court and plead guilty to a misdemeanor on the Holmesburg escape in Spaeth's court, they wouldn't fight us on the other two cases. They were offering to dispose of the whole thing in one package. And no risk that the Supreme Court might fool both of us, or that the DA's office would appeal any of the decisions.

Judge Spaeth had already approved that kind of a solution in principle, they could tell us, and had indeed already set a hearing date for the morning of Friday, November 14, so that we could get it done before the Supreme Court heard the appeal. Judge Spaeth, however, had set one condition. I had to be there. He was going to have to look at me and see for himself whether I was so desperately ill. And, I surmised, legitimize the habeas corpus proceedings by having the body in court.

They were ready to wrap the whole thing up, and the final roadblock came from where we were least expecting it. Judge Farrell.

Farrell had made it clear from the beginning that he was not going to sign any order allowing me to leave his jurisdiction unless he had something in writing that guaranteed he was going to get me back. Atta-boy, Judge! That was just what we had wanted. *Don't let them take me to Philadelphia.* But now the situation had turned completely around and we wanted to go to Philadelphia and get the thing over with, once and for all. The judge wasn't budging an inch. He still wanted something in writing. All the DA's man was able to offer him were "certain assurances" from Judge Spaeth, and it wasn't enough.

I could understand that. Farrell was right in the middle. Originally, you will remember, he had set the date for resentencing at May 21, 1968. When he had promised Katherine as much time as she needed to fight the Battle of Philadelphia, he had not had anything like eighteen months in mind. He had given us so many continuances that nobody knew which sentence I was serving any more, the one on which I had been conditionally paroled or the one that was being held in abeyance.

But Judge Spaeth had good reason for feeling slighted, himself. He had wanted something in writing from Farrell at the time of the hearing to satisfy himself that it was really only the Philadelphia detainers that were preventing him from suspending my sentence and, needless to say, Judge Farrell was hardly going to put anything like that in writing. Instead, Spaeth had been forced to take Kreppein's carefully worded statement that he himself was convinced "from his conversations with Judge Farrell" that it was what the judge wanted to do.

He had taken Kreppein's "assurances" that he was speaking for Farrell. Why, he could be excused for asking, shouldn't Farrell now take the DA's "assurances" that he was speaking for him?

I had two judges, both of whom wanted to let me go, and they were at an impasse.

Still, Farrell had promised Katherine that if she could find a legal way to shake me free from Philadelphia he'd go along. "There's always a way in the law," he told her. "It's up to you to find it."

Katherine went upstairs to the office of the Chief Clerk, Len Capone, who had a reputation for being very good at that kind of thing. "What if he was subpoenaed?" Capone said. If Spaeth sent a subpoena directly to Farrell, then it would be a recognition that he was in Farrell's custody and a commitment of sorts that he was going to send him back.

Okay. How do you subpoena a prisoner to appear at a hearing he himself has petitioned for and fought for? "What if we have him called as a material witness in his own case?" Katherine asked. Sure. If Spaeth subpoenaed me as a material witness, what would be more natural than for the subpoena to carry the date on which I would be wanted and the date on which I would be returned?

"Do you think we could get away with it?" Katherine asked him.

Well, Philadelphia wanted me there and all Farrell wanted was to find a way. So who was going to challenge it?

The DA's man headed right back to Philadelphia to get to work on it, and Katherine and Harmelin headed for the hospital to give me the good news.

In the corridor outside my room, the doctor handed them the bad news that the court appearance was going to have to wait. "If he doesn't have that operation on Thursday," he told Katherine, "he's going to lose that leg. At his age, in his condition, the shock of an amputation will probably kill him."

She told me it was my decision to make. "Don't even ask me what I think," Katherine pleaded. "I don't want to have any part in that kind of decision."

There really wasn't that much to think about. There had never been an escape where it hadn't been on the basis that I was going to bust out or die trying. The judge wanted to see a sick man, didn't he? Well, I was never going to look any sicker than I did right now. "I'd rather have one day of freedom," I told her, "than spend another whole lifetime locked up."

When Katherine told the doctor he was going to have to cancel the operation he went absolutely livid with rage. "Stupid woman lawyer," he screamed.

"Stupid woman lawyer sticking her nose into things she doesn't know about! He's going to lose the leg, you stupid woman! You're going to kill him!"

On Wednesday, November 12, the subpoena came into Farrell's office and he issued an order to the city Commissioner of Corrections in which he was careful to note the very limited purpose for which I was being allowed to leave the state. He then directed that "the said William Sutton be delivered to the custody of the duly authorized representatives of the Commonwealth of Pennsylvania on the morning of the 14th. I further order the representatives of the Department of Corrections, State of New York, be at Kings County Hospital at 9 A.M. and remain with the person of William Sutton at all times during his stay in the Commonwealth of Pennsylvania and return with him immediately upon conclusion of proceedings in the city of Philadelphia to the Kings County Hospital."

Early Friday morning, I was on the train to Philadelphia, with two Philadelphia detectives and two New York corrections officers. At the station, there was a van, complete with wire-cage backing, waiting to take me to the courthouse. By the time I got there I felt so cold and numb and clammy that I was taken to a small dispensary off the corridor where they put me on a cot and gave me oxygen.

The first thing Katherine did when she came in with Kreppein and Joan Harnes was to put her hand on my leg. Just by the way she winced, I could see that I was as cold on the outside as I felt on the inside. I gave her a big smile. "We made it," I said. "One more step and I'll be free. I'm going to spend Christmas outside of prison, Katherine."

They took me to the courtroom in a wheelchair, and it was like going through wall-to-wall cops. Through an ocean of blue. From the hatred that was in their eyes, it was as if they were all children of Harry McDevitt. The New York police may have come to view me with some affection, but as far as the law-enforcement people in Philadelphia were concerned, I was an outsider who had come into their town and made fools of them. Kreppein had warned me about that. The only people in Philadelphia who hated me more than the young assistant DAs, he had told me, were the young cops. And the younger the cop, the stronger the hatred. "Why do you hate him so much?" Kreppein had asked them. "You don't even know him. You weren't even born when he was operating in Philadelphia."

The hearing, conducted by Harmelin, took little more than thirty minutes, and the only two witnesses were Kreppein, who restated his belief that Judge Farrell was only waiting for the resolution of the cases in Philadelphia, and a medical doctor who was put on the stand to testify to the state of my health. Now that he had been able to look at me, Judge Spaeth voided the 1934 conviction on the Constitutional grounds and set aside the sentence for escaping from Eastern State. On the Holmesburg break he placed me on probation for two years and immediately gave me credit for twenty-two months and seven days served. Which left me with less than two months' actual probation, although he did order me not to return to the state for the full two years.

If he had made it for the rest of my life, it would have been even better.

Do you know when it really hit me that I had been set free? On the way back to New York. Freedom is riding on a train without being handcuffed. The two New York corrections officers chatted amiably with me and even bought me a drink, and I never could quite figure out what to do with my hands.

Nothing remained except to go back into court in Queens and Brooklyn for the resentencings that had been put off so many times. I wasn't about to delay it again by letting them operate on me. Not even after the doctor warned me that if I didn't have the operation within thirty days I was going to lose the leg. There was an easy answer to that one. Let me out so that I can have it. Joan Harnes's husband was a doctor and he had already made arrangements at Lenox Hill Hospital in Manhattan to have me operated on by one of the city's leading specialists. It wasn't that I questioned the ability of the doctors at Kings County Hospital. I just wanted to give Katherine the chance to go into court if it should become necessary and say in all honesty, "If this man isn't free to have an operation by a doctor of his own choosing he's going to die on your hands."

Kings County Hospital wasn't going to let me die on their hands. The day after I turned down the operation they transferred me to the hospital on Riker's Island.

On the morning of November 25, the day I was supposed to be resentenced, Kreppein called Katherine to tell her there was no sense coming in. Another indictment had just popped up. The Corn Exchange Bank in 1933. Indictments had been popping up all over the place for eighteen months. There had been one, in particular, on Staten Island, for a milk-company robbery. "I know I didn't do that one," I could tell Katherine. "If it was a bank, yeah. But I've never robbed any milk company in my life." Turned out that the place had been robbed back in 1950, and as soon as they found I had been living nearby they had gone to the grand jury and got an indictment without even having to put a witness in front of them.

The Corn Exchange Bank was a valid indictment. That was the one where I'd had all the fun with the girls. It was also thirty-six years old, and Katherine was able to go into court and get it dismissed.

December 1—Finally, I was in Judge Farrell's court, and I suspect it was a tossup which of us was the happier. Farrell went through the medical reports and then let the record show that the only occasions I had been cited for violation of rules at Attica were for performing legal work for other inmates. That done, he sentenced me to "not less than fifteen years and no more than twenty years" and stayed execution of the sentence during my good behavior.

Twenty months after he had called me down from Attica, he directed that after I had appeared before Judge Barshay's court I be returned to the jurisdiction of the New York State Board of Parole. You could almost hear the sigh of relief.

December 2—Judge Hyman Barshay had become

the final hurdle. While not exactly an unknown quantity, he had been the tail of the dog up to now, following Judge Farrell's lead as one would expect from a judge who was handling the lesser charge. Kreppein had spoken to him upon our return from Philadelphia. All he could tell us was that he had found him sympathetic but noncommittal. As our eyes swung toward Brooklyn, I suddenly realized how important Barshay was to the strategy we had devised. The other judges had simply been dismissing charges against me. *Barshay was the judge on whom the onus was going to fall for setting me free* and Barshay sat in a court in Brooklyn, where Arnold Schuster had been shot down.

Hyman Barshay had been one of the city's great criminal lawyers, probably second only to Sam Liebowitz. Unlike Liebowitz, who had become a hanging judge upon his ascension to the bench, Barshay was supposed to have great compassion for the kind of people he had once represented. "Everybody still calls him Hymie," Kreppein told me. "What have you got to fear from a judge who everybody calls Hymie?"

It was not that cut and dried. Not by a long shot. Katherine made a straight plea for mercy. The District Attorney, who had let it be known that he was going to ask for a stiff sentence, had a woman assistant DA there, Martha Prince, and she was not there to overflow with the milk of human kindness. She recalled to the court what Judge Goldstein had said upon sentencing me. She cited the long list of major armed robberies I was known to have participated in. And then she began to talk about the murder of Arnold Schuster. "And I add now," she said as she finished, "that Mr. Sutton refused any cooperation with the police department or with the District Attorney's office in attempting to apprehend the murderer of this young man." Absolutely untrue, of course. Terribly unfair. She was simply repeating what the DA's office in Queens had said at the time of my original appearance before Judge Farrell.

Katherine was livid. "I think it is time this is

stopped," she snapped, "and it is going to be stopped here and now." To stop it, Katherine brandished a file of newspaper clippings she had collected quoting various police officials as saying that there was not the slightest evidence that I had anything to do with the murder. The DA's office of Brooklyn most certainly had access to police reports not available to us, she pointed out, and she challenged Miss Prince to produce a single document which either linked me with the murder or showed any lack of cooperation with any law-enforcement agency.

Barshay was impossible to read. He had sent for exactly such a report, he now revealed, and it had arrived on his desk that very morning. He had found only suspicion, rumor, and surmise. "Hundreds of investigations have resulted, and there is not a single matter of proof that he was connected with the Schuster killing. I cannot substitute suspicion, rumor, surmise, and guess for proof." He also felt called upon, however, to let the record show that he agreed with the judge who had said, "I only regret that I can't sentence you to the electric chair." And then clouded what he was agreeing to by observing that it was the legislature which fixed the penalties, after all, not the court. "No judge can increase the penalty imposed by law."

"Now, Miss Bitses," he said, looking down at Katherine. And from the change in his voice and manner it was clear that the lawyers' work was over and he was now getting down to the business of handing down his decision. "The only good fortune that your client has had is the dedication of his lawyers." Every agency of the law that I had come into contact with, he told her, sternly, had been kinder to me than I had been to my victims. "I cannot hold any brief for your client because the probation report indicates he has probably the worst criminal record of any man who has ever appeared before me in forty-five years in the administration of justice. That he is getting the just desserts of the law is right and proper. That he has been given the legal rights that he is entitled to is only proof positive of the true administration of justice."

I'm dead, I thought. Twenty months I had gone through this and after all the plotting and scheming it was ending on a cold winter morning in a Brooklyn court, only a few miles from where I had been born. I should never have listened to Katherine. I should have stuck to my original plan and fought it out case by case through the federal courts. I should have known that I always had to do everything the hard way.

Judge Barshay's eyes shifted from Katherine to me. "But I must consider," he said, "as Judge Farrell did, the only ground upon which I will give mercy to him, and that is the medical reports. I shall read them into the record for fear that someone may later say that the matter was not thoroughly investigated."

It was going to be all right. He was going to let me go but he wanted the record to show that he was only following behind Farrell. He was reading from the probation report that had been submitted to him by John Kreppein. *It was going to be all right.* He read on and on, and when he was finished he looked at Katherine again and said, "I am convinced that these doctors have given the correct diagnosis of this defendant's condition. The parole board is the one to determine whether he will be free to breathe the air you speak of or not."

He had found himself an out, after all. He was going to put the onus on the parole board. He was talking now for the newspapers, of course, and he still wasn't finished. "There is only one thing I want to add. They all speak of his tremendous ability. I sum it up differently. He began to believe his own publicity, that was the disease he suffered from. The fact that he was not right is indicated by the number of times he was caught, and the number of years he has been in prison. But he was glamorized. That is a sad state. He was glamorized through the entire time."

Having protected himself in every possible way, he sentenced me to from fifteen to twenty years on both charges, suspended both sentences, and placed me on probation. I had to look at the man with admiration as he rose to leave the bench. Kreppein had been right about that. Hymie Barshay must have been one hell of a lawyer.

It was now only a matter of going back to Attica to have the parole finalized on the Rosenthal sentence. With the parole board meeting in exactly a week, I'd still be able to come back to New York and have my leg operated on within the thirty-day limit the doctor had set. The technicality was that by the terms of the parole, I was supposed to be serving out the remainder of that sentence concurrently with the Queens sentence, and since there were no more sentences for anything to run concurrently with, they were going to have to rewrite the terms. That's all.

I went back to Attica practically singing. Everybody was congratulating me, guards and inmates alike. "If there was anybody in the world I'd have bet didn't have a chance, Willie," they all said, "it was you." McGinnis, the state Commissioner of Corrections, wanted to send me to Sing Sing to be operated on, and I practically laughed at him. I was going to be operated on by my doctor, I said. In New York. After the parole.

The reservations had already been made for me at Lenox Hill Hospital. On the day before the board was scheduled to meet, Katherine came up so that she'd be on hand to take me back immediately and put me in. When I was brought down to the visiting room in my wheelchair I could see that she was fuming.

"What's the matter, Katherine?"

She had been asked to go to Warden Mancusi's office on the way in, and he had said to her, "I don't know, Katherine. You know Willie is a very good actor. There's a whole lot of people around here who don't think he's anywhere near as sick as you say he is."

Oh? Like who?

Himself, for one. "Personally, I have a lot of doubt that he's that sick."

Isn't that sick? He had the medical reports, didn't he? Hadn't he bothered to read them?

"Forget it, Katherine," I said. "There's a lot of stupid SOB's around here."

The following day, the three members of the board of parole arrived at the institution, and I was brought before them in a wheelchair. The hearing was quite lengthy by normal standards, and all the talk was about the complicated court procedures I had just gone through, the state of my health, and what I intended to do if I were released. Not a word was said about my criminal record. I had every reason to believe that it was just a matter of setting the date.

The decisions of the parole board are written out on a sheet of paper which is then folded over, stapled, and delivered with the regular mail. They don't go out on a day-by-day basis, it is the custom to wait until everybody has been interviewed so that they can all be delivered at the same time. The following evening, as the tier guard was coming toward my cell in the hospital block with the mail I could see that he was carrying a folded-over and stapled sheet of paper.

I had to read it four or five times before I could believe my eyes. The board had denied my application and decreed that I would not be eligible to apply again until August 1971. Two years.

The decision to grant parole has to be unanimous. No reason is given for being turned down, the voting of the members is not made public, and there is no appeal. I had died once on the operating table and half known it. I knew now what it was to die and know I had died. When they brought me dinner I told them to take it away. The way I felt, I was never going to eat again. If I was going to die, I was going to get it over with in a hurry and at least die on my own terms.

Katherine had heard about it even before the letter was delivered. Since the nearest hotel was in Batavia, seventeen miles away, whenever she visited any clients at Attica she boarded with an elderly couple, the Marleys, who had a home right across from the prison. She had been sitting in the kitchen, having coffee with Mrs. Marley, when the announcement came over the radio. The next morning she went storming into the warden's office. "I think that you are the most cruel, most vicious, the lousiest, and the most rotten kind of individual that anybody could be. How dare they release the fact that his parole had been denied on the radio when I knew nothing about it and he knew nothing about it!"

Mancusi insisted that he'd had nothing to do with it. "Believe me, Katherine," he said. "But you've got to make him eat."

"You've got to eat," Katherine told me. "The fight isn't over. It's just begun. You've got to keep fighting them, that's all."

I said, "The angel on your shoulder, Katherine, has forgotten me. Stop kidding yourself, there's nothing we can do about it any more."

"Oh yes there is," she said. "I told Mancusi the next time he sees me you'll be a first offender. Let me see them keep you in then."

Katherine has a way of talking to God which she knows has always amused me. So she looked up to the sky and said, "If you've ever done anything for me do it now—my God! Thirty-six years, isn't that enough punishment? A miracle now, God, please."

I almost did smile. "What else do you think you can cook up?" I sighed. "How about the 1926 conviction? Remember the legality I told you about there. . . ."

Sure. That was it. That was the ticket. "We have no time to bemoan our fate. We've got to get right to work on it." Sure. We'd knock out the first conviction, and that would make me a first offender on the Rosenthal conviction. As a first offender, I'd have already served all my time. We wouldn't have to ask to suspend any sentence to time served, we wouldn't have to ask for parole. They'd have no right to hold me. They'd be forced to let me go.

Each of us was putting on an act for the other, and still . . . for just one minute there I'm sure that we both believed it.

I'd eat, I told her. But there would be no operation. "I don't care if gangrene sets in. It can fall off me, and I won't let them touch it. They're going to have to let me out or I'm going to die on them."

"Good. I'll use that. *Look* sick, but don't die on me."

Before she left, she went to the prison doctor and to the warden and to the priest and to each of them she said, "Look, this man is going to die on your hands if you don't watch him carefully and treat him properly." She told them what the doctor's prognosis had been at the Kings County Hospital. The thirty days were almost up. "If he dies, look at the disgrace and the talk there will be. Dying right in your institution for lack of care. I'll be the first one to say it. I'll shout it from the skies!"

It was no good, though. As soon as I got back to my cell I knew it was no good. It took months and years to get a case through the courts, and I was down to the hours and days. The response to my refusal to be operated on was to move me from the hospital block to the invalid block. If I was so anxious to die, they were as much as saying, I could go ahead and die.

When Katherine got back to New York she whipped off an angry four-page letter to Governor Rockefeller which began, "On December 9, 1969, at Attica State Prison, three members of the New York State Parole Board, sitting as a Committee, pronounced a death sentence upon my client William Sutton." She explained to him that I had sought to finalize the 1930 parole, "so as to take advantage of superlative medical and surgical services proffered to him gratis by a first-rate hospital in New York City and specialists connected with that hospital in an attempt to save his life." She pointed out as forcefully as possible that the opinions and decisions of any number of "eminent elected jurists in two states" had been overruled by a parole board whose members had been appointed, and ended by saying, "I appeal to you because I am sure that unless you intervene, the death sentence of the parole board will be carried out for William Sutton will not live to keep his date in August of 1971."

The letter received an enormous amount of publicity, and when she followed it up by appearing on television to ask the viewers to write to Rockefeller, hundreds of letters were sent to him. As much as I appreciated her efforts, I didn't believe it would do any good. In the history of the parole board, it had never been pressured into changing a decision.

Pete Hamill of the *New York Post* wrote an open letter to Governor Rockefeller in his column on behalf of the Free Willie Sutton Committee (which consisted of himself and four other writers and was, I suspect, formed ad lib and ad hoc around the corner table of a West Side tavern). The newspaper was handed to me, open to the column, by one of the guards on the morning of December 24, the day after it had appeared. Christmas Eve day. I read it and as one who had made out a lot of writs myself, I could see that it was a powerful plea. One by one, he hit every significant point: my age, my health, the thirty-five years I had already spent in prison, and the undisputed fact that I had never hurt anyone. But more than that, he was able to hit it exactly the right tone:

"We know what Willie did, but then he never made any secret of it. . . . When asked for an occupation, he once told a judge: 'It was of an illegal nature. It was bank robbing.' There were times when he was less than cooperative with authorities, but this was at least based upon principle. . . ."

He wrote: "In his extracurricular activities he was always a gentleman, a suave dresser, an expert on psychology, Irish history, and chess, and a gallant with women. He had an aversion to steam table food to be sure and three times broke out of jail. . . ."

He wrote: "If the state prisons are anything they must be institutions which go beyond punishment. There is much lip service to this concept these days; acknowledging that this man has paid for his crimes would be a chance to show it. If Willie Sutton had been a GE board member or a former water commissioner, instead of the son of an Irish blacksmith, he would be on the street now."

He wrote: "This is frankly an appeal for mercy and human feeling. Willie Sutton should be able to sit and watch the ducks in Prospect Park one more time or go to Nathan's for a hotdog, or call up some old girl for a drink. . . . Letting Willie out won't gain you a vote, but it would be a hell of a thing if the old bank robber could take a look at the Christmas tree in Rockefeller Center for one last time."

I don't know whether Katherine's letter or the Hamill column had any effect. But I don't know that they didn't, either. All I do know is that a few hours later they practically threw me out of the place.

Sometime before noon, the tier officer came down to my cell and told me that the front office had sent for my records. "I don't want to raise your hopes, Willie, because I can always be wrong. But they only do this when they're getting ready to release somebody." About an hour later he stopped by again, even more excited. "Don't quote me, but I think you're going home. There's a lot of activity going on."

All right, I wouldn't quote him. I figured they were getting ready to ship me to Sing Sing so they could operate immediately in case I changed my mind. Within minutes, though, he was back again. "This is it, Willie, they want you down in administration."

Mr. Lenox, the officer in charge of the clothing department, was waiting for me. "Come in and sit down," he said. "You want a cup of coffee?"

I sat down and for the first time, really, there was a little bit of hope beginning to percolate inside me along with the coffee. "Willie," he said, beaming broadly. "I was notified to measure you for a civilian suit." That's what they do when you're being released. They measure you up for a civilian suit and topcoat. He stuck out his hand. "Congratulations."

It was as quick as that. I went back up for a bath and shave and was processed through. What that means is that they take your prints and picture again when you're leaving, because if you've been there a long time there can be a great change in your appearance. On the way back to administration to pick up my suit I stopped in at the parole agent's office to find out what the rush was all about. "Well," he said. "They found a decision that they overlooked and it gives you more time off your sentence than they originally thought."

"What's the name of the decision?" I asked. Because naturally I wondered what we could have overlooked.

"Offhand, I can't tell you. It came out a long time ago."

That didn't make any sense at all. But what was I going to do, argue with him?

Back to administration. Given the suit and topcoat. Handed a check for $169, half the amount I had earned through the fifteen years I had been confined there. Given the $40 check that everybody gets upon their release, the price of a bus ticket to New York City. And then I was being ushered through the front gate into the frigid December air.

The parole board never would admit that they had changed their decision. Paul D. McGinnis, the State Correction Commissioner, answered all questions by stating that he personally had ordered my release after checking through my records and finding that I was entitled by law to be set free. His decision, he insisted, had been based upon information not available to the parole board, although exactly what information was never made clear. Any more than it was ever made clear by what authority a commissioner of correction was entitled to go around discharging prisoners.

The story I heard in later years was that McGinnis, who didn't want me to die in his prison, called Rockefeller to urge him to give me a Christmas pardon, and Rockefeller, who had been trying desperately to pressure the parole board into getting him off the hook, either told him straight out or left him with the unmistakable impression that if he wanted to go ahead on his own and present everybody with an accomplished fact, not only wouldn't anybody be mad at him they would be downright grateful.

Needless to say, the parole board eventually did have to quietly legitimize it and place me under their control.

There was a television crew waiting for me just outside the gate, along with a clutch of reporters. A microphone was stuck into my face, and the first question I was asked was, "How does it feel to be a free man again?"

I told them, quite truthfully, that it was going to take a little time before I realized that I was.

A car was honking in the background, and when I looked over I could see that it was a friend of mine from Buffalo, Dominick Tassarella. Dominick had been an inmate at Attica for about three years, we had remained in touch, and he was such a good guy that whenever Katherine was coming up to see me he would be there at the train station in Batavia to drive her to the Marleys. The bewildering thing about seeing him there was that as an ex-con, Dominick wasn't supposed to come to the prison. Any more than I, as an ex-con, was supposed to associate with him. It was Katherine who had called him, of course. Not to pick her up this time, but to pick me up.

Katherine had been cleaning up her house for Christmas, the first time she had done any housework in months, when the phone rang and the caller identified himself as Commissioner McGinnis.

Katherine, who had been getting a lot of crank calls, said, "Cut the baloney," and slammed the receiver down.

A few moments later it rang again. "This is Commissioner McGinnis," he repeated. "You know who I am, don't you, Katherine? I'm calling to tell you that Willie Sutton is going to be on the front steps of Attica prison at four o'clock." If she didn't believe it, she could call up Attica herself. "In fact," he said, "turn on the radio. It will be coming over in about ten minutes." He had put out the story with a two-thirty release time on it to make sure he'd have time to notify her first.

She put in a call to the warden's office, got the dep, and said, "Do you realize it's zero degrees outside? What's all this I hear that he's going to be on the front step at four o'clock?"

That was the way it was going to be, the dep said. "He's being discharged at four o'clock sharp. Make your arrangements."

"What arrangements? I don't know anybody who lives in Buffalo except a convict friend of Willie's."

That, he said, was against the rules.

Katherine told him what he could do with his rules.

After she had thrown her fur coat over her dungarees and gone out to her office, she realized that she had no money and that the banks were closed. So she did the first thing that came to her mind. She picked up the phone, called the *New York Daily News,* and said, "You have a plane, don't you? Good. Well, I have a client in Buffalo who's going to be on the steps of Attica prison at four o'clock. That's right, Willie Sutton." Their plane for an exclusive story, even up. It wasn't until she had hung up that she remembered that she had never flown in a plane before and was in deathly fear of flying.

They were supposed to pick her up in fifteen minutes. When I called her from the first tavern Dominick and I saw she was still in her office, waiting. In fact, she was in the middle of being interviewed over television. Dominick was taking me home with him to spend Christmas Eve with his family, I told her. They were having a party there for their closest friends and their kids.

They made it seem as if the party had been planned especially to welcome me out, Dominick and his wife, Josie. The things you miss most in prison. A home, a family, white tablecloth, and happy, laughing children. A real Italian feast, with a long table piled high with food. The first thing Dominick did was hand me a huge goblet of sparkling red wine so that we could drink a toast in celebration of my release. And then another toast to Katherine. And then a toast to all the people who had written to Rockefeller . . . and a toast to Pete Hamill and the Free Willie Sutton Committee . . . and a toast to all the people who had prayed for me . . . and then I sat down, all woozy, and realized, amidst the laughter, that I couldn't go that route any more.

They made me the guest of honor, they treated me like a king. They even had a present to give me, gift-wrapped and everything. A sweater. And when Katherine arrived with the *News* reporter, Ed Kirkman, and the photographer, Gordon Rynders, Josie made them sit down and join in on the festivities.

It was after midnight before we got to the airport for the trip back. It had begun to snow by then and I was shivering in the thin topcoat they had given me. No sooner had we settled into the little five-seater than the pilot told us that the heater wasn't working and we were going to have to stay in a motel overnight while it was being fixed.

"No, we're not," I told him. "We're going to go to New York."

"Do you mind freezing? Look, if you want to brave the cold I'll brave it too, but I want you to know that if you think it's cold down here on the ground it's a lot colder up there."

I didn't care. "On Christmas Eve I've got to be in New York. If the reindeer can take it, so can I."

Well, we weren't in the air for ten minutes when the heater suddenly started to work. It was, no question about it, my day for miracles.

We came in over LaGuardia at about two o'clock in the morning and it was a sight I'll never forget. The whole city was still lit up. I saw a million colored lights illuminating the oblong squares of the city streets; I saw a thousand necklaces of red, green, amber, and white strewn across the town. I saw huge crosses of lighted bulbs standing out in bold relief against the towering skyscrapers. And in the harbor I saw the Statue of Liberty holding her torch up high.

It was such a breathtaking spectacle that for the first time in the entire trip Katherine forgot how scared she was and let go of her death's grip on my hand. "Do you now believe in miracles?" she squealed. "Do you now believe that the angel on my shoulder was telling the truth? Do you now believe in God?"

I believed, I believed. I believed in miracles. I believed in the angel on her shoulder. I believed in God. "But just remember, Katherine," I said as the little plane flattened out and headed for the runway. "We had a plan."